# PRO SE PRISONER:
# GUIDE TO BUILD WEALTH

## Taxes & Banking

C.A. Knuckles

**Freebird Publishers**

221 Pearl St., Ste. 541, North Dighton, MA 02764

Info@FreebirdPublishers.com

www.FreebirdPublishers.com

All Freebird Publishers titles, imprints, and distributed lines are available at special quantity discounts for bulk purchases for sales promotions, premiums, fundraising, educational, or institutional use.

ISBN: 978-1-952159-46-6

Printed in the United States of America

# DEDICATION

To those lost in the cycle of poverty, incarceration, and poverty-stricken ghettos. Behind me is a strong woman who has pushed me to do great things. I will never forget the role you played in my success. I love you and thank you!

.

# ACKNOWLEDGEMENT

Thanks to Freebird Publishers for their support. I want to extend my appreciation to all the people who helped with research for this book series. I am grateful to all the prisoners who became pro se prisoners by purchasing my books in the Pro Se Prisoners: Guide to Build Wealth series. I sincerely thank you for your continued support, and I will keep providing knowledge.

Thank you. The Forgotten Voices!

# CONTENTS

# WHAT IS MONEY?

One thing many people use every day but know so little about is MONEY! Lives have been taken, communities have been destroyed, and markets have been manipulated, while at the same time, people have built wealth and people have benefited from money. But do you really know and understand what happened to this form of value that makes people rich and poor at the same time?

So, what is money? All money is debt! Well, a little history is needed to show you what you thought wasn't money fully. In 1913, over 100 wealthy Americans met at Jekyll Island in Georgia and decided how the fed was going to work. Thus, the Federal Reserve Bank was created, which consisted of 12 banks spread across the country. These banks were set up because J.P. Morgan had just bailed America out of a financial crisis, and the fact that one man held that much control didn't sit well with some people. (More on this later). Another primary reason money is in debt is because, in 1971, President Nixon took our money off the Gold Standard. What this means is that before 1971, the USD was tied to gold at a price of $35 a (oz.). However, even under this gold standard, only countries and central banks could exchange for gold. This means of exchange, exclusive to these central banks, paved the way after 1971 when the U.S. removed itself from the gold standard and started its quest to suppress the price of gold to keep fiat currency alive for decades. Once we got off the gold standard, we moved to fiat currency, which is "money that's backed by nothing but a government promise." Fiat is a Latin word that means "currency circulating by force." U.S.A. moved towards Fiat currency because multiple countries started to see what was happening in the U.S., mainly America started spending because of wars, so these countries started requesting that America give them physical gold for their money, so Nixon suspended the Gold Standard, which then stopped "convertibility" of currency to gold. As were these countries right before 1971, today no country uses money; they only use currency! Value is only determined in relation to each other. Because the U.S. dollar is the World Reserve currency, every country values its currency against the U.S. dollar. Studying these financial history stories will help you to be financially educated and cure your "Ignorance: Destitute of Knowledge." This is the single most important thing that keeps people poor. The Gold Standard allowed the government to spend only what they collected from taxes; once it was put to rest in 1971, the government started running up deficits, spending money they didn't have, and using the Federal Reserve to print money and give out IOU's to people buying government bonds. Fiat currency allows the government to control the currency; the government then takes money from people who make money, it doesn't make money itself. What the

U.S.A. government does is really a Ponzi scheme similar to what Bernie Madoff went to prison for.

Governments borrow money as we do, and because of this borrowing, America is $28 trillion in debt. Because money is currency now, 95% of all money is numbers and digits in a computer system. So, back to the Ponzi Scheme earlier, this is how the American government engages in the same practices that it prosecutes citizens for every year. First, the Federal Reserve Bank isn't a bank – you can't store money there. It isn't Federal. Second, if the government wants $800 billion to bail out banks, they call the Federal Reserve Bank and tell them to print $800 billion; this will be in the form of a loan. Federal Reserve prints the money; by law, the Federal Reserve is the only place that can legally print money for the U.S.A. Okay! The Federal Reserve gets an IOU from taxpayers in the form of Government Bonds, and bondholders keep the monetary system going. (Rinse, wash, repeat)

We borrow all our currency into existence. Example: If you borrow the first $1 into existence, the only dollar that exists on the planet, but you promise to pay it back with interest, where do you get the second $1? You would have to borrow that too. It's a Ponzi Scheme on steroids because you can never pay it off; thus, we keep going deeper into debt. Since 1971, the U.S. has been running trade deficits with the rest of the world. We buy more from other countries than they buy from the U.S.

- Japan/Korea sells us cars/electronics.
- Middle East sells us oil
- China sells us everything at Walmart and Costco.

Remember, America has been running a Ponzi scheme since 1971, so here's how the above nations fit into the scheme, and without them, it (America) would fall down.

U.S. buys goods with U.S. Dollars. Then, they loan the profits back to the U.S. by buying government bonds! Money that enters our economic system without wealth being created reduces the individual value of each dollar. (Hence inflation). Who pays for it? Regular citizens, which is a hidden tax that's passed down to them. After the dollar is reduced due to inflation, supply chains get disrupted because citizens are buying more goods than usual because of higher prices. Other areas of your life will be affected, such as gas prices and rent, and even that raise at work gets watered down because it can't keep up with inflation. What's being described is real financial history; without it, your perspective will stay the same about money. Proving the point about "Inflation" being a problem, just today, July 27, 2022, the Federal Reserve Bank raised interest rates by 0.75%, an aggressive move to slow down inflation without causing a recession.

Think of money like credit, which is nothing more than the (power to spend). Once you spend it, you create debt. Why save money when they are printing it?

**Pro se Tip:** (!)   [Inflation] When the value of your dollar drops.

Federal Reserve ⟹ Print Money ⟹ $⇑ Increase Amount of Money out there ⟹ $⇓ Without increase in wealthy, this causes inflation.

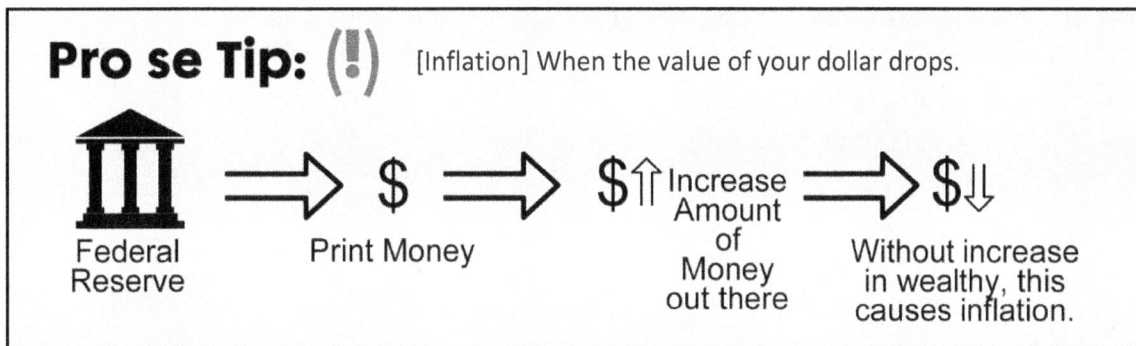

If you listen to all the talking heads on T.V. promoting some sort of financial knowledge, they will tell you, just as the banks say, 2%-3% inflation is better than 0%! Your head should explode! While also having you believe that wages are going up by 2%-3%, the same as inflation, the reality of all of this is that wages are actually going down by that much, not increasing. Not to get too into the weeds about inflation, but there are two important metrics you should know about—core Inflation – 2% target (doesn't matter). Pay attention to Headline Inflation, which includes energy prices and sudden tax rises, which will give you a better picture of what's going on in the economy and the value of your currency. Money of this type affects the most vulnerable and the financially uneducated; when they keep the inflation low 2%-3%, they give out less to social security benefiters, while also keeping the deficit low. So, the printing of money has its pros and cons, but right now, it's out of control, with the economy hanging on by slim threads.

When America was on the Gold Standard, it protected citizens from reckless spending. Since 1971, when money became a debt, the USA has run a deficit every year, which has devalued the dollar bit by bit. As long as the U.S. Dollar had the backing of gold, the Federal Reserve was tamed from printing money. As long as we keep using currency, we will always have to borrow money to keep up with inflation.

Money is complex, but now that we have gotten our history lesson, we need to move on to using debt (money) to build wealth in this current system. Knowing that since 1971, money is debt, you have been provided the financial education to help you build wealth. The wealthy use debt and tax to build wealth. To understand how the financial system works, you must ask questions. Debt used by the rich is simple: when debt is tied to an asset that goes up in value, it's considered good debt. So, a quick example of this process the rich use is this: let's say you buy a house for 100k all cash that appreciates at 10%, and your return on investment is 10%. However, how the rich use debt is different because they know what money is. The wealthy will look at a 100k house, finance it with $20,000 of their own cash, and get the bank to loan the rest; with a 10% appreciation, they make a 50% return on their money. This is called increasing return on debt. Understanding that money is a debt, you need to leverage it to get assets that produce income.

The power of debt allows the borrower [you] to gain full control over the asset without owning it yet— control over revenue, appreciation, depreciation, etc. Remember, because of inflation, our currency is a depreciating asset, something the rich and financially educated know. So, the rich borrow this depreciating asset to purchase appreciating assets, specifically assets that they can control. Examples of what to invest in are:

```
        Yourself
          /\
         /  \
        /Good\
       /Uses \
      / of    \
     / Debt    \
    /_____\
Your Business  Real Estate
```

Leveraging debt for the rich is easy because they understand money, and now so do you. How do you leverage debt to build wealth? Quick outline.

- 🏠 = valued at $100,000
- 🏠 = seller sells to you for $80,000
- 🏠 = you put 20% down = $16,000
- 🏠 = get/leverage the other $64,000 from the bank [80%]
- Interest rate on loan = 5%
- Term 30 years on loan
- Monthly payment on loan $344.00
- Give you control of = Revenue, Appreciation, Tax Advantages, Business Deductions
- Find a tenant to rent for $1,200/month
- Mortgage is $344.00; use rent, pay down debt that's amortization at work.

We used debt to create income, used that income to pay off debt, and also used the tax advantages of Real Estate to offset debt payments. Tax advantages, let's not forget, include:

- Cost of borrowing money
- Management costs
- Depreciation, and
- Other allowable business costs

Hold for three years with a 5.4% appreciation rate. Refinance real estate increases loan amount, withdraws money, and uses it to buy more real estate or assets. When you take out debt against an asset, it's tax-free! This makes the return on investment greater than the interest you pay on the debt. Keep reading to dig deeper into a system lost to use. Wow, being taught to you by someone in a cell like you is successful enough to explain "what is money?" to you in the simplest terms. MONEY IS DEBT.

Pro se Prisoner

C.A. Knuckles

# USING THE TAX CODE TO BUILD WEALTH

# BASIC UNDERSTANDING

One of the oldest and best ways to build wealth is to use the 95% of the tax code that doesn't raise taxes. Every day, people wake up, go to work, invest in a 401(k), save money in a bank, and repeat this again and again. Looking at taxes like this, of a repeated cycle of working and feeling like your money is being stolen by the government. For 30% of your life, you will work to pay taxes to the government. 3 hours out of an 8-hour shift goes to the government every day. Sitting in prison allows you not to have to pay taxes, right? Wrong, the state will get money back some way; the commissary makes you pay taxes on food items; right now, inflation is up 8.5% in April 2022, and this eats up your dollar/purchasing power. So as a result, commissary prices are raised because the dollar is weak, and the cost of goods is higher. Are there ways to not pay taxes? Yes, of course. Before we get started, remember that the government uses the tax law as an incentive for entrepreneurs to grow the economy by doing business with it to provide a multitude of services that will stimulate economic growth.

But how would you know this? If your whole life has been defined by a poverty mindset and people telling you that taxes are out to get you and you can't avoid it! So, to build wealth by lowering your taxes, you must first understand the tax code (knowledge) and take (action) on that knowledge to benefit you in the long run. When first imposed, tax laws didn't take money from the average person earning wages. Soon thereafter, that changed, and the employee pays the highest taxes while the employer pays the lowest. Taxes began to become more of an incentive for families (child tax credit), oil production, building/real estate, and areas that are essential to the country. Still, in areas the government didn't want to be involved in, they would just give a tax credit to people and investors to do it for them. To build wealth, taxes are key, so stop saying life is unfair, and just understand the tax code and take advantage of it the same way the wealthy do. Most of the biggest tax benefits are in producing jobs (employers), housing, and oil development.

The last major tax reform happened in 2017, within the body of that text, written by the Republican-led Congress. If you work a 9 to 5, you lose those needed reductions for moving, investment expenses, home mortgage interest, and important state income deductions. Corporations saw gains because of the reduction of taxes from 35% to 21%; owners of small businesses had gains with a 20% net income deduction, real estate with a greater depreciation incentive, and last but not least, 20% net income given to other small businesses.

Remember, being a Pro se Prisoner is about seeing what's happening and gaining the knowledge to execute it without delay. Working a 9 to 5 and applying for jobs upon your release should be a last resort when you have the time now to learn and build a business and wealth by understanding the tax laws that exist right now. Not to rain on any of you who have visions of going home and working. If you are going to do it, choose to specialize in a particular field (i.e., HVAC, etc.), be an independent contractor, and you will get the 20% small business deduction that the wealthy got above. Even service professionals can become a C-Corporation and reduce their tax rate to 21%. Turn the tax law around until it fits your current status in the business world, never settle for what people say, do your research, and stop being talked into being scared of government tax laws.

---

## Pro se Tip: (!)

TOP 3 areas that have the biggest tax breaks are:

1.  Start a Business (hire employees).
2.  Real Estate Investors
3.  Energy (oil and gas/coal; renewable energy)

---

Use the tax law; reduce your taxes. It's pretty simple for wealth building. Taxes make the rich – rich; make the poor – poorer. The only difference is the knowledge and study of the tax laws. The rich do it. The poor don't or rather don't know how. As a prisoner, you have two things going against you: the majority of prisoners are, first, poor, and second, you're a prisoner. Both are good things, in my opinion. Being poor allows you to know the bottom, which breeds that relentless yearning to succeed, and being a prisoner allows you to sit down and focus, which is basically unlimited time to learn.

Our goal is to learn and use our time to learn how to pay little or no tax at all. The only way to do this has nothing to do with anything illegal. All it takes is understanding how tax law works, which means utilizing your time in prison now to learn it.

---

## Pro se Tip: (!)

95% of the tax code is meant not to raise your taxes. It's meant to give a boost to energy, agriculture, economic, and housing activities that the government doesn't want to be involved in personally.

---

The tax code should be looked at as another form of investing for wealth building. Taxes must be a part of that to stimulate the economy and push it to grow. Let's get this out of the way now: "Yes, taxes were created and written for the wealthy!" Breathe. You were right on that point alone. But remember, there are two sides to every coin; the moment has come when you realize that and stop listening to these politicians who are in debt or are using your voice while they rake in millions behind your back using the same tax code they tell you that's rigged against you.

Your facts now define how the IRS looks at you for tax purposes. You are poor, you don't own a business, and you are in prison! Even if you take my advice and buy stocks while in prison. You still look forward to your (ROI) Return On Investment instead of first factoring in Investment after Taxes. Just know that taxes are your biggest expense until we learn why/how to use the tax code. Globally, citizens pay 30-45% of their income in taxes. With governments, 50-70% of the world's wealth is legally given to governments around the world. Think about that!

There are 5,800 pages of tax law in the U.S.A., with 25-30 pages geared toward raising taxes. So, if you read the other 5,770 pages, you will learn that it gives you a map to build wealth by lowering taxes. That means that 99% of the tax code is for reducing your taxes; you can't get a better percentage than that anywhere in the world.

## Pro se Tip: (!)

You can deduct almost anything! Business or personal. Business can reduce quarterly. Personal taxes can be immediately, because you can reduce how much come out of your check every payday.

Also equally important is the fact that the IRS allows citizens to file [AMENDED] tax returns and correct or fix errors on tax returns for up to three years (the previous three years) if they were generous enough to pay the IRS too much money in a previous year. Remember, it's your money, not the IRS!

Another good thing about the tax code is that if you want a refund now, you can also carry back a loss from the present year to a prior year and then use that loss to offset the prior year's income. The cash you would be able to get refunded immediately. Simply put, learning how to use income and knowing the difference between the good/bad kind, along with turning expenses into tax deductions (you will learn that later), which, at this point, 95% of your expenses can be turned into ways to reduce your taxes, you can essentially build wealth through the tax code.

Turning a personal expense into a business deduction could reduce your expenses by 15-25%. Using a business card to buy gas gives you a minimum 15-25% deduction. Your choices determine how much you save. As the pro se prisoner, I will teach you the knowledge, but it's up to you to use that knowledge and take action to get deductions on your taxes. Building wealth using the tax code is as easy as following a map on Google to a particular destination. But just as Google gives you directions, you still must walk or drive there alone. Google can't do that for you, just as I can't get you to sit in a cell and read, learn, and take action. That's up to you and only you from this point forward.

# GETTING STARTED: DEDUCTIONS

Whether you pay taxes now while in prison or while you were on the streets prior to being incarcerated, taxes were your biggest expense and seemed unfair. Having a family, a job, a mortgage/rent may seem like you were the ideal person the government would give the biggest tax breaks to. Because you rely on tax advisors or software like TurboTax® to prepare your taxes, you only get benefits such as the "Standard Deduction" or "Itemized Deductions" (i.e., mortgage interest and charitable contributions). Learning the tax code and living a different kind of life based on what you learned is the only way to rise up and change your circumstances. When you apply the knowledge of the tax code, you will get better at reducing your taxes and stop looking at the tax code as a scam only for the rich.

## Pro se Tip: (!)

"When you know you do better."

"Gain the benefits of your knowledge."

It's not a scam! Investors put money into the economy to produce. No benefit is gained from the tax code for you because you "consume." Hence, this is the reason why the government and news reporters call you "Consumers." It's 2022, and inflation is high; the Federal Reserve raised interest rates again (0.75%), but they determine inflation by how high the "Consumer Price Index" is. Our economy is based on the "consumer." Remember, investors produce while consumers consume. The producer gets the deduction, while the one who consumes gets expenses.

So, the 1st rule of deduction is to make your expense deductible. You must always make it an investment or business expense to accomplish this correctly. These types of expenses are deemed to be in furtherance to produce more income.

## Pro se Tip: (!)

Net income? Income after deductions.

There are several types of deductions we will get into later. But remember, deductions come from expenses, and the best expenses to deduct as business expenses are real estate expenses, stock market, and energy expenses, which are okay, depending on the circumstances. In my personal opinion, I won't ever tell you, as a prisoner, to go home after spending years in prison, to fill out applications at Amazon, etc., and work for somebody else when you have all day to sit in prison and gain financial freedom by reading and learning how to build wealth and run a business for yourself. Becoming an entrepreneur/business owner allows you to take advantage of the tax code and is your first step to wealth building. So, I'm not saying don't go home and find a job, but if you do, still become an entrepreneur to get the benefits. Starting now while you are here puts you ahead of people already in society doing nothing.

Deductions come from expenses, so when you spend money, make sure you have a business purpose for your expenses. Tax law or, for that matter, deductions are all based on your intent. Intent on the purpose of your spending. Make it in furtherance of your business, and it's a deduction for tax purposes.

---

## Pro se Tip: (❗)

Passive Income: Dividends, rents, and business.

Earned Income: Appreciation/Capital gains, or your paycheck.

---

Actively investing in passive income is a great way to build wealth through the tax code, which allows you to get those deductions. Our whole lives, our family and I have been living in the repeated cycle of (Income → Taxes → Expenses) when there is another more profitable way to build wealth (Income → Expenses → Taxes). Financial literacy allows us to learn how to properly get deductions like the (1%) do and not like people who work check to check, and taxes are taken before they see their check.

Some other deductions include:

- Business Supplies
- Business Equipment
- Vehicle for Business
- Marketing Expenses
- Meals (Business)
- Home Office Expenses (ex: 1,000 sq. ft. house/250 sq. ft. used =25%)
- Mortgage Interest
- Charitable Donations
- Property Taxes
- Travel
- Business Start-Up Tax write-off (up to $5,000 can be deducted, and $5,000 of organizational costs)
- Cell Phone and Cell Phone Services Expenses

- Cost of Goods Sold
- All Labor Costs (W-2/1099 Form)
- Business Mileage (client meetings)
- Retirement Contributions (401k for employees, traditional IRAs)
- Health Savings Contributions (Health Savings Account, your contributions are tax write-offs. Use for health, 100% write-off)
- Self-Employment Taxes (must pay self-employment taxes on these earnings, up to about $130,000). If you earn around $130,000, you can reduce your self-employment taxes by simply incorporating it into an S-Corporation.
- Qualified Business Income Deduction: write off 20% of business income on taxes.
- Carry Forward: Carry deduction to future tax years.
    1. Net Operating Loss – Carry losses from prior years where they had more "expenses than revenue, " resulting in a loss.
    2. Capital loss – Allows you to offset capital gains.
    3. Tax Credit – Allows you to offset tax dollar for dollar.
- Vehicle Tax Deductions – If you buy a vehicle worth over 6,000 pounds, you are able to write off 100% in the first year through accelerated depreciation (IRS section 179). Buy in the business name; if you buy it, depreciate it over five years. If you lease it, you deduct the payments.
- Contractor Expenses: You can deduct the expenses incurred from hiring contractors on your taxes.
- Education: Must own a business that is not a corporation.

While this number of deductions is a lot, there are over 450+ tax deductions that you can take for your business. IRS.gov provides a full list if further interest is warranted. This list shows why following the ways the wealthy build wealth using taxes is important. These deductions should be applied by taking the amount of the expense and subtracting that from your income. Most employees were required to pay income taxes and other taxes like employment taxes, which took money out of their checks before they even cashed it. (More on this in a minute.)

Take note that the way to build wealth using taxes is based on what kind of income you bring, and that will determine how it's taxed and what kind of deductions can be claimed. Just take, for instance, if you have a 401(k), pension plan, or any retirement account – as most Americans have. For tax purposes, you will still pay a higher tax rate, but you won't have to pay the employment tax. Where you always want to be is in the income category, which includes capital gains, interest, dividends, and passive income.

---

## Pro se Tip: (!)

Business Deductions: all these types of deductions must be an expense with a business purpose. Next, the expense must be ordinary. Lastly, the expense must be necessary (make more money for your business).

---

Remember that the rules the wealthy follow don't discriminate, as you probably have been told. No matter your color, age, background, or zip code, these rules are written in the laws and tax codes regulated by the same people you or your family vote into office every year. Our problem is that we are taught that wealthy people got there by cheating lower-income people out of something. So, you grew up looking for ways to hate (i.e., the 1%) instead of trying to get the proper financial education that shows you how the tax laws work, how to pay less in taxes and get deductions for your expenses. The only thing that has discriminated is the education system that fed you lies about money and the upbringing that fed you stories that led you to hate the (1%). These deductions will allow you to play on the same field as the wealthy while obtaining real financial freedom for yourself.

## Pro se Tip: (!)

In 1913 two things happened that you should be aware of. 1) The U.S. Federal Reserve Bank was created (they control money and interest rates); 2) The Internal Revenue Service (I.R.S.) was created after the 16th Amendment was ratified.

Simply put, financial freedom can only be obtained by investing in your financial education, and taxes should be at the top of that list. We can't talk about taxes without going back to the "Income" that's being taxed in the first place. Working a 9 to 5, saving money in a bank, or saving for a 401(k) is considered the worst kind of income; you will always pay the highest taxes because the government has never given a tax incentive for you to just be an employee, work, and save money. The best you get is a 401(k) being deferred in case you decide to pull it out. If you decide to pull it out before then (retirement age), you will be penalized on top of the fact that it's already being taxed at the regular tax rate. This concept makes you work for money, and you get very little deductions on this form of regular income.

## Pro se Tip: (!)

Since 1971, all money became debt in the U.S.A. That's why the Federal Reserve just prints it like it grows on trees.

The next form of income we talked about is "Capital Gains." Whenever you buy low and sell high, capital gains are triggered. For instance, buying a stock or real estate for $100 and then selling it for $700, your capital gain = $600. Make sure to compare the regular income above (i.e., working for money) and capital gains (i.e., investing and selling for money). In the U.S., this form of income is taxed at around 20%, lower than regular 9 to 5 income. Lastly is "Passive Income," which is cash from an asset; once your asset produces income, it becomes passive income. As always with taxes, all roads lead to real estate. Rental income is passive income and is the lowest taxed income, so low it can be organized to be 0%! The lesson here about deductions, taxes, and income is never working for money (regular income); allowing money to

PRO SE PRISONER: GUIDE TO BUILD WEALTH   CREDIT & TAXES

work for you through investments and assets that produce income that allows you to organize your financial affairs in such a way that you get all the deductions on your income so that you are paying the very minimum in taxes. History classes in schools love to tell you about America. This great country was built and fought for through many wars, but one of those is important to the current tax code. However, World War II changed the world and America's financial well-being. In 1943, Congress passed "The Current Payment Act," which was proposed and passed as a temporary tax on workers. But under all that war talk and the need to fund it – wars are expensive – was the true intent behind the law, and that was the first time the government started removing taxes directly from paychecks, even before the check was given to the worker. The law required the business to take the money from the government. Believe it or not, this started the wealth gap between the middle class/poor and the rich. Fast forward to 2022, the tax is permanent, and since 1940, how much the government takes has increased rapidly, and a worker (employee) can't do anything to stop it but gain financial education and earn other forms of income where your money works for you.

---

## Pro se Tip: (!)

These states do not have individual income tax: Florida, Nevada, Washington, South Dakota, and Wyoming.

---

Since the law was enacted, 70% of every dollar goes directly to some tax the government has deemed necessary. That law set into motion today's current tax scheme, where the employee pays the highest tax percentage. Become an active investor and get over the average reality you currently live in because nothing is being gained in this closed-off reality. A white family's median wealth is $142k, and a black family's median wealth is $36,000, not that race isn't known as a factor, on top of the fact that the FHA denied loans to black families due to redlining. It's good to still see the numbers up close because the numbers don't give the biggest view of the real cause of this gap: Black people lack financial education. So, I plan to reveal all the wealth-building deductions and forms the rich use to grow their wealth; white and black wealthy people use these deduction strategies. Let's move on to one of the best deductions!

# DEPRECIATION AS A DEDUCTION

Deduct for no cost to you; that's the basis for this deduction. You can deduct a portion of any asset that produces income for you each year. The I.R.S. allows you to write off this because of the natural value of said property going down. Depreciation applies to what the I.R.S. calls,

**Pro se Tip:** (!)

Under this depreciation deduction, your personal residence doesn't qualify for this deduction. Rental properties/investment properties qualify.

or deems tangible assets, like real estate or equipment, etc. The government wanted investors and businesses to buy buildings and construct them; all the government cared about was creating jobs & housing. (i.e., Depreciation created an incentive)

Look at depreciation this way: say you purchase a commercial building and the land it sits on for $400,000; the building costs $300,000, while the land costs $100,000. Under the IRS code for depreciation, the value of the land ($100,000) cannot be deducted as depreciation, but the commercial building ($300,000) cost will get you a deduction equal to a portion of the $300,000. Under current laws, the government will allow you to depreciate that building over a "39-year" period. It's time for a little math; back to middle school, we go. 300,000 ÷ 39 = (7,692), so you would be able to deduct that amount each year. This qualifies for a lot more deductions under the I.R.S. code, such as the money you put into the building and the loan from the bank that was also put into the building. If you get all the money from the bank for the entire cost of the building, you get the same deduction! One other thing that's important is everything that was bought with the building. All items inside and outside the building can be deducted faster than the building itself! Faster depreciation means more money in your bank account at an even faster pace without putting your money down on the cost of anything! For items like furniture, etc., you will get up to a 15-20% deduction every year because the $300,000 cost was $50,000 for everything (items) in the building. That will get you an extra $10,000 to $15,000 a year deduction. For the equipment and items in the building, that's a faster deduction, allowing you to put that money back into your business or invest in other properties, which is a tax-free event because you are producing for the government by putting income back into the business to provide housing and jobs.

Real estate investing in residential property works the same way, and it depreciates at a rate of 3.0-3.6% per year. So, the story to take away here is that when you buy an asset, it begins to lose value over time. Once you choose to write it off as a loss on your financial statement, it is claimed as an expense, which in turn can be deducted, and the loss is written off on your taxes.

# Pro se Tip: (!)

Depreciation: Tangible Assets (Real Estate)

Amortization: Intangible Assets (Computer Software and Recipes)

Just like depreciation, the same rules apply to amortization. You still get a deduction for a portion of the cost of the asset over a similar amount of years as depreciation. Depreciation applies to tangible assets, and amortization applies to intangible assets. Remember that documentation is important when filing these deductions. You must elect to deduct amortizations.

# Pro se Tip: (!)

Amortization on Cost of Computer Software

| Cost of Computer Software | $25,000 |
|---|---|
| Dividend by 15 Years ÷ | 15 |
| Equals deduction = | $1,666 |

Shown above is a breakdown of how amortization works based on the cost of an intangible asset like computer software. Amortization also reduces your debt; when you make a loan or credit card payment, it is amortized. Real Estate is the perfect example of how this works to perfection, instead of doing what people who work paycheck to paycheck to pay off credit cards/debt by using their own money, real estate investors with financial education use their tenants to pay off the debt they owe (amortized). Read that again! That's the true power of amortization. As we wrap up this deduction section, let's go back to regular people making a regular income. As you continue making regular income, you will live your life controlled by the paycheck. Reading about deductions shows you the real financial education of the wealthy. The tax code has 5,800 pages. How many people are living paycheck to paycheck? Do you read those pages to reduce taxes? How many of you sat in prison and read it? I'm giving you years of the financial education I amassed by reading these books and going over financial statements so I can help us level the playing field for re-entry back into society with wealth or a wealth plan. While you sit in prison with time on your hands, fix your financial education so you won't come out of prison searching for a job as an ex-felon, and when you can't find one, you go back to the streets to die or come back in here with me. A study conducted showed that. 70% of American prisoners cannot read above a 4th-grade level! But even more crazy than that is the fact that Maryland prisons pay prisoners and give them "good conduct credits" to go to school each day in hopes of obtaining their GED. They pay you and shorten your sentence! Nowhere outside these walls does this occur for citizens; some take advantage of it and learn to read and get their GED, while others still blame others for sitting around on a tier all day or sleeping in their cell for not knowing or understanding something. Learning about taxes, deductions, and financial freedom starts with you. Money has no brain to say who gets it; you are not a victim of the tax system. Here is your chance to learn how the rich pay less in taxes and build wealth. The I.R.S. website and law libraries around the prison have tax code books that can be ordered for free. The wealthy aren't holding it in a safe in a mansion; it's only for them. It's public information. If Keefe Commissary starts selling noodles for $0.05, you would rush to buy up all of them because the price dropped by $0.40. So why can't you use the same logic when looking at stocks dropping? When the stock market crashes, you run away and say it's not the right time to buy; why? Bitcoin dropped to $20,000 this week from up to $60,000 6 months ago. Everybody in my prison, including correctional officers, asked me if it was a good time to buy. Some suggested waiting until it came back up! Those drops that people are scared of are why the rich get richer. Warren Buffett's people buy companies like crazy because he is financially educated, and those prisoners and officers are not. Because of the lack of financial literacy, we fail to see the opportunity in front of our eyes, or we believe it's a scam. By studying the tax code, financial literacy allows you to see these opportunities and pay less taxes.

# TAX CREDIT 101:
# $1 FOR $1

Some people think it's crazy to say that prison was the greatest thing that happened to me - when it happened. On the streets at a young age, I sold drugs while destroying my neighborhood. Prison was the first time I sat down and let my brain relax and breathe. Prison is a messed up, dangerous place, but that wasn't my concern. My concern was using this time as a time to sit down and learn, study, and change my circumstances.

I was out of survival mode and now entering knowledge-seeking mode. In prison, I never wanted to fit in because that would have stopped my growth; I was an "Outlier." Financial education is an investment that we all in prison should take. Have a desire to make a change? I'm you, and you are me! Poor is a state of mind, just as being broke is a temporary situation. Every day, I see prisoners mismanage money from something simple as a prison job. Or never get it and go home and come right back to prison within 2-3 years because they lacked financial education or didn't give themselves a chance. Hence, why Pro se Prisoner was created. D.O.C. hasn't realized that the real danger to public safety is a prisoner going home financially illiterate. We enter prison with no financial education, just street ways to make money; we earn on average $0.30 an hour, with no real expenses, leave prison with $50.00 in our hands, and leave prison with no real financial plan. What are you supposed to do? Those are the facts; let's get to how to change it once and for all.

Taxes aren't about just one thing; they deal with many subsections, such as tax credits. Tax credits are dollar for dollar, regardless of your tax bracket. Remember, the tax deductions we talked about earlier reduce your taxable income. The tax credit is directly against your taxes, so the $1 for $1 talk is about what it says "$1 for $1". For example, if the government gives you a tax credit for $10,000, your taxes will instantly be reduced by $10,000. When Congress wants something done specifically, they usually give out subsidies, which is the same as credit toward your income tax return. These tax credits are special for wealth building because of the $1 for $1 against your taxes. Within the tax credit world, there are two types of tax credits; one is a "refundable credit," which doesn't require any taxes to be due to obtain them. The second one is a "nonrefundable credit." This form of tax credit requires that you have taxes due to obtain this type of credit. Be careful when trying to apply for these tax credits because you must have sufficient income to claim these credits. You can lose these credits if you don't have enough income being produced to claim these credits correctly. That's why you need to document everything so you can look down the road to see your full financial health.

Some of these credits include family credits, education credits, charity credits, working poor credits, and investment tax credits. The U.S.A. wants you to have kids, so they offer credits to reward you for raising and having kids. Also, the same principles apply to the other credits here, like the working poor credit, which allows the receiving of credits for helping the working poor. Charity credits are designed to give back to the community or other charities. Understanding that the tax code was designed to get citizens to build businesses to hire and invest to build things that the government deemed necessary tells you all you need to know about why the biggest tax credit is the investment tax credit. Here is what I was talking about earlier in regard to the opportunity to see it and capitalize on it. Right now, inflation is ripping the rug right out from under the feet of people. However, savvy investors use tax credits and deductions to do the government bidding and build wealth. One of the best ways to involve the investment tax credit for building low-income housing (which is needed right now) and buying equipment while also getting credits for research and development. Irs.gov has a lot more credits associated with this form of wealth.

When building wealth like this, always look for what the government wants done because you will always find deductions and $1 for $1 credits to offset taxes. Always! Many of our hoods/ghettos need housing, and the best way to provide for that need and make money is to invest money into low-income housing. Real Estate investments like this will credit you the highest $1 for a $1 offset on your taxes. Credits don't just reduce taxes when combined with tax deductions; the credit of $1 for $1 offset allows you to really gain profit, and the right set of investments will ultimately double your profits. Tax benefits are cool, but make sure your cash flow is pouring in on top of the tax/credit benefits. So, remember, the main advantage is the dollar-for-dollar reduction of taxes.

# TAX BENEFITS OF COMMODITIES

Wars have been started more for oil than any other reason. The dollar (U.S.) has become the currency of all oil around the world since 1974. Also, in the 1970s, the U.S. dollar was no longer backed by gold, thus making the U.S. dollar nothing but debt. Wars that we were fed lies about were about oil; remember, World War II was so expensive that the U.S. created a tax scheme that directly, for the first time, removed taxes from the paychecks of American citizens. Oh, by the way, that war was about oil; the U.S. cut off Japan from oil. Vietnam was about them selling oil to China directly, something the U.S. didn't want.

As such, America gives enormous tax breaks to help the government reduce dependence on foreign oil. Normally, regular citizens invest in oil and gas companies through the stock market. (i.e., Exxon Mobile, Chevron, BP, and Shell) these types of investments don't give you the tax benefit you want when starting out building wealth. Stocks are a start, but we must study the 11% ways of getting 100% tax deductions when building wealth. One area of investment is domestic "wildcat" drilling. It is a fitting name because the taxes you receive are wild compared to the rest of the tax code. These expenses are associated with "equipment" bought to do the drilling and all other "Intangible Drilling Costs," this also brings in the labor cost, survey cost, ground clearing cost, fuel cost, and any and all repairs. This expense allows you special treatment under the tax code because the government wants you to invest in domestic oil production. This special treatment allows you to deduct both the "Intangible Drilling Cost" and "Equipment" cost in the year you will spend the money. No other tax code rule allows for such a thing; this means that a person can deduct 100% of their investment in the drilling in the year the investment was made! This is called doing business with the government! The U.S.A. gives you a $50,000 deduction for a $50,000 investment in the operation. So, any money invested is in the first year (no matter the amount); $50,000 above is just an example, but you get the equivalent deduction for the amount invested. Take the (Investment X Tax rate=Deduction). Facts are facts! Stop thinking as 90% of Americans do, and stop locking your brain into going home and working paycheck to paycheck when you can build wealth by understanding how the wealthy do it. Moving on to the next tax benefit, you can deduct 15% of gross income from the well every year. [e.g., Depletion]. It doesn't matter if you already deducted equipment and Intangible Drilling Costs; you still get to use depletion.

**Pro se Tip: (!)**

Sale proceeds from oil and gas (Gross income – expenses = net income. Gross income X 15% depletion = taxes that must be paid on income.)

You qualify for intangible drilling costs, depletion deductions, and equipment by owning a direct interest in a drilling operation while also investing in the operation as a General Partnership or Sole Proprietorship. Several other types of commodities offer tax benefits to help you build wealth. One is mining operations, which offer similar tax benefits such as the depletion of gross income, deductions for mining operation development expenses, and deductions for equipment costs.

---

## Pro se Tip: (!)

Remember, if you buy stocks or options in oil and gas or commodities section, that type of investment doesn't apply to the tax benefits talked about above. Only direct investment in the operations.

---

Another tax benefit is mining, which really has somewhat of the same tax breaks as oil and gas. Depletion is available on gross income from the sale of the minerals. Under the new law passed by Congress in the Budget Reconciliation Bill [which is over 700 pages], there are incentives for mining companies. Companies will be able to write 10% of the cost of the operations if they produce any amount of "critical minerals" [minerals essential for national security]. They must produce at least one type of these minerals [i.e., lithium, cobalt, and nickel]. Mining companies are critical to switching the U.S. from fossil fuels to electric vehicles/hydrogen fuel cells. If you lease federal land to mine minerals critical to the government, you will never pay royalties to the Federal government. When thinking about wealth building, I'm putting everything in here. Some things you can do now, but others need a well-drawn-out plan to accomplish this feat. Starting a mining company is the next generation's goal, and materials are needed for the renewable energy sector in the future. Renewable energy taxes enjoy some good tax benefits. This sector includes wind turbines, solar energy, and electric cars. Some include tax credits for wind turbines, credits for solar panels on homes, and credits for purchasing electric vehicles. For instance, the Inflation Reduction Act of 2022 will give consumers even more tax credits for these renewable energy practices, such as a tax credit of $7,500 for people who buy "clean" vehicles like Tesla's. This will last through 2032. Also, the bill creates a tax credit for used vehicles (clean vehicles); you can receive up to $4,000 or 30% of the sale price, whichever is less. The vehicle price can't exceed $25,000 (used). If you own a home as an investment or live in it, under this new law, you get a 30% tax credit for solar panels and wind energy, which will also extend to battery storage systems. Keeping with the trend, you will get up to $2,000 a year for installing efficient exterior windows, skylights, exterior doors, water heaters, and other items. Up to $1,200 a year and $2,000 with larger projects must meet an Energy Star rating. These projects include installing electric or natural gas heat pumps, electric or natural gas water heaters, and biomass stoves or boilers. To receive the $2,000 annually through 2032. Another part of this bill is the two rebate programs, which are grant programs that state energy offices would administer. Each state would have to apply for the 8.8-billion-dollar total. One program is the "Home Rebate Program", which calls on you to cut home energy use through insulation and HVAC installations. Doing this makes you eligible for 50% of the cost of these projects, up to a dollar cap. Cut energy by 20% and get a $2,000 rebate or half of the retrofit cost. Cut by 35% and get an extra $4,000 rebate for lower-income households that doubles to $8,000, but their income must be 80% or less of an area's median income to qualify. The second rebate is the "High-Efficiency Electric Home Rebate Program," up to $14,000 for buying efficient electric appliances: $1,750 for a heat pump clothes dryer. It also applies to non-appliance upgrades: $4,000 for an electric load service center upgrade, $1,600 for insulation, air sealing, and ventilation, and $2,500 for electric wiring. Low-income citizens below 80% of the area median can claim a rebate for the full cost of their upgrades, up to a $14,000 cap. If you are a low-income homeowner who falls between 80% - 150% of the area median income, you are still eligible for rebates of 50% of your cost, up to $14,000. These are what are called point-of-sale rebates for consumers.

Consumers and low-income citizens will benefit from this new bill. Still, companies that invest in wind, solar, geothermal, nuclear, and hydrogen energy, biofuels, and technology that capture carbon fossil fuels from power plants also receive incentives based on workers' pay and U.S. manufacturing of steel, iron, and other precious metals. There are a vast many resources for Renewable Energy under the new law as well as old laws; oh yeah, equipment used in business is 100% deductible in the year purchased, a little bonus for you.

Agricultural tax benefits also fit into the commodities tax benefit. Many benefits exist, but the deductions for the expenses of running a farm, orchard, or ranch are the most important. Let's start with farms, shall we?

1. Prepaid Farm Supplies – this includes feed, seed, fertilizer, and supplies (even poultry) you bought this year but haven't used can be deducted. You can claim 50% of your total deductible farm expenses in one year.

2. Prepaid Livestock Feed – Several rules apply here:

    a. Is it for the purchase of feed rather than just a deposit?

    b. Does it have a business purpose rather than just tax avoidance?

    c. Will the deduction result in a distortion/misrepresentation of your income?

3. Labor – The wages you pay to people who work on your farm are deductible, as are any costs associated with boarding, health insurance, workers' compensation, etc.

4. Repairs and Maintenance – This includes expenses made for the routine upkeep of your buildings and vehicles can be deducted. Any improvement to depreciable property would be considered capital expenditures.

5. Interest—You can deduct any interest paid or accrued this year on loans for mortgages or farm-related purchases as a farm business expense.

6. Breeding Fees – These are deductible, but if the breeder guarantees live offspring, you will have to make capitalization adjustments as the cost basis of the offspring.

7. Fertilizer and Lime – If soil improvements to the farmland last a year or less, you can deduct the full cost of any materials you purchased for that reason. If they last over a year, you must Capitalize the improvements and take smaller deductions.

8. Taxes—Real Estate, property, social security, Medicare, unemployment taxes, and taxes on any farm assets that apply are deductible for the year you are filing.

9. Insurance - Premiums you pay for various types of insurance for running the farm are deductible.

10. Rent and Leasing – Rent and lease payments can be deducted from property and equipment needed to operate your agricultural business.

11. Depreciation – Anything you purchase that lasts more than a year is deducted gradually.

12. Business Use of Your Home—Regularly use your home to conduct business; you can

deduct a portion from your taxes. You must show the difference between personal and business use.

13. Truck and Car Expenses – Gas, oil, licenses, repairs, etc. can be deducted from your taxes, or you can choose the standard mileage rate of 56 cents [For more than 5 vehicles you operate, you must deduct actual expenses]

14. Travel Expenses – Travel to conduct business for a farm [i.e., transporting cattle or harvest], and you are away for a day; those expenses can be deducted.

While this may not be an exhaustive list, they are some of the most important in the business. Other forms of this Agricultural tax benefit extend to livestock and crops. Under current tax laws, you don't have to add any cost to your inventory for crops and livestock. This is because the I.R.S. allows you to deduct them whenever you spend money on them. As was discussed at the start of this book, the government uses the tax code to incentivize people and businesses to do what the government doesn't want to do. Agriculture is no different. To encourage investments in this field and because the government doesn't want to rely on other countries for their food supply for National Security purposes, they give agriculture special treatment in the tax code to conduct this activity on their behalf.

Just like depreciation, the I.R.S. allows [100% of the cost of the equipment to be deductible in the year you acquire it]. Even farming operations. Some are not taxable and can even be pushed to a later year if earned through cooperatives. Other taxes include special tax breaks for certain crops, such as citrus groves. So, look into buying land for farms, orchards, and ranches because these deductions for running a farm, orchard, or ranch take away these expenses; depreciation deduction, along with full expensing for equipment, is another benefit. You will get special tax benefits if you allow your kids to inherit a farm or ranch under the estate tax. Some include the fact that your kids who inherit a farm or ranch get to pay estate tax over several years instead of right away. Still, the asset protection measures like trust, etc., would allow you to really not pay tax at all if your kids inherit your land, farm, or ranch; 1031 Exchanges are good.

---

## Pro se Tip: (!)

The "Rat-Race", much talked about, always not told completely as to what it means. Living on some sort of financial edge, living one paycheck away from broke constantly [75% of Americans live paycheck to pay-check constantly.] The more responsibility you have, the more this race gets difficult. It's about living on the edge, chasing the next thing, putting your goals aside, living paycheck to paycheck.

---

Precious metal tax perks are okay; remember, in the "What is Money?" part at the start of this book, we talked about money. Around 1970, President Nixon removed the U.S. Dollar from the Gold Standard. Since then, U.S. tax policy hasn't given incentives or encouraged ownership of gold and silver because they want to control the gold prices, so it's never an option to go back to this option because of dire debt issues in the U.S. and abroad. Gold and silver are good investments as hedges against rising inflation. The I.R.S. policies discourage investments outside of owning physical gold bars and silver. Whatever the government tries to do to restrict some form of wealth being built tells me that it's a good investment even with the higher tax rate on it, compared to other long-term capital gains tax rates. The tax rate for gold and silver is 28%, double that of other capital gains. Precious metals are considered "collectibles" by the I.R.S., hence the 28% long-term capital gains rate. But as the

---

## Pro se Tip: (!)

Other "collectibles" include works of art, rugs, antiques, metals [gold, silver, platinum, and palladium bullion] gems, stamps, coins, alcoholic beverages, and certain tangible property.

---

government hides behind these crazy tax policies against ownership of these precious metals; all it takes is well-rounded, smart, wealth-building citizens to figure out how to avoid these high taxes. One way is the "short-term" capital gains tax, which means if you sell precious metals for less than a year, it's considered "short-term" gains and can be only taxed as ordinary income. But if you do not want to sell in a year and hold on to your gold and silver, etc., You can use what's known as a [1031 Exchange]; see [book 3] for more on this. 1031 exchange will allow you to defer capital gains if you reinvest profits in another investment asset. You will also have 45 days under the I.R.S. tax policy to sell the old one to make a new investment; if it is gold or silver, you must reinvest in precious metals. The most important part is the collection of the money; before you sell, make sure that your goal is to use a 1031 Exchange because you will need an intermediary to hold the money from the sale because as soon as the capital gains hit your bank account, it becomes taxable. This process is nothing but rolling one investment into another.

Another way to avoid paying taxes is to use your status as an employee for your business and set up an I.R.A. to hold your own gold and silver inside the plan. This allows you to hold precious metals long-term without taxes. Using a Roth IRA, you can postpone the tax through this government–qualified retirement plan. Owning a Roth IRA means you will never pay taxes on the increase in value of your gold and silver. With this strategy, you can protect against currency deflation and be used as a hedge against inflation.

---

## Pro se Tip: (!)

Taxes will make you wealthy or poor. It's really up to you!

---

# SECTION 179

While I jumped ahead a little, section 179 needed to be separated from the Agricultural Tax Benefits section so that it could be fully explained with a little more detail. Section 179 allows small and medium-sized businesses [including agricultural operations] to deduct the costs of vehicles, software, and other equipment they use in the course of running their companies. Section 179 of the I.R.S. code also allows full deduction on the purchase price of software purchased during a tax year. Even leased qualified equipment can be deducted from your gross income at the full purchase price. Being a farmer or owning a farm can save a lot because the cost associated with the specialized equipment can be used and become a massive tax break. To use this bonus feature, you must use up to the maximum allowable cap of $2,700,000. Once that amount is reached, the bonus depreciation under section 179 goes into effect. Section 179 deduction limit for 2022 is $1,080,000 [new and used equipment and software]. The 2022 spending cap on equipment purchases is $2,700,000. That's when the bonus depreciation kicks in, which is 100% for 2022, once the cap is reached. Section 179 completely goes away once $3,700,000 in purchases are reached. These incentives are for businesses to buy equipment and invest in their business.

## Pro se Tip: (!)

To produce wealth, you understand:

1. Compound Interest

2. Leverage: When you earn interest on your money, but most importantly on someone else's money.

3. Velocity: In business this means keep your money moving!

# ADDITIONAL TAX BENEFITS

Getting into these additional tax benefits, some of these words might have been said in previous sections or will be in other sections as well.

## Real Estate Tax Benefits

For the purpose of not saying or writing about this multiple times, check out Book 3, "Pro se Prisoner: Guide to Build Wealth (Cryptocurrency, Real Estate, and Business)," for the full real estate benefit of 1031 exchanges. However, to build wealth like the 1%, we have to combine 1031 exchange with depreciation to never pay taxes from the sale of real estate again. Briefly, suppose you have five houses with positive cash flow, but you then use a 1031 exchange with a "Qualified Intermediary" to buy 3 apartment buildings from the sale of the five houses. The apartment buildings are also producing even more cash flow, plus the added bonus of depreciation, which allows your cash flow to be closed off from income taxes. I recently read a couple of real estate books and tax papers and saw that if you invest in Walgreens, you can live a good life. An explanation is needed; remember, we are using the 1031 Exchange + Depreciation to avoid paying taxes on our real estate sales. We had 5 houses with positive cash flow, sold after several years, and purchased 3 apartment buildings, so we sold our 3 apartment buildings to buy a Walgreens property. Yes, a Walgreens store. Here is the thing: Walgreens builds the building, sells the land with the building to an investor like you, and leases it to you for 30 years. Walgreens handles the maintenance and all the expenses; all you do is pay the mortgage. Because Walgreens guarantees the lease, banks will throw extra money at you for the purchase. Every month, Walgreens sends you a check. How would this fit into the above tax strategy? By owning the houses and apartment buildings over the years, you took depreciation deductions, even on Walgreens. All this did was shelter your cash flow generated from the assets from income taxes! Reading up on this, I noticed a couple of examples of this strategy, so let's say your total deduction over the years from depreciation was $3 million. You would have to reduce the tax basis [the property's purchase price less all of the depreciation you take on the property over the years], which calculates the capital gain when selling the property. Say you paid $4 million for Walgreens, and you depreciated $3 million; your tax basis is $1 million. To eliminate this capital gain, you can just hold it until you pass away, "Generational Wealth," because your tax basis is automatically increased to the property's value. The I.R.S. calls this a "Basis Step-Up." If you have valued the property at $5 million, your basis will be $5 million upon death. Even if your kids sell the Walgreens, you have set them up beforehand to recoup tax-free money from your assets. You benefited from depreciation; your children won't have to pay taxes upon your death!

While you have all this value in your assets, get cash from a bank, thus borrow against Walgreens and do it all over again using O.P.M. [Other People's Money]; this keeps money building up, cash flow coming in, and assets in a generational cycle for your kids and family. While we are in banks, remember, in real estate, we benefit from not being taxed on loans. So, you can refinance and won't pay tax on that money. Refinancing allows you to get a tax-free loan to buy other real estate while still owning the asset you refinanced!

One more tax benefit from real estate is that you know that in the U.S.A., there is no tax on the sale of a personal residence so long as you have lived in it for two out of the past five years. Savvy real estate investors buy fixer-uppers, use them as personal residences, fix them up, stay there for two years, and sell them tax-free. This works best with fixer-uppers that you buy cheap and fix-up because the gain upon the sale can't exceed $500,000; if it doesn't exceed $500,000 [gain], it's tax-free. Just something to think about on your wealth-building journey while you are still in prison or upon release: keep educating yourself; fail, make mistakes, and build wealth using these tax benefits.

## Stock Tax Benefits

Actively investing in the stock market has its benefits from a tax perspective. One of the most important things to remember from a tax point of view is that gains made from actively trading stocks are "Capital Gains," which means that you will only pay taxes when you sell them.

The goal is long-term capital gains because that's how you get the lower tax rate. Long-term in the U.S.A. is [1 year and a day]. Also, any losses from stocks are considered "Capital Losses." In the U.S.A., you are allowed to use 3,000 per year in capital losses to offset other income when you don't have enough capital gains to offset. Remember, one of the reasons the wealthy don't pay taxes is because they have the best tax advisors who get paid millions of dollars, so their clients don't pay taxes from investments.

## Pro se Tip: (!)

Every dollar you spend about 75% goes directly or indirectly to some kind of tax to the government. Regular citizens not the wealthy.

# TAXES MAKE THE WEALTHY...WEALTHY

Way back in 1773, the Boston Tea Party led to the Revolutionary War. Our founding of the U.S.A. came because of a tax revolt. We were founded because Americans didn't want to pay taxes. From 1773 to 1943, America had little taxes until the Current Tax Payment Act, and World War II was expensive. So, what the wealthy do legally, by using current laws not to pay taxes, was actually how we became a country in the first place. Everybody knows how to spend money but doesn't know how to make it. Knowing how to make money, with knowledge about financial literacy, will help you know how to spend your money to buy assets and allow your money to work for you and not the other way around. Wealthy people starting out had to seek knowledge about money and taxes to be successful. Right now, the wealthy can hire the best tax advisors in the world. Where you are starting on your journey won't allow you to do such a thing, but what it allows you to do. At the same time, you have the time to do it is read the tax code yourself and study it until you grasp the fact that all expenses can be deducted; you have to use what the wealthy use [tax code] to make sure the expense is an ordinary and necessary business expense.

The key to building wealth using the tax code is to understand that the I.R.S. wants you to produce energy, food, and housing. Anybody can also obtain the proper financial knowledge the wealthy have. Starting with taxes, you have started to understand what the wealthy already know: "Taxes are incentives."

To be wealthy, you must first invest in your financial education. Sitting in that hole of a cell, playing video games, and spending your money at a commissary is the old poverty mindset. We are Pro se Prisoners, so we have a wealthy mindset. You have invested in your financial education by purchasing or borrowing this book. It seems as though "taxes are incentives" and are set up for you to do business with the government by providing services for the government [i.e., housing (real estate)], energy [oil and gas, solar, etc.], food that they don't want to be involved in because it's better for the economy to give out "tax incentives" to businesses to provide such services. This is the main reason the poor and middle class work 9 to 5 and pay the highest taxes because they are employees. You are happier with getting more money in your check (income), staying there for 3 years, and moving up in the company only to receive higher pay and bonuses. Thus, it makes you work for money instead of making money work for you. Instead, making money works for you via tax incentives, which in turn allows you to make more money. Because the government needs jobs, you, as a business owner, get a tax break for hiring employees. They do this for the tax that comes from the employer checks. So, becoming a business owner who hires employees is better than being the employee who already pays the highest taxes and now has other taxes out of your check before you get it. Hence, I keep saying, "Make money work for you," and "Taxes are incentives." These are wealth principles developed through financial education.

The same applies to real estate; it's cheaper for the government to give "ABC Real Estate Group" a tax incentive to build housing for people than for the government to do so because it would cost taxpayers too much money. Yes, the poor and middle class get some incentives, too. For example, if you purchase a house, you can deduct the interest expense on your tax return. If you save for retirement, you can deduct your investment through IRAs. Also, you can deduct charity donations. However, building wealth, such as the 1% tax incentives, is vaster because you are performing vitally and helping the economy improve. Whether it's jobs, food, or energy, it is vital to the economy and life. Financial knowledge about tax incentives allows you to put yourself in the right environment to build wealth and use the tax code to build wealth like the wealthy.

The U.S. tax system taxes "income." Selling stocks generates "income," so the wealthy avoid this by using other forms of the tax code to define it differently. Another way the wealthy build wealth is by borrowing against their income because borrowing isn't "taxable." Others use Roth IRAs accounts that shield income from taxes. Even buying a sports team allows the wealthy to write off everything, even players' contracts. These owners, who have businesses, pay less in taxes than their players and employees in the stadium. Some take pay cuts on salaries and categorize the money instead as pass-through income, as most businesses can take. Financial education allowed about 20 billionaires to get stimulus checks in 2020 because of tax returns that reported income of less than $150,000, which was cut off for a married couple written in the stimulus bill. Now, don't get upset; look at the lessons in these stories because you can do the same. It's all "LEGAL"; this stuff doesn't send you to prison for robbery for 25 years. Most commonly used strategies by the 1% allow them to use "TRUST" in "Estate Planning" to create generational wealth that's tax-free when it gets to your heirs. Unknown to many but the wealthy, one of their best secrets to building wealth using the tax system is "The Buy, Borrow, Die" strategy. Buying an asset is the first step to building a company or inheriting a fortune; as long as they don't sell, they can't be taxed. They keep income as low as possible because every dollar earned can be taxed. Next is Borrowing; once you learn about this, you will keep your money while using someone else's. They borrow against their holdings, and banks give them a bargain deal on a loan. [ex. $10 million for 3% interest] Loan money = not income = not taxed. Part 3 is DIE; billionaires set up trusts that are tax-free and use charities that are tax-free. So, the lesson here is that you can do the same just by getting started with an LLC that produces income and builds up. The net lesson is that once you choose to work as an employee and work a regular job, you will get a paycheck and pay income taxes because you own nothing that you can use to offset that taxable income. Federal income taxes are at a maximum rate of 37% when the financial knowledge here allows you to pay less. Following these examples of wealth building using taxes, the wealthy financial education

**Pro se Tip: (!)**

57% of U.S. households paid no federal income taxes for 2021, due to COVID-relief funds, tax credits and stimulus.

is in arms reach. Would you want a $1 million dollar salary a year or real estate worth $1 million? If you want to make $1 million in salary, you are an employee who will get taxed approximately 40% on that $1 million salary. With $1 million in real estate, you won't pay taxes, and you can leverage it to get more money to continue asset building. Knowing the difference of these levels of playing is important because it's financial education. Once the wealthy create the cash flow, they know they control their taxes. Wealthy tax tools!

# DEBT/TAXES

I want to discuss debt and its association with taxes briefly. I was going to wait to have a whole section about it in my next book, but a little needs to be explained here. It will be more in-depth in my next book.

Debt and taxes are the reason for the long gap between the wealthy and every class under them. Once the Internal Revenue Service was created after the 16th Amendment was ratified, debt and taxes became the revenue source for the government and became a tool for the wealthy and a mechanism for people to stay in poverty because they didn't have the financial education to understand the tax code. Even the government of the U.S.A. isn't immune from being touched by debt. The National debt is created by people who have no financial education. If you take anything from this book, remember that real financial education is about debt and taxes because although it keeps the middle-class and working poor in poverty, with financial education, you can use debt and taxes to become rich!

Debt is tax-free! Read that again because that's the most important rule about using debt to build wealth. So, the wealthy use debt because it's "TAX-FREE." So, if you borrow $20,000 from the bank to use as a down payment for some real estate, it's tax-free. But if you use your own after-tax money, and depending on your tax bracket, $20,000 is really about $30,000 or $35,000 because $10,000 to $15,000 went to the government in taxes. My goal is to show how to advance from using your money to buy stocks and ETFs to borrowing money from the bank [DEBT] tax-free to buy bigger and bigger assets without ever using your own money. Reading up on debt, one paper said that you are renting money rather than working to earn it, and it's tax-free. The same thing happens with Amortization, which is the reduction of your debt. Whether it's a mortgage credit card payment or loan balance, it's being amortized [paid-off]. Using your house tenants to pay down your debt means that debt is tax-free, and getting someone else to pay it off is the key to real wealth building. Get the loan and allow the tenants to amortize your debt. Remember that because it further uses debt to grow your wealth. Debt is money that can write its own ticket if you use it correctly.

Another thing about real estate and debt is that when you allow the bank to value your property, they look at your "Net Operating Income." Once you increase that, return to the bank and refinance the property; because debt is tax-free, all proceeds distributed to you are tax-free. Talking about debt makes the average person have a negative reaction to it. When I first heard about it, I had a poverty mindset, and I thought that it was the key to wealth building. Student loan debt is over $1 trillion and is the biggest income stream for the U.S.A. government. So, when you purchase something on a credit card, remember there is no money on that card; all it is credit. Once you use it, debt is created. For these credit card companies, it's a win-win because the economy grows when you create money from borrowing. The opposite happens when you pay off your debt and the economy gets smaller.

The method of using debt to build wealth and not a more negative debt is using leverage [a strategy of using borrowed money] to multiply returns on the investment you purchase with the debt. This is what the wealthy call financial leverage because you are leveraging debt from your company to fund an asset. Also, if you want to purchase a house, you take out a mortgage, and getting a loan from the bank means you are leveraging to buy an asset. This is called personal finance leveraging.

Another feature of debt is "Debt Recycling," where, as you pay off your loan, you redraw the equity from the asset [real estate] you have built up to invest in other properties. Making bad debt and good debt can earn your income and be used to pay back the loan and provide tax breaks. Any excess income can be put back into your home loan to pay that off quicker, which will, in turn, make further interest savings. Debt allows you to do amazing things. For instance, why would you buy one investment property for $100,000, paying cash, when you could buy 5 $100,000 dollar properties by borrowing 80% of the purchase price for each and putting down $20,000 a piece? Even better, this debt can improve your cash-on-cash returns. While this isn't an exhaustive run down about debt, it will allow you to have a basic understanding of how powerful a tool debt can be.

---

## Pro se Tip: (!)

1) Use debt to buy assets, not liabilities;
2) Borrow money for an investment, it's tax-free money;
3) Debt is not income, so it can't be taxed.

---

Now you understand why the wealthy use tax codes to build wealth. You have the financial education to level the playing field. Remember, "When you gain knowledge, there are no more excuses. Plot, plan, and execute!" Check out all of the tax forms below you must understand to start building wealth using taxes.

# TAX FORMS INDEX

- 2022 Tax Table [Morgan Stanley]
  - Form 941
  - SS4 Form
  - Form 8824
  - Form 4562
  - Form W-4
  - Form 1040
  - Form W-9
    - Form 4506-T
  - Form 5695 Instructions
- Publication 535 Business Expenses
  - Form Schedule K-1
  - Form Schedule C
    - Form 1065

# Morgan Stanley

# Tax Tables 2022 Edition

## 2022 Tax Rate Schedule

| TAXABLE INCOME ($) OVER | NOT OVER | BASE AMOUNT OF TAX ($) | PLUS | MARGINAL TAX RATE | OF THE AMOUNT OVER ($) |
|---|---|---|---|---|---|
| **SINGLE** | | | | | |
| $0 | $10,275 | $0 | + | 10.0 | $0 |
| $10,275 | $41,775 | $1,027.50 | + | 12.0 | $10,275 |
| $41,775 | $89,075 | $4,807.50 | + | 22.0 | $41,775 |
| $89,075 | $170,050 | $15,213.50 | + | 24.0 | $89,075 |
| $170,050 | $215,950 | $34,647.50 | + | 32.0 | $170,050 |
| $215,950 | $539,950 | $47,843 | + | 35.0 | $215,950 |
| $539,900 | | $162,718 | + | 37.0 | $539,900 |
| **HEAD OF HOUSEHOLD** | | | | | |
| $0 | $14,650 | $0 | + | 10.0 | $0 |
| $14,650 | $55,900 | $1,465 | + | 12.0 | $14,650 |
| $55,900 | $89,050 | $6,415 | + | 22.0 | $55,900 |
| $89,050 | $170,050 | $13,708 | + | 24.0 | $89,050 |
| $170,050 | $215,950 | $33,148 | + | 32.0 | $170,050 |
| $215,950 | $539,900 | $47,836 | + | 35.0 | $215,950 |
| $539,900 | | $161,218.50 | + | 37.0 | $539,900 |
| **MARRIED FILING JOINTLY AND SURVIVING SPOUSES** | | | | | |
| $0 | $20,550 | $0 | + | 10.0 | $0 |
| $20,550 | $83,550 | $2,055 | + | 12.0 | $20,550 |
| $83,550 | $178,150 | $9,615 | + | 22.0 | $83,550 |
| $178,150 | $340,100 | $30,427 | + | 24.0 | $178,150 |
| $340,100 | $431,900 | $69,295 | + | 32.0 | $340,100 |
| $431,900 | $628,300 | $98,671 | + | 35.0 | $431,900 |
| $647,850 | | $174,253.50 | + | 37.0 | $647,850 |
| **MARRIED FILING SEPARATELY** | | | | | |
| $0 | $10,275 | $0 | + | 10.0 | $0 |
| $10,275 | $41,775 | $1,027.50 | + | 12.0 | $10,275 |
| $41,775 | $89,075 | $4,807.50 | + | 22.0 | $41,775 |
| $89,075 | $170,050 | $15,213.50 | + | 24.0 | $89,075 |
| $170,050 | $215,950 | $34,647.50 | + | 32.0 | $170,050 |
| $215,950 | $323,925 | $49,335.50 | + | 35.0 | $215,950 |
| $323,925 | | $87,126.75 | + | 37.0 | $323,925 |
| **ESTATES AND TRUSTS** | | | | | |
| $0 | $2,750 | $0 | + | 10.0 | $0 |
| $2,750 | $9,850 | $275 | + | 24.0 | $2,750 |
| $9,850 | $13,450 | $1,979 | + | 35.0 | $9,850 |
| $13,450 | | $3,239 | + | 37.0 | $13,450 |

Kiddie Tax: all net unearned income over a threshold amount of $2,300 for 2022 is taxed using the brackets and rates of the child's parents

## Tax Rates on Long-Term Capital Gains and Qualified Dividends

| LTCG TAX | SINGLE FILERS | MARRIED FILING JOINTLY | HEAD OF HOUSEHOLD | MARRIED FILING SEPARATELY |
|---|---|---|---|---|
| 0% | $0 – $41,675 | $0 – $83,350 | $0 – $55,800 | $0 – $41,675 |
| 15% | $41,676 – $459,750 | $83,351 – $517,200 | $55,801 – $488,500 | $41,676 – $258,600 |
| 20% | $459,751 or more | $517,201 or more | $488,501 or more | $258,601 or more |

## Net Investment Income Tax

3.8% tax on the lesser of: (1) Net Investment Income, or (2) MAGI in excess of $200,000 for single filers or head of households, $250,000 for married couples filing jointly, and $125,000 for married couples filing separately.

## Standard Deductions & Personal Exemption

| FILING STATUS | STANDARD DEDUCTION | PERSONAL EXEMPTION | PHASEOUTS BEGIN AT AGI OF: |
|---|---|---|---|
| Single | $12,950 | N/A | N/A |
| Head of household | $19,400 | N/A | N/A |
| Married, filing jointly and qualifying widow(er)s | $25,900 | N/A | N/A |
| Married, filing separately | $12,950 | N/A | N/A |
| Dependent filing own tax return | $1,150* | N/A | N/A |
| **ADDITIONAL DEDUCTIONS FOR NON-ITEMIZERS** | | | |
| Blind or over 65 Married Filing Jointly | | | Add $1,400 |
| Blind or over 65 and unmarried and not a surviving spouse | | | Add $1,750 |

*For taxable years beginning in 2022, the standard deduction amount under § 63(c)(5) for an individual who may be claimed as a dependent by another taxpayer cannot exceed the greater of (1) $1,150, or (2) the sum of $400 and the individual's earned income.

## Alternative Minimum Tax

### EXEMPTION AMOUNTS AND PHASEOUTS

| | EXEMPTION AMOUNT/ PHASEOUT AMOUNT BEGINS AT: |
|---|---|
| Single | $75,900 / $539,900 |
| Married, filing jointly or surviving spouses | $118,100 / $1,079,800 |
| Married, filing separately | $59,050 / $539,900 |
| Estates and trusts | $26,500 / $88,300 |

### AMT TAX RATES

| | MARRIED FILING SEPARATELY | ALL OTHERS |
|---|---|---|
| 26% tax rate applies to income at or below: | $103,050 | $206,100 |
| 28% tax rate applies to income over: | | |

## Child Tax Credit

| CREDIT | MAXIMUM CREDIT | INCOME PHASEOUTS BEGIN AT MAGI OF: |
|---|---|---|
| Child Tax Credit* | $2,000 per qualifying child | $400,000 – married filing jointly $200,000 – all others |

*Subject to eligibility requirements

## Gift and Estate Tax Exclusions and Credits

| | |
|---|---|
| Gift tax annual exclusion | $16,000 |
| Estate, gift & generation skipping transfer tax exclusion amount (per taxpayer) | $12,060,000 |
| Exclusion on gifts to non-citizen spouse | $164,000 |
| Maximum estate, gift & generation skipping transfer tax rate | 40% |

## Tax Deadlines

Jan 18, 2022 – 4th installment deadline to pay 2021 estimated taxes due

April 18, 2022 – Last day to file amended return for 2018 (subject to limited exceptions); Last day to contribute to most employer-sponsored retirement plans, including SEPs and profit-sharing plans for 2021 if the federal income tax return deadline for the business that maintains such plans is April 18, 2022 (unless the federal income tax return filing deadline for the business has been extended). Tax filing deadline to request an extension until Oct. 17, 2022 for businesses whose tax return deadline is April 18, 2022. 1st installment deadline to pay 2022 estimated taxes due. Last day to file federal income tax returns for individuals. Tax filing deadline to request an extension until Oct. 17, 2022 for individuals whose tax return deadline is April 18, 2022. Last day to contribute to Roth or traditional IRA or HSA for 2021. Note: Kentucky, Illinois, and Tennessee tornado victims have until May 16, 2022 to file 2021 individual income tax returns, as well as various 2021 business returns.

June 15, 2022 – 2nd installment deadline to pay 2022 estimated taxes due

Sep 15, 2022 – 3rd installment deadline to pay 2022 estimated taxes due

Oct 17, 2022 – Last day to file federal income tax return if 6-month extension was requested by April 18, 2022. Last day to recharacterize an eligible Traditional IRA or Roth IRA contribution from 2021 if extension was filed or tax return was filed by April 18, 2022 (and certain conditions were met). Last day to contribute to most employer-sponsored retirement plans, including SEPs and profit-sharing plans for 2021 if the federal income tax return deadline for the business that maintains such plans is April 18, 2022, and federal income tax return extension was filed for such business.

Dec 31, 2022 – Last day to: 1) pay expenses for itemized deductions for 2022; 2) complete transactions for capital gains or losses. Note: last 2022 trade date is December 30.

# Morgan Stanley

## Tax Tables 2022 Edition

### Traditional IRA Deductibility Limits

The max. contribution limit for IRAs is **$6,000**; the catch up at age 50+ is **$1,000**

| FILING STATUS | MODIFIED AGI | CONTRIBUTION |
|---|---|---|
| Single/HOH covered by a plan at work | $68,000 or Less | Fully Deductible |
| | $68,001 – $77,999 | Partially Deductible |
| | $78,000 or More | Not Deductible |
| Married Filing Jointly and covered by a plan at work | $109,000 or Less | Fully Deductible |
| | $109,001 – $128,999 | Partially Deductible |
| | $129,000 or More | Not Deductible |
| Married Filing Jointly not covered by a plan at work and spouse is covered by a plan at work | $204,000 or Less | Fully Deductible |
| | $204,001 – $213,999 | Partially Deductible |
| | $214,000 or More | Not Deductible |
| Married Filing Separately and you or your spouse are covered by plan at work * | Less than $10,000 | Partially Deductible |
| | $10,000 or More | Not Deductible |

If not covered by a plan, single, HOH and married filing jointly/separately (both spouses not covered by a plan) tax filers are able to take a full deduction on their IRA contribution.
*If spouses did not live together at any time during the year, their filing status is considered Single for purposes of IRA deductions.

### Roth IRAs Contribution Limits

The maximum contribution limit for IRAs is **$6,000**; the catch up at age 50+ is **$1,000**.

| Allowable Contribution | Modified Adjusted Gross Income | | |
|---|---|---|---|
| | Single/HOH | Married Filing Jointly | Married Filing Separately |
| Full | ≤ $129,000 | ≤ $204,000 | N/A |
| Partial | $129,001 – $143,999 | $204,001 – $213,999 | $0 – $9,999 |
| None | ≥ $144,000 | ≥ $214,000 | ≥ $10,000 |

*Roth conversion income is not included in Modified Adjusted Gross Income

### Other Retirement Plans Contribution Limits

| RETIREMENT PLAN TYPE | MAX. CONTRIBUTION LIMIT | CATCH-UP (50+) | INCOME RESTRICTIONS ON CONTRIBUTIONS |
|---|---|---|---|
| SEP IRA | The lesser of 25% of compensation or $61,000 | N/A | Employer contributions cannot take into account compensation in excess of $305,000 |
| SIMPLE IRA | $14,000 | $3,000 | No limit except for the 2% non-elective contributions capped at $305,000 |
| Defined Benefit Plan | $245,000 | N/A | Capped at $305,000, or lower limit defined in the plan |
| 401(k) | $20,500 | $6,500 | Employer contributions cannot take into account compensation in excess of $305,000 |
| 403(b), 457(b), Roth 401(k) | $20,500 | $6,500 | Employer contributions cannot take into account compensation in excess of $305,000 |

### Health Savings Accounts*

| ANNUAL LIMIT | MAXIMUM CONTRIBUTION |
|---|---|
| Self-Only HDHP Coverage | $3,650 |
| Family HDHP Coverage | $7,300 |
| Catch-up for 55 and older by end of calendar year | $1,000 |

*HSAs are only available for taxpayers enrolled in a qualifying high-deductible health plan (HDHP)

### Education Credits & Exclusions

| CREDIT / EXCLUSION | MAXIMUM CREDIT / EXCLUSION | INCOME PHASEOUTS AT MAGI OF |
|---|---|---|
| American Opportunity Tax Credit/Hope | $2,500 credit | $160,000 – $180,000 joint $80,000 – $90,000 all others |
| Lifetime Learning Credit | $2,000 credit | $160,000 – $180,000 joint $80,000 – $90,000 all others |
| Savings bond interest tax-free if used for education | Exclusion limited to amount of qualified expenses | $128,650 – $158,650 joint $85,800 – $100,800 all others |

### Social Security

| FILING STATUS | PROVISIONAL INCOME | AMOUNT OF SS SUBJECT TO TAXES |
|---|---|---|
| **TAX ON SOCIAL SECURITY BENEFITS: INCOME BRACKETS** | | |
| Single, head of household, qualifying widow(er), married filing separately and living apart from spouse | Under $25,000 | 0 |
| | $25,000 – $34,000 | up to 50% |
| | Over $34,000 | up to 85% |
| Married filing jointly | Under $32,000 | 0 |
| | $32,000 – $44,000 | up to 50% |
| | Over $44,000 | up to 85% |
| Married filing separately and living with spouse | Over $0 | up to 85% |

### FICA

| SS TAX PAID ON INCOME UP TO $147,000 | PERCENTAGE WITHHELD | MAXIMUM TAX PAYABLE |
|---|---|---|
| **Tax (FICA)** | | |
| Employer pays | 6.2% | $9,114.00 |
| Employee pays | 6.2% | $9,114.00 |
| Self-employed pays | 12.4% | $18,228.00 |

### Medicare Tax

| SS TAX PAID ON INCOME | PERCENTAGE WITHHELD |
|---|---|
| Employer pays | 1.45% |
| Employee pays | 1.45% + 0.9% on wages over $200,000 (single) or $250,000 (joint) |
| Self-employed pays | 2.90% + 0.9% on self-employment income over $200,000 (single) or $250,000 (joint) |

### Reduction of Social Security Benefits Before Full Retirement Age

| AGE WHEN BENEFITS BEGIN | PERCENTAGE OF SOCIAL SECURITY BENEFITS | |
|---|---|---|
| | FRA of 66* | FRA of 67 |
| 62 | 75.0% | 70.0% |
| 63 | 80.0% | 75.0% |
| 64 | 86.7% | 80.0% |
| 65 | 93.3% | 86.7% |
| 66 | 100.0% | 93.3% |
| 67 | 100.0% | 100.0% |

*Full retirement age determined by year of birth. Source SSA.Gov

### Retirement Earnings Exempt Amounts

| | |
|---|---|
| Before Full Retirement Age (FRA) | $19,560 |
| During the year in which FRA is reached | $51,960 |
| After FRA | No limit after FRA |

### Deductibility of Long-Term Care Premiums on Qualified Policies

| ATTAINED AGE BEFORE CLOSE OF TAX YEAR | AMOUNT OF LTC PREMIUMS THAT QUALIFY AS MEDICAL EXPENSES IN 2022 |
|---|---|
| 40 or less | $450 |
| 41 to 50 | $850 |
| 51 to 60 | $1,690 |
| 61 to 70 | $4,510 |
| Over 70 | $5,640 |

**Form 941 for 2023:** **Employer's QUARTERLY Federal Tax Return**
(Rev. March 2023)   Department of the Treasury — Internal Revenue Service

950122

OMB No. 1545-0029

**Employer identification number (EIN)** ☐☐ – ☐☐☐☐☐☐☐

**Name** *(not your trade name)*

**Trade name** *(if any)*

**Address**

| | | |
|---|---|---|
| Number | Street | Suite or room number |
| City | State | ZIP code |
| Foreign country name | Foreign province/county | Foreign postal code |

**Report for this Quarter of 2023**
(Check one.)

☐ **1:** January, February, March

☐ **2:** April, May, June

☐ **3:** July, August, September

☐ **4:** October, November, December

Go to *www.irs.gov/Form941* for instructions and the latest information.

Read the separate instructions before you complete Form 941. Type or print within the boxes.

**Part 1:**   **Answer these questions for this quarter.**

**1**   Number of employees who received wages, tips, or other compensation for the pay period including: *Mar. 12 (Quarter 1), June 12 (Quarter 2), Sept. 12 (Quarter 3),* or *Dec. 12 (Quarter 4)*   **1** _____

**2**   Wages, tips, and other compensation . . . . . . . . . .   **2** _____

**3**   Federal income tax withheld from wages, tips, and other compensation . . . .   **3** _____

**4**   If no wages, tips, and other compensation are subject to social security or Medicare tax   ☐ Check and go to **line 6.**

| | Column 1 | | Column 2 | |
|---|---|---|---|---|
| **5a** Taxable social security wages* . . | _____ | × 0.124 = | _____ | |
| **5a** (i)  Qualified sick leave wages* . . | _____ | × 0.062 = | _____ | |
| **5a** (ii) Qualified family leave wages* . . | _____ | × 0.062 = | _____ | |
| **5b** Taxable social security tips . . . | _____ | × 0.124 = | _____ | |
| **5c** Taxable Medicare wages & tips . . | _____ | × 0.029 = | _____ | |
| **5d** Taxable wages & tips subject to Additional Medicare Tax withholding | _____ | × 0.009 = | _____ | |

*Include taxable qualified sick and family leave wages paid in this quarter of 2023 for leave taken after March 31, 2021, and before October 1, 2021, on line 5a. Use lines 5a(i) and 5a(ii) **only** for taxable qualified sick and family leave wages paid in this quarter of 2023 for leave taken after March 31, 2020, and before April 1, 2021.

**5e**   Total social security and Medicare taxes. Add Column 2 from lines 5a, 5a(i), 5a(ii), 5b, 5c, and 5d   **5e** _____

**5f**   Section 3121(q) Notice and Demand—Tax due on unreported tips (see instructions) . .   **5f** _____

**6**   Total taxes before adjustments. Add lines 3, 5e, and 5f . . . . . . . . . .   **6** _____

**7**   Current quarter's adjustment for fractions of cents . . . . . . . . . . .   **7** _____

**8**   Current quarter's adjustment for sick pay . . . . . . . . . . . . .   **8** _____

**9**   Current quarter's adjustments for tips and group-term life insurance . . . . . .   **9** _____

**10**   Total taxes after adjustments. Combine lines 6 through 9 . . . . . . . . .   **10** _____

**11a**   Qualified small business payroll tax credit for increasing research activities. Attach Form 8974   **11a** _____

**11b**   Nonrefundable portion of credit for qualified sick and family leave wages for leave taken before April 1, 2021 . . . . . . . . . . . . . . . . . . . .   **11b** _____

**11c**   Reserved for future use . . . . . . . . . . . . . . . . . .   **11c** _____

You MUST complete all three pages of Form 941 and SIGN it.

For Privacy Act and Paperwork Reduction Act Notice, see the back of the Payment Voucher.   Cat. No. 17001Z   Form **941** (Rev. 3-2023)

951222

| Name (not your trade name) | Employer identification number (EIN) |
|---|---|
| | — |

**Part 1:** Answer these questions for this quarter. *(continued)*

**11d** Nonrefundable portion of credit for qualified sick and family leave wages for leave taken after March 31, 2021, and before October 1, 2021 . . . . . . . . . . . . . . **11d** [_____ .]

**11e** Reserved for future use . . . . . . . . . . . . . . **11e** [_____ .]

**11f** Reserved for future use . . . . . . . . . [_____]

**11g** Total nonrefundable credits. Add lines 11a, 11b, and 11d . . . . . . . . . . **11g** [_____ .]

**12** Total taxes after adjustments and nonrefundable credits. Subtract line 11g from line 10 . **12** [_____ .]

**13a** Total deposits for this quarter, including overpayment applied from a prior quarter and overpayments applied from Form 941-X, 941-X (PR), 944-X, or 944-X (SP) filed in the current quarter **13a** [_____ .]

**13b** Reserved for future use . . . . . . . . . . . . . . **13b** [_____ .]

**13c** Refundable portion of credit for qualified sick and family leave wages for leave taken before April 1, 2021 . . . . . . . . . . . . . . . . . . **13c** [_____ .]

**13d** Reserved for future use . . . . . . . . . . . . . . **13d** [_____ .]

**13e** Refundable portion of credit for qualified sick and family leave wages for leave taken after March 31, 2021, and before October 1, 2021 . . . . . . . . . . **13e** [_____ .]

**13f** Reserved for future use . . . . . . . . . . . . . . **13f** [_____ .]

**13g** Total deposits and refundable credits. Add lines 13a, 13c, and 13e . . . . . . . . **13g** [_____ .]

**13h** Reserved for future use . . . . . . . . . . . . . . **13h** [_____ .]

**13i** Reserved for future use . . . . . . . . . . . . . . **13i** [_____ .]

**14** Balance due. If line 12 is more than line 13g, enter the difference and see instructions . . . **14** [_____ .]

**15** Overpayment. If line 13g is more than line 12, enter the difference [_____ .] Check one: ☐ Apply to next return. ☐ Send a refund.

**Part 2:** Tell us about your deposit schedule and tax liability for this quarter.

If you're unsure about whether you're a monthly schedule depositor or a semiweekly schedule depositor, see section 11 of Pub. 15.

**16** Check one: ☐ Line 12 on this return is less than $2,500 or line 12 on the return for the prior quarter was less than $2,500, and you didn't incur a $100,000 next-day deposit obligation during the current quarter. If line 12 for the prior quarter was less than $2,500 but line 12 on this return is $100,000 or more, you must provide a record of your federal tax liability. If you're a monthly schedule depositor, complete the deposit schedule below; if you're a semiweekly schedule depositor, attach Schedule B (Form 941). Go to Part 3.

☐ You were a monthly schedule depositor for the entire quarter. Enter your tax liability for each month and total liability for the quarter, then go to Part 3.

Tax liability: Month 1 [_____ .]

Month 2 [_____ .]

Month 3 [_____ .]

Total liability for quarter [_____ .] Total must equal line 12.

☐ You were a semiweekly schedule depositor for any part of this quarter. Complete Schedule B (Form 941), Report of Tax Liability for Semiweekly Schedule Depositors, and attach it to Form 941. Go to Part 3.

You MUST complete all three pages of Form 941 and SIGN it.

950922

| Name *(not your trade name)* | Employer identification number (EIN) |
|---|---|
| | – |

**Part 3:** Tell us about your business. If a question does NOT apply to your business, leave it blank.

17 If your business has closed or you stopped paying wages . . . . . . . . . . . . . ☐ Check here, and

enter the final date you paid wages [ / / ] ; also attach a statement to your return. See instructions.

18 If you're a seasonal employer and you don't have to file a return for every quarter of the year . . . ☐ Check here.

19 Qualified health plan expenses allocable to qualified sick leave wages for leave taken before April 1, 2021   19 [ . ]

20 Qualified health plan expenses allocable to qualified family leave wages for leave taken before April 1, 2021   20 [ . ]

21 Reserved for future use . . . . . . . . . . . . . .   21 [ . ]

22 Reserved for future use . . . . . . . . . . . . . .   22 [ . ]

23 Qualified sick leave wages for leave taken after March 31, 2021, and before October 1, 2021   23 [ . ]

24 Qualified health plan expenses allocable to qualified sick leave wages reported on line 23   24 [ . ]

25 Amounts under certain collectively bargained agreements allocable to qualified sick leave wages reported on line 23 . . . . . . . . . . .   25 [ . ]

26 Qualified family leave wages for leave taken after March 31, 2021, and before October 1, 2021   26 [ . ]

27 Qualified health plan expenses allocable to qualified family leave wages reported on line 26   27 [ . ]

28 Amounts under certain collectively bargained agreements allocable to qualified family leave wages reported on line 26 . . . . . . . . . . . . . .   28 [ . ]

**Part 4:** May we speak with your third-party designee?

Do you want to allow an employee, a paid tax preparer, or another person to discuss this return with the IRS? See the instructions for details.

☐ Yes. Designee's name and phone number

Select a 5-digit personal identification number (PIN) to use when talking to the IRS. ☐ ☐ ☐ ☐ ☐

☐ No.

**Part 5:** Sign here. You MUST complete all three pages of Form 941 and SIGN it.

Under penalties of perjury, I declare that I have examined this return, including accompanying schedules and statements, and to the best of my knowledge and belief, it is true, correct, and complete. Declaration of preparer (other than taxpayer) is based on all information of which preparer has any knowledge.

**Sign your name here**

Print your name here

Print your title here

Date [ / / ]   Best daytime phone

**Paid Preparer Use Only**   Check if you're self-employed . . . ☐

| Preparer's name | | PTIN | |
| Preparer's signature | | Date | / / |
| Firm's name (or yours if self-employed) | | EIN | |
| Address | | Phone | |
| City | State | ZIP code | |

Page 3   Form **941** (Rev. 3-2023)

44

# Form 941-V,
# Payment Voucher

## Purpose of Form

Complete Form 941-V if you're making a payment with Form 941. We will use the completed voucher to credit your payment more promptly and accurately, and to improve our service to you.

## Making Payments With Form 941

To avoid a penalty, make your payment with Form 941 **only if**:

• Your total taxes after adjustments and nonrefundable credits (Form 941, line 12) for either the current quarter or the preceding quarter are less than $2,500, you didn't incur a $100,000 next-day deposit obligation during the current quarter, and you're paying in full with a timely filed return; or

• You're a monthly schedule depositor making a payment in accordance with the Accuracy of Deposits Rule. See section 11 of Pub. 15 for details. In this case, the amount of your payment may be $2,500 or more.

Otherwise, you must make deposits by electronic funds transfer. See section 11 of Pub. 15 for deposit instructions. Don't use Form 941-V to make federal tax deposits.

⚠ **CAUTION** Use Form 941-V when making any payment with Form 941. However, if you pay an amount with Form 941 that should've been deposited, you may be subject to a penalty. See Deposit Penalties in section 11 of Pub. 15.

## Specific Instructions

**Box 1—Employer identification number (EIN).** If you don't have an EIN, you may apply for one online by visiting the IRS website at *www.irs.gov/EIN*. You may also apply for an EIN by faxing or mailing Form SS-4 to the IRS. If you haven't received your EIN by the due date of Form 941, write "Applied For" and the date you applied in this entry space.

**Box 2—Amount paid.** Enter the amount paid with Form 941.

**Box 3—Tax period.** Darken the circle identifying the quarter for which the payment is made. Darken only one circle.

**Box 4—Name and address.** Enter your name and address as shown on Form 941.

• Enclose your check or money order made payable to "United States Treasury." Be sure to enter your EIN, "Form 941," and the tax period ("1st Quarter 2023," "2nd Quarter 2023," "3rd Quarter 2023," or "4th Quarter 2023") on your check or money order. Don't send cash. Don't staple Form 941-V or your payment to Form 941 (or to each other).

• Detach Form 941-V and send it with your payment and Form 941 to the address in the Instructions for Form 941.

**Note:** You must also complete the entity information above Part 1 on Form 941.

---

**Detach Here and Mail With Your Payment and Form 941.**

| Form **941-V**<br>Department of the Treasury<br>Internal Revenue Service | **Payment Voucher**<br>Don't staple this voucher or your payment to Form 941. | OMB No. 1545-0029<br>20**23** |
|---|---|---|

| 1 Enter your employer identification number (EIN).<br>— | 2 **Enter the amount of your payment.**<br>Make your check or money order payable to "**United States Treasury**." | Dollars | Cents |
|---|---|---|---|

| 3 Tax Period | | 4 Enter your business name (individual name if sole proprietor). |
|---|---|---|
| ○ 1st Quarter | ○ 3rd Quarter | Enter your address. |
| ○ 2nd Quarter | ○ 4th Quarter | Enter your city, state, and ZIP code; or your city, foreign country name, foreign province/county, and foreign postal code. |

Form 941 (Rev. 3-2023)

**Privacy Act and Paperwork Reduction Act Notice.**
We ask for the information on Form 941 to carry out the Internal Revenue laws of the United States. We need it to figure and collect the right amount of tax. Subtitle C, Employment Taxes, of the Internal Revenue Code imposes employment taxes on wages and provides for income tax withholding. Form 941 is used to determine the amount of taxes that you owe. Section 6011 requires you to provide the requested information if the tax is applicable to you. Section 6109 requires you to provide your identification number. If you fail to provide this information in a timely manner, or provide false or fraudulent information, you may be subject to penalties.

You're not required to provide the information requested on a form that is subject to the Paperwork Reduction Act unless the form displays a valid OMB control number. Books and records relating to a form or its instructions must be retained as long as their contents may become material in the administration of any Internal Revenue law.

Generally, tax returns and return information are confidential, as required by section 6103. However, section 6103 allows or requires the IRS to disclose or give the information shown on your tax return to others as described in the Code. For example, we may disclose your tax information to the Department of Justice for civil and criminal litigation, and to cities, states, the District of Columbia, and U.S. commonwealths and possessions for use in administering their tax laws. We may also disclose this information to other countries under a tax treaty, to federal and state agencies to enforce federal nontax criminal laws, or to federal law enforcement and intelligence agencies to combat terrorism.

The time needed to complete and file Form 941 will vary depending on individual circumstances. The estimated average time is:

**Recordkeeping** . . . . . . . . . . . 22 hr., 28 min.

**Learning about the law or the form** . . . . 53 min.

**Preparing, copying, assembling, and sending the form to the IRS** . . . . . 1 hr., 18 min.

If you have comments concerning the accuracy of these time estimates or suggestions for making Form 941 simpler, we would be happy to hear from you. You can send us comments from *www.irs.gov/FormComments*. Or you can send your comments to Internal Revenue Service, Tax Forms and Publications Division, 1111 Constitution Ave. NW, IR-6526, Washington, DC 20224. Don't send Form 941 to this address. Instead, see *Where Should You File?* in the Instructions for Form 941.

| Form **SS-4**<br>(Rev. December 2019)<br>Department of the Treasury<br>Internal Revenue Service | **Application for Employer Identification Number**<br>(For use by employers, corporations, partnerships, trusts, estates, churches,<br>government agencies, Indian tribal entities, certain individuals, and others.)<br>▶ Go to *www.irs.gov/FormSS4* for instructions and the latest information.<br>▶ See separate instructions for each line.  ▶ Keep a copy for your records. | OMB No. 1545-0003<br><br>EIN |
|---|---|---|

| | | |
|---|---|---|
| 1 | Legal name of entity (or individual) for whom the EIN is being requested | |

| 2 | Trade name of business (if different from name on line 1) | 3 | Executor, administrator, trustee, "care of" name |
|---|---|---|---|
| 4a | Mailing address (room, apt., suite no. and street, or P.O. box) | 5a | Street address (if different) (Don't enter a P.O. box.) |
| 4b | City, state, and ZIP code (if foreign, see instructions) | 5b | City, state, and ZIP code (if foreign, see instructions) |
| 6 | County and state where principal business is located | | |
| 7a | Name of responsible party | 7b | SSN, ITIN, or EIN |

**8a** Is this application for a limited liability company (LLC) (or a foreign equivalent)? ☐ Yes ☐ No  **8b** If 8a is "Yes," enter the number of LLC members ▶

**8c** If 8a is "Yes," was the LLC organized in the United States? ☐ Yes ☐ No

**9a** Type of entity (check only one box). Caution: If 8a is "Yes," see the instructions for the correct box to check.
☐ Sole proprietor (SSN) _____ ☐ Estate (SSN of decedent) _____
☐ Partnership ☐ Plan administrator (TIN) _____
☐ Corporation (enter form number to be filed) ▶ _____ ☐ Trust (TIN of grantor) _____
☐ Personal service corporation ☐ Military/National Guard ☐ State/local government
☐ Church or church-controlled organization ☐ Farmers' cooperative ☐ Federal government
☐ Other nonprofit organization (specify) ▶ ☐ REMIC ☐ Indian tribal governments/enterprises
☐ Other (specify) ▶ Group Exemption Number (GEN) if any ▶

**9b** If a corporation, name the state or foreign country (if applicable) where incorporated | State | Foreign country

**10** Reason for applying (check only one box)
☐ Started new business (specify type) ▶ ☐ Banking purpose (specify purpose) ▶
☐ Changed type of organization (specify new type) ▶
☐ Purchased going business
☐ Hired employees (Check the box and see line 13.) ☐ Created a trust (specify type) ▶
☐ Compliance with IRS withholding regulations ☐ Created a pension plan (specify type) ▶
☐ Other (specify) ▶

**11** Date business started or acquired (month, day, year). See instructions. | **12** Closing month of accounting year
**14** If you expect your employment tax liability to be $1,000 or less in a full calendar year **and** want to file Form 944 annually instead of Forms 941 quarterly, check here. (Your employment tax liability generally will be $1,000 or less if you expect to pay $5,000 or less in total wages.) If you don't check this box, you must file Form 941 for every quarter. ☐

**13** Highest number of employees expected in the next 12 months (enter -0- if none). If no employees expected, skip line 14.

| Agricultural | Household | Other |
|---|---|---|
| | | |

**15** First date wages or annuities were paid (month, day, year). Note: If applicant is a withholding agent, enter date income will first be paid to nonresident alien (month, day, year) ▶

**16** Check **one** box that best describes the principal activity of your business. ☐ Health care & social assistance ☐ Wholesale-agent/broker
☐ Construction ☐ Rental & leasing ☐ Transportation & warehousing ☐ Accommodation & food service ☐ Wholesale-other ☐ Retail
☐ Real estate ☐ Manufacturing ☐ Finance & insurance ☐ Other (specify) ▶

**17** Indicate principal line of merchandise sold, specific construction work done, products produced, or services provided.

**18** Has the applicant entity shown on line 1 ever applied for and received an EIN? ☐ Yes ☐ No
If "Yes," write previous EIN here ▶

| **Third Party Designee** | Complete this section **only** if you want to authorize the named individual to receive the entity's EIN and answer questions about the completion of this form. | |
|---|---|---|
| | Designee's name | Designee's telephone number (include area code) |
| | Address and ZIP code | Designee's fax number (include area code) |

Under penalties of perjury, I declare that I have examined this application, and to the best of my knowledge and belief, it is true, correct, and complete. | Applicant's telephone number (include area code)
Name and title (type or print clearly) ▶
Signature ▶ Date ▶ | Applicant's fax number (include area code)

For Privacy Act and Paperwork Reduction Act Notice, see separate instructions. | Cat. No. 16055N | Form **SS-4** (Rev. 12-2019)

# Do I Need an EIN?

File Form SS-4 if the applicant entity doesn't already have an EIN but is required to show an EIN on any return, statement, or other document.[1] See also the separate instructions for each line on Form SS-4.

| IF the applicant... | AND... | THEN... |
|---|---|---|
| started a new business | doesn't currently have (nor expect to have) employees | complete lines 1, 2, 4a–8a, 8b–c (if applicable), 9a, 9b (if applicable), and 10–14 and 16–18. |
| hired (or will hire) employees, including household employees | doesn't already have an EIN | complete lines 1, 2, 4a–6, 7a–b, 8a, 8b–c (if applicable), 9a, 9b (if applicable), 10–18. |
| opened a bank account | needs an EIN for banking purposes only | complete lines 1–5b, 7a–b, 8a, 8b–c (if applicable), 9a, 9b (if applicable), 10, and 18. |
| changed type of organization | either the legal character of the organization or its ownership changed (for example, you incorporate a sole proprietorship or form a partnership)[2] | complete lines 1–18 (as applicable). |
| purchased a going business[3] | doesn't already have an EIN | complete lines 1–18 (as applicable). |
| created a trust | the trust is other than a grantor trust or an IRA trust[4] | complete lines 1–18 (as applicable). |
| created a pension plan as a plan administrator[5] | needs an EIN for reporting purposes | complete lines 1, 3, 4a–5b, 7a–b, 9a, 10, and 18. |
| is a foreign person needing an EIN to comply with IRS withholding regulations | needs an EIN to complete a Form W-8 (other than Form W-8ECI), avoid withholding on portfolio assets, or claim tax treaty benefits[6] | complete lines 1–5b, 7a–b (SSN or ITIN as applicable), 8a, 8b–c (if applicable), 9a, 9b (if applicable), 10, and 18. |
| is administering an estate | needs an EIN to report estate income on Form 1041 | complete lines 1–7b, 9a, 10–12, 13–17 (if applicable), and 18. |
| is a withholding agent for taxes on nonwage income paid to an alien (that is, individual, corporation, or partnership, etc.) | is an agent, broker, fiduciary, manager, tenant, or spouse who is required to file Form 1042, Annual Withholding Tax Return for U.S. Source Income of Foreign Persons | complete lines 1, 2, 3 (if applicable), 4a–5b, 7a–b, 8a, 8b–c (if applicable), 9a, 9b (if applicable), 10, and 18. |
| is a state or local agency | serves as a tax reporting agent for public assistance recipients under Rev. Proc. 80-4, 1980-1 C.B. 581[7] | complete lines 1, 2, 4a–5b, 7a–b, 9a, 10, and 18. |
| is a single-member LLC (or similar single-member entity) | needs an EIN to file Form 8832, Entity Classification Election, for filing employment tax returns and excise tax returns, or for state reporting purposes[8], or is a foreign-owned U.S. disregarded entity and needs an EIN to file Form 5472, Information Return of a 25% Foreign-Owned U.S. Corporation or a Foreign Corporation Engaged in a U.S. Trade or Business | complete lines 1–18 (as applicable). |
| is an S corporation | needs an EIN to file Form 2553, Election by a Small Business Corporation[9] | complete lines 1–18 (as applicable). |

[1] For example, a sole proprietorship or self-employed farmer who establishes a qualified retirement plan, or is required to file excise, employment, alcohol, tobacco, or firearms returns, must have an EIN. A partnership, corporation, REMIC (real estate mortgage investment conduit), nonprofit organization (church, club, etc.), or farmers' cooperative must use an EIN for any tax-related purpose even if the entity doesn't have employees.

[2] However, don't apply for a new EIN if the existing entity only (a) changed its business name, (b) elected on Form 8832 to change the way it is taxed (or is covered by the default rules), or (c) terminated its partnership status because at least 50% of the total interests in partnership capital and profits were sold or exchanged within a 12-month period. The EIN of the terminated partnership should continue to be used. See Regulations section 301.6109-1(d)(2)(iii).

[3] Don't use the EIN of the prior business unless you became the "owner" of a corporation by acquiring its stock.

[4] However, grantor trusts that don't file using Optional Method 1 and IRA trusts that are required to file Form 990-T, Exempt Organization Business Income Tax Return, must have an EIN. For more information on grantor trusts, see the Instructions for Form 1041.

[5] A plan administrator is the person or group of persons specified as the administrator by the instrument under which the plan is operated.

[6] Entities applying to be a Qualified Intermediary (QI) need a QI-EIN even if they already have an EIN. See Rev. Proc. 2000-12.

[7] See also *Household employer agent* in the instructions. **Note:** State or local agencies may need an EIN for other reasons, for example, hired employees.

[8] See *Disregarded entities* in the instructions for details on completing Form SS-4 for an LLC.

[9] An existing corporation that is electing or revoking S corporation status should use its previously-assigned EIN.

**Form 8824**

Department of the Treasury
Internal Revenue Service

**Like-Kind Exchanges**
(and section 1043 conflict-of-interest sales)
Attach to your tax return.
Go to *www.irs.gov/Form8824* for instructions and the latest information.

OMB No. 1545-1190

**2022**

Attachment Sequence No. **109**

Name(s) shown on tax return | Identifying number

**Part I    Information on the Like-Kind Exchange**

**Note:** Only real property should be described on lines 1 and 2. If the property described on line 1 or line 2 is real property located outside the United States, indicate the country.

**1**  Description of like-kind property given up:

**2**  Description of like-kind property received:

**3**  Date like-kind property given up was originally acquired (month, day, year) . . . . . . . . . | **3** | MM/DD/YYYY

**4**  Date you actually transferred your property to the other party (month, day, year) . . . . . . | **4** | MM/DD/YYYY

**5**  Date like-kind property you received was identified by written notice to another party (month, day, year). See instructions for 45-day written identification requirement . . . . . . . . . . | **5** | MM/DD/YYYY

**6**  Date you actually received the like-kind property from other party (month, day, year). See instructions | **6** | MM/DD/YYYY

**7**  Was the exchange of the property given up or received made with a related party, either directly or indirectly (such as through an intermediary)? See instructions. If "Yes," complete Part II. If "No," go to Part III . . . ☐ **Yes**   ☐ **No**

**Note:** Do not file this form if a related party sold property into the exchange, directly or indirectly (such as through an intermediary); that property became your replacement property; and none of the exceptions on line 11 applies to the exchange. Instead, report the disposition of the property as if the exchange had been a sale. If one of the exceptions on line 11 applies to the exchange, complete Part II.

**Part II    Related Party Exchange Information**

**8**  Name of related party | Relationship to you | Related party's identifying number

Address (no., street, and apt., room, or suite no.; city or town; state; and ZIP code)

**9**  During this tax year (and before the date that is 2 years after the last transfer of property that was part of the exchange), did the related party sell or dispose of any part of the like-kind property received from you (or an intermediary) in the exchange? . . . . . . . . . . . . . . . . . . . . . . ☐ **Yes**   ☐ **No**

**10**  During this tax year (and before the date that is 2 years after the last transfer of property that was part of the exchange), did you sell or dispose of any part of the like-kind property you received? . . . . . . ☐ **Yes**   ☐ **No**

*If both lines 9 and 10 are "No" and this is the year of the exchange, go to Part III. If both lines 9 and 10 are "No" and this is **not** the year of the exchange, stop here. If either line 9 or line 10 is "Yes," complete Part III and report on this year's tax return the deferred gain or (loss) from line 24 **unless** one of the exceptions on line 11 applies.*

**11**  If one of the exceptions below applies to the disposition, check the applicable box.

**a**  ☐ The disposition was after the death of either of the related parties.

**b**  ☐ The disposition was an involuntary conversion, and the threat of conversion occurred after the exchange.

**c**  ☐ You can establish to the satisfaction of the IRS that neither the exchange nor the disposition had tax avoidance as one of its principal purposes. If this box is checked, attach an explanation. See instructions.

For Paperwork Reduction Act Notice, see the instructions.      Cat. No. 12311A      Form **8824** (2022)

| Name(s) shown on tax return. Do not enter name and social security number if shown on other side. | Your social security number |
|---|---|

## Part III — Realized Gain or (Loss), Recognized Gain, and Basis of Like-Kind Property Received

**Caution:** If you transferred **and** received (**a**) more than one group of like-kind properties, or (**b**) cash or other (not like-kind) property, see *Reporting of multi-asset exchanges* in the instructions.

**Note:** Complete lines 12 through 14 **only** if you gave up property that was not like-kind. Otherwise, go to line 15.

| | | | |
|---|---|---|---|
| 12 | Fair market value (FMV) of other property given up. See instructions | 12 | |
| 13 | Adjusted basis of other property given up | 13 | |
| 14 | Gain or (loss) recognized on other property given up. Subtract line 13 from line 12. Report the gain or (loss) in the same manner as if the exchange had been a sale | 14 | |

**Caution:** If the property given up was used previously or partly as a home, see *Property used as home* in the instructions.

| | | | |
|---|---|---|---|
| 15 | Cash received, FMV of other property received, plus net liabilities assumed by other party, reduced (but not below zero) by any exchange expenses you incurred. See instructions | 15 | |
| 16 | FMV of like-kind property you received | 16 | |
| 17 | Add lines 15 and 16 | 17 | |
| 18 | Adjusted basis of like-kind property you gave up, net amounts paid to other party, plus any exchange expenses **not** used on line 15. See instructions | 18 | |
| 19 | **Realized gain or (loss).** Subtract line 18 from line 17 | 19 | |
| 20 | Enter the smaller of line 15 or line 19, but not less than zero | 20 | |
| 21 | Ordinary income under recapture rules. Enter here and on Form 4797, line 16. See instructions | 21 | |
| 22 | Subtract line 21 from line 20. If zero or less, enter -0-. If more than zero, enter here and on Schedule D or Form 4797, unless the installment method applies. See instructions | 22 | |
| 23 | **Recognized gain.** Add lines 21 and 22 | 23 | |
| 24 | Deferred gain or (loss). Subtract line 23 from line 19. If a related party exchange, see instructions | 24 | |
| 25 | **Basis of like-kind property received.** Subtract line 15 from the sum of lines 18 and 23. See instructions | 25 | |

## Part IV — Deferral of Gain From Section 1043 Conflict-of-Interest Sales

**Note:** This part is to be used **only** by officers or employees of the executive branch of the federal government or judicial officers of the federal government (including certain spouses, minor or dependent children, and trustees as described in section 1043) for reporting nonrecognition of gain under section 1043 on the sale of property to comply with the conflict-of-interest requirements. This part can be used **only** if the cost of the replacement property is more than the basis of the divested property.

| | | | |
|---|---|---|---|
| 26 | Enter the number from the upper right corner of your certificate of divestiture. (**Do not** attach a copy of your certificate. Keep the certificate with your records.) | | — |
| 27 | Description of divested property | | |
| 28 | Description of replacement property | | |
| 29 | Date divested property was sold (month, day, year) | 29 | MM/DD/YYYY |
| 30 | Sales price of divested property. See instructions | 30 | |
| 31 | Basis of divested property | 31 | |
| 32 | **Realized gain.** Subtract line 31 from line 30 | 32 | |
| 33 | Cost of replacement property purchased within 60 days after date of sale | 33 | |
| 34 | Subtract line 33 from line 30. If zero or less, enter -0- | 34 | |
| 35 | Ordinary income under recapture rules. Enter here and on Form 4797, line 10. See instructions | 35 | |
| 36 | Subtract line 35 from line 34. If zero or less, enter -0-. If more than zero, enter here and on Schedule D or Form 4797. See instructions | 36 | |
| 37 | **Deferred gain.** Subtract the sum of lines 35 and 36 from line 32 | 37 | |
| 38 | **Basis of replacement property.** Subtract line 37 from line 33 | 38 | |

Form **8824** (2022)

| Form **4562** | **Depreciation and Amortization** | OMB No. 1545-0172 |
|---|---|---|
| Department of the Treasury<br>Internal Revenue Service | (Including Information on Listed Property)<br>**Attach to your tax return.**<br>**Go to www.irs.gov/Form4562 for instructions and the latest information.** | 20**22**<br>Attachment<br>Sequence No. **179** |

| Name(s) shown on return | Business or activity to which this form relates | Identifying number |
|---|---|---|

### Part I — Election To Expense Certain Property Under Section 179

**Note:** If you have any listed property, complete Part V before you complete Part I.

| | | | |
|---|---|---|---|
| 1 | Maximum amount (see instructions) . . . . . . . . . . . | **1** | |
| 2 | Total cost of section 179 property placed in service (see instructions) . . . . . . . | **2** | |
| 3 | Threshold cost of section 179 property before reduction in limitation (see instructions) . . . . . . | **3** | |
| 4 | Reduction in limitation. Subtract line 3 from line 2. If zero or less, enter -0- . . . . . . . . | **4** | |
| 5 | Dollar limitation for tax year. Subtract line 4 from line 1. If zero or less, enter -0-. If married filing separately, see instructions . . . . . . . . . . . . . | **5** | |

| 6 | (a) Description of property | (b) Cost (business use only) | (c) Elected cost |
|---|---|---|---|
| | | | |
| | | | |

| | | | |
|---|---|---|---|
| 7 | Listed property. Enter the amount from line 29 . . . . . . . . | **7** | |
| 8 | Total elected cost of section 179 property. Add amounts in column (c), lines 6 and 7 . . . . . | **8** | |
| 9 | Tentative deduction. Enter the **smaller** of line 5 or line 8 . . . . . . . . . . | **9** | |
| 10 | Carryover of disallowed deduction from line 13 of your 2021 Form 4562 . . . . . . . | **10** | |
| 11 | Business income limitation. Enter the smaller of business income (not less than zero) or line 5. See instructions | **11** | |
| 12 | Section 179 expense deduction. Add lines 9 and 10, but don't enter more than line 11 . . . . . . | **12** | |
| 13 | Carryover of disallowed deduction to 2023. Add lines 9 and 10, less line 12 . | **13** | |

**Note:** Don't use Part II or Part III below for listed property. Instead, use Part V.

### Part II — Special Depreciation Allowance and Other Depreciation (Don't include listed property. See instructions.)

| | | | |
|---|---|---|---|
| 14 | Special depreciation allowance for qualified property (other than listed property) placed in service during the tax year. See instructions . . . . . . . . . . . . . . . | **14** | |
| 15 | Property subject to section 168(f)(1) election . . . . . . . . . . . | **15** | |
| 16 | Other depreciation (including ACRS) . . . . . . . . . . . . . | **16** | |

### Part III — MACRS Depreciation (Don't include listed property. See instructions.)

#### Section A

| | | | |
|---|---|---|---|
| 17 | MACRS deductions for assets placed in service in tax years beginning before 2022 . . . . . . | **17** | |
| 18 | If you are electing to group any assets placed in service during the tax year into one or more general asset accounts, check here . . . . . . . . . . . . . . . . ☐ | | |

#### Section B—Assets Placed in Service During 2022 Tax Year Using the General Depreciation System

| (a) Classification of property | (b) Month and year placed in service | (c) Basis for depreciation (business/investment use only—see instructions) | (d) Recovery period | (e) Convention | (f) Method | (g) Depreciation deduction |
|---|---|---|---|---|---|---|
| 19a   3-year property | | | | | | |
| b    5-year property | | | | | | |
| c    7-year property | | | | | | |
| d   10-year property | | | | | | |
| e   15-year property | | | | | | |
| f   20-year property | | | | | | |
| g   25-year property | | | 25 yrs. | | S/L | |
| h   Residential rental | | | 27.5 yrs. | MM | S/L | |
|      property | | | 27.5 yrs. | MM | S/L | |
| i   Nonresidential real | | | 39 yrs. | MM | S/L | |
|      property | | | | MM | S/L | |

#### Section C—Assets Placed in Service During 2022 Tax Year Using the Alternative Depreciation System

| | | | | | | |
|---|---|---|---|---|---|---|
| 20a   Class life | | | | | S/L | |
| b   12-year | | | 12 yrs. | | S/L | |
| c   30-year | | | 30 yrs. | MM | S/L | |
| d   40-year | | | 40 yrs. | MM | S/L | |

### Part IV — Summary (See instructions.)

| | | | |
|---|---|---|---|
| 21 | Listed property. Enter amount from line 28 . . . . . . . . . . . . | **21** | |
| 22 | **Total.** Add amounts from line 12, lines 14 through 17, lines 19 and 20 in column (g), and line 21. Enter here and on the appropriate lines of your return. Partnerships and S corporations—see instructions . | **22** | |
| 23 | For assets shown above and placed in service during the current year, enter the portion of the basis attributable to section 263A costs . . . . . . . . . | **23** | |

**For Paperwork Reduction Act Notice, see separate instructions.**     Cat. No. 12906N     Form **4562** (2022)

C.A. KNUCKLES

Form 4562 (2022)                                                                                          Page **2**

**Part V**  **Listed Property** (Include automobiles, certain other vehicles, certain aircraft, and property used for entertainment, recreation, or amusement.)

**Note:** For any vehicle for which you are using the standard mileage rate or deducting lease expense, complete **only** 24a, 24b, columns (a) through (c) of Section A, all of Section B, and Section C if applicable.

**Section A—Depreciation and Other Information (Caution: See the instructions for limits for passenger automobiles.)**

**24a** Do you have evidence to support the business/investment use claimed? ☐ **Yes** ☐ **No**  **24b** If "Yes," is the evidence written? ☐ **Yes** ☐ **No**

| (a) Type of property (list vehicles first) | (b) Date placed in service | (c) Business/investment use percentage | (d) Cost or other basis | (e) Basis for depreciation (business/investment use only) | (f) Recovery period | (g) Method/Convention | (h) Depreciation deduction | (i) Elected section 179 cost |
|---|---|---|---|---|---|---|---|---|
| **25** Special depreciation allowance for qualified listed property placed in service during the tax year and used more than 50% in a qualified business use. See instructions . | | | | | **25** | | | |
| **26** Property used more than 50% in a qualified business use: | | | | | | | | |
| | | % | | | | | | |
| | | % | | | | | | |
| | | % | | | | | | |
| **27** Property used 50% or less in a qualified business use: | | | | | | | | |
| | | % | | | | S/L – | | |
| | | % | | | | S/L – | | |
| | | % | | | | S/L – | | |
| **28** Add amounts in column (h), lines 25 through 27. Enter here and on line 21, page 1 . | | | | | **28** | | | |
| **29** Add amounts in column (i), line 26. Enter here and on line 7, page 1 . . . . . . . . . . . . . | | | | | | | **29** | |

**Section B—Information on Use of Vehicles**

Complete this section for vehicles used by a sole proprietor, partner, or other "more than 5% owner," or related person. If you provided vehicles to your employees, first answer the questions in Section C to see if you meet an exception to completing this section for those vehicles.

| | (a) Vehicle 1 | | (b) Vehicle 2 | | (c) Vehicle 3 | | (d) Vehicle 4 | | (e) Vehicle 5 | | (f) Vehicle 6 | |
|---|---|---|---|---|---|---|---|---|---|---|---|---|
| **30** Total business/investment miles driven during the year (**don't** include commuting miles) . | | | | | | | | | | | | |
| **31** Total commuting miles driven during the year | | | | | | | | | | | | |
| **32** Total other personal (noncommuting) miles driven . . . . . . . . . | | | | | | | | | | | | |
| **33** Total miles driven during the year. Add lines 30 through 32 . . . . . . | | | | | | | | | | | | |
| **34** Was the vehicle available for personal use during off-duty hours? . . . | Yes | No | Yes | No | Yes | No | Yes | No | Yes | No | Yes | No |
| **35** Was the vehicle used primarily by a more than 5% owner or related person? . | | | | | | | | | | | | |
| **36** Is another vehicle available for personal use? | | | | | | | | | | | | |

**Section C—Questions for Employers Who Provide Vehicles for Use by Their Employees**

Answer these questions to determine if you meet an exception to completing Section B for vehicles used by employees who **aren't** more than 5% owners or related persons. See instructions.

| | Yes | No |
|---|---|---|
| **37** Do you maintain a written policy statement that prohibits all personal use of vehicles, including commuting, by your employees? . . . . . . . . . . . . . . . . . . . . . . . . | | |
| **38** Do you maintain a written policy statement that prohibits personal use of vehicles, except commuting, by your employees? See the instructions for vehicles used by corporate officers, directors, or 1% or more owners . . | | |
| **39** Do you treat all use of vehicles by employees as personal use? . . . . . . . . . . | | |
| **40** Do you provide more than five vehicles to your employees, obtain information from your employees about the use of the vehicles, and retain the information received? . . . . . . . . . . . . . | | |
| **41** Do you meet the requirements concerning qualified automobile demonstration use? See instructions . . . . | | |

**Note:** If your answer to 37, 38, 39, 40, or 41 is "Yes," don't complete Section B for the covered vehicles.

**Part VI**  **Amortization**

| (a) Description of costs | (b) Date amortization begins | (c) Amortizable amount | (d) Code section | (e) Amortization period or percentage | (f) Amortization for this year |
|---|---|---|---|---|---|
| **42** Amortization of costs that begins during your 2022 tax year (see instructions): | | | | | |
| | | | | | |
| | | | | | |
| **43** Amortization of costs that began before your 2022 tax year . . . . . . . . . | | | | **43** | |
| **44** **Total.** Add amounts in column (f). See the instructions for where to report . . . . . . . | | | | **44** | |

Form **4562** (2022)

52

| Form **W-4** | **Employee's Withholding Certificate** | OMB No. 1545-0074 |
|---|---|---|
| Department of the Treasury<br>Internal Revenue Service | Complete Form W-4 so that your employer can withhold the correct federal income tax from your pay.<br>**Give Form W-4 to your employer.**<br>**Your withholding is subject to review by the IRS.** | 2023 |

**Step 1:**
**Enter Personal Information**

| (a) First name and middle initial | Last name | (b) Social security number |
|---|---|---|

| Address | | Does your name match the name on your social security card? If not, to ensure you get credit for your earnings, contact SSA at 800-772-1213 or go to *www.ssa.gov*. |
|---|---|---|
| City or town, state, and ZIP code | | |

(c) ☐ **Single** or **Married filing separately**

☐ **Married filing jointly** or **Qualifying surviving spouse**

☐ **Head of household** (Check only if you're unmarried and pay more than half the costs of keeping up a home for yourself and a qualifying individual.)

**Complete Steps 2–4 ONLY if they apply to you; otherwise, skip to Step 5.** See page 2 for more information on each step, who can claim exemption from withholding, other details, and privacy.

**Step 2:**
**Multiple Jobs or Spouse Works**

Complete this step if you (1) hold more than one job at a time, or (2) are married filing jointly and your spouse also works. The correct amount of withholding depends on income earned from all of these jobs.

Do **only one** of the following.

(a) Reserved for future use.

(b) Use the Multiple Jobs Worksheet on page 3 and enter the result in Step 4(c) below; **or**

(c) If there are only two jobs total, you may check this box. Do the same on Form W-4 for the other job. This option is generally more accurate than (b) if pay at the lower paying job is more than half of the pay at the higher paying job. Otherwise, (b) is more accurate . . . . . . . . . . . . . . . . . ☐

**TIP:** If you have self-employment income, see page 2.

**Complete Steps 3–4(b) on Form W-4 for only ONE of these jobs.** Leave those steps blank for the other jobs. (Your withholding will be most accurate if you complete Steps 3–4(b) on the Form W-4 for the highest paying job.)

**Step 3:**
**Claim Dependent and Other Credits**

| If your total income will be $200,000 or less ($400,000 or less if married filing jointly): | | |
|---|---|---|
| Multiply the number of qualifying children under age 17 by $2,000 $ _____ | | |
| Multiply the number of other dependents by $500 . . . . . $ _____ | | |
| Add the amounts above for qualifying children and other dependents. You may add to this the amount of any other credits. Enter the total here . . . . . . . . . . | 3 | $ |

**Step 4 (optional):**
**Other Adjustments**

| (a) **Other income (not from jobs).** If you want tax withheld for other income you expect this year that won't have withholding, enter the amount of other income here. This may include interest, dividends, and retirement income . . . . . . . . | 4(a) | $ |
|---|---|---|
| (b) **Deductions.** If you expect to claim deductions other than the standard deduction and want to reduce your withholding, use the Deductions Worksheet on page 3 and enter the result here . . . . . . . . . . . . . . . . . . | 4(b) | $ |
| (c) **Extra withholding.** Enter any additional tax you want withheld each **pay period** . . | 4(c) | $ |

**Step 5:**
**Sign Here**

Under penalties of perjury, I declare that this certificate, to the best of my knowledge and belief, is true, correct, and complete.

_____

**Employee's signature** (This form is not valid unless you sign it.)

**Date**

| **Employers Only** | Employer's name and address | First date of employment | Employer identification number (EIN) |
|---|---|---|---|

**For Privacy Act and Paperwork Reduction Act Notice, see page 3.**  Cat. No. 10220Q  Form **W-4** (2023)

# General Instructions

Section references are to the Internal Revenue Code.

## Future Developments

For the latest information about developments related to Form W-4, such as legislation enacted after it was published, go to *www.irs.gov/FormW4.*

## Purpose of Form

Complete Form W-4 so that your employer can withhold the correct federal income tax from your pay. If too little is withheld, you will generally owe tax when you file your tax return and may owe a penalty. If too much is withheld, you will generally be due a refund. Complete a new Form W-4 when changes to your personal or financial situation would change the entries on the form. For more information on withholding and when you must furnish a new Form W-4, see Pub. 505, Tax Withholding and Estimated Tax.

**Exemption from withholding.** You may claim exemption from withholding for 2023 if you meet both of the following conditions: you had no federal income tax liability in 2022 **and** you expect to have no federal income tax liability in 2023. You had no federal income tax liability in 2022 if (1) your total tax on line 24 on your 2022 Form 1040 or 1040-SR is zero (or less than the sum of lines 27, 28, and 29), or (2) you were not required to file a return because your income was below the filing threshold for your correct filing status. If you claim exemption, you will have no income tax withheld from your paycheck and may owe taxes and penalties when you file your 2023 tax return. To claim exemption from withholding, certify that you meet both of the conditions above by writing "Exempt" on Form W-4 in the space below Step 4(c). Then, complete Steps 1(a), 1(b), and 5. Do not complete any other steps. You will need to submit a new Form W-4 by February 15, 2024.

**Your privacy.** If you have concerns with Step 2(c), you may choose Step 2(b); if you have concerns with Step 4(a), you may enter an additional amount you want withheld per pay period in Step 4(c).

**Self-employment.** Generally, you will owe both income and self-employment taxes on any self-employment income you receive separate from the wages you receive as an employee. If you want to pay income and self-employment taxes through withholding from your wages, you should enter the self-employment income on Step 4(a). Then compute your self-employment tax, divide that tax by the number of pay periods remaining in the year, and include that resulting amount per pay period on Step 4(c). You can also add half of the annual amount of self-employment tax to Step 4(b) as a deduction. To calculate self-employment tax, you generally multiply the self-employment income by 14.13% (this rate is a quick way to figure your self-employment tax and equals the sum of the 12.4% social security tax and the 2.9% Medicare tax multiplied by 0.9235). See Pub. 505 for more information, especially if the sum of self-employment income multiplied by 0.9235 and wages exceeds $160,200 for a given individual.

**Nonresident alien.** If you're a nonresident alien, see Notice 1392, Supplemental Form W-4 Instructions for Nonresident Aliens, before completing this form.

# Specific Instructions

**Step 1(c).** Check your anticipated filing status. This will determine the standard deduction and tax rates used to compute your withholding.

**Step 2.** Use this step if you (1) have more than one job at the same time, or (2) are married filing jointly and you and your spouse both work.

If you (and your spouse) have a total of only two jobs, you may check the box in option **(c)**. The box must also be checked on the Form W-4 for the other job. If the box is checked, the standard deduction and tax brackets will be cut in half for each job to calculate withholding. This option is roughly accurate for jobs with similar pay; otherwise, more tax than necessary may be withheld, and this extra amount will be larger the greater the difference in pay is between the two jobs.

⚠️ **CAUTION**   *Multiple jobs. Complete Steps 3 through 4(b) on only one Form W-4. Withholding will be most accurate if you do this on the Form W-4 for the highest paying job.*

**Step 3.** This step provides instructions for determining the amount of the child tax credit and the credit for other dependents that you may be able to claim when you file your tax return. To qualify for the child tax credit, the child must be under age 17 as of December 31, must be your dependent who generally lives with you for more than half the year, and must have the required social security number. You may be able to claim a credit for other dependents for whom a child tax credit can't be claimed, such as an older child or a qualifying relative. For additional eligibility requirements for these credits, see Pub. 501, Dependents, Standard Deduction, and Filing Information. You can also include **other tax credits** for which you are eligible in this step, such as the foreign tax credit and the education tax credits. To do so, add an estimate of the amount for the year to your credits for dependents and enter the total amount in Step 3. Including these credits will increase your paycheck and reduce the amount of any refund you may receive when you file your tax return.

**Step 4 (optional).**

  **Step 4(a).** Enter in this step the total of your other estimated income for the year, if any. You shouldn't include income from any jobs or self-employment. If you complete Step 4(a), you likely won't have to make estimated tax payments for that income. If you prefer to pay estimated tax rather than having tax on other income withheld from your paycheck, see Form 1040-ES, Estimated Tax for Individuals.

  **Step 4(b).** Enter in this step the amount from the Deductions Worksheet, line 5, if you expect to claim deductions other than the basic standard deduction on your 2023 tax return and want to reduce your withholding to account for these deductions. This includes both itemized deductions and other deductions such as for student loan interest and IRAs.

  **Step 4(c).** Enter in this step any additional tax you want withheld from your pay **each pay period**, including any amounts from the Multiple Jobs Worksheet, line 4. Entering an amount here will reduce your paycheck and will either increase your refund or reduce any amount of tax that you owe.

## Step 2(b)—Multiple Jobs Worksheet *(Keep for your records.)*

If you choose the option in Step 2(b) on Form W-4, complete this worksheet (which calculates the total extra tax for all jobs) on **only ONE** Form W-4. Withholding will be most accurate if you complete the worksheet and enter the result on the Form W-4 for the highest paying job. To be accurate, submit a new Form W-4 for all other jobs if you have not updated your withholding since 2019.

**Note:** If more than one job has annual wages of more than $120,000 or there are more than three jobs, see Pub. 505 for additional tables.

1   **Two jobs.** If you have two jobs or you're married filing jointly and you and your spouse each have one job, find the amount from the appropriate table on page 4. Using the "Higher Paying Job" row and the "Lower Paying Job" column, find the value at the intersection of the two household salaries and enter that value on line 1. Then, **skip** to line 3 . . . . . . . . .   **1** $ _____

2   **Three jobs.** If you and/or your spouse have three jobs at the same time, complete lines 2a, 2b, and 2c below. Otherwise, skip to line 3.

   a   Find the amount from the appropriate table on page 4 using the annual wages from the highest paying job in the "Higher Paying Job" row and the annual wages for your next highest paying job in the "Lower Paying Job" column. Find the value at the intersection of the two household salaries and enter that value on line 2a . . . . . . . . . . . . .   **2a** $ _____

   b   Add the annual wages of the two highest paying jobs from line 2a together and use the total as the wages in the "Higher Paying Job" row and use the annual wages for your third job in the "Lower Paying Job" column to find the amount from the appropriate table on page 4 and enter this amount on line 2b . . . . . . . . . . . . . . . . . . .   **2b** $ _____

   c   Add the amounts from lines 2a and 2b and enter the result on line 2c . . . . . . . .   **2c** $ _____

3   Enter the number of pay periods per year for the highest paying job. For example, if that job pays weekly, enter 52; if it pays every other week, enter 26; if it pays monthly, enter 12, etc. . . . . .   **3** _____

4   **Divide** the annual amount on line 1 or line 2c by the number of pay periods on line 3. Enter this amount here and in **Step 4(c)** of Form W-4 for the highest paying job (along with any other additional amount you want withheld) . . . . . . . . . . . . . . . . .   **4** $ _____

## Step 4(b)—Deductions Worksheet *(Keep for your records.)*

1   Enter an estimate of your 2023 itemized deductions (from Schedule A (Form 1040)). Such deductions may include qualifying home mortgage interest, charitable contributions, state and local taxes (up to $10,000), and medical expenses in excess of 7.5% of your income . . . . . . . . . . . .   **1** $ _____

2   Enter:  { • $27,700 if you're married filing jointly or a qualifying surviving spouse
           • $20,800 if you're head of household
           • $13,850 if you're single or married filing separately }   . . . .   **2** $ _____

3   If line 1 is greater than line 2, subtract line 2 from line 1 and enter the result here. If line 2 is greater than line 1, enter "-0-" . . . . . . . . . . . . . .   **3** $ _____

4   Enter an estimate of your student loan interest, deductible IRA contributions, and certain other adjustments (from Part II of Schedule 1 (Form 1040)). See Pub. 505 for more information . . . .   **4** $ _____

5   **Add** lines 3 and 4. Enter the result here and in **Step 4(b)** of Form W-4 . . . . . . . . . . .   **5** $ _____

## Married Filing Jointly or Qualifying Surviving Spouse

| Higher Paying Job Annual Taxable Wage & Salary | Lower Paying Job Annual Taxable Wage & Salary | | | | | | | | | | | |
|---|---|---|---|---|---|---|---|---|---|---|---|---|
| | $0 - 9,999 | $10,000 - 19,999 | $20,000 - 29,999 | $30,000 - 39,999 | $40,000 - 49,999 | $50,000 - 59,999 | $60,000 - 69,999 | $70,000 - 79,999 | $80,000 - 89,999 | $90,000 - 99,999 | $100,000 - 109,999 | $110,000 - 120,000 |
| $0 - 9,999 | $0 | $0 | $850 | $850 | $1,000 | $1,020 | $1,020 | $1,020 | $1,020 | $1,020 | $1,020 | $1,870 |
| $10,000 - 19,999 | 0 | 930 | 1,850 | 2,000 | 2,200 | 2,220 | 2,220 | 2,220 | 2,220 | 2,220 | 3,200 | 4,070 |
| $20,000 - 29,999 | 850 | 1,850 | 2,920 | 3,120 | 3,320 | 3,340 | 3,340 | 3,340 | 3,340 | 4,320 | 5,320 | 6,190 |
| $30,000 - 39,999 | 850 | 2,000 | 3,120 | 3,320 | 3,520 | 3,540 | 3,540 | 3,540 | 4,520 | 5,520 | 6,520 | 7,390 |
| $40,000 - 49,999 | 1,000 | 2,200 | 3,320 | 3,520 | 3,720 | 3,740 | 3,740 | 4,720 | 5,720 | 6,720 | 7,720 | 8,590 |
| $50,000 - 59,999 | 1,020 | 2,220 | 3,340 | 3,540 | 3,740 | 3,760 | 4,750 | 5,750 | 6,750 | 7,750 | 8,750 | 9,610 |
| $60,000 - 69,999 | 1,020 | 2,220 | 3,340 | 3,540 | 3,740 | 4,750 | 5,750 | 6,750 | 7,750 | 8,750 | 9,750 | 10,610 |
| $70,000 - 79,999 | 1,020 | 2,220 | 3,340 | 3,540 | 4,720 | 5,750 | 6,750 | 7,750 | 8,750 | 9,750 | 10,750 | 11,610 |
| $80,000 - 99,999 | 1,020 | 2,220 | 4,170 | 5,370 | 6,570 | 7,600 | 8,600 | 9,600 | 10,600 | 11,600 | 12,600 | 13,460 |
| $100,000 - 149,999 | 1,870 | 4,070 | 6,190 | 7,390 | 8,590 | 9,610 | 10,610 | 11,660 | 12,860 | 14,060 | 15,260 | 16,330 |
| $150,000 - 239,999 | 2,040 | 4,440 | 6,760 | 8,160 | 9,560 | 10,780 | 11,980 | 13,180 | 14,380 | 15,580 | 16,780 | 17,850 |
| $240,000 - 259,999 | 2,040 | 4,440 | 6,760 | 8,160 | 9,560 | 10,780 | 11,980 | 13,180 | 14,380 | 15,580 | 16,780 | 17,850 |
| $260,000 - 279,999 | 2,040 | 4,440 | 6,760 | 8,160 | 9,560 | 10,780 | 11,980 | 13,180 | 14,380 | 15,580 | 16,780 | 18,140 |
| $280,000 - 299,999 | 2,040 | 4,440 | 6,760 | 8,160 | 9,560 | 10,780 | 11,980 | 13,180 | 14,380 | 15,870 | 17,870 | 19,740 |
| $300,000 - 319,999 | 2,040 | 4,440 | 6,760 | 8,160 | 9,560 | 10,780 | 11,980 | 13,470 | 15,470 | 17,470 | 19,470 | 21,340 |
| $320,000 - 364,999 | 2,040 | 4,440 | 6,760 | 8,550 | 10,750 | 12,770 | 14,770 | 16,770 | 18,770 | 20,770 | 22,770 | 24,640 |
| $365,000 - 524,999 | 2,970 | 6,470 | 9,890 | 12,390 | 14,890 | 17,220 | 19,520 | 21,820 | 24,120 | 26,420 | 28,720 | 30,880 |
| $525,000 and over | 3,140 | 6,840 | 10,460 | 13,160 | 15,860 | 18,390 | 20,890 | 23,390 | 25,890 | 28,390 | 30,890 | 33,250 |

## Single or Married Filing Separately

| Higher Paying Job Annual Taxable Wage & Salary | Lower Paying Job Annual Taxable Wage & Salary | | | | | | | | | | | |
|---|---|---|---|---|---|---|---|---|---|---|---|---|
| | $0 - 9,999 | $10,000 - 19,999 | $20,000 - 29,999 | $30,000 - 39,999 | $40,000 - 49,999 | $50,000 - 59,999 | $60,000 - 69,999 | $70,000 - 79,999 | $80,000 - 89,999 | $90,000 - 99,999 | $100,000 - 109,999 | $110,000 - 120,000 |
| $0 - 9,999 | $310 | $890 | $1,020 | $1,020 | $1,020 | $1,860 | $1,870 | $1,870 | $1,870 | $1,870 | $2,030 | $2,040 |
| $10,000 - 19,999 | 890 | 1,630 | 1,750 | 1,750 | 2,600 | 3,600 | 3,600 | 3,600 | 3,600 | 3,760 | 3,960 | 3,970 |
| $20,000 - 29,999 | 1,020 | 1,750 | 1,880 | 2,720 | 3,720 | 4,720 | 4,730 | 4,730 | 4,890 | 5,090 | 5,290 | 5,300 |
| $30,000 - 39,999 | 1,020 | 1,750 | 2,720 | 3,720 | 4,720 | 5,720 | 5,730 | 5,890 | 6,090 | 6,290 | 6,490 | 6,500 |
| $40,000 - 59,999 | 1,710 | 3,450 | 4,570 | 5,570 | 6,570 | 7,700 | 7,910 | 8,110 | 8,310 | 8,510 | 8,710 | 8,720 |
| $60,000 - 79,999 | 1,870 | 3,600 | 4,730 | 5,860 | 7,060 | 8,260 | 8,460 | 8,660 | 8,860 | 9,060 | 9,260 | 9,280 |
| $80,000 - 99,999 | 1,870 | 3,730 | 5,060 | 6,260 | 7,460 | 8,660 | 8,860 | 9,060 | 9,260 | 9,460 | 10,430 | 11,240 |
| $100,000 - 124,999 | 2,040 | 3,970 | 5,300 | 6,500 | 7,700 | 8,900 | 9,110 | 9,610 | 10,610 | 11,610 | 12,610 | 13,430 |
| $125,000 - 149,999 | 2,040 | 3,970 | 5,300 | 6,500 | 7,700 | 9,610 | 10,610 | 11,610 | 12,610 | 13,610 | 14,900 | 16,020 |
| $150,000 - 174,999 | 2,040 | 3,970 | 5,610 | 7,610 | 9,610 | 11,610 | 12,610 | 13,750 | 15,050 | 16,350 | 17,650 | 18,770 |
| $175,000 - 199,999 | 2,720 | 5,450 | 7,580 | 9,580 | 11,580 | 13,870 | 15,180 | 16,480 | 17,780 | 19,080 | 20,380 | 21,490 |
| $200,000 - 249,999 | 2,900 | 5,930 | 8,360 | 10,660 | 12,960 | 15,260 | 16,570 | 17,870 | 19,170 | 20,470 | 21,770 | 22,880 |
| $250,000 - 399,999 | 2,970 | 6,010 | 8,440 | 10,740 | 13,040 | 15,340 | 16,640 | 17,940 | 19,240 | 20,540 | 21,840 | 22,960 |
| $400,000 - 449,999 | 2,970 | 6,010 | 8,440 | 10,740 | 13,040 | 15,340 | 16,640 | 17,940 | 19,240 | 20,540 | 21,840 | 22,960 |
| $450,000 and over | 3,140 | 6,380 | 9,010 | 11,510 | 14,010 | 16,510 | 18,010 | 19,510 | 21,010 | 22,510 | 24,010 | 25,330 |

## Head of Household

| Higher Paying Job Annual Taxable Wage & Salary | Lower Paying Job Annual Taxable Wage & Salary | | | | | | | | | | | |
|---|---|---|---|---|---|---|---|---|---|---|---|---|
| | $0 - 9,999 | $10,000 - 19,999 | $20,000 - 29,999 | $30,000 - 39,999 | $40,000 - 49,999 | $50,000 - 59,999 | $60,000 - 69,999 | $70,000 - 79,999 | $80,000 - 89,999 | $90,000 - 99,999 | $100,000 - 109,999 | $110,000 - 120,000 |
| $0 - 9,999 | $0 | $620 | $860 | $1,020 | $1,020 | $1,020 | $1,020 | $1,650 | $1,870 | $1,870 | $1,890 | $2,040 |
| $10,000 - 19,999 | 620 | 1,630 | 2,060 | 2,220 | 2,220 | 2,220 | 2,850 | 3,850 | 4,070 | 4,090 | 4,290 | 4,440 |
| $20,000 - 29,999 | 860 | 2,060 | 2,490 | 2,650 | 2,650 | 3,280 | 4,280 | 5,280 | 5,520 | 5,720 | 5,920 | 6,070 |
| $30,000 - 39,999 | 1,020 | 2,220 | 2,650 | 2,810 | 3,440 | 4,440 | 5,440 | 6,460 | 6,880 | 7,080 | 7,280 | 7,430 |
| $40,000 - 59,999 | 1,020 | 2,220 | 3,130 | 4,290 | 5,290 | 6,290 | 7,480 | 8,680 | 9,100 | 9,300 | 9,500 | 9,650 |
| $60,000 - 79,999 | 1,500 | 3,700 | 5,130 | 6,290 | 7,480 | 8,680 | 9,880 | 11,080 | 11,500 | 11,700 | 11,900 | 12,050 |
| $80,000 - 99,999 | 1,870 | 4,070 | 5,690 | 7,050 | 8,250 | 9,450 | 10,650 | 11,850 | 12,260 | 12,460 | 12,870 | 13,820 |
| $100,000 - 124,999 | 2,040 | 4,440 | 6,070 | 7,430 | 8,630 | 9,830 | 11,030 | 12,230 | 13,190 | 14,190 | 15,190 | 16,150 |
| $125,000 - 149,999 | 2,040 | 4,440 | 6,070 | 7,430 | 8,630 | 9,980 | 11,980 | 13,980 | 15,190 | 16,190 | 17,270 | 18,530 |
| $150,000 - 174,999 | 2,040 | 4,440 | 6,070 | 7,980 | 9,980 | 11,980 | 13,980 | 15,980 | 17,420 | 18,720 | 20,020 | 21,280 |
| $175,000 - 199,999 | 2,190 | 5,390 | 7,820 | 9,980 | 11,980 | 14,060 | 16,360 | 18,660 | 20,170 | 21,470 | 22,770 | 24,030 |
| $200,000 - 249,999 | 2,720 | 6,190 | 8,920 | 11,380 | 13,680 | 15,980 | 18,280 | 20,580 | 22,090 | 23,390 | 24,690 | 25,950 |
| $250,000 - 449,999 | 2,970 | 6,470 | 9,200 | 11,660 | 13,960 | 16,260 | 18,560 | 20,860 | 22,380 | 23,680 | 24,980 | 26,230 |
| $450,000 and over | 3,140 | 6,840 | 9,770 | 12,430 | 14,930 | 17,430 | 19,930 | 22,430 | 24,150 | 25,650 | 27,150 | 28,600 |

**Form 1040**
Department of the Treasury—Internal Revenue Service
**U.S. Individual Income Tax Return** **2022** OMB No. 1545-0074 | IRS Use Only—Do not write or staple in this space.

| Filing Status Check only one box. | ☐ Single ☐ Married filing jointly ☐ Married filing separately (MFS) ☐ Head of household (HOH) ☐ Qualifying surviving spouse (QSS) |

If you checked the MFS box, enter the name of your spouse. If you checked the HOH or QSS box, enter the child's name if the qualifying person is a child but not your dependent:

| Your first name and middle initial | Last name | Your social security number |
|---|---|---|
| If joint return, spouse's first name and middle initial | Last name | Spouse's social security number |

| Home address (number and street). If you have a P.O. box, see instructions. | Apt. no. |
|---|---|

**Presidential Election Campaign**
Check here if you, or your spouse if filing jointly, want $3 to go to this fund. Checking a box below will not change your tax or refund.
☐ You ☐ Spouse

| City, town, or post office. If you have a foreign address, also complete spaces below. | State | ZIP code |
|---|---|---|

| Foreign country name | Foreign province/state/county | Foreign postal code |
|---|---|---|

**Digital Assets** At any time during 2022, did you: (a) receive (as a reward, award, or payment for property or services); or (b) sell, exchange, gift, or otherwise dispose of a digital asset (or a financial interest in a digital asset)? (See instructions.) ☐ Yes ☐ No

**Standard Deduction** Someone can claim: ☐ You as a dependent ☐ Your spouse as a dependent
☐ Spouse itemizes on a separate return or you were a dual-status alien

**Age/Blindness** You: ☐ Were born before January 2, 1958 ☐ Are blind **Spouse:** ☐ Was born before January 2, 1958 ☐ Is blind

**Dependents** (see instructions):
If more than four dependents, see instructions and check here . . ☐

| (1) First name    Last name | (2) Social security number | (3) Relationship to you | (4) Check the box if qualifies for (see instructions): |  |
|---|---|---|---|---|
|  |  |  | Child tax credit | Credit for other dependents |
|  |  |  | ☐ | ☐ |
|  |  |  | ☐ | ☐ |
|  |  |  | ☐ | ☐ |
|  |  |  | ☐ | ☐ |

**Income**

Attach Form(s) W-2 here. Also attach Forms W-2G and 1099-R if tax was withheld.

If you did not get a Form W-2, see instructions.

| | | | | |
|---|---|---|---|---|
| 1a | Total amount from Form(s) W-2, box 1 (see instructions) | | 1a | |
| b | Household employee wages not reported on Form(s) W-2 | | 1b | |
| c | Tip income not reported on line 1a (see instructions) | | 1c | |
| d | Medicaid waiver payments not reported on Form(s) W-2 (see instructions) | | 1d | |
| e | Taxable dependent care benefits from Form 2441, line 26 | | 1e | |
| f | Employer-provided adoption benefits from Form 8839, line 29 | | 1f | |
| g | Wages from Form 8919, line 6 | | 1g | |
| h | Other earned income (see instructions) | | 1h | |
| i | Nontaxable combat pay election (see instructions) | 1i | | |
| z | Add lines 1a through 1h | | 1z | |

Attach Sch. B if required.

| | | | | | | | |
|---|---|---|---|---|---|---|---|
| 2a | Tax-exempt interest | 2a | | b | Taxable interest | 2b | |
| 3a | Qualified dividends | 3a | | b | Ordinary dividends | 3b | |
| 4a | IRA distributions | 4a | | b | Taxable amount | 4b | |
| 5a | Pensions and annuities | 5a | | b | Taxable amount | 5b | |
| 6a | Social security benefits | 6a | | b | Taxable amount | 6b | |

**Standard Deduction for—**
• Single or Married filing separately, $12,950
• Married filing jointly or Qualifying surviving spouse, $25,900
• Head of household, $19,400
• If you checked any box under *Standard Deduction,* see instructions.

| | | | |
|---|---|---|---|
| c | If you elect to use the lump-sum election method, check here (see instructions) ☐ | | |
| 7 | Capital gain or (loss). Attach Schedule D if required. If not required, check here ☐ | 7 | |
| 8 | Other income from Schedule 1, line 10 | 8 | |
| 9 | Add lines 1z, 2b, 3b, 4b, 5b, 6b, 7, and 8. This is your **total income** | 9 | |
| 10 | Adjustments to income from Schedule 1, line 26 | 10 | |
| 11 | Subtract line 10 from line 9. This is your **adjusted gross income** | 11 | |
| 12 | **Standard deduction or itemized deductions** (from Schedule A) | 12 | |
| 13 | Qualified business income deduction from Form 8995 or Form 8995-A | 13 | |
| 14 | Add lines 12 and 13 | 14 | |
| 15 | Subtract line 14 from line 11. If zero or less, enter -0-. This is your **taxable income** | 15 | |

For Disclosure, Privacy Act, and Paperwork Reduction Act Notice, see separate instructions. Cat. No. 11320B Form **1040** (2022)

Form 1040 (2022) | Page **2**

| | | | |
|---|---|---|---|
| **Tax and Credits** | 16 | **Tax** (see instructions). Check if any from Form(s): 1 ☐ 8814   2 ☐ 4972   3 ☐ _____ . . | 16 | |
| | 17 | Amount from Schedule 2, line 3 . . . . . . . . . . . . . . . . . . | 17 | |
| | 18 | Add lines 16 and 17 . . . . . . . . . . . . . . . . . . . . . | 18 | |
| | 19 | Child tax credit or credit for other dependents from Schedule 8812 . . . . . . . . | 19 | |
| | 20 | Amount from Schedule 3, line 8 . . . . . . . . . . . . . . . . . | 20 | |
| | 21 | Add lines 19 and 20 . . . . . . . . . . . . . . . . . . . . . | 21 | |
| | 22 | Subtract line 21 from line 18. If zero or less, enter -0- . . . . . . . . . . . . | 22 | |
| | 23 | Other taxes, including self-employment tax, from Schedule 2, line 21 . . . . . . . | 23 | |
| | 24 | Add lines 22 and 23. This is your **total tax** . . . . . . . . . . . . . . | 24 | |

| | | | | |
|---|---|---|---|---|
| **Payments** | 25 | Federal income tax withheld from: | | |
| | a | Form(s) W-2 . . . . . . . . . . . . . . . . . | 25a | |
| | b | Form(s) 1099 . . . . . . . . . . . . . . . . | 25b | |
| | c | Other forms (see instructions) . . . . . . . . . . | 25c | |
| | d | Add lines 25a through 25c . . . . . . . . . . . . . . . . . . | 25d | |
| *If you have a qualifying child, attach Sch. EIC.* | 26 | 2022 estimated tax payments and amount applied from 2021 return . . . . . . . | 26 | |
| | 27 | Earned income credit (EIC) . . . . . . . . . . . | 27 | |
| | 28 | Additional child tax credit from Schedule 8812 . . . . | 28 | |
| | 29 | American opportunity credit from Form 8863, line 8 . . . | 29 | |
| | 30 | Reserved for future use . . . . . . . . . . . . | 30 | |
| | 31 | Amount from Schedule 3, line 15 . . . . . . . . . | 31 | |
| | 32 | Add lines 27, 28, 29, and 31. These are your **total other payments and refundable credits** . | 32 | |
| | 33 | Add lines 25d, 26, and 32. These are your **total payments** . . . . . . . . | 33 | |

| | | | | |
|---|---|---|---|---|
| **Refund** | 34 | If line 33 is more than line 24, subtract line 24 from line 33. This is the amount you **overpaid** . . | 34 | |
| | 35a | Amount of line 34 you want **refunded to you**. If Form 8888 is attached, check here . . . ☐ | 35a | |
| *Direct deposit? See instructions.* | b | Routing number [ ][ ][ ][ ][ ][ ][ ][ ][ ]   c Type: ☐ Checking  ☐ Savings | | |
| | d | Account number [ ][ ][ ][ ][ ][ ][ ][ ][ ] | | |
| | 36 | Amount of line 34 you want applied to your **2023 estimated tax** . . . | 36 | |

| | | | | |
|---|---|---|---|---|
| **Amount You Owe** | 37 | Subtract line 33 from line 24. This is the **amount you owe**. For details on how to pay, go to *www.irs.gov/Payments* or see instructions . . . . . . . | 37 | |
| | 38 | Estimated tax penalty (see instructions) . . . . . . . . . | 38 | |

| | |
|---|---|
| **Third Party Designee** | Do you want to allow another person to discuss this return with the IRS? See instructions . . . . . . . . . . . . . . . . . . . . . . . . . ☐ **Yes.** Complete below.  ☐ **No** |
| | Designee's name _____   Phone no. _____   Personal identification number (PIN) [ ][ ][ ][ ][ ] |

| | |
|---|---|
| **Sign Here** | Under penalties of perjury, I declare that I have examined this return and accompanying schedules and statements, and to the best of my knowledge and belief, they are true, correct, and complete. Declaration of preparer (other than taxpayer) is based on all information of which preparer has any knowledge. |
| *Joint return? See instructions. Keep a copy for your records.* | Your signature _____   Date _____   Your occupation _____   If the IRS sent you an Identity Protection PIN, enter it here (see inst.) [ ][ ][ ][ ][ ][ ] |
| | Spouse's signature. If a joint return, **both** must sign. _____   Date _____   Spouse's occupation _____   If the IRS sent your spouse an Identity Protection PIN, enter it here (see inst.) [ ][ ][ ][ ][ ][ ] |
| | Phone no. _____   Email address _____ |

| | | | | |
|---|---|---|---|---|
| **Paid Preparer Use Only** | Preparer's name _____ | Preparer's signature _____ | Date _____   PTIN _____ | Check if: ☐ Self-employed |
| | Firm's name _____ | | Phone no. _____ | |
| | Firm's address _____ | | Firm's EIN _____ | |

Go to *www.irs.gov/Form1040* for instructions and the latest information.   Form **1040** (2022)

**Form W-9**
(Rev. October 2018)
Department of the Treasury
Internal Revenue Service

## Request for Taxpayer Identification Number and Certification

▶ Go to *www.irs.gov/FormW9* for instructions and the latest information.

**Give Form to the requester. Do not send to the IRS.**

**1** Name (as shown on your income tax return). Name is required on this line; do not leave this line blank.

**2** Business name/disregarded entity name, if different from above

**3** Check appropriate box for federal tax classification of the person whose name is entered on line 1. Check only **one** of the following seven boxes.

☐ Individual/sole proprietor or single-member LLC

☐ C Corporation   ☐ S Corporation   ☐ Partnership   ☐ Trust/estate

☐ Limited liability company. Enter the tax classification (C=C corporation, S=S corporation, P=Partnership) ▶ _____

**Note:** Check the appropriate box in the line above for the tax classification of the single-member owner. Do not check LLC if the LLC is classified as a single-member LLC that is disregarded from the owner unless the owner of the LLC is another LLC that is **not** disregarded from the owner for U.S. federal tax purposes. Otherwise, a single-member LLC that is disregarded from the owner should check the appropriate box for the tax classification of its owner.

☐ Other (see instructions) ▶

**4** Exemptions (codes apply only to certain entities, not individuals; see instructions on page 3):

Exempt payee code (if any) _____

Exemption from FATCA reporting code (if any) _____

*(Applies to accounts maintained outside the U.S.)*

**5** Address (number, street, and apt. or suite no.) See instructions.

**6** City, state, and ZIP code

Requester's name and address (optional)

**7** List account number(s) here (optional)

Print or type. See **Specific Instructions** on page 3.

### Part I    Taxpayer Identification Number (TIN)

Enter your TIN in the appropriate box. The TIN provided must match the name given on line 1 to avoid backup withholding. For individuals, this is generally your social security number (SSN). However, for a resident alien, sole proprietor, or disregarded entity, see the instructions for Part I, later. For other entities, it is your employer identification number (EIN). If you do not have a number, see *How to get a TIN*, later.

**Note:** If the account is in more than one name, see the instructions for line 1. Also see *What Name and Number To Give the Requester* for guidelines on whose number to enter.

**Social security number**
☐☐☐ – ☐☐ – ☐☐☐☐

**or**

**Employer identification number**
☐☐ – ☐☐☐☐☐☐☐

### Part II    Certification

Under penalties of perjury, I certify that:

1. The number shown on this form is my correct taxpayer identification number (or I am waiting for a number to be issued to me); and
2. I am not subject to backup withholding because: (a) I am exempt from backup withholding, or (b) I have not been notified by the Internal Revenue Service (IRS) that I am subject to backup withholding as a result of a failure to report all interest or dividends, or (c) the IRS has notified me that I am no longer subject to backup withholding; and
3. I am a U.S. citizen or other U.S. person (defined below); and
4. The FATCA code(s) entered on this form (if any) indicating that I am exempt from FATCA reporting is correct.

**Certification instructions.** You must cross out item 2 above if you have been notified by the IRS that you are currently subject to backup withholding because you have failed to report all interest and dividends on your tax return. For real estate transactions, item 2 does not apply. For mortgage interest paid, acquisition or abandonment of secured property, cancellation of debt, contributions to an individual retirement arrangement (IRA), and generally, payments other than interest and dividends, you are not required to sign the certification, but you must provide your correct TIN. See the instructions for Part II, later.

**Sign Here**   Signature of U.S. person ▶     Date ▶

## General Instructions

Section references are to the Internal Revenue Code unless otherwise noted.

**Future developments.** For the latest information about developments related to Form W-9 and its instructions, such as legislation enacted after they were published, go to *www.irs.gov/FormW9*.

## Purpose of Form

An individual or entity (Form W-9 requester) who is required to file an information return with the IRS must obtain your correct taxpayer identification number (TIN) which may be your social security number (SSN), individual taxpayer identification number (ITIN), adoption taxpayer identification number (ATIN), or employer identification number (EIN), to report on an information return the amount paid to you, or other amount reportable on an information return. Examples of information returns include, but are not limited to, the following.

• Form 1099-INT (interest earned or paid)

• Form 1099-DIV (dividends, including those from stocks or mutual funds)
• Form 1099-MISC (various types of income, prizes, awards, or gross proceeds)
• Form 1099-B (stock or mutual fund sales and certain other transactions by brokers)
• Form 1099-S (proceeds from real estate transactions)
• Form 1099-K (merchant card and third party network transactions)
• Form 1098 (home mortgage interest), 1098-E (student loan interest), 1098-T (tuition)
• Form 1099-C (canceled debt)
• Form 1099-A (acquisition or abandonment of secured property)

Use Form W-9 only if you are a U.S. person (including a resident alien), to provide your correct TIN.

*If you do not return Form W-9 to the requester with a TIN, you might be subject to backup withholding. See What is backup withholding, later.*

Cat. No. 10231X      Form **W-9** (Rev. 10-2018)

By signing the filled-out form, you:

1. Certify that the TIN you are giving is correct (or you are waiting for a number to be issued),

2. Certify that you are not subject to backup withholding, or

3. Claim exemption from backup withholding if you are a U.S. exempt payee. If applicable, you are also certifying that as a U.S. person, your allocable share of any partnership income from a U.S. trade or business is not subject to the withholding tax on foreign partners' share of effectively connected income, and

4. Certify that FATCA code(s) entered on this form (if any) indicating that you are exempt from the FATCA reporting, is correct. See *What is FATCA reporting,* later, for further information.

**Note:** If you are a U.S. person and a requester gives you a form other than Form W-9 to request your TIN, you must use the requester's form if it is substantially similar to this Form W-9.

**Definition of a U.S. person.** For federal tax purposes, you are considered a U.S. person if you are:

• An individual who is a U.S. citizen or U.S. resident alien;

• A partnership, corporation, company, or association created or organized in the United States or under the laws of the United States;

• An estate (other than a foreign estate); or

• A domestic trust (as defined in Regulations section 301.7701-7).

**Special rules for partnerships.** Partnerships that conduct a trade or business in the United States are generally required to pay a withholding tax under section 1446 on any foreign partners' share of effectively connected taxable income from such business. Further, in certain cases where a Form W-9 has not been received, the rules under section 1446 require a partnership to presume that a partner is a foreign person, and pay the section 1446 withholding tax. Therefore, if you are a U.S. person that is a partner in a partnership conducting a trade or business in the United States, provide Form W-9 to the partnership to establish your U.S. status and avoid section 1446 withholding on your share of partnership income.

In the cases below, the following person must give Form W-9 to the partnership for purposes of establishing its U.S. status and avoiding withholding on its allocable share of net income from the partnership conducting a trade or business in the United States.

• In the case of a disregarded entity with a U.S. owner, the U.S. owner of the disregarded entity and not the entity;

• In the case of a grantor trust with a U.S. grantor or other U.S. owner, generally, the U.S. grantor or other U.S. owner of the grantor trust and not the trust; and

• In the case of a U.S. trust (other than a grantor trust), the U.S. trust (other than a grantor trust) and not the beneficiaries of the trust.

**Foreign person.** If you are a foreign person or the U.S. branch of a foreign bank that has elected to be treated as a U.S. person, do not use Form W-9. Instead, use the appropriate Form W-8 or Form 8233 (see Pub. 515, Withholding of Tax on Nonresident Aliens and Foreign Entities).

**Nonresident alien who becomes a resident alien.** Generally, only a nonresident alien individual may use the terms of a tax treaty to reduce or eliminate U.S. tax on certain types of income. However, most tax treaties contain a provision known as a "saving clause." Exceptions specified in the saving clause may permit an exemption from tax to continue for certain types of income even after the payee has otherwise become a U.S. resident alien for tax purposes.

If you are a U.S. resident alien who is relying on an exception contained in the saving clause of a tax treaty to claim an exemption from U.S. tax on certain types of income, you must attach a statement to Form W-9 that specifies the following five items.

1. The treaty country. Generally, this must be the same treaty under which you claimed exemption from tax as a nonresident alien.

2. The treaty article addressing the income.

3. The article number (or location) in the tax treaty that contains the saving clause and its exceptions.

4. The type and amount of income that qualifies for the exemption from tax.

5. Sufficient facts to justify the exemption from tax under the terms of the treaty article.

*Example.* Article 20 of the U.S.-China income tax treaty allows an exemption from tax for scholarship income received by a Chinese student temporarily present in the United States. Under U.S. law, this student will become a resident alien for tax purposes if his or her stay in the United States exceeds 5 calendar years. However, paragraph 2 of the first Protocol to the U.S.-China treaty (dated April 30, 1984) allows the provisions of Article 20 to continue to apply even after the Chinese student becomes a resident alien of the United States. A Chinese student who qualifies for this exception (under paragraph 2 of the first protocol) and is relying on this exception to claim an exemption from tax on his or her scholarship or fellowship income would attach to Form W-9 a statement that includes the information described above to support that exemption.

If you are a nonresident alien or a foreign entity, give the requester the appropriate completed Form W-8 or Form 8233.

## Backup Withholding

**What is backup withholding?** Persons making certain payments to you must under certain conditions withhold and pay to the IRS 24% of such payments. This is called "backup withholding." Payments that may be subject to backup withholding include interest, tax-exempt interest, dividends, broker and barter exchange transactions, rents, royalties, nonemployee pay, payments made in settlement of payment card and third party network transactions, and certain payments from fishing boat operators. Real estate transactions are not subject to backup withholding.

You will not be subject to backup withholding on payments you receive if you give the requester your correct TIN, make the proper certifications, and report all your taxable interest and dividends on your tax return.

**Payments you receive will be subject to backup withholding if:**

1. You do not furnish your TIN to the requester,

2. You do not certify your TIN when required (see the instructions for Part II for details),

3. The IRS tells the requester that you furnished an incorrect TIN,

4. The IRS tells you that you are subject to backup withholding because you did not report all your interest and dividends on your tax return (for reportable interest and dividends only), or

5. You do not certify to the requester that you are not subject to backup withholding under 4 above (for reportable interest and dividend accounts opened after 1983 only).

Certain payees and payments are exempt from backup withholding. See *Exempt payee code,* later, and the separate Instructions for the Requester of Form W-9 for more information.

Also see *Special rules for partnerships,* earlier.

## What is FATCA Reporting?

The Foreign Account Tax Compliance Act (FATCA) requires a participating foreign financial institution to report all United States account holders that are specified United States persons. Certain payees are exempt from FATCA reporting. See *Exemption from FATCA reporting code,* later, and the Instructions for the Requester of Form W-9 for more information.

## Updating Your Information

You must provide updated information to any person to whom you claimed to be an exempt payee if you are no longer an exempt payee and anticipate receiving reportable payments in the future from this person. For example, you may need to provide updated information if you are a C corporation that elects to be an S corporation, or if you no longer are tax exempt. In addition, you must furnish a new Form W-9 if the name or TIN changes for the account; for example, if the grantor of a grantor trust dies.

## Penalties

**Failure to furnish TIN.** If you fail to furnish your correct TIN to a requester, you are subject to a penalty of $50 for each such failure unless your failure is due to reasonable cause and not to willful neglect.

**Civil penalty for false information with respect to withholding.** If you make a false statement with no reasonable basis that results in no backup withholding, you are subject to a $500 penalty.

**Criminal penalty for falsifying information.** Willfully falsifying certifications or affirmations may subject you to criminal penalties including fines and/or imprisonment.

**Misuse of TINs.** If the requester discloses or uses TINs in violation of federal law, the requester may be subject to civil and criminal penalties.

# Specific Instructions

## Line 1

You must enter one of the following on this line; **do not** leave this line blank. The name should match the name on your tax return.

If this Form W-9 is for a joint account (other than an account maintained by a foreign financial institution (FFI)), list first, and then circle, the name of the person or entity whose number you entered in Part I of Form W-9. If you are providing Form W-9 to an FFI to document a joint account, each holder of the account that is a U.S. person must provide a Form W-9.

**a. Individual.** Generally, enter the name shown on your tax return. If you have changed your last name without informing the Social Security Administration (SSA) of the name change, enter your first name, the last name as shown on your social security card, and your new last name.

**Note: ITIN applicant:** Enter your individual name as it was entered on your Form W-7 application, line 1a. This should also be the same as the name you entered on the Form 1040/1040A/1040EZ you filed with your application.

**b. Sole proprietor or single-member LLC.** Enter your individual name as shown on your 1040/1040A/1040EZ on line 1. You may enter your business, trade, or "doing business as" (DBA) name on line 2.

**c. Partnership, LLC that is not a single-member LLC, C corporation, or S corporation.** Enter the entity's name as shown on the entity's tax return on line 1 and any business, trade, or DBA name on line 2.

**d. Other entities.** Enter your name as shown on required U.S. federal tax documents on line 1. This name should match the name shown on the charter or other legal document creating the entity. You may enter any business, trade, or DBA name on line 2.

**e. Disregarded entity.** For U.S. federal tax purposes, an entity that is disregarded as an entity separate from its owner is treated as a "disregarded entity." See Regulations section 301.7701-2(c)(2)(iii). Enter the owner's name on line 1. The name of the entity entered on line 1 should never be a disregarded entity. The name on line 1 should be the name shown on the income tax return on which the income should be reported. For example, if a foreign LLC that is treated as a disregarded entity for U.S. federal tax purposes has a single owner that is a U.S. person, the U.S. owner's name is required to be provided on line 1. If the direct owner of the entity is also a disregarded entity, enter the first owner that is not disregarded for federal tax purposes. Enter the disregarded entity's name on line 2, "Business name/disregarded entity name." If the owner of the disregarded entity is a foreign person, the owner must complete an appropriate Form W-8 instead of a Form W-9. This is the case even if the foreign person has a U.S. TIN.

## Line 2

If you have a business name, trade name, DBA name, or disregarded entity name, you may enter it on line 2.

## Line 3

Check the appropriate box on line 3 for the U.S. federal tax classification of the person whose name is entered on line 1. Check only one box on line 3.

| IF the entity/person on line 1 is a(n) . . . | THEN check the box for . . . |
|---|---|
| • Corporation | Corporation |
| • Individual<br>• Sole proprietorship, or<br>• Single-member limited liability company (LLC) owned by an individual and disregarded for U.S. federal tax purposes. | Individual/sole proprietor or single-member LLC |
| • LLC treated as a partnership for U.S. federal tax purposes,<br>• LLC that has filed Form 8832 or 2553 to be taxed as a corporation, or<br>• LLC that is disregarded as an entity separate from its owner but the owner is another LLC that is not disregarded for U.S. federal tax purposes. | Limited liability company and enter the appropriate tax classification. (P= Partnership; C= C corporation; or S= S corporation) |
| • Partnership | Partnership |
| • Trust/estate | Trust/estate |

## Line 4, Exemptions

If you are exempt from backup withholding and/or FATCA reporting, enter in the appropriate space on line 4 any code(s) that may apply to you.

**Exempt payee code.**

• Generally, individuals (including sole proprietors) are not exempt from backup withholding.

• Except as provided below, corporations are exempt from backup withholding for certain payments, including interest and dividends.

• Corporations are not exempt from backup withholding for payments made in settlement of payment card or third party network transactions.

• Corporations are not exempt from backup withholding with respect to attorneys' fees or gross proceeds paid to attorneys, and corporations that provide medical or health care services are not exempt with respect to payments reportable on Form 1099-MISC.

The following codes identify payees that are exempt from backup withholding. Enter the appropriate code in the space in line 4.

1—An organization exempt from tax under section 501(a), any IRA, or a custodial account under section 403(b)(7) if the account satisfies the requirements of section 401(f)(2)

2—The United States or any of its agencies or instrumentalities

3—A state, the District of Columbia, a U.S. commonwealth or possession, or any of their political subdivisions or instrumentalities

4—A foreign government or any of its political subdivisions, agencies, or instrumentalities

5—A corporation

6—A dealer in securities or commodities required to register in the United States, the District of Columbia, or a U.S. commonwealth or possession

7—A futures commission merchant registered with the Commodity Futures Trading Commission

8—A real estate investment trust

9—An entity registered at all times during the tax year under the Investment Company Act of 1940

10—A common trust fund operated by a bank under section 584(a)

11—A financial institution

12—A middleman known in the investment community as a nominee or custodian

13—A trust exempt from tax under section 664 or described in section 4947

The following chart shows types of payments that may be exempt from backup withholding. The chart applies to the exempt payees listed above, 1 through 13.

| IF the payment is for . . . | THEN the payment is exempt for . . . |
|---|---|
| Interest and dividend payments | All exempt payees except for 7 |
| Broker transactions | Exempt payees 1 through 4 and 6 through 11 and all C corporations. S corporations must not enter an exempt payee code because they are exempt only for sales of noncovered securities acquired prior to 2012. |
| Barter exchange transactions and patronage dividends | Exempt payees 1 through 4 |
| Payments over $600 required to be reported and direct sales over $5,000[1] | Generally, exempt payees 1 through 5[2] |
| Payments made in settlement of payment card or third party network transactions | Exempt payees 1 through 4 |

[1] See Form 1099-MISC, Miscellaneous Income, and its instructions.

[2] However, the following payments made to a corporation and reportable on Form 1099-MISC are not exempt from backup withholding: medical and health care payments, attorneys' fees, gross proceeds paid to an attorney reportable under section 6045(f), and payments for services paid by a federal executive agency.

**Exemption from FATCA reporting code.** The following codes identify payees that are exempt from reporting under FATCA. These codes apply to persons submitting this form for accounts maintained outside of the United States by certain foreign financial institutions. Therefore, if you are only submitting this form for an account you hold in the United States, you may leave this field blank. Consult with the person requesting this form if you are uncertain if the financial institution is subject to these requirements. A requester may indicate that a code is not required by providing you with a Form W-9 with "Not Applicable" (or any similar indication) written or printed on the line for a FATCA exemption code.

A—An organization exempt from tax under section 501(a) or any individual retirement plan as defined in section 7701(a)(37)

B—The United States or any of its agencies or instrumentalities

C—A state, the District of Columbia, a U.S. commonwealth or possession, or any of their political subdivisions or instrumentalities

D—A corporation the stock of which is regularly traded on one or more established securities markets, as described in Regulations section 1.1472-1(c)(1)(i)

E—A corporation that is a member of the same expanded affiliated group as a corporation described in Regulations section 1.1472-1(c)(1)(i)

F—A dealer in securities, commodities, or derivative financial instruments (including notional principal contracts, futures, forwards, and options) that is registered as such under the laws of the United States or any state

G—A real estate investment trust

H—A regulated investment company as defined in section 851 or an entity registered at all times during the tax year under the Investment Company Act of 1940

I—A common trust fund as defined in section 584(a)

J—A bank as defined in section 581

K—A broker

L—A trust exempt from tax under section 664 or described in section 4947(a)(1)

M—A tax exempt trust under a section 403(b) plan or section 457(g) plan

**Note:** You may wish to consult with the financial institution requesting this form to determine whether the FATCA code and/or exempt payee code should be completed.

### Line 5

Enter your address (number, street, and apartment or suite number). This is where the requester of this Form W-9 will mail your information returns. If this address differs from the one the requester already has on file, write NEW at the top. If a new address is provided, there is still a chance the old address will be used until the payor changes your address in their records.

### Line 6

Enter your city, state, and ZIP code.

## Part I. Taxpayer Identification Number (TIN)

**Enter your TIN in the appropriate box.** If you are a resident alien and you do not have and are not eligible to get an SSN, your TIN is your IRS individual taxpayer identification number (ITIN). Enter it in the social security number box. If you do not have an ITIN, see *How to get a TIN* below.

If you are a sole proprietor and you have an EIN, you may enter either your SSN or EIN.

If you are a single-member LLC that is disregarded as an entity separate from its owner, enter the owner's SSN (or EIN, if the owner has one). Do not enter the disregarded entity's EIN. If the LLC is classified as a corporation or partnership, enter the entity's EIN.

**Note:** See *What Name and Number To Give the Requester,* later, for further clarification of name and TIN combinations.

**How to get a TIN.** If you do not have a TIN, apply for one immediately. To apply for an SSN, get Form SS-5, Application for a Social Security Card, from your local SSA office or get this form online at *www.SSA.gov.* You may also get this form by calling 1-800-772-1213. Use Form W-7, Application for IRS Individual Taxpayer Identification Number, to apply for an ITIN, or Form SS-4, Application for Employer Identification Number, to apply for an EIN. You can apply for an EIN online by accessing the IRS website at *www.irs.gov/Businesses* and clicking on Employer Identification Number (EIN) under Starting a Business. Go to *www.irs.gov/Forms* to view, download, or print Form W-7 and/or Form SS-4. Or, you can go to *www.irs.gov/OrderForms* to place an order and have Form W-7 and/or SS-4 mailed to you within 10 business days.

If you are asked to complete Form W-9 but do not have a TIN, apply for a TIN and write "Applied For" in the space for the TIN, sign and date the form, and give it to the requester. For interest and dividend payments, and certain payments made with respect to readily tradable instruments, generally you will have 60 days to get a TIN and give it to the requester before you are subject to backup withholding on payments. The 60-day rule does not apply to other types of payments. You will be subject to backup withholding on all such payments until you provide your TIN to the requester.

**Note:** Entering "Applied For" means that you have already applied for a TIN or that you intend to apply for one soon.

**Caution:** A disregarded U.S. entity that has a foreign owner must use the appropriate Form W-8.

## Part II. Certification

To establish to the withholding agent that you are a U.S. person, or resident alien, sign Form W-9. You may be requested to sign by the withholding agent even if item 1, 4, or 5 below indicates otherwise.

For a joint account, only the person whose TIN is shown in Part I should sign (when required). In the case of a disregarded entity, the person identified on line 1 must sign. Exempt payees, see *Exempt payee code,* earlier.

**Signature requirements.** Complete the certification as indicated in items 1 through 5 below.

**1. Interest, dividend, and barter exchange accounts opened before 1984 and broker accounts considered active during 1983.** You must give your correct TIN, but you do not have to sign the certification.

**2. Interest, dividend, broker, and barter exchange accounts opened after 1983 and broker accounts considered inactive during 1983.** You must sign the certification or backup withholding will apply. If you are subject to backup withholding and you are merely providing your correct TIN to the requester, you must cross out item 2 in the certification before signing the form.

**3. Real estate transactions.** You must sign the certification. You may cross out item 2 of the certification.

**4. Other payments.** You must give your correct TIN, but you do not have to sign the certification unless you have been notified that you have previously given an incorrect TIN. "Other payments" include payments made in the course of the requester's trade or business for rents, royalties, goods (other than bills for merchandise), medical and health care services (including payments to corporations), payments to a nonemployee for services, payments made in settlement of payment card and third party network transactions, payments to certain fishing boat crew members and fishermen, and gross proceeds paid to attorneys (including payments to corporations).

**5. Mortgage interest paid by you, acquisition or abandonment of secured property, cancellation of debt, qualified tuition program payments (under section 529), ABLE accounts (under section 529A), IRA, Coverdell ESA, Archer MSA or HSA contributions or distributions, and pension distributions.** You must give your correct TIN, but you do not have to sign the certification.

## What Name and Number To Give the Requester

| For this type of account: | Give name and SSN of: |
|---|---|
| 1. Individual | The individual |
| 2. Two or more individuals (joint account) other than an account maintained by an FFI | The actual owner of the account or, if combined funds, the first individual on the account[1] |
| 3. Two or more U.S. persons (joint account maintained by an FFI) | Each holder of the account |
| 4. Custodial account of a minor (Uniform Gift to Minors Act) | The minor[2] |
| 5. a. The usual revocable savings trust (grantor is also trustee) | The grantor-trustee[1] |
| b. So-called trust account that is not a legal or valid trust under state law | The actual owner[1] |
| 6. Sole proprietorship or disregarded entity owned by an individual | The owner[3] |
| 7. Grantor trust filing under Optional Form 1099 Filing Method 1 (see Regulations section 1.671-4(b)(2)(i)(A)) | The grantor* |

| For this type of account: | Give name and EIN of: |
|---|---|
| 8. Disregarded entity not owned by an individual | The owner |
| 9. A valid trust, estate, or pension trust | Legal entity[4] |
| 10. Corporation or LLC electing corporate status on Form 8832 or Form 2553 | The corporation |
| 11. Association, club, religious, charitable, educational, or other tax-exempt organization | The organization |
| 12. Partnership or multi-member LLC | The partnership |
| 13. A broker or registered nominee | The broker or nominee |

| For this type of account: | Give name and EIN of: |
|---|---|
| 14. Account with the Department of Agriculture in the name of a public entity (such as a state or local government, school district, or prison) that receives agricultural program payments | The public entity |
| 15. Grantor trust filing under the Form 1041 Filing Method or the Optional Form 1099 Filing Method 2 (see Regulations section 1.671-4(b)(2)(i)(B)) | The trust |

[1] List first and circle the name of the person whose number you furnish. If only one person on a joint account has an SSN, that person's number must be furnished.

[2] Circle the minor's name and furnish the minor's SSN.

[3] You must show your individual name and you may also enter your business or DBA name on the "Business name/disregarded entity" name line. You may use either your SSN or EIN (if you have one), but the IRS encourages you to use your SSN.

[4] List first and circle the name of the trust, estate, or pension trust. (Do not furnish the TIN of the personal representative or trustee unless the legal entity itself is not designated in the account title.) Also see *Special rules for partnerships,* earlier.

***Note:** The grantor also must provide a Form W-9 to trustee of trust.

**Note:** If no name is circled when more than one name is listed, the number will be considered to be that of the first name listed.

## Secure Your Tax Records From Identity Theft

Identity theft occurs when someone uses your personal information such as your name, SSN, or other identifying information, without your permission, to commit fraud or other crimes. An identity thief may use your SSN to get a job or may file a tax return using your SSN to receive a refund.

To reduce your risk:

• Protect your SSN,

• Ensure your employer is protecting your SSN, and

• Be careful when choosing a tax preparer.

If your tax records are affected by identity theft and you receive a notice from the IRS, respond right away to the name and phone number printed on the IRS notice or letter.

If your tax records are not currently affected by identity theft but you think you are at risk due to a lost or stolen purse or wallet, questionable credit card activity or credit report, contact the IRS Identity Theft Hotline at 1-800-908-4490 or submit Form 14039.

For more information, see Pub. 5027, Identity Theft Information for Taxpayers.

Victims of identity theft who are experiencing economic harm or a systemic problem, or are seeking help in resolving tax problems that have not been resolved through normal channels, may be eligible for Taxpayer Advocate Service (TAS) assistance. You can reach TAS by calling the TAS toll-free case intake line at 1-877-777-4778 or TTY/TDD 1-800-829-4059.

**Protect yourself from suspicious emails or phishing schemes.** Phishing is the creation and use of email and websites designed to mimic legitimate business emails and websites. The most common act is sending an email to a user falsely claiming to be an established legitimate enterprise in an attempt to scam the user into surrendering private information that will be used for identity theft.

The IRS does not initiate contacts with taxpayers via emails. Also, the IRS does not request personal detailed information through email or ask taxpayers for the PIN numbers, passwords, or similar secret access information for their credit card, bank, or other financial accounts.

If you receive an unsolicited email claiming to be from the IRS, forward this message to *phishing@irs.gov*. You may also report misuse of the IRS name, logo, or other IRS property to the Treasury Inspector General for Tax Administration (TIGTA) at 1-800-366-4484. You can forward suspicious emails to the Federal Trade Commission at *spam@uce.gov* or report them at *www.ftc.gov/complaint*. You can contact the FTC at *www.ftc.gov/idtheft* or 877-IDTHEFT (877-438-4338). If you have been the victim of identity theft, see *www.IdentityTheft.gov* and Pub. 5027.

Visit *www.irs.gov/IdentityTheft* to learn more about identity theft and how to reduce your risk.

## Privacy Act Notice

Section 6109 of the Internal Revenue Code requires you to provide your correct TIN to persons (including federal agencies) who are required to file information returns with the IRS to report interest, dividends, or certain other income paid to you; mortgage interest you paid; the acquisition or abandonment of secured property; the cancellation of debt; or contributions you made to an IRA, Archer MSA, or HSA. The person collecting this form uses the information on the form to file information returns with the IRS, reporting the above information. Routine uses of this information include giving it to the Department of Justice for civil and criminal litigation and to cities, states, the District of Columbia, and U.S. commonwealths and possessions for use in administering their laws. The information also may be disclosed to other countries under a treaty, to federal and state agencies to enforce civil and criminal laws, or to federal law enforcement and intelligence agencies to combat terrorism. You must provide your TIN whether or not you are required to file a tax return. Under section 3406, payers must generally withhold a percentage of taxable interest, dividend, and certain other payments to a payee who does not give a TIN to the payer. Certain penalties may also apply for providing false or fraudulent information.

Form **4506-T**
(June 2023)
Department of the Treasury
Internal Revenue Service

### Request for Transcript of Tax Return

▶ **Do not sign this form unless all applicable lines have been completed.**
▶ **Request may be rejected if the form is incomplete or illegible.**
▶ **For more information about Form 4506-T, visit** *www.irs.gov/form4506t.*

OMB No. 1545-1872

**Tip: Get faster service:** Online at www.irs.gov, **Get Your Tax Record** (Get Transcript) or by calling **1-800-908-9946** for specialized assistance. We have teams available to assist. **Note:** Taxpayers may register to use Get Transcript to view, print, or download the following transcript types: **Tax Return Transcript** (shows most line items including Adjusted Gross Income (AGI) from your original Form 1040-series tax return as filed, along with any forms and schedules), **Tax Account Transcript** (shows basic data such as return type, marital status, AGI, taxable income and all payment types), **Record of Account Transcript** (combines the tax return and tax account transcripts into one complete transcript), **Wage and Income Transcript** (shows data from information returns we receive such as Forms W-2, 1099, 1098 and Form 5498), and **Verification of Non-filing Letter** (provides proof that the IRS has no record of a filed Form 1040-series tax return for the year you request).

| | |
|---|---|
| **1a** Name shown on tax return. If a joint return, enter the name shown first. | **1b** First social security number on tax return, individual taxpayer identification number, or employer identification number (see instructions) |
| **2a** If a joint return, enter spouse's name shown on tax return. | **2b** Second social security number or individual taxpayer identification number if joint tax return |

**3** Current name, address (including apt., room, or suite no.), city, state, and ZIP code (see instructions)

**4** Previous address shown on the last return filed if different from line 3 (see instructions)

**5** Customer file number (if applicable) (see instructions)

**Note:** Effective July 2019, the IRS will mail tax transcript requests only to your address of record. See **What's New** under **Future Developments** on Page 2 for additional information.

**6** **Transcript requested.** Enter the tax form number here (1040, 1065, 1120, etc.) and check the appropriate box below. Enter only one tax form number per request. ▶ _____

**a** **Return Transcript,** which includes most of the line items of a tax return as filed with the IRS. A tax return transcript does not reflect changes made to the account after the return is processed. Transcripts are only available for the following returns: Form 1040 series, Form 1065, Form 1120, Form 1120-A, Form 1120-H, Form 1120-L, and Form 1120S. Return transcripts are available for the current year and returns processed during the prior 3 processing years. Most requests will be processed within 10 business days . . . . . . ☐

**b** **Account Transcript,** which contains information on the financial status of the account, such as payments made on the account, penalty assessments, and adjustments made by you or the IRS after the return was filed. Return information is limited to items such as tax liability and estimated tax payments. Account transcripts are available for most returns. Most requests will be processed within 10 business days ☐

**c** **Record of Account,** which provides the most detailed information as it is a combination of the Return Transcript and the Account Transcript. Available for current year and 3 prior tax years. Most requests will be processed within 10 business days . . . . . . ☐

**7** **Verification of Nonfiling,** which is proof from the IRS that you did not file a return for the year. Current year requests are only available after June 15th. There are no availability restrictions on prior year requests. Most requests will be processed within 10 business days . . ☐

**8** **Form W-2, Form 1099 series, Form 1098 series, or Form 5498 series transcript.** The IRS can provide a transcript that includes data from these information returns. State or local information is not included with the Form W-2 information. The IRS may be able to provide this transcript information for up to 10 years. Information for the current year is generally not available until the year after it is filed with the IRS. For example, W-2 information for 2016, filed in 2017, will likely not be available from the IRS until 2018. If you need W-2 information for retirement purposes, you should contact the Social Security Administration at 1-800-772-1213. Most requests will be processed within 10 business days . ☐

**Caution:** If you need a copy of Form W-2 or Form 1099, you should first contact the payer. To get a copy of the Form W-2 or Form 1099 filed with your return, you must use Form 4506 and request a copy of your return, which includes all attachments.

**9** **Year or period requested.** Enter the end date of the tax year or period requested in mm/dd/yyyy format. This may be a calendar year, fiscal year or quarter. Enter each quarter requested for quarterly returns. Example: Enter 12/31/2018 for a calendar year 2018 Form 1040 transcript.

| / / | / / | / / | / / |
|---|---|---|---|

**Caution:** Do not sign this form unless all applicable lines have been completed.

**Signature of taxpayer(s).** I declare that I am either the taxpayer whose name is shown on line 1a or 2a, or a person authorized to obtain the tax information requested. If the request applies to a joint return, at least one spouse must sign. If signed by a corporate officer, 1 percent or more shareholder, partner, managing member, guardian, tax matters partner, executor, receiver, administrator, trustee, or party other than the taxpayer, I certify that I have the authority to execute Form 4506-T on behalf of the taxpayer. **Note:** This form must be received by IRS within 120 days of the signature date.

☐ **Signatory attests that he/she has read the attestation clause and upon so reading declares that he/she has the authority to sign the Form 4506-T.** See instructions.

Phone number of taxpayer on line 1a or 2a

**Sign Here**

▶ **Signature** (see instructions)                    Date

▶ **Title** (if line 1a above is a corporation, partnership, estate, or trust)

▶ **Spouse's signature**                    Date

**For Privacy Act and Paperwork Reduction Act Notice, see page 2.**          Cat. No. 37667N          Form **4506-T** (Rev. 6-2023)

Section references are to the Internal Revenue Code unless otherwise noted.

## Future Developments

For the latest information about Form 4506-T and its instructions, go to *www.irs.gov/form4506t*. Information about any recent developments affecting Form 4506-T (such as legislation enacted after we released it) will be posted on that page.

The filing location for the Form 4506-T has changed. **Please see Chart for individual transcripts or Chart for all other transcripts** for the correct mailing location.

**What's New.** As part of its ongoing efforts to protect taxpayer data, the Internal Revenue Service announced that in July 2019, it will stop all third-party mailings of requested transcripts. After this date masked Tax Transcripts will only be mailed to the taxpayer's address of record.

If a third-party is unable to accept a Tax Transcript mailed to the taxpayer, they may either contract with an existing IVES participant or become an IVES participant themselves. For additional information about the IVES program, go to *www.irs.gov* and search IVES.

## General Instructions

**Caution:** Do not sign this form unless all applicable lines have been completed.

**Purpose of form.** Use Form 4506-T to request tax return information. Taxpayers using a tax year beginning in one calendar year and ending in the following year (fiscal tax year) must file Form 4506-T to request a return transcript.

**Note:** If you are unsure of which type of transcript you need, request the Record of Account, as it provides the most detailed information.

**Customer File Number.** The transcripts provided by the IRS have been modified to protect taxpayers' privacy. Transcripts only display partial personal information, such as the last four digits of the taxpayer's Social Security Number. Full financial and tax information, such as wages and taxable income, are shown on the transcript.

An optional Customer File Number field is available to use when requesting a transcript. This number will print on the transcript. See Line 5 instructions for specific requirements. The customer file number is an optional field and not required.

**Tip.** Use Form 4506, Request for Copy of Tax Return, to request copies of tax returns.

**Automated transcript request.** You can quickly request transcripts by using our automated self-help service tools. Please visit us at IRS.gov and click on "Get a Tax Transcript..." under "Tools" or call 1-800-908-9946.

**Where to file.** Mail or fax Form 4506-T to the address below for the state you lived in, or the state your business was in, when that return was filed. There are two address charts: one for individual transcripts (Form 1040 series and Form W-2) and one for all other transcripts.

If you are requesting more than one transcript or other product and the chart shows two different addresses, send your request to the address based on the address of your most recent return.

**Line 1b.** Enter your employer identification number (EIN) if your request relates to a business return. Otherwise, enter the first social security number (SSN) or your individual taxpayer identification number (TTIN) shown on the return. For example, if you are requesting Form 1040 that includes Schedule C (Form 1040), enter your SSN.

**Line 3.** Enter your current address. If you use a P.O. box, include it on this line.

**Line 4.** Enter the address shown on the last return filed if different from the address entered on line 3.

**Note:** If the addresses on lines 3 and 4 are different and you have not changed your address with the IRS, file Form 8822, Change of Address. For a business address, file Form 8822-B, Change of Address or Responsible Party — Business.

**Line 5.** Enter up to 10 numeric characters to create a unique customer file number that will appear on the transcript. The customer file number **should not** contain an SSN. Completion of this line is not required.

**Note.** If you use an SSN, name or combination of both, we will not input the information and the customer file number will reflect a generic entry of "9999999999" on the transcript.

**Line 6.** Enter only one tax form number per request.

**Signature and date.** Form 4506-T must be signed and dated by the taxpayer listed on line 1a or 2a. The IRS must receive Form 4506-T within 120 days of the date signed by the taxpayer or it will be rejected. Ensure that all applicable lines are completed before signing.

*You must check the box in the signature area to acknowledge you have the authority to sign and request the information. The form will not be processed and returned to you if the box is unchecked.*

*Individuals.* Transcripts of jointly filed tax returns may be furnished to either spouse. Only one signature is required. Sign Form 4506-T exactly as your name appeared on the original return. If you changed your name, also sign your current name.

*Corporations.* Generally, Form 4506-T can be signed by: (1) an officer having legal authority to bind the corporation, (2) any person designated by the board of directors or other governing body, or (3) any officer or employee on written request by any principal officer and attested to by the secretary or other officer. A bona fide shareholder of record owning 1 percent or more of the outstanding stock of the corporation may submit a Form 4506-T but must provide documentation to support the requester's right to receive the information.

*Partnerships.* Generally, Form 4506-T can be signed by any person who was a member of the partnership during any part of the tax period requested on line 9.

*All others.* See section 6103(e) if the taxpayer has died, is insolvent, is a dissolved corporation, or if a trustee, guardian, executor, receiver, or administrator is acting for the taxpayer.

**Note:** If you are Heir at law, Next of kin, or Beneficiary you must be able to establish a material interest in the estate or trust.

**Documentation.** For entities other than individuals, you must attach the authorization document. For example, this could be the letter from the principal officer authorizing an employee of the corporation or the letters testamentary authorizing an individual to act for an estate.

**Signature by a representative.** A representative can sign Form 4506-T for a taxpayer only if the taxpayer has specifically delegated this authority to the representative on Form 2848, line 5. The representative must attach Form 2848 showing the delegation to Form 4506-T.

**Privacy Act and Paperwork Reduction Act Notice.** We ask for the information on this form to establish your right to gain access to the requested tax information under the Internal Revenue Code. We need this information to properly identify the tax information and respond to your request. You are not required to request any transcript; if you do request a transcript, sections 6103 and 6109 and their regulations require you to provide this information, including your SSN or EIN. If you do not provide this information, we may not be able to process your request. Providing false or fraudulent information may subject you to penalties.

Routine uses of this information include giving it to the Department of Justice for civil and criminal litigation, and cities, states, the District of Columbia, and U.S. commonwealths and possessions for use in administering their tax laws. We may also disclose this information to other countries under a tax treaty, to federal and state agencies to enforce federal nontax criminal laws, or to federal law enforcement and intelligence agencies to combat terrorism.

You are not required to provide the information requested on a form that is subject to the Paperwork Reduction Act unless the form displays a valid OMB control number. Books or records relating to a form or its instructions must be retained as long as their contents may become material in the administration of any Internal Revenue law. Generally, tax returns and return information are confidential, as required by section 6103.

The time needed to complete and file Form 4506-T will vary depending on individual circumstances. The estimated average time is: **Learning about the law or the form,** 10 min.; **Preparing the form,** 12 min.; and **Copying, assembling, and sending the form to the IRS,** 20 min.

If you have comments concerning the accuracy of these time estimates or suggestions for making Form 4506-T simpler, we would be happy to hear from you. You can write to:

Internal Revenue Service
Tax Forms and Publications Division
1111 Constitution Ave. NW, IR-6526

Washington, DC 20224

Do not send the form to this address. Instead, see *Where to file* on this page.

## Chart for individual transcripts (Form 1040 series and Form W-2 and Form 1099)

| If you filed an individual return and lived in: | Mail or fax to: |
|---|---|
| Alabama, Arkansas, Florida, Georgia, Louisiana, Mississippi, North Carolina, Oklahoma, South Carolina, Tennessee, Texas, a foreign country, American Samoa, Puerto Rico, Guam, the Commonwealth of the Northern Mariana Islands, the U.S. Virgin Islands, or A.P.O. or F.P.O. address | Internal Revenue Service RAIVS Team Stop 6716 AUSC Austin, TX 73301  855-587-9604 |
| Delaware, Illinois, Indiana, Iowa, Kentucky, Maine, Massachusetts, Minnesota, Missouri, New Hampshire, New Jersey, New York, Vermont, Virginia, Wisconsin | Internal Revenue Service RAIVS Team Stop 6705 S-2 Kansas City, MO 64999  855-821-0094 |
| Alaska, Arizona, California, Colorado, Connecticut, District of Columbia, Hawaii, Idaho, Kansas, Maryland, Michigan, Montana, Nebraska, Nevada, New Mexico, North Dakota, Ohio, Oregon, Pennsylvania, Rhode Island, South Dakota, Utah, Washington, West Virginia, Wyoming | Internal Revenue Service RAIVS Team P.O. Box 9941 Mail Stop 6734 Ogden, UT 84409  855-298-1145 |

## Chart for all other transcripts

| If you lived in or your business was in: | Mail or fax to: |
|---|---|
| Alabama, Alaska, Arizona, Arkansas, California, Colorado, Florida, Hawaii, Idaho, Iowa, Kansas, Louisiana, Minnesota, Mississippi, Missouri, Montana, Nebraska, Nevada, New Mexico, North Dakota, Oklahoma, Oregon, South Dakota, Texas, Utah, Washington, Wyoming, a foreign country, American Samoa, Puerto Rico, Guam, the Commonwealth of the Northern Mariana Islands, the U.S. Virgin Islands, A.P.O. or F.P.O. address | Internal Revenue Service RAIVS Team P.O. Box 9941 Mail Stop 6734 Ogden, UT 84409  855-298-1145 |
| Connecticut, Delaware, District of Columbia, Georgia, Illinois, Indiana, Kentucky, Maine, Maryland, Massachusetts, Michigan, New Hampshire, New Jersey, New York, North Carolina, Ohio, Pennsylvania, Rhode Island, South Carolina, Tennessee, Vermont, Virginia, West Virginia, Wisconsin | Internal Revenue Service RAIVS Team Stop 6705 S-2 Kansas City, MO 64999  855-821-0094 |

# 20**21**

# Instructions for Form 5695

**Residential Energy Credits**

Department of the Treasury
Internal Revenue Service

Section references are to the Internal Revenue Code unless otherwise noted.

## General Instructions

### Future Developments

For the latest information about developments related to Form 5695 and its instructions, such as legislation enacted after they were published, go to *IRS.gov/Form5695*.

### What's New

**The Consolidated Appropriations Act, 2021:**

1. Extends the residential energy efficient property credit to qualified biomass fuel property costs on line 5, and provides definitions in these instructions.

2. Extends the 26 percent residential energy efficient property credit rate to property placed in service in 2021 and 2022.

3. Disallows the nonbusiness energy property credit for a stove which uses the burning of biomass fuel on line 22a, and we deleted the related definitions from these instructions.

4. Extends the balance of the nonbusiness energy property credit to property placed in service in 2021.

### Purpose of Form

Use Form 5695 to figure and take your residential energy credits. The residential energy credits are:
• The residential energy efficient property credit, and
• The nonbusiness energy property credit.

Also use Form 5695 to take any residential energy efficient property credit carryforward from 2020 or to carry the unused portion of the credit to 2022.

### Who Can Take the Credits

You may be able to take the credits if you made energy saving improvements to your home located in the United States in 2021.

**Home.** A home is where you lived in 2021 and can include a house, houseboat, mobile home, cooperative apartment, condominium, and a manufactured home that conforms to Federal Manufactured Home Construction and Safety Standards.

You must reduce the basis of your home by the amount of any credit allowed.

**Main home.** Your main home is generally the home where you live most of the time. A temporary absence due to special circumstances, such as illness, education, business, military service, or vacation, won't change your main home.

**Costs.** For purposes of both credits, costs are treated as being paid when the original installation of the item is completed, or, in the case of costs connected with the reconstruction of your home, when your original use of the reconstructed home begins. For purposes of the residential energy efficient property credit only, costs connected with the construction of a home are treated as being paid when your original use of the constructed home begins. If less than 80% of the use of an item is for

nonbusiness purposes, only that portion of the costs that is allocable to the nonbusiness use can be used to determine either credit.

⚠️ *Only the residential energy efficient property credit (Part I) is available for both existing homes and homes being constructed. The nonbusiness energy property credit (Part II) is only available for existing homes.*

⚠️ *IRS guidance issued with respect to the energy credit under section 48, such as Notice 2018-59, does not apply to the residential energy credits.*

**Association or cooperative costs.** If you are a member of a condominium management association for a condominium you own or a tenant-stockholder in a cooperative housing corporation, you are treated as having paid your proportionate share of any costs of such association or corporation.

⚠️ *If you received a subsidy from a public utility for the purchase or installation of an energy conservation product and that subsidy wasn't included in your gross income, you must reduce your cost for the product by the amount of that subsidy before you figure your credit. This rule also applies if a third party (such as a contractor) receives the subsidy on your behalf.*

## Residential Energy Efficient Property Credit (Part I)

If you made energy saving improvements to more than one home that you used as a residence during 2021, enter the total of those costs on the applicable line(s) of one Form 5695. For qualified fuel cell property, see *Lines 7a and 7b*, later.

You may be able to take a credit of 26% of your costs of qualified solar electric property, solar water heating property, small wind energy property, geothermal heat pump property, biomass fuel property, and fuel cell property. Include any labor costs properly allocable to the onsite preparation, assembly, or original installation of the residential energy efficient property and for piping or wiring to interconnect such property to the home. The credit amount for costs paid for qualified fuel cell property is limited to $500 for each one-half kilowatt of capacity of the property.

**Qualified solar electric property costs.** Qualified solar electric property costs are costs for property that uses solar energy to generate electricity for use in your home located in the United States. No costs relating to a solar panel or other property installed as a roof (or portion thereof) will fail to qualify solely because the property constitutes a structural component of the structure on which it is installed. Some solar roofing tiles and solar roofing shingles serve the function of both traditional roofing and solar electric collectors, and thus serve functions of both solar electric generation and structural support. These solar roofing tiles and solar roofing shingles can qualify for the credit. This is in contrast to structural components such as a roof's decking or rafters that serve only a roofing or structural function and thus do not qualify for the credit. The home doesn't have to be your main home.

**Qualified solar water heating property costs.** Qualified solar water heating property costs are costs for property to heat water

Jan 07, 2022                    Cat. No. 66412C

for use in your home located in the United States if at least half of the energy used by the solar water heating property for such purpose is derived from the sun. No costs relating to a solar panel or other property installed as a roof (or portion thereof) will fail to qualify solely because the property constitutes a structural component of the structure on which it is installed. Some solar roofing tiles and solar roofing shingles serve the function of both traditional roofing and solar electric collectors, and thus serve functions of both solar electric generation and structural support. These solar roofing tiles and solar roofing shingles can qualify for the credit. This is in contrast to structural components such as a roof's decking or rafters that serve only a roofing or structural function and thus do not qualify for the credit. To qualify for the credit, the property must be certified for performance by the nonprofit Solar Rating Certification Corporation or a comparable entity endorsed by the government of the state in which the property is installed. The home doesn't have to be your main home.

**Qualified small wind energy property costs.** Qualified small wind energy property costs are costs for property that uses a wind turbine to generate electricity for use in connection with your home located in the United States. The home doesn't have to be your main home.

**Qualified geothermal heat pump property costs.** Qualified geothermal heat pump property costs are costs for qualified geothermal heat pump property installed on or in connection with your home located in the United States. Qualified geothermal heat pump property is any equipment that uses the ground or ground water as a thermal energy source to heat your home or as a thermal energy sink to cool your home. To qualify for the credit, the geothermal heat pump property must meet the requirements of the Energy Star program that are in effect at the time of purchase. The home doesn't have to be your main home.

**Qualified biomass fuel property costs.** Qualified biomass fuel property costs are costs for property which uses the burning of biomass fuel to heat a dwelling unit located in the United States and used as a residence by the taxpayer, or to heat water for use in such a dwelling unit, and has a thermal efficiency rating of at least 75 percent (measured by the higher heating value of the fuel). Biomass fuel means any plant derived fuel available on a renewable or recurring basis.

**Qualified fuel cell property costs.** Qualified fuel cell property costs are costs for qualified fuel cell property installed on or in connection with your main home located in the United States. Qualified fuel cell property is an integrated system comprised of a fuel cell stack assembly and associated balance of plant components that converts a fuel into electricity using electrochemical means. To qualify for the credit, the fuel cell property must have a nameplate capacity of at least one-half kilowatt of electricity using an electrochemical process and an electricity-only generation efficiency greater than 30%.

⚠ *Costs allocable to a swimming pool, hot tub, or any other energy storage medium which has a function other than the function of such storage don't qualify for the residential energy efficient property credit.*

**Joint occupancy.** If you occupied your home jointly with someone other than your spouse, each occupant must complete his or her own Form 5695. To figure the credit, the maximum qualifying costs that can be taken into account by all occupants for qualified fuel cell property costs is $1,667 for each one-half kilowatt of capacity of the property. The amount allocable to you for qualified fuel cell property costs is the lesser of:

1. The amount you paid, or
2. The maximum qualifying cost of the property multiplied by a fraction. The numerator is the amount you paid and the

denominator is the total amount paid by you and all other occupants.

These rules don't apply to married individuals filing a joint return.

*Example.* Taxpayer A owns a house with Taxpayer B where they both reside. In 2021, they installed qualified fuel cell property at a cost of $20,000 with a kilowatt capacity of 5. Taxpayer A paid $12,000 towards the cost of the property and Taxpayer B paid the remaining $8,000. The amount to be allocated is $16,670 ($1,667 x 10 (kilowatt capacity x 2)). The amount of cost allocable to Taxpayer A is $10,002 ($16,670 x $12,000/$20,000). The amount of cost allocable to Taxpayer B is $6,668 ($16,670 x $8,000/$20,000).

# Nonbusiness Energy Property Credit (Part II)

You may be able to take a credit equal to the sum of:

1. 10% of the amount paid or incurred for qualified energy efficiency improvements installed during 2021, and

2. Any residential energy property costs paid or incurred in 2021

However, this credit is limited as follows.
* A total combined credit limit of $500 for all tax years after 2005.
* A combined credit limit of $200 for windows for all tax years after 2005.
* A credit limit for residential energy property costs for 2021 of $50 for any advanced main air circulating fan; $150 for any qualified natural gas, propane, or oil furnace or hot water boiler; and $300 for any item of energy efficient building property.

⚠ *If the total of any nonbusiness energy property credits you have taken in previous years (after 2005) is more than $500, you generally can't take the credit in 2021.*

**Subsidized energy financing.** Any amounts provided for by subsidized energy financing can't be used to figure the nonbusiness energy property credit. This is financing provided under a federal, state, or local program, the principal purpose of which is to provide subsidized financing for projects designed to conserve or produce energy.

**Qualified energy efficiency improvements.** Qualified energy efficiency improvements are the following building envelope components installed on or in your main home that you owned during 2021 located in the United States if the original use of the component begins with you, the component can be expected to remain in use at least 5 years, and the component meets certain energy standards.
* Any insulation material or system that is specifically and primarily designed to reduce heat loss or gain of a home when installed in or on such a home.
* Exterior windows and skylights.
* Exterior doors.
* Any metal roof with appropriate pigmented coatings or asphalt roof with appropriate cooling granules that are specifically and primarily designed to reduce the heat gain of your home.

For purposes of figuring the credit, don't include amounts paid for the onsite preparation, assembly, or original installation of the building envelope component.

⚠ *To qualify for the credit, qualified energy efficiency improvements must meet certain energy efficiency requirements. See Lines 19a Through 19h, later, for details.*

**Residential energy property costs.** Residential energy property costs are costs of new qualified energy property that is

Instructions for Form 5695 (2021)

installed on or in connection with your main home that you owned during 2021 located in the United States. Include any labor costs properly allocable to the onsite preparation, assembly, or original installation of the energy property. Qualified energy property is any of the following.

• Certain electric heat pump water heaters; electric heat pumps; central air conditioners; and natural gas, propane, or oil water heaters.

• Qualified natural gas, propane, or oil furnaces and qualified natural gas, propane, or oil hot water boilers.

• Certain advanced main air circulating fans used in natural gas, propane, or oil furnaces.

⚠️ To qualify for the credit, qualified energy property must meet certain energy efficiency requirements. See Lines 22a through 22c, later, for details.

**Joint ownership of qualified property.** If you and a neighbor shared the cost of qualifying property to benefit each of your main homes, both of you can take the nonbusiness energy property credit. You figure your credit on the part of the cost you paid. The limit on the amount of the credit applies to each of you separately.

**Married taxpayers with more than one home.** If both you and your spouse owned and lived apart in separate main homes, the limit on the amount of the credit applies to each of you separately. If you are filing separate returns, both of you would complete a separate Form 5695. If you are filing a joint return, figure your nonbusiness energy property credit as follows.

1. Complete lines 17a through 17c and 19 through 24 of a separate Form 5695 for each main home.

2. Figure the amount to be entered on line 24 of both forms (but not more than $500 for each form) and enter the combined amount on line 24 of one of the forms.

3. On line 25 of the form with the combined amount on line 24, cross out the preprinted $500 and enter $1,000.

4. On the dotted line to the left of line 25, enter "More than one main home." Then, complete the rest of this form, including line 18. The amount on line 18 can exceed $500.

5. Attach both forms to your return.

**Joint occupancy.** If you owned your home jointly with someone other than your spouse, each owner must complete his or her own Form 5695. To figure the credit, there are no maximum qualifying costs for insulation, exterior doors, and a metal or asphalt roof. Enter the amounts you paid for these items on the appropriate lines of Form 5695, Part II. For windows and residential energy property costs, the amount allocable to you is the smaller of:

1. The amount you paid, or

2. The maximum qualifying cost" of the property multiplied by a fraction. The numerator is the amount you paid and the denominator is the total amount paid by you and all other owners.

* $2,000 for windows; $300 for energy-efficient building property; $150 for qualified natural gas, propane, or oil furnace or hot water boiler; or $50 for an advanced main air circulating fan.

# Specific Instructions
## Part I
## Residential Energy Efficient Property Credit

### Before you begin Part I.

Figure the amount of the credits shown in the credit limitation worksheet if you take those credits on your return.

**TIP** Also, include on lines 1 through 5, and 8, any labor costs properly allocable to the onsite preparation, assembly, or original installation of the property and for piping or wiring to interconnect such property to the home.

### Line 1

Enter the amounts you paid for qualified solar electric property. See *Qualified solar electric property costs*, earlier.

### Line 2

Enter the amounts you paid for qualified solar water heating property. See *Qualified solar water heating property costs*, earlier.

### Line 3

Enter the amounts you paid for qualified small wind energy property. See *Qualified small wind energy property costs*, earlier.

### Line 4

Enter the amounts you paid for qualified geothermal heat pump property. See *Qualified geothermal heat pump property costs*, earlier.

### Line 5

Enter the amounts you paid for qualified biomass fuel property. See *Qualified biomass fuel property costs*, earlier.

### Lines 7a and 7b

Any qualified fuel cell property costs must have been for your main home located in the United States. See *Main home*, earlier. If you check the "No" box, you can't include any fuel cell property costs on line 8.

If you check the "Yes" box, enter the full address of your main home during 2021 on line 7b.

If you and your spouse are filing jointly and you each have different main homes with qualified fuel cell property costs, provide on line 7b the address of your main home. Add a sheet providing the address of your spouse's main home. You and your spouse should add your qualified fuel cell property costs together on line 8 of one Form 5695.

### Line 8

Enter the amounts you paid for qualified fuel cell property. See *Qualified fuel cell property costs*, earlier.

### Line 14

Complete the following worksheet to figure the amount to enter on line 14.

**Residential Energy Efficient Property Credit Limit Worksheet—Line 14**

1. Enter the amount from Form 1040, 1040-SR, or 1040-NR, line 18 ... **1** _____

2. Enter the total of the following credit(s)/adjustment(s) if you are taking the credit(s)/adjustment(s) on your 2021 income tax return:

   + Negative Form 8978 Adjustment, Schedule 3 (Form 1040), Part I, line 6 ...... _____

   + Foreign Tax Credit, Schedule 3 (Form 1040), Part I, line 1 ...... _____

   + Credit for Child and Dependent Care Expenses, Schedule 3 (Form 1040), Part I, line 2 ...... _____

   + Credit for the Elderly or the Disabled, Schedule R (Form 1040), line 22 ...... _____

   + Nonrefundable Education Credits, Schedule 3 (Form 1040), Part I, line 3 ...... _____

   + Retirement Savings Contributions Credit, Schedule 3 (Form 1040), Part I, line 4 ...... _____

   + Nonbusiness Energy Property Credit, Form 5695, Part II, line 30 ...... _____

   + Alternative Motor Vehicle Credit, Personal use part, Form 8910, Part III, line 15 ...... _____

   + Qualified Plug-in Electric Drive Motor Vehicle Credit (including Qualified Two-Wheeled Plug-in Electric Vehicles), Personal use part, Form 8936, Part III, line 23 ...... _____

   + Nonrefundable child tax credit and credit for other dependents, Form 1040, 1040-SR, or 1040-NR, line 19* ...... _____

   + Mortgage Interest Credit, Form 8396, line 9 ...... _____

   + Adoption Credit, Form 8839, line 16 ...... _____

   + Carryforward of the District of Columbia First-Time Homebuyer Credit, Form 8859, line 3 ...... _____

   **Note.** *Enter the total of the preceding credit(s)/adjustment(s), only if allowed and taken on your 2021 income tax return. Not all credits/adjustments are available for all years nor for all filers. See the instructions for your 2021 income tax return.* **2** _____

3. Subtract line 2 from line 1. Also enter this amount on Form 5695, line 14. If zero or less, enter -0- on Form 5695, lines 14 and 15. **3** _____

* Include the amount from Schedule 8812 (Form 1040), Credit Limit Worksheet B, line 14, instead of the amount from Form 1040, 1040-SR, or 1040-NR, line 19, if the instructions for Schedule 8812 (Form 1040) direct you to complete Credit Limit Worksheet B.

**Manufacturer's certification.** For purposes of taking the credit, you can rely on the manufacturer's certification in writing that a product is qualifying property for the credit. Don't attach the certification to your return. Keep it for your records.

## Line 16

If you can't use all of the credit because of the tax liability limit (that is, line 14 is less than line 13), you can carry the unused portion of the credit to 2022.

File this form even if you can't use any of your credit in 2021.

# Part II
# Nonbusiness Energy Property Credit

### Before you begin Part II.

Figure the amount of the credits shown in the credit limitation worksheet if you take those credits on your return.

### Lines 17a Through 17c

**Line 17a.** To qualify for the credit, any qualified energy efficiency improvements or residential energy property costs must have been for your main home located in the United States. See *Main home*, earlier. If you check the "No" box, you can't take the nonbusiness energy property credit.

**Line 17b.** Enter the full address of your main home during 2021.

**Line 17c.** You may only include expenses for qualified improvements for an existing home or for an addition or renovation to an existing home, and not for a newly constructed home. If you check the "Yes" box, you can't claim any expenses for qualified improvements that are related to the construction of your home, even if the improvement is installed after you have moved into the home.

## Line 18

If you took a nonbusiness energy property credit in 2006, 2007, 2009, 2010, 2011, 2012, 2013, 2014, 2015, 2016, 2017, 2018, 2019, or 2020, complete the following worksheet to figure the amount to enter on line 18. If the total of the credits on the worksheet is $500 or more, you generally can't take this credit for 2021.

-4-

## Lifetime Limitation Worksheet—Line 18

1. Enter the amount, if any, from your 2006 Form 5695, line 12 ........... 1. _____

2. Enter the amount, if any, from your 2007 Form 5695, line 15 ........... 2. _____

3. Enter the amount, if any, from your 2009 Form 5695, line 11 ........... 3. _____

4. Enter the amount, if any, from your 2010 Form 5695, line 11 ........... 4. _____

5. Enter the amount, if any, from your 2011 Form 5695, line 14 ........... 5. _____

6. Enter the amount, if any, from your 2012 Form 5695, line 32 ........... 6. _____

7. Enter the amount, if any, from your 2013 Form 5695, line 30 ........... 7. _____

8. Enter the amount, if any, from your 2014 Form 5695, line 30 ........... 8. _____

9. Enter the amount, if any, from your 2015 Form 5695, line 30 ........... 9. _____

10. Enter the amount, if any, from your 2016 Form 5695, line 30 ........... 10. _____

11. Enter the amount, if any, from your 2017 Form 5695, line 30 ........... 11. _____

12. Enter the amount, if any, from your 2018 Form 5695, line 30 ........... 12. _____

13. Enter the amount, if any, from your 2019 Form 5695, line 30 ........... 13. _____

14. Enter the amount, if any, from your 2020 Form 5695, line 30 ........... 14. _____

15. Add lines 1 through 14. Also enter this amount on Form 5695, line 18. If $500 or more, **stop;** you can't take the nonbusiness energy property credit ........... 15. _____

## Lines 19a Through 19h

**Note.** A reference to the IECC is a reference to the 2009 International Energy Conservation Code as in effect (with supplements) on February 17, 2009.

⚠ *Don't include on lines 19a through 19d any amounts paid for the onsite preparation, assembly, or original installation of the components.*

**Line 19a.** Enter the amounts you paid for any insulation material or system (including any vapor retarder or seal to limit infiltration) that is specifically and primarily designed to reduce the heat loss or gain of your home when installed in or on such home and meets the prescriptive criteria established by the IECC.

⚠ *A component isn't specifically and primarily designed to reduce the heat loss or gain of your home if it provides structural support or a finished surface (such as drywall or siding) or its principal purpose is to serve any function unrelated to the reduction of heat loss or gain.*

**Line 19b.** Enter the amounts you paid for exterior doors that meet or exceed the version 6.0 Energy Star program requirements.

**Line 19c.** Enter the amounts you paid for a metal roof with the appropriate pigmented coatings or an asphalt roof with the appropriate cooling granules that are specifically and primarily designed to reduce the heat gain of your home, and the roof meets or exceeds the Energy Star program requirements in effect at the time of purchase or installation.

**Line 19d.** Enter the amounts you paid for exterior windows and skylights that meet or exceed the version 6.0 Energy Star program requirements.

⚠ *If you took the credit for windows in 2006, 2007, 2009, 2010, 2011, 2012, 2013, 2014, 2015, 2016, 2017, 2018, 2019, or 2020, you may not be able to include window expenses this year.*

**Line 19f.** If you reported expenses on your 2006 Form 5695, line 2b; 2007 Form 5695, line 2d; 2009 Form 5695, line 2b; 2010 Form 5695, line 2b; 2011 Form 5695, line 3d; 2012 Form 5695, line 21d; 2013 Form 5695, line 19d; 2014 Form 5695, line 19d; 2015 Form 5695, line 19d; 2016 Form 5695, line 19d; 2017 Form 5695, line 19d; 2018 Form 5695, line 19d; 2019 Form 5695, line 19d; or 2020 Form 5695, line 19d, then use the worksheet next to figure the amount to enter on line 19f.

## Window Expense Worksheet—Line 19f

1. Enter the amount from your 2006 Form 5695, line 2b — 1. ____
2. Enter the amount from your 2007 Form 5695, line 2d — 2. ____
3. Enter the amount from your 2009 Form 5695, line 2b — 3. ____
4. Enter the amount from your 2010 Form 5695, line 2b — 4. ____
5. Add lines 3 and 4 — 5. ____
6. Multiply line 5 by 3.0 — 6. ____
7. Enter the amount from your 2011 Form 5695, line 3d — 7. ____
8. Enter the amount from your 2012 Form 5695, line 21d — 8. ____
9. Enter the amount from your 2013 Form 5695, line 19d — 9. ____
10. Enter the amount from your 2014 Form 5695, line 19d — 10. ____
11. Enter the amount from your 2015 Form 5695, line 19d — 11. ____
12. Enter the amount from your 2016 Form 5695, line 19d — 12. ____
13. Enter the amount from your 2017 Form 5695, line 19d — 13. ____
14. Enter the amount from your 2018 Form 5695, line 19d — 14. ____
15. Enter the amount from your 2019 Form 5695, line 19d — 15. ____
16. Enter the amount from your 2020 Form 5695, line 19d — 16. ____
17. Add lines 1, 2, and 6 through 16. Also enter this amount on Form 5695, line 19f — 17. ____

**Manufacturer's certification.** For purposes of taking the credit, you can rely on a manufacturer's certification in writing that a building envelope component is an eligible building envelope component. Don't attach the certification to your return. Keep it for your records.

## Lines 22a Through 22c

**TIP** Also include on lines 22a through 22c any labor costs properly allocable to the onsite preparation, assembly, or original installation of the property.

**Line 22a.** Enter the amounts you paid for energy-efficient building property. Energy-efficient building property is any of the following.
• An electric heat pump water heater that yields a Uniform Energy Factor of at least 2.2 in the standard Department of Energy test procedure.
• An electric heat pump that achieves the highest efficiency tier established by the Consortium for Energy Efficiency (CEE) as in effect on January 1, 2009.
• A central air conditioner that achieves the highest efficiency tier that has been established by the CEE as in effect on January 1, 2009.
• A natural gas, propane, or oil water heater that has a Uniform Energy Factor of at least 0.82 or a thermal efficiency of at least 90%.

Don't enter more than $300 on line 22a.

**Line 22b.** Enter the amounts you paid for a natural gas, propane, or oil furnace or hot water boiler that achieves an annual fuel utilization rate of at least 95.

Don't enter more than $150 on line 22b.

**Line 22c.** Enter the amounts you paid for an advanced main air circulating fan used in a natural gas, propane, or oil furnace that has an annual electricity use of no more than 2% of the total annual energy use of the furnace (as determined in the standard Department of Energy test procedures).

Don't enter more than $50 on line 22c.

**Manufacturer's certification.** For purposes of taking the credit, you can rely on a manufacturer's certification in writing that a product is qualified energy property. Don't attach the certification to your return. Keep it for your records.

## Line 25

If the rules discussed earlier for joint occupancy apply, cross out the preprinted $500 on line 25, and enter on line 25 the smaller of

1. The amount on line 24, or
2. $500 multiplied by a fraction. The numerator is the amount on line 24. The denominator is the total amount from line 24 for all owners.

For more details, see *Joint occupancy*, earlier.

## Line 29

Complete the worksheet below to figure the amount to enter on line 29.

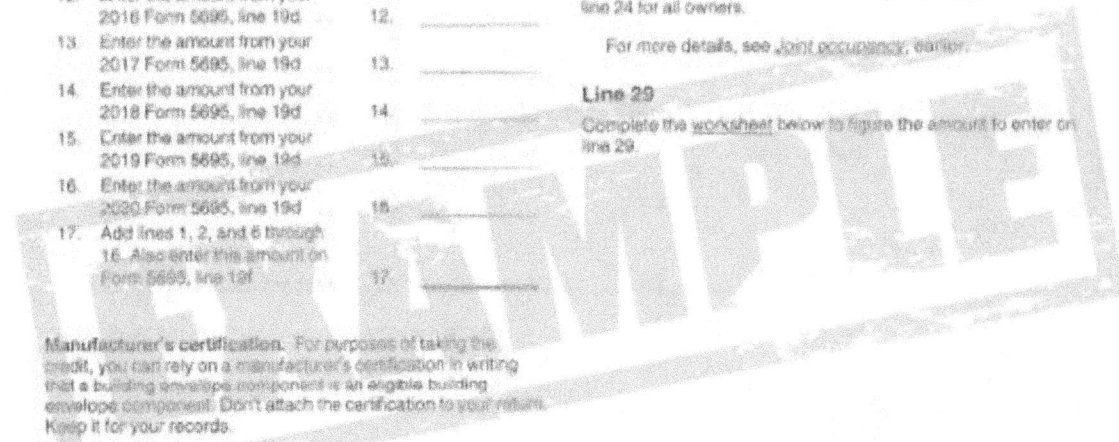

Instructions for Form 5695 (2021)

72

**Nonbusiness Energy Property Credit Limit Worksheet—Line 29**

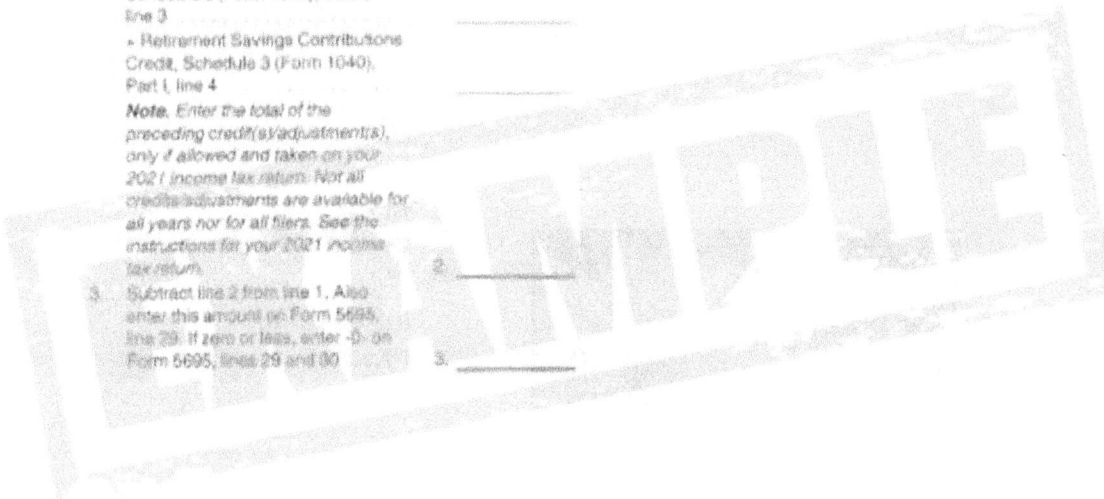

1. Enter the amount from Form 1040, 1040-SR, or 1040-NR, line 18 ... **1.** _____

2. Enter the total of the following credit(s)/adjustment(s) if you are taking the credit(s)/adjustment(s) on your 2021 income tax return:

   + Negative Form 8978 Adjustment, Schedule 3 (Form 1040), Part I, line 6l _____

   + Foreign Tax Credit, Schedule 3 (Form 1040), Part I, line 1 _____

   + Credit for Child and Dependent Care Expenses, Schedule 3 (Form 1040), Part I, line 2 _____

   + Credit for the Elderly or the Disabled, Schedule R (Form 1040), line 22 _____

   + Nonrefundable Education Credits, Schedule 3 (Form 1040), Part I, line 3 _____

   + Retirement Savings Contributions Credit, Schedule 3 (Form 1040), Part I, line 4 _____

   **Note.** Enter the total of the preceding credit(s)/adjustment(s), only if allowed and taken on your 2021 income tax return. Not all credits/adjustments are available for all years nor for all filers. See the instructions for your 2021 income tax return. ... **2.** _____

3. Subtract line 2 from line 1. Also enter this amount on Form 5695, line 29. If zero or less, enter -0- on Form 5695, lines 29 and 30) ... **3.** _____

**Publication 535**
Cat. No. 15065Z

Department
of the
Treasury

**Internal
Revenue
Service**

# Business Expenses

For use in preparing

**2022** Returns

**Get forms and other information faster and easier at:**
- *IRS.gov* (English)
- *IRS.gov/Spanish* (Español)
- *IRS.gov/Chinese* (中文)
- *IRS.gov/Korean* (한국어)
- *IRS.gov/Russian* (Русский)
- *IRS.gov/Vietnamese* (Tiếng Việt)

## Contents

## Introduction

This publication discusses common business expenses and explains what is and is not deductible. The general rules for deducting business expenses are discussed in the opening chapter. The chapters that follow cover specific expenses and list other publications and forms you may need.

**Note.** Section references within this publication are to the Internal Revenue Code and regulation references are to the Income Tax Regulations under the Code.

**Comments and suggestions.** We welcome your comments about this publication and your suggestions for future editions.

You can send us comments through *IRS.gov/FormComments*. Or you can write to the Internal Revenue Service, Tax Forms and Publications, 1111 Constitution Ave. NW, IR-6526, Washington, DC 20224.

Although we cannot respond individually to each comment received, we do appreciate your feedback and will consider your comments and suggestions as we revise our tax forms, instructions, and publications. **Don't** send tax questions, tax returns, or payments to the above address.

*Getting answers to your tax questions.* If you have a tax question not answered by this publication or the *How To Get Tax Help* section at the end of this publication, go to the IRS Interactive Tax Assistant page at *IRS.gov/Help/ITA* where you can find topics by using the search feature or viewing the categories listed.

**Getting tax forms, instructions, and publications.** Go to *IRS.gov/Forms* to download current and prior-year forms, instructions, and publications.

**Ordering tax forms, instructions, and publications.** Go to *IRS.gov/OrderForms* to order current forms, instructions, and publications; call 800-829-3676 to order prior-year forms and instructions. The IRS will process your order for forms and publications as soon as possible. **Don't** resubmit requests you've already sent us. You can get forms and publications faster online.

## Future Developments

For the latest information about developments related to Pub. 535, such as legislation enacted after it was published, go to *IRS.gov/Pub535*.

## What's New for 2022

The following items highlight some changes in the tax law for 2022.

**Form 1099-K reporting transition period.** The transition period described in *Notice 2023-10* delays the reporting of transactions in excess of $600 to transactions that occur after calendar year 2022. The transition period is intended to facilitate an orderly transition for TPSO tax compliance, as well as individual payee compliance with income tax reporting. A participating payee, in the case of a third-party network transaction, is any person who accepts payment from a third-party settlement organization for a business transaction.

**The COVID-19 related credit for qualified sick and family leave wages is limited to leave taken after March 31, 2020, and before October 1, 2021.** Generally, the credit for qualified sick and family leave wages, as enacted under the Families First Coronavirus Response Act (FFCRA) and amended and extended by the COVID-related Tax Relief Act of 2020, for leave taken after March 31, 2020, and before April 1, 2021, and the credit for qualified sick and family leave wages under sections 3131, 3132, and 3133 of the Internal Revenue Code, as enacted under the American Rescue Plan Act of 2021 (the ARP), for leave taken after March 31, 2021, and before October 1, 2021, have expired. However, employers that pay qualified sick and family leave wages in 2022 for leave taken after March 31, 2020, and before October 1, 2021, are eligible to claim a credit for qualified sick and family leave wages in 2022. For more information, see *chapter 2*.

**The COVID-19 related employee retention credit has expired.** The employee retention credit enacted under the Coronavirus Aid, Relief, and Economic Security (CARES) Act and amended and extended by the Taxpayer Certainty and Disaster Tax Relief Act of 2020 was limited to qualified wages paid after March 12,

2020, and before July 1, 2021. The employee retention credit under section 3134 of the Internal Revenue Code, as enacted by the ARP and amended by the Infrastructure Investment and Jobs Act, was limited to wages paid after June 30, 2021, and before October 1, 2021, unless the employer was a recovery startup business. An employer that was a recovery startup business could also claim the employee retention credit for wages paid after September 30, 2021, and before January 1, 2022. For more information, see *chapter 2*.

**Credit for COBRA premium assistance payments is limited to periods of coverage beginning on or after April 1, 2021, through periods of coverage beginning on or before September 30, 2021.** Section 9501 of the ARP provides for COBRA premium assistance in the form of a full reduction in the premium otherwise payable by certain individuals and their families who elect COBRA continuation coverage due to a loss of coverage as the result of a reduction in hours or an involuntary termination of employment (assistance eligible individuals). This COBRA premium assistance is available for periods of coverage beginning on or after April 1, 2021, through periods of coverage beginning on or before September 30, 2021. For more information, see *chapter 2*.

**Advance payment of COVID-19 credits extended.** You may no longer request an advance payment of any credit on Form 7200, Advance Payment of Employer Credits Due to COVID-19. For more information, see *chapter 2*.

**Research and experimental costs.** Beginning January 1, 2022, research and experimental expenditures, generally, have to be amortized over a 5-year period. A business cannot elect to deduct their total research expenses in the current year. For more information, see *chapter 7*.

**Amortization of research and experimental expenditures.** Specified research or experimental costs paid or incurred in tax years beginning after 2021 must be capitalized and amortized ratably over a 5-year period (15-year period for any expenditures related to foreign research). For more information, see *chapter 8*.

**Corporate alternative minimum tax reinstated in 2023.** P.L. 117-169, dated August 16, 2022, amended section 55 to impose a corporate alternative minimum tax. The amendment applies to tax years beginning after 2022. For more information, see *chapter 9*.

**Excise tax on Black Lung Benefits now permanent.** P.L. 117-169 also amended section 4121 to eliminate the reduction in tax on coal from mines located in the United States by the producer. The amendment applies to sales in calendar quarters beginning after August 17, 2022. For more information, see *chapter 9*.

**Standard mileage rate.** For tax year 2022, the standard mileage rate for *the cost of operating your car*, van, pickup, or panel truck for each mile of business use is:
- 58.5 cents per mile from January 1, 2022, through June 30, 2022; and
- 62.5 cents per mile from July 1, 2022, through December 31, 2022.

For more information, see *chapter 11*.

## What's New for 2023

The following item highlights a change in the tax law for 2023.

**Most current standard mileage rate.** For the most current standard mileage rates, go to *IRS.gov/Tax-Professionals/Standard-Mileage-Rates*.

The following item highlights a change regarding this publication.

**Final revision.** Pub. 535 will no longer be revised and published. The 2022 edition will be the final revision available.

## Reminders

The following reminders and other items may help you file your tax return.

### IRS *e-file* (Electronic Filing)

You can file your tax returns electronically using an IRS *e-file* option. The benefits of IRS *e-file* include faster refunds, increased accuracy, and acknowledgment of IRS receipt of your return. You can use one of the following IRS *e-file* options.
- Use an authorized IRS *e-file* provider.
- Use a personal computer.
- Visit a Volunteer Income Tax Assistance (VITA) or Tax Counseling for the Elderly (TCE) site.

For details on these fast filing methods, see your income tax package.

**Form 1099-MISC.** File Form 1099-MISC, Miscellaneous Income, for each person to whom you have paid during the year in the course of your trade or business at least $600 in rents, prizes and awards, other income payments, medical and health care payments, and crop insurance proceeds. See the Instructions for Forms 1099-MISC and 1099-NEC for more information and additional reporting requirements.

**Form 1099-NEC.** File Form 1099-NEC, Nonemployee Compensation, for each person to whom you have paid during the year in the course of your trade or business at least $600 in services (including parts and materials), who is not your employee. See the Instructions for Forms 1099-MISC and 1099-NEC for more information and additional reporting requirements.

**Gig Economy Tax Center.** The IRS Gig Economy Tax Center on IRS.gov can help people in this growing area meet their tax obligations through more streamlined information.

The gig economy is also known as the sharing, on-demand, or access economy. It usually includes businesses that operate an app or website to connect people to provide services to customers. While there are many types of gig economy businesses, ride-sharing and home rentals are two of the most popular.

The Gig Economy Tax Center streamlines various resources, making it easier for taxpayers to find information about the tax implications for the companies that provide the services and the individuals who perform them. It offers tips and resources on a variety of topics including:

- Filing requirements;
- Making quarterly estimated income tax payments;
- Paying self-employment taxes;
- Paying FICA, Medicare, and Additional Medicare taxes;
- Deductible business expenses; and
- Special rules for reporting vacation home rentals.

For more information, go to the *Gig Economy Tax Center* at *IRS.gov/Gig*.

**Photographs of missing children.** The Internal Revenue Service is a proud partner with the *National Center for Missing & Exploited Children® (NCMEC)*. Photographs of missing children selected by the Center may appear in this publication on pages that would otherwise be blank. You can help bring these children home by looking at the photographs and calling 1-800-THE-LOST (1-800-843-5678) (24 hours a day, 7 days a week) if you recognize a child.

**Preventing slavery and human trafficking.** Human trafficking is a form of modern-day slavery, and involves the use of force, fraud, or coercion to exploit human beings for some type of labor or commercial sex purpose. The United States is a source, transit, and destination country for men, women, and children, both U.S. citizens and foreign nationals, who are subjected to the injustices of slavery and human trafficking, including forced labor, debt bondage, involuntary servitude, "mail-order" marriages, and sex trafficking. Trafficking in persons can occur in both lawful and illicit industries or markets, including in hotel services, hospitality, agriculture, manufacturing, janitorial services, construction, health and elder care, domestic service, brothels, massage parlors, and street prostitution, among others.

The *President's Interagency Task Force to Monitor and Combat Trafficking in Persons (PITF)* brings together federal departments and agencies to ensure a whole-of-government approach that addresses all aspects of human trafficking. Online resources for recognizing and reporting trafficking activities, and assisting victims include the Department of Homeland Security (DHS) Blue Campaign at *DHS.gov/blue-campaign*, the Department of State Office to Monitor and Combat Trafficking in Persons at *State.gov/j/tip*, and the National Human Trafficking Resource Center (NHTRC) at *humantraffickinghotline.org*. DHS is responsible for investigating human trafficking, arresting traffickers, and protecting victims. DHS also provides *immigration relief* to non-U.S. citizen victims of human trafficking. DHS uses a *victim-centered approach* to combating human trafficking, which places equal value on identifying and stabilizing victims and on investigating and prosecuting traffickers. Victims are crucial to investigations and prosecutions; each case and every conviction changes lives. DHS understands how difficult it can be for victims to come forward and work with law enforcement due to their trauma. DHS is committed to helping victims feel stable, safe, and secure.

To report suspected human trafficking, call the DHS domestic 24-hour toll-free number at 866-DHS-2-ICE (866-347-2423) or 802-872-6199 (non-toll-free international). For help from the NHTRC, call the National Human Trafficking Hotline toll free at 888-373-7888 or text HELP or INFO to BeFree (233733).

The U.S. Department of the Treasury's Financial Crimes Enforcement Network (FinCEN) has issued a public advisory to financial institutions that contains red flag indicators for potential suspicious financial activity associated with human trafficking. If warranted, financial institutions should file a Suspicious Activity Report (FinCEN 112) with FinCEN to report these activities. For more information, go to *Fincen.gov/Sites/default/files/advisory/FIN-2014-A008.pdf*.

# 1.

# Deducting Business Expenses

## Introduction

This chapter covers the general rules for deducting business expenses. Business expenses are the costs of carrying on a trade or business, and they are usually deductible if the business is operated to make a profit.

## Topics
This chapter discusses:

- What you can deduct
- How much you can deduct
- When you can deduct
- Not-for-profit activities

## Useful Items
You may want to see:

### Publication

- ❑ **334** Tax Guide for Small Business
- ❑ **463** Travel, Gift, and Car Expenses
- ❑ **525** Taxable and Nontaxable Income
- ❑ **529** Miscellaneous Deductions
- ❑ **536** Net Operating Losses (NOLs) for Individuals, Estates, and Trusts
- ❑ **538** Accounting Periods and Methods
- ❑ **542** Corporations
- ❑ **547** Casualties, Disasters, and Thefts
- ❑ **583** Starting a Business and Keeping Records
- ❑ **587** Business Use of Your Home
- ❑ **925** Passive Activity and At-Risk Rules
- ❑ **936** Home Mortgage Interest Deduction
- ❑ **946** How To Depreciate Property

### Form (and Instructions)

- ❑ **Schedule A (Form 1040)** Itemized Deductions
- ❑ **5213** Election To Postpone Determination as To Whether the Presumption Applies That an Activity Is Engaged in for Profit

See chapter 12 for information about getting publications and forms.

## What Can I Deduct?

To be deductible, a business expense must be both ordinary and necessary. An ordinary expense is one that is common and accepted in your industry. A necessary expense is one that is helpful and appropriate for your trade or business. An expense does not have to be indispensable to be considered necessary.

Even though an expense may be ordinary and necessary, you may not be allowed to deduct the expense in the year you paid or incurred it. In some cases, you may not be allowed to deduct the expense at all. Therefore, it is important to distinguish usual business expenses from expenses that include the following.

- The expenses used to figure cost of goods sold.
- Capital expenses.
- Personal expenses.

## Cost of Goods Sold

If your business manufactures products or purchases them for resale, you must generally value inventory at the beginning and end of each tax year to determine your cost of goods sold. Some of your business expenses may be included in figuring cost of goods sold. Cost of goods sold is deducted from your gross receipts to figure your gross profit for the year. If you include an expense in the cost of goods sold, you cannot deduct it again as a business expense.

The following are types of expenses that go into figuring cost of goods sold.

- The cost of products or raw materials, including freight.
- Storage.
- Direct labor (including contributions to pension or annuity plans) for workers who produce the products.
- Factory overhead.

Under the uniform capitalization rules, you must capitalize the direct costs and part of the indirect costs for certain production or resale activities. Indirect costs include rent, interest, taxes, storage, purchasing, processing, repackaging, handling, and administrative costs.

This rule does not apply to small business taxpayers. You qualify as a small business taxpayer if you (a) have average annual gross receipts of $27 million or less for the 3 prior tax years, and (b) are not a tax shelter (as defined in section 448(d)(3)). If your business has not been in existence for all of the 3-tax-year period used in figuring average gross receipts, base your average on the period it has existed, and if your business has a predecessor entity, include the gross receipts of the predecessor entity from the 3-tax-year period when figuring average gross receipts. If your business (or predecessor entity) had short tax years for any of the 3-tax-year period, annualize your business' gross receipts for the short tax years that are part of the 3-tax-year period. See Pub. 538 for more information.

For more information, see the following sources.
- Cost of goods sold—chapter 6 of Pub. 334.
- Inventories—Pub. 538.
- Uniform capitalization rules—Pub. 538 and section 263A and the related regulations.

## Capital Expenses

You must capitalize, rather than deduct, some costs. These costs are a part of your investment in your business and are called "capital expenses." Capital expenses are considered assets in your business. In general, you capitalize three types of costs.
- Business startup costs (see Tip below).
- Business assets.
- Improvements.

**TIP** *You can elect to deduct or amortize certain business startup costs. See* chapters 7 *and* 8.

**Cost recovery.** Although you generally cannot take a current deduction for a capital expense, you may be able to recover the amount you spend through depreciation, amortization, or depletion. These recovery methods allow you to deduct part of your cost each year. In this way, you are able to recover your capital expense. See *Amortization* (chapter 8) and *Depletion* (chapter 9) in this publication. A taxpayer can elect to deduct a portion of the costs of certain depreciable property as a section 179 deduction. A greater portion of these costs can be deducted if the property is qualified disaster assistance property. See Pub. 946 for details.

### Going Into Business

The costs of getting started in business, before you actually begin business operations, are capital expenses. These costs may include expenses for advertising, travel, or wages for training employees.

**If you go into business.** When you go into business, treat all costs you had to get your business started as capital expenses.

Usually, you recover costs for a particular asset through depreciation. Generally, you cannot recover other costs until you sell the business or otherwise go out of business. However, you can choose to amortize certain costs for setting up your business. See *Starting a Business* in chapter 8 for more information on business startup costs.

**If your attempt to go into business is unsuccessful.** If you are an individual and your attempt to go into business is not successful, the expenses you had in trying to establish yourself in business fall into two categories.

1. The costs you had before making a decision to acquire or begin a specific business. These costs are personal and nondeductible. They include any costs incurred during a general search for, or preliminary investigation of, a business or investment possibility.

2. The costs you had in your attempt to acquire or begin a specific business. These costs are capital expenses and you can deduct them as a capital loss.

If you are a corporation and your attempt to go into a new trade or business is not successful, you may be able to deduct all investigatory costs as a loss.

The costs of any assets acquired during your unsuccessful attempt to go into business are a part of your basis in the assets. You cannot take a deduction for these costs. You will recover the costs of these assets when you dispose of them.

### Business Assets

There are many different kinds of business assets, for example, land, buildings, machinery, furniture, trucks, patents, and franchise rights. You must fully capitalize the cost of these assets, including freight and installation charges.

Certain property you produce for use in your trade or business must be capitalized under the uniform capitalization rules. See Regulations section 1.263A-2 for information on these rules.

### De Minimis Safe Harbor for Tangible Property

Although you must generally capitalize costs to acquire or produce real or tangible personal property used in your trade or business, such as buildings, equipment, or furniture, you can elect to use a de minimis safe harbor to deduct the costs of some tangible property. Under the de minimis safe harbor for tangible property, you can deduct de minimis amounts paid to acquire or produce certain tangible business property if these amounts are deducted by you for financial accounting purposes or in keeping your books and records. See the following for the requirements for the de minimis safe harbor.

**You have an applicable financial statement.** If you elect the de minimis safe harbor for the tax year, you can deduct amounts paid to acquire or produce certain tangible business property if:
- You have a trade or business or are a corporation, partnership, or S corporation that has an applicable financial statement;
- You have, at the beginning of the tax year, written accounting procedures treating as an expense for nontax purposes:
  - Amounts paid for property costing less than a certain dollar amount, or

- Amounts paid for property with an economic useful life of 12 months or less;
- You treat the amount paid during the tax year for which you make the election as an expense on your applicable financial statements in accordance with your written accounting procedures;
- The amount paid for the property does not exceed $5,000 per invoice (or per item substantiated by invoice); and
- The uniform capitalization rules do not apply to the amount.

**You do not have an applicable financial statement.** If you elect the de minimis safe harbor for the tax year, you can deduct amounts paid to acquire or produce certain tangible business property if:
- You have a trade or business, partnership, or S corporation that does not have an applicable financial statement;
- You have, at the beginning of the tax year, accounting procedures treating as an expense for nontax purposes:
  - Amounts paid for property costing less than a certain dollar amount, or
  - Amounts paid for property with an economic useful life of 12 months or less;
- You treat the amounts paid for the property as an expense on your books and records in accordance with your accounting procedures;
- The amount paid for the property does not exceed $2,500 per invoice (or per item substantiated by invoice); and
- The uniform capitalization rules do not apply to the amounts.

**How to make the de minimis safe harbor election.** To elect the de minimis safe harbor for the tax year, attach a statement to the taxpayer's timely filed original tax return (including extensions) for the tax year when qualifying amounts were paid. The statement must be titled "Section 1.263(a)-1(f) de minimis safe harbor election" and must include your name, address, taxpayer identification number (TIN), and a statement that you are making the de minimis safe harbor election under section 1.263(a)-1(f). In the case of a consolidated group filing a consolidated income tax return, the election is made for each member of the consolidated group.

In the case of a consolidated group filing a consolidated income tax return, the election is made for each member of the consolidated group. In the case of an S corporation or a partnership, the election is made by the S corporation or the partnership and not by the shareholders or partners. The election applies only for the tax year for which it is made.

*Example.* In 2022, you do not have an applicable financial statement and you purchase five laptop computers for use in your trade or business. You paid $2,000 each for a total cost of $10,000 and these amounts are substantiated in an invoice. You had an accounting procedure in place at the beginning of 2022 to expense the cost of tangible property if the property costs $2,000 or less. You treat each computer as an expense on your books and records for 2022 in accordance with this policy. If you elect the de minimis safe harbor in your tax returns for your 2022 tax year, you can deduct the cost of each $2,000 computer.

## Improvements

Generally, you must capitalize the costs of making improvements to a business asset if the improvements result in a betterment to the unit of property, restore the unit of property, or adapt the unit of property to a new or different use.

Some examples of improvements include rewiring or replumbing of a building, replacing an entire roof, increasing the production output of your equipment, putting an addition on your building, strengthening the foundation of a building so you can use it for a new purpose, or replacing a major component or substantial structural part of a machine.

However, you may currently deduct the costs of repairs or maintenance that do not improve a unit of property. This generally includes the costs of routine repairs and maintenance to your property that result from your use of the property and that keep your property in an ordinary, efficient operating condition. For example, deductible repairs include costs such as painting exteriors or interiors of business buildings, repairing broken windowpanes, replacing worn-out minor parts, sealing cracks and leaks, and changing oil or other fluids to maintain business equipment.

**Routine maintenance safe harbor.** If you determine that your cost was for an improvement to a building or equipment, you can deduct your cost under the routine maintenance safe harbor. Under the routine maintenance safe harbor, you can deduct the costs of an improvement that meets all of the following criteria.

- It is paid for recurring activities performed on tangible property.
- It arises from the use of the property in your trade or business.
- It keeps your property in an ordinary, efficient operating condition.
- You reasonably expect, at the time the property is placed in service, to perform this activity:

  – For buildings and building systems, more than once during the 10-year period after you place the building in service; or
  – For other property, more than once during the class life of the particular type of property. For class lives, see Revenue Procedure 88-57, 1987-2 C.B. 674.

**Costs incurred during an improvement.** You must capitalize both the direct and indirect costs of an improvement. Indirect costs include repairs and other expenses that directly benefit or are incurred by reason of your improvement. For example, if you improve the electrical system in your building, you must also capitalize the costs of repairing the holes that you made in walls to install the new wiring. This rule applies even if this work, performed by itself, would otherwise be treated as currently deductible repair costs.

**Election to capitalize repair and maintenance costs.** You can elect to capitalize and depreciate certain amounts paid for repair and maintenance of tangible property, even if they do not improve your property. To qualify for this election, you must treat these amounts as capital expenditures on your books and records used in figuring your income. If you make this election, you must apply it to all repair and maintenance costs of tangible property that you treat as capital expenditures on your books and records for this tax year. To make the election to treat repairs and maintenance as capital expenditures, attach a statement titled "Section 1.263(a)-3(n) Election" to your timely filed original tax return (including extensions) and include your name and address, TIN, and a statement that you elect to capitalize repair and maintenance costs under section 1.263(a)-3(n). You must treat these amounts as improvements to your tangible property and begin to depreciate these amounts when the improvement is placed in service.

## Capital Versus Deductible Expenses

To help you distinguish between capital and deductible expenses, different examples are given below.

**Motor vehicles.** You usually capitalize the cost of a motor vehicle you use in your business. You can recover its cost through annual deductions for depreciation.

There are dollar limits on the depreciation you can claim each year on passenger automobiles used in your business. See Pub. 463 for more information.

Generally, repairs you make to your business vehicle are currently deductible. However, amounts you pay to improve your business vehicle are generally capital expenditures and are recovered through depreciation.

**Roads and driveways.** The cost of building a private road on your business property and the cost of replacing a gravel driveway with a concrete one are capital expenses you may be able to depreciate. The cost of maintaining a private road on your business property is a deductible expense.

**Tools.** Unless the uniform capitalization rules apply, amounts spent for tools used in your business are deductible expenses if the tools have a life expectancy of less than 1 year or they cost $200 or less per item or invoice.

**Machinery parts.** Unless the uniform capitalization rules apply, the cost of replacing short-lived parts of a machine to keep it in good working condition, but not to improve the machine, is a deductible expense.

**Heating equipment.** The cost of changing from one heating system to another is a capital expense.

**Deduction for qualified business income.** For tax years beginning after 2017, you may be entitled to take a deduction of up to 20% of your qualified business income from your qualified trade or business, plus 20% of the aggregate amount of qualified real estate investment trust (REIT) and qualified publicly traded partnership income. The deduction is subject to various limitations, such as limitations based on the type of your trade or business, your taxable income, the amount of W-2 wages paid with respect to the qualified trade or business, and the unadjusted basis of qualified property held by your trade or business. You will claim this deduction on Form 1040 or 1040-SR, not on Schedule C. Unlike other deductions, this deduction can be taken in addition to the standard or itemized deductions. For more information, see the Instructions for Form 1040.

## Personal Versus Business Expenses

Generally, you cannot deduct personal, living, or family expenses. However, if you have an expense for something that is used partly for business and partly for personal purposes, divide the total cost between the business and personal parts. You can deduct the business part.

For example, if you borrow money and use 70% of it for business and the other 30% for a family vacation, you can generally deduct 70% of the interest as a business expense. The remaining 30% is personal interest and is generally not deductible. See chapter 4 for information on deducting interest and the allocation rules.

**Business use of your home.** If you use part of your home for business, you may be able to deduct expenses for the business use of your home. These expenses may include mortgage interest, insurance, utilities, repairs, and depreciation.

To qualify to claim expenses for the business use of your home, you must meet both of the following tests.

1. The business part of your home must be used exclusively and regularly for your trade or business.

2. The business part of your home must be:

   a. Your principal place of business;

   b. A place where you meet or deal with patients, clients, or customers in the normal course of your trade or business; or

   c. A separate structure (not attached to your home) used in connection with your trade or business.

You generally do not have to meet the exclusive use test for the part of your home that you regularly use either for the storage of inventory or product samples, or as a daycare facility.

Your home office qualifies as your principal place of business if you meet the following requirements.

- You use the office exclusively and regularly for administrative or management activities of your trade or business.

- You have no other fixed location where you conduct substantial administrative or management activities of your trade or business.

If you have more than one business location, determine your principal place of business based on the following factors.

- The relative importance of the activities performed at each location.
- If the relative importance factor does not determine your principal place of business, consider the time spent at each location.

**Optional safe harbor method.** Individual taxpayers can use the optional safe harbor method to determine the amount of deductible expenses attributable to certain business use of a residence during the tax year. This method is an alternative to the calculation, allocation, and substantiation of actual expenses.

The deduction under the optional method is limited to $1,500 per year based on $5 per square foot for up to 300 square feet. Under this method, you claim your allowable mortgage interest, real estate taxes, and casualty losses on the home as itemized deductions on Schedule A (Form 1040). You are not required to allocate these deductions between personal and business use, as is required under the regular method. If you use the optional method, you cannot depreciate the portion of your home used in a trade or business.

Business expenses unrelated to the home, such as advertising, supplies, and wages paid to employees, are still fully deductible. All of the requirements discussed earlier under *Business use of your home* still apply.

For more information on the deduction for business use of your home, including the optional safe harbor method, see Pub. 587.

⚠ **CAUTION** *If you were entitled to deduct depreciation on the part of your home used for business, you cannot exclude the part of the gain from the sale of your home that equals any depreciation you deducted (or could have deducted) for periods after May 6, 1997.*

**Business use of your car.** If you use your car exclusively in your business, you can deduct car expenses. If you use your car for both business and personal purposes, you must divide your expenses based on actual mileage. Generally, commuting expenses between your home and your business location, within the area of your tax home, are not deductible.

You can deduct actual car expenses, which include depreciation (or lease payments), gas and oil, tires, repairs, tune-ups, insurance, and registration fees. Or, instead of figuring the business part of these actual expenses, you may be able to use the standard mileage rate to figure your deduction. For 2022, the standard mileage rate is 58.5 cents per mile before July 1, 2022, and 62.5 cents per mile on or after July 1, 2022. To find the standard mileage rate for 2023, go to *IRS.gov/Tax-Professionals/Standard-Mileage-Rates*.

If you are self-employed, you can also deduct the business part of interest on your car loan, state and local personal property tax on the car, parking fees, and tolls, whether or not you claim the standard mileage rate.

For more information on car expenses and the rules for using the standard mileage rate, see Pub. 463.

# How Much Can I Deduct?

Generally, you can deduct the full amount of a business expense if it meets the criteria of ordinary and necessary and it is not a capital expense.

**Recovery of amount deducted (tax benefit rule).** If you recover part of an expense in the same tax year in which you would have claimed a deduction, reduce your current year expense by the amount of the recovery. If you have a recovery in a later year, include the recovered amount in income in that year. However, if part of the deduction for the expense did not reduce your tax, you do not have to include that part of the recovered amount in income.

For more information on recoveries and the tax benefit rule, see Pub. 525.

**Payments in kind.** If you provide services to pay a business expense, the amount you can deduct is limited to your out-of-pocket costs. You cannot deduct the cost of your own labor.

Similarly, if you pay a business expense in goods or other property, you can deduct only what the property costs you. If these costs are included in the cost of goods sold, do not deduct them again as a business expense.

**Limits on losses.** If your deductions for an investment or business activity are more than the income it brings in, you have a loss. There may be limits on how much of the loss you can deduct.

**Not-for-profit limits.** If you carry on your business activity without the intention of making a profit, you cannot use a loss from it to offset other income. For more information, see *Not-for-Profit Activities*, later.

**At-risk limits.** Generally, a deductible loss from a trade or business or other income-producing activity is limited to the investment you have "at risk" in the activity. You are at risk in any activity for the following.

1. The money and adjusted basis of property you contribute to the activity.

2. Amounts you borrow for use in the activity if:

   a. You are personally liable for repayment, or

   b. You pledge property (other than property used in the activity) as security for the loan.

For more information, see Pub. 925.

**Passive activities.** Generally, you are in a passive activity if you have a trade or business activity in which you do not materially participate, or a rental activity. In general, deductions for losses from passive activities only offset income from passive activities. You cannot use any excess deductions to offset other income.

In addition, passive activity credits can only offset the tax on net passive income. Any excess loss or credits are carried over to later years. Suspended passive losses are fully deductible in the year you completely dispose of the activity. For more information, see Pub. 925.

**Net operating loss (NOL).** If your deductions are more than your income for the year, you may have an NOL. You can use an NOL to lower your taxes in other years. See Pub. 536 for more information.

See Pub. 542 for information about NOLs of corporations.

# When Can I Deduct an Expense?

When you can deduct an expense depends on your accounting method. An accounting method is a set of rules used to determine when and how income and expenses are reported. The two basic methods are the cash method and the accrual method. Whichever method you choose must clearly reflect income.

For more information on accounting methods, see Pub. 538.

**Cash method.** Under the cash method of accounting, you generally deduct business expenses in the tax year you pay them.

**Accrual method.** Under the accrual method of accounting, you generally deduct business expenses when both of the following apply.

1. The all-events test has been met. The test is met when:

   a. All events have occurred that fix the fact of liability, and

   b. The liability can be determined with reasonable accuracy.

2. Economic performance has occurred.

**Economic performance.** You generally cannot deduct or capitalize a business expense until economic performance occurs. If your expense is for property or services provided to you, or for your use of property, economic performance occurs as the property or services are provided, or the property is used. If your expense is for property or services you provide to others, economic performance occurs as you provide the property or services.

**Example.** Your tax year is the calendar year. In December 2022, the Field Plumbing Company did some repair work at your place of business and sent you a bill for $600. You paid it by check in January 2023. If you use the accrual method of accounting, deduct the $600 on your tax return for 2022 because all events have occurred to "fix" the fact of liability (in this case, the work was completed), the liability can be determined, and economic performance occurred in that year.

If you use the cash method of accounting, deduct the expense on your 2023 tax return.

**Prepayment.** You generally cannot deduct expenses in advance, even if you pay them in advance. This applies to prepaid interest, prepaid insurance premiums, and any other prepaid expense that creates an intangible asset. If you pay an amount that creates an intangible asset, then you must capitalize the amounts paid and begin to amortize the payment over the appropriate period.

However, you do not have to capitalize amounts for creating an intangible asset if the right or benefit created does not extend beyond the earlier of 12 months after the date that you first receive the right or benefit or the end of the tax year following the year in which you made the advance payment. If you are a cash method taxpayer and your advance payment qualifies for this exception, then you can generally deduct the amount when paid. If you are an accrual method taxpayer, you cannot deduct the amount until the all-events test has been met and economic performance has occurred.

**Example 1.** In 2022, you sign a 10-year lease and immediately pay your rent for the first 3 years. Even though you paid the rent for 2022, 2023, and 2024, you can only deduct the rent for 2022 on your 2022 tax return. You can deduct the rent for 2023 and 2024 on your tax returns for those years.

**Example 2.** You are a cash method calendar year taxpayer. On December 1, 2022, you sign a 12-month lease, effective beginning January 1, 2023, and immediately pay your rent for the entire 12-month period that begins on January 1, 2023. The right or benefit attributable to the payment neither extends more than 12 months beyond January 1, 2023 (the first day that you are entitled to use the property) nor beyond the tax year ending December 31, 2023 (the year following the year in which you made the advance payment). Therefore, your prepayment does not have to be capitalized, and you can deduct the entire payment in the year you pay it.

**Contested liability.** Under the cash method, you can deduct a contested liability only in the year you pay the liability. Under the accrual method, you can deduct contested liabilities such as taxes (except foreign or U.S. possession income, war profits, and excess profits taxes) either in the tax year you pay the liability (or transfer money or other property to satisfy the obligation) or in the tax year you settle the contest. However, to take the deduction in the year of payment or transfer, you must meet certain conditions. See Regulations section 1.461-2.

**Related person.** Under the accrual method of accounting, you generally deduct expenses when you incur them, even if you have not yet paid them. However, if you and the person you owe are related and that person uses the cash method of accounting, you must pay the expense before you can deduct it. Your deduction is allowed when the amount is includible in income by the related cash method payee. For more information, see *Related Persons* in Pub. 538.

## Not-for-Profit Activities

If you do not carry on your business or investment activity to make a profit, you cannot use a loss from the activity to offset other income. Activities you do as a hobby, or mainly for sport or recreation, are often not entered into for profit.

The limit on not-for-profit losses applies to individuals, partnerships, estates, trusts, and S corporations. It does not apply to corporations other than S corporations.

In determining whether you are carrying on an activity for profit, several factors are taken into account. No one factor alone is decisive. Among the factors to consider are whether:

- You carry on the activity in a businesslike manner,
- The time and effort you put into the activity indicate you intend to make it profitable,
- You depend on the income for your livelihood,
- Your losses are due to circumstances beyond your control (or are normal in the startup phase of your type of business),
- You change your methods of operation in an attempt to improve profitability,
- You (or your advisors) have the knowledge needed to carry on the activity as a successful business,
- You were successful in making a profit in similar activities in the past,
- The activity makes a profit in some years, and
- You can expect to make a future profit from the appreciation of the assets used in the activity.

**Presumption of profit.** An activity is presumed carried on for profit if it produced a profit in at least 3 of the last 5 tax years, including the current year. Activities that consist primarily of breeding, training, showing, or racing horses are presumed carried on for profit if they produced a profit in at least 2 of the last 7 tax years, including the current year. The activity must be substantially the same for each year within this period. You have a profit when the gross income from an activity exceeds the deductions.

If a taxpayer dies before the end of the 5-year (or 7-year) period, the "test" period ends on the date of the taxpayer's death.

If your business or investment activity passes this 3- (or 2-) years-of-profit test, the IRS will presume it is carried on for profit. This means the limits discussed here will not apply. You can take all your business deductions from the activity, even for the years that you have a loss. You can rely on this presumption unless the IRS later shows it to be invalid.

**Using the presumption later.** If you are starting an activity and do not have 3 (or 2) years showing a profit, you can elect to have the presumption made after you have the 5 (or 7) years of experience allowed by the test.

You can elect to do this by filing Form 5213. Filing this form postpones any determination that your activity is not carried on for profit until 5 (or 7) years have passed since you started the activity.

The benefit gained by making this election is that the IRS will not immediately question whether your activity is engaged in for profit. Accordingly, it will not restrict your deductions. Rather, you will gain time to earn a profit in the required number of years. If you show 3 (or 2) years of profit at the end of this period, your deductions are not limited under these rules. If you do not have 3 (or 2) years of profit, the limit can be applied retroactively to any year with a loss in the 5-year (or 7-year) period.

Filing Form 5213 automatically extends the period of limitations on any year in the 5-year (or 7-year) period to 2 years after the due date of the tax return for the last year of the period. The period is extended only for deductions of the activity and any related deductions that might be affected.

**TIP** *You must file Form 5213 within 3 years after the due date of your tax return (determined without extensions) for the year in which you first carried on the activity, or, if earlier, within 60 days after receiving written notice from the IRS proposing to disallow deductions attributable to the activity.*

## Gross Income

Gross income from a not-for-profit activity includes the total of all gains from the sale, exchange, or other disposition of property, and all other gross receipts derived from the activity. Gross income from the activity also includes capital gains and rents received for the use of property that is held in connection with the activity.

You can determine gross income from any not-for-profit activity by subtracting the cost of goods sold from your gross receipts. However, if you determine gross income by subtracting cost of goods sold from gross receipts, you must do so consistently, and in a manner that follows generally accepted methods of accounting.

## Limit on Deductions

**CAUTION** *You can no longer claim any miscellaneous itemized deductions. Miscellaneous itemized deductions are those deductions that would have been subject to the 2%-of-adjusted-gross-income limitation. You can still claim certain expenses as itemized deductions on Schedule A (Form 1040).*

Deductions you can take for personal as well as for business activities are allowed in full. For individuals, all nonbusiness deductions, such as those for home mortgage interest, taxes, and casualty losses, may also be deducted. Deduct them on the appropriate lines of Schedule A (Form 1040).

For the limits that apply to home mortgage interest, see Pub. 936.

Generally, you can deduct a casualty loss on property you own for personal use only to the extent each casualty loss is more than $100, and the total of all casualty losses exceeds 10% of your adjusted gross income (AGI). See Pub. 547 for more information on casualty losses.

***Disaster tax relief.*** For personal casualty losses resulting from federally declared disasters that occurred before 2018, you may be entitled to disaster tax relief. As a result, you may be required to figure your casualty loss differently. For tax years beginning after 2017, casualty and theft losses are allowed only to the extent it is attributable to a federally declared disaster. For more information, see Pub. 976, Disaster Relief.

**Partnerships and S corporations.** If a partnership or S corporation carries on a not-for-profit activity, these limits apply at the partnership or S corporation level. They are reflected in the individual shareholder's or partner's distributive shares.

**More than one activity.** If you have several undertakings, each may be a separate activity or several undertakings may be combined. The following are the most significant facts and circumstances in making this determination.
- The degree of organizational and economic interrelationship of various undertakings.
- The business purpose that is (or might be) served by carrying on the various undertakings separately or together in a business or investment setting.
- The similarity of the undertakings.

The IRS will generally accept your characterization if it is supported by facts and circumstances.

**TIP** *If you are carrying on two or more different activities, keep the deductions and income from each one separate. Figure separately whether each is a not-for-profit activity. Then figure the limit on deductions and losses separately for each activity that is not for profit.*

# 2.

# Employees' Pay

## What's New

**The COVID-19 related credit for qualified sick and family leave wages is limited to leave taken after March 31, 2020, and before October 1, 2021.** Generally, the credit for qualified sick and family leave wages, as enacted under the Families First Coronavirus Response Act (FFCRA) and amended and extended by the COVID-related Tax Relief Act of 2020, for leave taken after March 31, 2020, and before April 1, 2021, and the credit for qualified sick and family leave wages under sections 3131, 3132, and 3133 of the Internal Revenue Code, as enacted under the American Rescue Plan Act of 2021 (the ARP), for leave taken after March 31, 2021, and before October 1, 2021, have expired. However, employers that pay

qualified sick and family leave wages in 2022 for leave taken after March 31, 2020, and before October 1, 2021, are eligible to claim a credit for qualified sick and family leave wages in 2022. For more information about the credit for qualified sick and family leave wages, go to *IRS.gov/PLC*.

**The COVID-19 related employee retention credit has expired.** The employee retention credit enacted under the Coronavirus Aid, Relief, and Economic Security (CARES) Act and amended and extended by the Taxpayer Certainty and Disaster Tax Relief Act of 2020 was limited to qualified wages paid after March 12, 2020, and before July 1, 2021. The employee retention credit under section 3134 of the Internal Revenue Code, as enacted by the ARP and amended by the Infrastructure Investment and Jobs Act, was limited to wages paid after June 30, 2021, and before October 1, 2021, unless the employer was a recovery startup business. An employer that was a recovery startup business could also claim the employee retention credit for wages paid after September 30, 2021, and before January 1, 2022.

**Credit for COBRA premium assistance payments is limited to periods of coverage beginning on or after April 1, 2021, through periods of coverage beginning on or before September 30, 2021.** Section 9501 of the ARP provides for COBRA premium assistance in the form of a full reduction in the premium otherwise payable by certain individuals and their families who elect COBRA continuation coverage due to a loss of coverage as the result of a reduction in hours or an involuntary termination of employment (assistance eligible individuals). This COBRA premium assistance is available for periods of coverage beginning on or after April 1, 2021, through periods of coverage beginning on or before September 30, 2021. A premium payee is entitled to the COBRA premium assistance credit at the time an eligible individual elects coverage. Therefore, due to the COBRA notice and election period requirements (generally, employers have 60 days to provide notice and assistance eligible individuals have 60 days to elect coverage), some employers may be eligible to claim the COBRA premium assistance credit on employment tax returns for the first quarter of 2022.

**Advance payment of COVID-19 credits ended.** Although you may pay qualified sick and family leave wages in 2022 for leave taken after March 31, 2020, and before October 1, 2021, or provide COBRA premium assistance payments in 2022, you may no longer request an advance payment of any credit on Form 7200, Advance Payment of Employer Credits Due to COVID-19.

## Introduction

You can generally deduct the amount you pay your employees for the services they perform. The pay may be in cash, property, or services. It may include wages, salaries, bonuses, commissions, or other noncash compensation such as vacation allowances and fringe benefits. For information about deducting employment taxes, see *chapter 5*.

**TIP** *You may be able to claim employment credits, such as the credits listed below, if you meet certain requirements.* You must reduce your deduction for employee wages by the amount of employment credits that you claim. For more information about these credits, see the instructions for the form on which the credit is claimed.

- *Work opportunity credit (Form 5884).*
- *Empowerment zone employment credit (Form 8844).*
- *Credit for employer differential wage payments (Form 8932).*
- *Employer credit for paid family and medical leave (Form 8994).*

## Topics
This chapter discusses:

- Tests for deducting pay
- Kinds of pay

## Useful Items
You may want to see:

**Publication**
- ❏ **15** Employer's Tax Guide
- ❏ **15-A** Employer's Supplemental Tax Guide
- ❏ **15-B** Employer's Tax Guide to Fringe Benefits

**Form (and Instructions)**
- ❏ **1099-NEC** Nonemployee Compensation
- ❏ **W-2** Wage and Tax Statement

See *chapter 12* for information about getting publications and forms.

## Tests for Deducting Pay

To be deductible, your employees' pay must be an ordinary and necessary business expense and you must pay or incur it. These and other requirements that apply to all business expenses are explained in *chapter 1*.

In addition, the pay must meet both of the following tests.
- ***Test 1.*** It must be reasonable.
- ***Test 2.*** It must be for services performed.

The form or method of figuring the pay doesn't affect its deductibility. For example, bonuses and commissions based on sales or earnings, and paid under an agreement made before the services were performed, are both deductible.

### Test 1—Reasonableness

You must be able to prove that the pay is reasonable. Whether the pay is reasonable depends on the circumstances that existed when you contracted for the services, not those that exist when reasonableness is questioned. If the pay is excessive, the excess pay is disallowed as a deduction.

**Factors to consider.** Determine the reasonableness of pay by the facts and circumstances.

81

Generally, reasonable pay is the amount that a similar business would pay for the same or similar services.

To determine if pay is reasonable, also consider the following items and any other pertinent facts.

- The duties performed by the employee.
- The volume of business handled.
- The character and amount of responsibility.
- The complexities of your business.
- The amount of time required.
- The cost of living in the locality.
- The ability and achievements of the individual employee performing the service.
- The pay compared with the gross and net income of the business, as well as with distributions to shareholders if the business is a corporation.
- Your policy regarding pay for all your employees.
- The history of pay for each employee.

**Compensation in excess of $1 million.** Publicly held corporations can't deduct compensation to a "covered employee" to the extent that the compensation for the tax year exceeds $1 million. For more information, including the definition of a "covered employee," see the Instructions for Form 1125-E and Regulations section 1.162-33.

## Test 2—For Services Performed

You must be able to prove the payment was made for services actually performed.

**Employee-shareholder salaries.** If a corporation pays an employee who is also a shareholder a salary that is unreasonably high considering the services actually performed, the excessive part of the salary may be treated as a constructive dividend to the employee-shareholder. The excessive part of the salary wouldn't be allowed as a salary deduction by the corporation. For more information on corporate distributions to shareholders, see Pub. 542.

## Kinds of Pay

Some of the ways you may provide pay to your employees in addition to regular wages or salaries are discussed next. For specialized and detailed information on employees' pay and the employment tax treatment of employees' pay, see Pubs. 15, 15-A, and 15-B.

## Awards

You can generally deduct amounts you pay to your employees as awards, whether paid in cash or property. If you give property to an employee as an employee achievement award, your deduction may be limited.

**Achievement awards.** An achievement award is an item of tangible personal property that meets all the following requirements.

- It is given to an employee for length of service or safety achievement.

- It is awarded as part of a meaningful presentation.
- It is awarded under conditions and circumstances that don't create a significant likelihood of disguised pay.

**Tangible personal property.** An award isn't an item of tangible personal property if it is an award of cash, cash equivalents, gift cards, gift coupons, or gift certificates (other than arrangements granting only the right to select and receive tangible personal property from a limited assortment of items preselected or preapproved by you). Also, tangible personal property doesn't include vacations, meals, lodging, tickets to theater or sporting events, stocks, bonds, other securities, and other similar items.

**Length-of-service award.** An award will qualify as a length-of-service award only if either of the following applies.

- The employee receives the award after their first 5 years of employment.
- The employee didn't receive another length-of-service award (other than one of very small value) during the same year or in any of the prior 4 years.

**Safety achievement award.** An award for safety achievement will qualify as an achievement award unless one of the following applies.

1. It is given to a manager, administrator, clerical employee, or other professional employee.

2. During the tax year, more than 10% of your employees, excluding those listed in (1), have already received a safety achievement award (other than one of very small value).

**Deduction limit.** Your deduction for the cost of employee achievement awards given to any one employee during the tax year is limited to the following.

- $400 for awards that aren't qualified plan awards.
- $1,600 for all awards, whether or not qualified plan awards.

A qualified plan award is an achievement award given as part of an established written plan or program that doesn't favor highly compensated employees as to eligibility or benefits.

A highly compensated employee is an employee who meets either of the following tests.

1. The employee was a 5% owner at any time during the year or the preceding year.

2. The employee received more than $130,000 in pay for the preceding year.

You can choose to ignore test (2) if the employee wasn't also in the top 20% of employees when ranked by pay for the preceding year.

An award isn't a qualified plan award if the average cost of all the employee achievement awards given during the tax year (that would be qualified plan awards except for this limit) is more than $400. To figure this average cost, ignore awards of nominal value.

Deduct achievement awards, up to the maximum amounts listed earlier, as a nonwage business expense on your return or business schedule.

**TIP** You may not owe employment taxes on the value of some achievement awards you provide to an employee. See Pub. 15-B.

## Bonuses

You can generally deduct a bonus paid to an employee if you intended the bonus as additional pay for services, not as a gift, and the services were performed. However, the total bonuses, salaries, and other pay must be reasonable for the services performed. If the bonus is paid in property, see *Property*, later.

**Gifts of nominal value.** If, to promote employee goodwill, you distribute merchandise of nominal value or other de minimis items to your employees at holidays, you can deduct the cost of these items as a nonwage business expense. See Pub. 15-B for additional information on de minimis fringe benefits. If you provide food to your employees, your business deduction may be limited; see *Meals and lodging*, later.

## Education Expenses

If you pay or reimburse education expenses for an employee, you can deduct the payments if they are part of a qualified educational assistance program. Deduct them on the "Employee benefit programs" or other appropriate line of your tax return. For information on educational assistance programs, see *Educational Assistance* in section 2 of Pub. 15-B.

**TIP** Section 2206 of the CARES Act expands the definition of educational assistance to include certain employer payments of student loans paid after March 27, 2020. The exclusion applies to the payment by an employer, whether paid to the employee or to a lender, of principal or interest on any qualified education loan incurred by the employee for the education of the employee. Qualified education loans are defined in chapter 10 of Pub. 970. This exclusion expires January 1, 2026, unless extended by future legislation.

## Fringe Benefits

A fringe benefit is a form of pay for the performance of services. You can generally deduct the cost of fringe benefits.

You may be able to exclude all or part of the value of some fringe benefits from your employees' pay. You also may not owe employment taxes on the value of the fringe benefits. See Table 2-1 in Pub. 15-B for details.

Generally, no deduction is allowed for activities generally considered entertainment, amusement, or recreation, or for a facility used in connection with such activity. However, you may deduct these expenses if the goods, services, or facilities are treated as compensation to the recipient and reported on Form W-2 for an employee or on Form 1099-NEC for an independent contractor. If the recipient is an officer, director, beneficial owner (directly or indirectly), or other "specified individual" (as defined in section 274(e)(2)(B) and Regulations section 1.274-9(b)), special rules apply. See section 274(e)(2) and Regulations sections 1.274-9 and 1.274-10.

Certain fringe benefits are discussed next. See Pub. 15-B for more details on these and other fringe benefits.

**Meals and lodging.** Generally, you can deduct 50% of certain meal expenses and 100% of certain lodging expenses provided to your employees. If the amounts are deductible, deduct the cost in whatever category the expense falls.

*Deduction limit on meals.* You can generally deduct only 50% of the cost of furnishing meals to your employees. However, you can deduct the full cost of certain meals; see section 274(n)(2) and Regulations section 1.274-12(c) for more information. For example, you can deduct the full cost of the following meals.

- Meals whose value you include in an employee's wages.
- Meals you furnish to your employees as part of the expense of providing recreational or social activities, such as holiday parties or annual picnics, when made primarily for the benefit of your employees other than employees who are officers, shareholders or other owners who own a 10% or greater interest in your business, or other highly compensated employees.
- Meals you furnish to your employees at the work site when you operate a restaurant or catering service.
- Meals you're required by federal law to furnish to crew members of certain commercial vessels (or would be required to furnish if the vessels were operated at sea). This doesn't include meals you furnish on vessels primarily providing luxury water transportation.
- Meals you furnish on an oil or gas platform or drilling rig located offshore or in Alaska. This includes meals you furnish at a support camp that is near and integral to an oil or gas drilling rig located in Alaska.

⚠️ *P.L. 115-97, Tax Cuts and Jobs Act, changed the rules for the deduction of food or beverage expenses that are excludable from employee income as a de minimis fringe benefit. For amounts incurred or paid after 2017, the 50% limit on deductions for food or beverage expenses also applies to food or beverage expenses excludable from employee income as a de minimis fringe benefit. While your business deduction may be limited, the rules that allow you to exclude certain de minimis meals and meals on your business premises from your employee's wages still apply. See Meals in section 2 of Pub. 15-B.*

*Food and beverage expense incurred together with entertainment expenses.* P.L. 115-97 changed the rules for the deduction of business entertainment expenses. For amounts incurred or paid after 2017, no business deduction is allowed for any item generally considered to be entertainment, amusement, or recreation. As discussed earlier, you can deduct 50% of the cost of business meals. If food and beverages are provided during or at an entertainment activity, and the food and beverages are purchased separately from the entertainment, or the cost of the food and beverages is stated separately from the cost of the entertainment on one or more bills, invoices, or receipts, you may continue to deduct 50% of the business meal expenses. The amount charged for food or beverages on a bill, invoice, or receipt must reflect the venue's usual selling cost for those items if they were to be purchased separately from the entertainment or must approximate the reasonable value of those items. If you purchase food and beverages together with entertainment expenses and the cost of the food and beverages isn't stated separately on the invoice, the cost of the food and beverages is also an entertainment expense and none of the expenses are deductible. For more information, including details about additional requirements that must be met for a business meal to be deductible, see Regulations sections 1.274-11 and 1.274-12(a).

💡 *Section 210 of the Taxpayer Certainty and Disaster Tax Relief Act of 2020 provides for the temporary allowance of a 100% business meal deduction for food or beverages provided by a restaurant and paid or incurred after December 31, 2020, and before January 1, 2023. For more information, see Notice 2021-25, 2021-17 I.R.B. 1118, available at IRS.gov/irb/2021-17_IRB#NOT-2021-25; and Notice 2021-63, 2021-49 I.R.B. 835, available at IRS.gov/irb/2021-49_IRB#NOT-2021-63.*

**Transportation (commuting) benefits.** If you provide your employees with qualified transportation benefits, such as transportation in a commuter highway vehicle, transit passes, or qualified parking, you may no longer deduct these amounts. P.L. 115-97 provides that no deduction is allowed for qualified transportation benefits (whether provided directly by you, through a bona fide reimbursement arrangement, or through a compensation reduction agreement) incurred or paid after 2017. Also, no deduction is allowed for any expense incurred for providing any transportation, or any payment or reimbursement to your employee, in connection with travel between your employee's residence and place of employment, except as necessary for ensuring the safety of your employee or for qualified bicycle commuting reimbursements as described in section 132(f)(5)(F). While you may no longer deduct payments for qualified transportation benefits, the fringe benefit exclusion rules still apply and the payments, except for qualified bicycle commuting reimbursements, may be excluded from your employee's wages. Although the value of a qualified transportation fringe benefit is relevant in determining the fringe benefit exclusion and whether the section 274(e)(2) exception for expenses treated as compensation applies, the deduction that is disallowed relates to the expense of providing a qualified transportation fringe, not its value. For more information, see Regulations sections 1.274-13 and 1.274-14. See Pub. 15-B for more information about qualified transportation benefits.

**Employee benefit programs.** Employee benefit programs include the following.

- Accident and health plans.
- Adoption assistance.
- Cafeteria plans.
- Dependent care assistance.
- Education assistance.
- Life insurance coverage.
- Welfare benefit funds.

You can generally deduct amounts you spend on employee benefit programs on the applicable line of your tax return. For example, if you provide dependent care by operating a dependent care facility for your employees, deduct your costs in whatever categories they fall (utilities, salaries, etc.).

*Life insurance coverage.* You can't deduct the cost of life insurance coverage for you, an employee, or any person with a financial interest in your business if you're directly or indirectly the beneficiary of the policy. See Regulations section 1.264-1 for more information.

*Welfare benefit funds.* A welfare benefit fund is a funded plan (or a funded arrangement having the effect of a plan) that provides welfare benefits to your employees, independent contractors, or their beneficiaries. Welfare benefits are any benefits other than deferred compensation or transfers of restricted property.

Your deduction for contributions to a welfare benefit fund is limited to the fund's qualified cost for the tax year. If your contributions to the fund are more than its qualified cost, carry the excess over to the next tax year.

Generally, the fund's "qualified cost" is the total of the following amounts, reduced by the after-tax income of the fund.

- The cost you would've been able to deduct using the cash method of accounting if you had paid for the benefits directly.
- The contributions added to a reserve account that are needed to fund claims incurred but not paid as of the end of the year. These claims can be for supplemental unemployment benefits, severance pay, or disability, medical, or life insurance benefits.

For more information, see sections 419(c) and 419A and the related regulations.

## Loans or Advances

You can generally deduct as wages an advance you make to an employee for services to be performed if you don't expect the employee to repay the advance. However, if the employee performs no services, treat the amount you advanced as a loan; if the employee doesn't repay the loan, treat it as income to the employee.

**Below-market interest rate loans.** On certain loans you make to an employee or shareholder, you're treated as having received interest income and as having paid compensation or dividends equal to that interest. See Below-Market Loans in chapter 4.

## Property

If you transfer property (including your company's stock) to an employee as payment for services, you can generally deduct it as wages. The amount you can deduct is the property's fair market value (FMV) on the date of the transfer less any amount the employee paid for the property.

You can claim the deduction only for the tax year in which your employee includes the property's value in their income. Your employee is deemed to have included the value in their income if you report it on their Form W-2 in a timely manner.

You treat the deductible amount as received in exchange for the property, and you must recognize any gain or loss realized on the transfer, unless it is the company's stock transferred as payment for services. Your gain or loss is the difference between the FMV of the property and its adjusted basis on the date of transfer.

These rules also apply to property transferred to an independent contractor for services, generally reported on Form 1099-NEC.

**Restricted property.** If the property you transfer for services is subject to restrictions that affect its value, you generally can't deduct it and don't report gain or loss until it is substantially vested in the recipient. However, if the recipient pays for the property, you must report any gain at the time of the transfer up to the amount paid.

"Substantially vested" means the property isn't subject to a substantial risk of forfeiture. This means that the recipient isn't likely to have to give up their rights in the property in the future.

## Reimbursements for Business Expenses

You can generally deduct the amount you pay or reimburse employees for business expenses incurred for your business. However, your deduction may be limited.

If you make the payment under an accountable plan, deduct it in the category of the expense paid. For example, if you pay an employee for travel expenses incurred on your behalf, deduct this payment as a travel expense. If you make the payment under a nonaccountable plan, deduct it as wages and include it on the employee's Form W-2.

See *Reimbursement of Travel and Non-Entertainment Related Meals* in chapter 11 for more information about deducting reimbursements and an explanation of accountable and nonaccountable plans.

## Sick and Vacation Pay

**Sick pay.** You can deduct amounts you pay to your employees for sickness and injury, including lump-sum amounts, as wages. However, your deduction is limited to amounts not compensated by insurance or other means.

**Vacation pay.** Vacation pay is an employee benefit. It includes amounts paid for unused vacation leave. You can deduct vacation pay only in the tax year in which the employee actually receives it. This rule applies regardless of whether you use the cash or accrual method of accounting.

# 3.

# Rent Expense

## Introduction

This chapter discusses the tax treatment of rent or lease payments you make for property you use in your business but do not own. It also discusses how to treat other kinds of payments you make that are related to your use of this property. These include payments you make for taxes on the property.

## Topics
This chapter discusses:

- The definition of rent
- Taxes on leased property
- The cost of getting a lease
- Improvements by the lessee
- Capitalizing rent expenses

## Useful Items
You may want to see:

### Publication
- ☐ **538** Accounting Periods and Methods
- ☐ **544** Sales and Other Dispositions of Assets
- ☐ **946** How To Depreciate Property

See chapter 12 for information about getting publications and forms.

## Rent

Rent is any amount you pay for the use of property you do not own. In general, you can deduct rent as an expense only if the rent is for property you use in your trade or business. If you have or will receive equity in or title to the property, the rent is not deductible.

**Unreasonable rent.** You can't take a rental deduction for unreasonable rent. Ordinarily, the issue of reasonableness arises only if you and the lessor are related. Rent paid to a related person is reasonable if it is the same amount you would pay to a stranger for use of the same property. Rent isn't unreasonable just because it is figured as a percentage of gross sales. For examples of related persons, see *Related persons* in chapter 2 of Pub. 544.

**Rent on your home.** If you rent your home and use part of it as your place of business, you may be able to deduct the rent you pay for that part. You must meet the requirements for business use of your home. For more information, see *Business use of your home* in chapter 1.

**Rent paid in advance.** Generally, rent paid for use of property in your trade or business is deductible in the year paid or incurred. If you are an accrual method taxpayer and pay rent in advance, you can deduct only the amount of rent that applies to your use of rented property during the tax year. You can deduct the rest of the rent payment only over the period to which it applies. If you are a cash method taxpayer, you may deduct the entire amount of rent you paid in advance in the year of payment if the payment applies to the right to use property that does not extend beyond the earlier of 12 months after the first date you have the right to use the property or the end of the tax year following the year in which you paid the advance rent. If your payment applies to the right to use property beyond this period, then you must capitalize the rent payment and deduct it over the period to which it applies.

*Example 1.* You are an accrual method calendar year taxpayer and you lease a building at a monthly rental rate of $1,000 beginning July 1, 2022. On June 30, 2022, you pay advance rent of $12,000 for the last 6 months of 2022 and the first 6 months of 2023. You can deduct only $6,000 for 2022, for the right to use property in 2022. You deduct the other $6,000 in 2023.

*Example 2.* Assume the same facts as *Example 1*, except you are a cash method calendar year taxpayer. You may deduct the entire $12,000 payment for 2022. The payment applies to your right to use the property that does not extend beyond 12 months after the date you received this right. If you deduct the $12,000 in 2022, you should not deduct any part of this payment in 2023.

*Example 3.* You are either a cash or accrual calendar year taxpayer. Last January, you leased property for 3 years for $6,000 per year. You pay the full $18,000 (3 x $6,000) during the first year of the lease. Because this amount is a prepaid expense that must be capitalized, you can deduct only $6,000 per year, the amount allocable to your use of the property in each year.

**Canceling a lease.** You can generally deduct as rent an amount you pay to cancel a business lease.

**Lease or purchase.** There may be instances in which you must determine whether your payments are for rent or for the purchase of the property. You must first determine whether your agreement is a lease or a conditional sales contract. Payments made under a conditional sales contract are not deductible as rent expense.

*Conditional sales contract.* Whether an agreement is a conditional sales contract depends on the intent of the parties. Determine intent based on the provisions of the agreement and the facts and circumstances that exist when you make the agreement. No single test, or special combination of tests, always applies. However, in general, an agreement may be considered a conditional sales contract rather than a lease if any of the following is true.

- The agreement applies part of each payment toward an equity interest you will receive.
- You get title to the property after you make a stated amount of required payments.
- The amount you must pay to use the property for a short time is a large part of the amount you would pay to get title to the property.
- You pay much more than the current fair rental value of the property.
- You have an option to buy the property at a nominal price compared to the value of the property when you may exercise the option. Determine this value when you make the agreement.
- You have an option to buy the property at a nominal price compared to the total amount you have to pay under the agreement.
- The agreement designates part of the payments as interest, or that part is easy to recognize as interest.

*Leveraged leases.* Leveraged lease transactions may not be considered leases. Leveraged leases generally involve three parties: a lessor, a lessee, and a lender to the lessor. Usually, the lease term covers a large part of the useful life of the leased property, and the lessee's payments to the lessor are enough to cover the lessor's payments to the lender.

If you plan to take part in what appears to be a leveraged lease, you may want to get an advance ruling.

- Revenue Procedure 2001-28 contains the guidelines the IRS will use to determine if a leveraged lease is a lease for federal income tax purposes.
- Revenue Procedure 2001-29 provides the information required to be furnished in a request for an advance ruling on a leveraged lease transaction.

These two revenue procedures can be found in I.R.B. 2001-19, which is available at *IRS.gov/pub/irs-irbs/irb01-19.pdf*.

For advance ruling purposes only, the IRS will consider the lessor in a leveraged lease transaction to be the owner of the property and the transaction to be a valid lease if all the factors in the revenue procedure are met, including the following.

- The lessor must maintain a minimum unconditional "at risk" equity investment in the property (at least 20% of the cost of the property) during the entire lease term.
- The lessee may not have a contractual right to buy the property from the lessor at less than FMV when the right is exercised.
- The lessee may not invest in the property, except as provided by Revenue Procedure 2001-28.
- The lessee may not lend any money to the lessor to buy the property or guarantee the loan used by the lessor to buy the property.
- The lessor must show that it expects to receive a profit apart from the tax deductions, allowances, credits, and other tax attributes.

The IRS may charge you a user fee for issuing a tax ruling. For more information, see Revenue Procedure 2022-1, available at *IRS.gov/irb/2022-01_IRB#REV-PROC-2022-1*.

*Leveraged leases of limited-use property.* The IRS won't issue advance rulings on leveraged leases of so-called limited-use property. Limited-use property is property not expected to be either useful to or usable by a lessor at the end of the lease term except for continued leasing or transfer to a lessee. See Revenue Procedure 2001-28 for examples of limited-use property and property that isn't limited-use property.

**Leases over $250,000.** Special rules are provided for certain leases of tangible property. The rules apply if the lease calls for total payments of more than $250,000 and any of the following apply.

- Rents increase during the lease.
- Rents decrease during the lease.
- Rents are deferred (rent is payable after the end of the calendar year following the calendar year in which the use occurs and the rent is allocated).
- Rents are prepaid (rent is payable before the end of the calendar year preceding the calendar year in which the use occurs and the rent is allocated).

These rules do not apply if your lease specifies equal amounts of rent for each month in the lease term and all rent payments are due in the calendar year to which the rent relates (or in the preceding or following calendar year).

Generally, if the special rules apply, you must use an accrual method of accounting (and time value of money principles) for your rental expenses, regardless of your overall method of accounting. In addition, in certain cases in which the IRS has determined that a lease was designed to achieve tax avoidance, you must take rent and stated or imputed interest into account under a constant rental accrual method in which the rent is treated as accruing ratably over the entire lease term. For details, see section 467.

# Taxes on Leased Property

If you lease business property, you can deduct as additional rent any taxes you have to pay to or for the lessor. When you can deduct these taxes as additional rent depends on your accounting method.

**Cash method.** If you use the cash method of accounting, you can deduct the taxes as additional rent only for the tax year in which you pay them.

**Accrual method.** If you use an accrual method of accounting, you can deduct the taxes as additional rent for the tax year in which you can determine all the following.

- That you have a liability for taxes on the leased property.
- How much the liability is.
- That economic performance occurred.

The liability and amount of taxes are determined by state or local law and the lease agreement. Economic performance occurs as you use the property.

*Example 1.* Oak Corporation is a calendar year taxpayer that uses an accrual method of accounting. Oak leases land for use in its business. Under state law, owners of real property become liable (incur a lien on the property) for real estate taxes for the year on January 1 of that year. However, they don't have to pay these taxes until July 1 of the next year (18 months later) when tax bills are issued. Under the terms of the lease, Oak becomes liable for the real estate taxes in the later year when the tax bills are issued. If the lease ends before the tax bill for a year is issued, Oak isn't liable for the taxes for that year.

Oak cannot deduct the real estate taxes as rent until the tax bill is issued. This is when Oak's liability under the lease becomes fixed.

*Example 2.* The facts are the same as in *Example 1*, except that, according to the terms of the lease, Oak becomes liable for the real estate taxes when the owner of the property becomes liable for them. As a result, Oak will deduct the real estate taxes as rent on its tax return for the earlier year. This is the year in which Oak's liability under the lease becomes fixed.

# Cost of Getting a Lease

You may either enter into a new lease with the lessor of the property or get an existing lease from another lessee. Very often when you get an existing lease from another lessee, you must pay the previous lessee money to get the lease, besides having to pay the rent on the lease.

If you get an existing lease on property or equipment for your business, you must generally amortize any amount you pay to get that lease over the remaining term of the lease. For example, if you pay $10,000 to get a lease and there are 10 years remaining on the lease with no option to renew, you can deduct $1,000 each year.

The cost of getting an existing lease of tangible property is not subject to the amortization rules for section 197 intangibles discussed in chapter 8.

**Option to renew.** The term of the lease for amortization includes all renewal options plus any other period for which you and the lessor reasonably expect the lease to be renewed. However, this applies only if less than 75% of the cost of getting the lease is for the term remaining on the purchase date (not including any period for which you may choose to renew, extend, or continue the lease). Allocate the lease cost to the original term and any option term based on the facts and circumstances. In some cases, it may be appropriate to make the allocation using a present value calculation. For more information, see Regulations section 1.178-1(b)(5).

**Example 1.** You paid $10,000 to get a lease with 20 years remaining on it and two options to renew for 5 years each. Of this cost, you paid $7,000 for the original lease and $3,000 for the renewal options. Because $7,000 is less than 75% of the total $10,000 cost of the lease (or $7,500), you must amortize the $10,000 over 30 years. That is the remaining life of your present lease plus the periods for renewal.

**Example 2.** The facts are the same as in *Example 1*, except that you paid $8,000 for the original lease and $2,000 for the renewal options. You can amortize the entire $10,000 over the 20-year remaining life of the original lease. The $8,000 cost of getting the original lease was not less than 75% of the total cost of the lease (or $7,500).

**Cost of a modification agreement.** You may have to pay an additional "rent" amount over part of the lease period to change certain provisions in your lease. You must capitalize these payments and amortize them over the remaining period of the lease. You can't deduct the payments as additional rent, even if they are described as rent in the agreement.

**Example.** You are a calendar year taxpayer and sign a 20-year lease to rent part of a building starting on January 1. However, before you occupy it, you decide that you really need less space. The lessor agrees to reduce your rent from $7,000 to $6,000 per year and to release the excess space from the original lease. In exchange, you agree to pay an additional rent amount of $3,000, payable in 60 monthly installments of $50 each.

You must capitalize the $3,000 and amortize it over the 20-year term of the lease. Your amortization deduction each year will be $150 ($3,000 ÷ 20). You can't deduct the $600 (12 × $50) that you will pay during each of the first 5 years as rent.

**Commissions, bonuses, and fees.** Commissions, bonuses, fees, and other amounts you pay to get a lease on property you use in your business are capital costs. You must amortize these costs over the term of the lease.

**Loss on merchandise and fixtures.** If you sell at a loss merchandise and fixtures that you bought solely to get a lease, the loss is a cost of getting the lease. You must capitalize the loss and amortize it over the remaining term of the lease.

## Improvements by Lessee

If you add buildings or make other permanent improvements to leased property, depreciate the cost of the improvements using the modified accelerated cost recovery system (MACRS). Depreciate the property over its appropriate recovery period. You can't amortize the cost over the remaining term of the lease.

If you don't keep the improvements when you end the lease, figure your gain or loss based on your adjusted basis in the improvements at that time.

For more information, see the discussion of MACRS in chapter 4 of Pub. 946.

**Assignment of a lease.** If a long-term lessee who makes permanent improvements to land later assigns all lease rights to you for money and you pay the rent required by the lease, the amount you pay for the assignment is a capital investment. If the rental value of the leased land increased since the lease began, part of your capital investment is for that increase in the rental value. The rest is for your investment in the permanent improvements.

The part that is for the increased rental value of the land is a cost of getting a lease, and you amortize it over the remaining term of the lease. You can depreciate the part that is for your investment in the improvements over the recovery period of the property as discussed earlier, without regard to the lease term.

## Capitalizing Rent Expenses

Under the uniform capitalization rules, you must capitalize the direct costs and part of the indirect costs for certain production or resale activities. Include these costs in the basis of property you produce or acquire for resale, rather than claiming them as a current deduction. You recover the costs through depreciation, amortization, or cost of goods sold when you use, sell, or otherwise dispose of the property.

Indirect costs include amounts incurred for renting or leasing equipment, facilities, or land.

**Uniform capitalization rules.** You may be subject to the uniform capitalization rules if you do any of the following, unless the property is produced for your use other than in a business or an activity carried on for profit.

1. Produce real property or tangible personal property.

2. Acquire property for resale. However, this rule does not apply to personal property if your average annual gross receipts are $27 million or less.

Effective for tax years beginning after 2017, if you are a small business taxpayer (see *Cost of Goods Sold* in chapter 1), you are not required to capitalize costs under section 263A. See section 263A(i).

**Producing property.** You produce property if you construct, build, install, manufacture, develop, improve, create, raise, or grow property. Property produced for you under a contract is treated as produced by you to the extent you make payments or otherwise incur costs in connection with the property.

**Example 1.** You rent construction equipment to build a storage facility. If you are subject to the uniform capitalization rules, you must capitalize as part of the cost of the building the rent you paid for the equipment. You recover your cost by claiming a deduction for depreciation on the building.

**Example 2.** You rent space in a facility to conduct your business of manufacturing tools. If you are subject to the uniform capitalization rules, you must include the rent you paid to occupy the facility in the cost of the tools you produce.

**More information.** For exceptions and more information on these rules, see *Uniform Capitalization Rules* in Pub. 538 and the regulations under section 263A.

# 4.

# Interest

## Introduction

This chapter discusses the tax treatment of business interest expense. **Business interest expense** is an amount charged for the use of money you borrowed for business activities.

## Topics
This chapter discusses:

- Allocation of interest
- Interest expense limitation
- Interest you can deduct
- Interest you cannot deduct
- Capitalization of interest
- When to deduct interest
- Below-market loans

## Useful Items
You may want to see:

**Publication**

❏ **537** Installment Sales

❏ **550** Investment Income and Expenses

❏ **936** Home Mortgage Interest Deduction

**Form (and Instructions)**

❏ **Schedule A (Form 1040)** Itemized Deductions

❏ **Schedule E (Form 1040)** Supplemental Income and Loss

❏ **Schedule K-1 (Form 1065)** Partner's Share of Income, Deductions, Credits, etc.

❏ **Schedule K-1 (Form 1120-S)** Shareholder's Share of Income, Deductions, Credits, etc.

❏ **1098** Mortgage Interest Statement

❏ **3115** Application for Change in Accounting Method

❏ **4952** Investment Interest Expense Deduction

❏ **8582** Passive Activity Loss Limitations

❏ **8990** Limitation on Business Interest Expense Under Section 163(j)

See chapter 12 for information about getting publications and forms.

## Allocation of Interest

The rules for deducting interest vary, depending on whether the loan proceeds are used for business, personal, or investment activities. If you use the proceeds of a loan for more than one type of expense, you must allocate the interest based on the use of the loan's proceeds.

Allocate your interest expense to the following categories.
- Nonpassive trade or business activity interest.
- Passive trade or business activity interest.
- Investment interest.
- Portfolio interest.
- Personal interest.

In general, you allocate interest on a loan the same way you allocate the loan proceeds. You allocate loan proceeds by tracing disbursements to specific uses.

**TIP** *The easiest way to trace disbursements to specific uses is to keep the proceeds of a particular loan separate from any other funds.*

**Secured loan.** The allocation of loan proceeds and the related interest is generally not affected by the use of property that secures the loan.

*Example.* Marge and Jeff secure a loan with property used in their business. They use the loan proceeds to buy an automobile for personal use. Jeff and Marge must allocate interest expense on the loan to personal use (purchase of the automobile) even though the loan is secured by business property.

**⚠ CAUTION** *P.L. 115-97, section 11043, limited the deduction for mortgage interest paid on home equity loans and line of credit. For more information, see Pub. 936.*

**Allocation period.** The period for which a loan is allocated to a particular use begins on the date the proceeds are used and ends on the earlier of the following dates.
- The date the loan is repaid.
- The date the loan is reallocated to another use.

**Proceeds not disbursed to borrower.** Even if the lender disburses the loan proceeds to a third party, the allocation of the loan is still based on your use of the funds. This applies whether you pay for property, services, or anything else by incurring a loan, or you take property subject to a debt.

**Proceeds deposited in borrower's account.** Treat loan proceeds deposited in an account as property held for investment. It does not matter whether the account pays interest. Any interest you pay on the loan is investment interest expense. If you withdraw the proceeds of the loan, you must reallocate the loan based on the use of the funds.

*Example.* Celina, a calendar-year taxpayer, borrows $100,000 on January 4 and immediately uses the proceeds to open a checking account. No other amounts are deposited in the account during the year and no part of the loan principal is repaid during the year. On April 2, Celina uses $20,000 from the checking account for a passive activity expenditure. On September 4, Celina uses an additional $40,000 from the account for personal purposes.

Under the interest allocation rules, the entire $100,000 loan is treated as property held for investment for the period from January 4 through April 1. From April 2 through September 3, Celina must treat $20,000 of the loan as used in the passive activity and $80,000 of the loan as property held for investment. From September 4 through December 31, she must treat $40,000 of the loan as used for personal purposes, $20,000 as used in the passive activity, and $40,000 as property held for investment.

**Order of funds spent.** Generally, you treat loan proceeds deposited in an account as used (spent) before either of the following amounts.
- Any unborrowed amounts held in the same account.
- Any amounts deposited after these loan proceeds.

*Example.* On January 9, Olena opened a checking account, depositing $500 of the proceeds of Loan A and $1,000 of unborrowed funds. The following table shows the transactions in her account during the tax year.

| Date | Transaction |
|---|---|
| January 9 | $500 proceeds of Loan A and $1,000 unborrowed funds deposited |
| January 14 | $500 proceeds of Loan B deposited |
| February 19 | $800 used for personal purposes |
| February 27 | $700 used for passive activity |
| June 19 | $1,000 proceeds of Loan C deposited |
| November 20 | $800 used for an investment |
| December 18 | $600 used for personal purposes |

Olena treats the $800 used for personal purposes as made from the $500 proceeds of Loan A and $300 of the proceeds of Loan B. She treats the $700 used for a passive activity as made from the remaining $200 proceeds of Loan B and $500 of unborrowed funds. She treats the $800 used for an investment as made entirely from the proceeds of Loan C. She treats the $600 used for personal purposes as made from the remaining $200 proceeds of Loan C and $400 of unborrowed funds.

For the periods during which loan proceeds are held in the account, Olena treats them as property held for investment.

**Payments from checking accounts.** Generally, you treat a payment from a checking or similar account as made at the time the check is written if you mail or deliver it to the payee within a reasonable period after you write it. You can treat checks written on the same day as written in any order.

**Amounts paid within 30 days.** If you receive loan proceeds in cash or if the loan proceeds are deposited in an account, you can treat any payment (up to the amount of the proceeds) made from any account you own, or from cash, as made from those proceeds. This applies to any payment made within 30 days before or after the proceeds are received in cash or deposited in your account.

If the loan proceeds are deposited in an account, you can apply this rule even if the rules stated earlier under Order of funds spent would otherwise require you to treat the proceeds as used for other purposes. If you apply this rule to any payments, disregard those payments (and the proceeds from which they are made) when applying the rules stated earlier under Order of funds spent.

If you received the loan proceeds in cash, you can treat the payment as made on the date you received the cash instead of the date you actually made the payment.

*Example.* Giovanni gets a loan of $1,000 on August 4 and receives the proceeds in cash. Giovanni deposits $1,500 in an account on August 8 and on August 18 writes a check on the account for a passive activity expense. Also, Giovanni deposits his paycheck, deposits other loan proceeds, and pays his bills during the same period. Regardless of these other transactions, Giovanni can treat $1,000 of the deposit he made on August 8 as being paid on August 4 from the loan proceeds. In addition, Giovanni can treat the passive activity expense he paid on August 18 as made from the $1,000 loan proceeds treated as deposited in the account.

**Optional method for determining date of reallocation.** You can use the following method to determine the date loan proceeds are reallocated to another use. You can treat all payments from loan proceeds in the account during any month as taking place on the later of the following dates.
- The first day of that month.
- The date the loan proceeds are deposited in the account.

However, you can use this optional method only if you treat all payments from the account during the same calendar month in the same way.

**Interest on a segregated account.** If you have an account that contains only loan proceeds and interest earned on the account, you can treat any payment from that account as being made first from the interest. When the interest earned is used up, any remaining payments are from loan proceeds.

*Example.* You borrowed $20,000 and used the proceeds of this loan to open a new savings account. When the account had earned interest of $867, you withdrew $20,000 for personal purposes. You can treat the withdrawal as coming first from the interest earned on the account, $867, and then from the loan proceeds, $19,133 ($20,000 – $867). All the interest charged on the loan from the time it was deposited in the account until the time of the withdrawal is investment interest expense. The interest charged on the part of the proceeds used for personal purposes ($19,133) from the time you withdrew it until you either repay it or reallocate it to another use is personal interest expense. The interest charged on the loan proceeds you left in the account ($867) continues to be investment interest expense until you either repay it or reallocate it to another use.

**Loan repayment.** When you repay any part of a loan allocated to more than one use, treat it as being repaid in the following order.

1. Personal use.

2. Investments and passive activities (other than those included in (3)).

3. Passive activities in connection with a rental real estate activity in which you actively participate.

4. Former passive activities.

5. Trade or business use and expenses for certain low-income housing projects.

**Line of credit (continuous borrowings).** The following rules apply if you have a line of credit or similar arrangement.

1. Treat all borrowed funds on which interest accrues at the same fixed or variable rate as a single loan.

2. Treat borrowed funds or parts of borrowed funds on which interest accrues at different fixed or variable rates as different loans. Treat these loans as repaid in the order shown on the loan agreement.

**Loan refinancing.** Allocate the replacement loan to the same uses to which the repaid loan was allocated. Make this allocation only to the extent you use the proceeds of the new loan to repay any part of the original loan.

**Debt-financed distribution.** A debt-financed distribution occurs when a partnership or S corporation borrows funds and allocates those funds to distributions made to partners or shareholders. The manner in which you report the interest expense associated with the distributed debt proceeds depends on your use of those proceeds.

*How to report.* If the proceeds were used in a nonpassive trade or business activity, report the interest on Schedule E (Form 1040), line 28; enter "interest expense" and the name of the partnership or S corporation in column (a) and the amount in column (i). If the proceeds were used in a passive activity, follow the Instructions for Form 8582 to determine the amount of interest expense that can be reported on Schedule E (Form 1040), line 28; enter "interest expense" and the name of the partnership in column (a) and the amount in column (g). If the proceeds were used in an investment activity, enter the interest on Form 4952. If the proceeds are used for personal purposes, the interest is generally not deductible.

# Interest Expense Limitation

You must generally limit business interest expense you pay or accrue during the tax year, unless an exception to the limitation is met.

The business interest expense deduction allowed for a tax year is generally limited to the sum of:

1. Business interest income,

2. 30% of the adjustable taxable income, and

3. Floor plan financing interest.

If the section 163(j) limitation applies, generally the amount of any business interest expense that is not allowed as a deduction under section 163(j) for the tax year is carried forward to the following year as a disallowed business interest expense carryforward. See the Instructions for Form 8990, Limitation on Business Interest Expense Under Section 163(j), for more information.

# Interest You Can Deduct

Your trade or business interest expense may be limited. See the Instructions for Form 8990 for more information. Interest relates to your trade or business if you use the proceeds of the loan for a trade or business expense. It does not matter what type of property secures the loan. You can deduct interest on a debt only if you meet all the following requirements.

- You are legally liable for that debt.
- Both you and the lender intend that the debt be repaid.
- You and the lender have a true debtor–creditor relationship.

**Partial liability.** If you are liable for part of a business debt, only your share of the total interest paid or accrued is included in your interest limitation calculation.

*Example.* You and your sibling borrow money. You are liable for 50% of the note. You use your half of the loan in your business, and you make one-half of the loan payments. Your business interest is half of the total interest payments. However, the current year interest expense deduction may be limited.

**Mortgage.** Generally, mortgage interest paid or accrued on real estate you own legally or equitably is deductible. However, rather than deducting the interest currently, you may have to add it to the cost basis of the property as explained later under *Capitalization of Interest*.

*Statement.* If you paid $600 or more of mortgage interest (including certain points) during the year on any one mortgage, you will generally receive a Form 1098 or a similar statement. You will receive the statement if you pay interest to a person (including a financial institution or a cooperative housing corporation) in the course of that person's trade or business. A governmental unit is a person for purposes of furnishing the statement.

If you receive a refund of interest you overpaid in an earlier year, this amount will be reported in box 4 of Form 1098. You cannot deduct this amount. For information on how to report this refund, see *Refunds of interest*, later, in this chapter.

*Expenses paid to obtain a mortgage.* Certain expenses you pay to obtain a mortgage cannot be deducted as interest. These expenses, which include mortgage commissions, abstract fees, and recording fees, are capital expenses. If the property mortgaged is business or income-producing property, you can amortize the costs over the life of the mortgage.

*Prepayment penalty.* If you pay off your mortgage early and pay the lender a penalty for doing this, you can deduct the penalty as interest.

**Interest on employment tax deficiency.** Interest charged on employment taxes assessed on your business is deductible.

**Original issue discount (OID).** OID is a form of interest. A loan (mortgage or other debt) generally has OID when its proceeds are less than its principal amount. The OID is the difference between the stated redemption price at maturity and the issue price of the loan.

A loan's stated redemption price at maturity is the sum of all amounts (principal and interest) payable on it other than qualified stated interest. Qualified stated interest is stated interest that is unconditionally payable in cash or property (other than another loan of the issuer) at least annually over the term of the loan at a single fixed rate.

You generally deduct OID over the term of the loan. Figure the amount to deduct each year using the constant-yield method, unless the OID on the loan is de minimis.

*De minimis OID.* The OID is de minimis if it is less than one-fourth of 1% (0.0025) of the stated redemption price of the loan at maturity multiplied by the number of full years from the date of original issue to maturity (the term of the loan).

If the OID is de minimis, you can choose one of the following ways to figure the amount you can deduct each year.

- On a constant-yield basis over the term of the loan.
- On a straight-line basis over the term of the loan.
- In proportion to stated interest payments.
- In its entirety at maturity of the loan.

You make this choice by deducting the OID in a manner consistent with the method chosen on your timely filed tax return for the tax year in which the loan is issued.

*Example.* On January 1, 2022, you took out a $100,000 discounted loan and received $98,500 in proceeds. The loan will mature on January 1, 2032 (a 10-year term), and the $100,000 principal is payable on that date. Interest of $10,000 is payable on January 1 of each year, beginning January 1, 2023. The $1,500 OID on the loan is de minimis because it is less than $2,500 ($100,000 × 0.0025 × 10). You choose to deduct the OID on a straight-line basis over the term of the loan. Beginning in 2022, you can deduct $150 each year for 10 years.

*Constant-yield method.* If the OID is not de minimis, you must use the constant-yield method to figure how much you can deduct each year. You figure your deduction for the first year using the following steps.

1. Determine the issue price of the loan. Generally, this equals the proceeds of the loan. If you paid points on the loan (as discussed later), the issue price is generally the difference between the proceeds and the points.

2. Multiply the result in (1) by the yield to maturity.

3. Subtract any qualified stated interest payments from the result in (2). This is the OID you can deduct in the first year.

To figure your deduction in any subsequent year, follow the steps above, except determine the adjusted issue price in step 1. To get the adjusted issue price, add to the issue price any OID previously deducted. Then follow steps 2 and 3 above.

The yield to maturity is generally shown in the literature you receive from your lender. If you do not have this information, consult your lender or tax advisor. In general, the yield to maturity is the discount rate that, when used in figuring the present value of all principal and interest payments, produces an amount equal to the principal amount of the loan.

*Example.* The facts are the same as in the previous example, except that you deduct the OID on a constant-yield basis over the term of the loan. The yield to maturity on your loan is 10.2467%, compounded annually. For 2022, you can deduct $93 [($98,500 × 0.102467) − $10,000]. For 2023, you can deduct $103 [($98,593 × 0.102467) − $10,000].

*Loan or mortgage ends.* If your loan or mortgage ends, you may be able to deduct any remaining OID in the tax year in which the loan or mortgage ends. A loan or mortgage may end due to a refinancing, prepayment, foreclosure, or similar event.

*If you refinance with the original lender, you generally cannot deduct the remaining OID in the year in which the refinancing occurs, but you may be able to deduct it over the term of the new mortgage or loan. See Interest paid with funds borrowed from original lender under Interest You Cannot Deduct, later.*

**Points.** The term "points" is used to describe certain charges paid, or treated as paid, by a borrower to obtain a loan or a mortgage. These charges are also called loan origination fees, maximum loan charges, discount points, or premium charges. If any of these charges (points) are solely for the use of money, they are interest.

Because points are prepaid interest, you generally cannot deduct the full amount in the year paid. However, you can choose to fully deduct points in the year paid if you meet certain

tests. For exceptions to the general rule, see Pub. 936.

The points reduce the issue price of the loan and result in OID, deductible as explained in the preceding discussion.

**Partial payments on a nontax debt.** If you make partial payments on a debt (other than a debt owed to the IRS), the payments are applied, in general, first to interest and any remainder to principal. You can deduct only the interest. This rule does not apply when it can be inferred that the borrower and lender understood that a different allocation of the payments would be made.

**Installment purchase.** If you make an installment purchase of business property, the contract between you and the seller generally provides for the payment of interest. If no interest or a low rate of interest is charged under the contract, a portion of the stated principal amount payable under the contract may be recharacterized as interest (unstated interest). The amount recharacterized as interest reduces your basis in the property and increases your interest expense. For more information on installment sales and unstated interest, see Pub. 537.

# Interest You Cannot Deduct

Certain interest payments cannot be deducted. In addition, certain other expenses that may seem to be interest, but are not, cannot be deducted as interest.

You cannot currently deduct interest that must be capitalized, and you generally cannot deduct personal interest.

**Interest paid with funds borrowed from original lender.** If you use the cash method of accounting, you cannot deduct interest you pay with funds borrowed from the original lender through a second loan, an advance, or any other arrangement similar to a loan. You can deduct the interest expense once you start making payments on the new loan.

When you make a payment on the new loan, you first apply the payment to interest and then to the principal. All amounts you apply to the interest on the first loan are deductible, along with any interest you pay on the second loan, subject to any limits that apply.

**Capitalized interest.** You cannot currently deduct interest you are required to capitalize under the uniform capitalization rules. See *Capitalization of Interest*, later. In addition, if you buy property and pay interest owed by the seller (for example, by assuming the debt and any interest accrued on the property), you cannot deduct the interest. Add this interest to the basis of the property.

**Commitment fees or standby charges.** Fees you incur to have business funds available on a standby basis, but not for the actual use of the funds, are not deductible as interest payments. You may be able to deduct them as business expenses.

If the funds are for inventory or certain property used in your business, the fees are indirect costs and you must generally capitalize them under the uniform capitalization rules. See *Capitalization of Interest*, later.

**Interest on income tax.** Interest charged on income tax assessed on your individual income tax return is not a business deduction even though the tax due is related to income from your trade or business. Treat this interest as a business deduction only in figuring a net operating loss deduction.

*Penalties.* Penalties on underpaid deficiencies and underpaid estimated tax are not interest. You cannot deduct them. Generally, you cannot deduct any fines or penalties.

**Interest on loans with respect to life insurance policies.** You generally cannot deduct interest on a debt incurred with respect to any life insurance, annuity, or endowment contract that covers any individual unless that individual is a key person.

If the policy or contract covers a key person, you can deduct the interest on up to $50,000 of debt for that person. However, the deduction for any month cannot be more than the interest figured using Moody's Composite Yield on Seasoned Corporate Bonds (formerly known as Moody's Corporate Bond Yield Average—Monthly Average Corporates) (Moody's rate) for that month.

*Who is a key person?* A "key person" is an officer or 20% owner. However, the number of individuals you can treat as key persons is limited to the greater of the following.

- Five individuals.
- The lesser of 5% of the total officers and employees of the company or 20 individuals.

*Exceptions for pre-June 1997 contracts.* You can generally deduct the interest if the contract was issued before June 9, 1997, and the covered individual is someone other than an employee, officer, or someone financially interested in your business. If the contract was purchased before June 21, 1986, you can generally deduct the interest no matter who is covered by the contract.

*Interest allocated to unborrowed policy cash value.* Corporations and partnerships generally cannot deduct any interest expense allocable to unborrowed cash values of life insurance, annuity, or endowment contracts. This rule applies to contracts issued after June 8, 1997, that cover someone other than an officer, director, employee, or 20% owner. For more information, see section 264(f).

# Capitalization of Interest

Under the uniform capitalization rules, you must generally capitalize interest on debt equal to your expenditures to produce real property or certain tangible personal property. The property must be produced by you for use in your trade or business or for sale to customers. You cannot capitalize interest related to property that you acquire in any other manner.

Interest you paid or incurred during the production period must be capitalized if the property produced is designated property. Designated property is any of the following.

- Real property.
- Tangible personal property with a class life of 20 years or more.
- Tangible personal property with an estimated production period of more than 2 years.
- Tangible personal property with an estimated production period of more than 1 year if the estimated cost of production is more than $1 million.

**Property you produce.** You produce property if you construct, build, install, manufacture, develop, improve, create, raise, or grow it. Treat property produced for you under a contract as produced by you up to the amount you pay or incur for the property.

**Carrying charges.** Carrying charges include taxes you pay to carry or develop real estate or to carry, transport, or install personal property. You can choose to capitalize carrying charges not subject to the uniform capitalization rules if they are otherwise deductible. For more information, see chapter 7.

**Capitalized interest.** Treat capitalized interest as a cost of the property produced. You recover your interest when you sell or use the property. If the property is inventory, recover capitalized interest through cost of goods sold. If the property is used in your trade or business, recover capitalized interest through an adjustment to basis, depreciation, amortization, or other method.

**Partnerships and S corporations.** The interest capitalization rules are applied first at the partnership or S corporation level. The rules are then applied at the partners' or shareholders' level to the extent the partnership or S corporation has insufficient debt to support the production or construction costs.

If you are a partner or a shareholder, you may have to capitalize interest you incur during the tax year for the production costs of the partnership or S corporation. You may also have to capitalize interest incurred by the partnership or S corporation for your own production costs. To properly capitalize interest under these rules, you must be given the required information in an attachment to the Schedule K-1 you receive from the partnership or S corporation.

**Additional information.** The procedures for applying the uniform capitalization rules are beyond the scope of this publication. For more information, see Regulations sections 1.263A-8 through 1.263A-15 and Notice 88-99, which is in Cumulative Bulletin 1988-2.

## When To Deduct Interest

If the uniform capitalization rules, discussed under Capitalization of Interest, earlier, and the business interest expense deduction limitation rules discussed under Interest Expense Limitation, earlier, do not apply, deduct interest as follows.

**Cash method.** Under the cash method, you can generally deduct only the interest you actually paid during the tax year. You cannot deduct a promissory note you gave as payment because it is a promise to pay and not an actual payment.

**Prepaid interest.** You generally cannot deduct any interest paid before the year it is due. Interest paid in advance can be deducted only in the tax year in which it is due.

**Discounted loan.** If interest or a discount is subtracted from your loan proceeds, it is not a payment of interest and you cannot deduct it when you get the loan. For more information, see Original issue discount (OID) under Interest You Can Deduct, earlier.

**Refunds of interest.** If you pay interest and then receive a refund in the same tax year of any part of the interest, reduce your interest deduction by the refund. If you receive the refund in a later tax year, include the refund in your income to the extent the deduction for the interest reduced your tax.

**Accrual method.** Under an accrual method, you can deduct only interest that has accrued during the tax year.

**Prepaid interest.** You generally cannot deduct any interest paid before the year it is due. Interest paid in advance can be deducted only in the tax year in which it is due.

**Discounted loan.** If interest or a discount is subtracted from your loan proceeds, it is not a payment of interest and you cannot deduct it when you get the loan. For more information, see Original issue discount (OID) under Interest You Can Deduct, earlier.

**Tax deficiency.** If you contest a federal income tax deficiency, interest does not accrue until the tax year the final determination of liability is made. If you do not contest the deficiency, then the interest accrues in the year the tax was asserted and agreed to by you.

However, if you contest but pay the proposed tax deficiency and interest, and you do not designate the payment as a cash bond, then the interest is deductible in the year paid.

**Related person.** If you use an accrual method, you cannot deduct interest owed to a related person who uses the cash method until payment is made and the interest is includible in the gross income of that person. The relationship is determined as of the end of the tax year for which the interest would otherwise be deductible. See section 267 for more information.

## Below-Market Loans

If you receive a below-market gift or demand loan and use the proceeds in your trade or business, you may be able to deduct the forgone interest. See Treatment of gift and demand loans, later, in this discussion.

A "below-market loan" is a loan on which no interest is charged or on which interest is charged at a rate below the applicable federal rate (AFR). A gift or demand loan that is a below-market loan is generally considered an arm's-length transaction in which you, the borrower, are considered as having received both of the following.

- A loan in exchange for a note that requires the payment of interest at the AFR.
- An additional payment in an amount equal to the forgone interest.

The additional payment is treated as a gift, dividend, contribution to capital, payment of compensation, or other payment, depending on the substance of the transaction.

**Forgone interest.** For any period, forgone interest is:

1. The interest that would be payable for that period if interest accrued on the loan at the AFR and was payable annually on December 31, minus
2. Any interest actually payable on the loan for the period.

**TIP** AFRs are published by the IRS each month in the Internal Revenue Bulletin (I.R.B.), which is available on the IRS website at IRS.gov/IRB. You can also contact an IRS office to get these rates.

**Loans subject to the rules.** The rules for below-market loans apply to the following.

1. Gift loans (below-market loans where the forgone interest is in the nature of a gift).
2. Compensation-related loans (below-market loans between an employer and an employee or between an independent contractor and a person for whom the contractor provides services).
3. Corporation-shareholder loans.
4. Tax avoidance loans (below-market loans where the avoidance of federal tax is one of the main purposes of the interest arrangement).
5. Loans to qualified continuing care facilities under a continuing care contract (made after October 11, 1985).

Except as noted in (5) above, these rules apply to demand loans (loans payable in full at any time upon the lender's demand) outstanding after June 6, 1984, and to term loans (loans that are not demand loans) made after that date.

**Treatment of gift and demand loans.** If you receive a below-market gift loan or demand loan, you are treated as receiving an additional payment (as a gift, dividend, etc.) equal to the forgone interest on the loan. You are then treated as transferring this amount back to the lender as interest. These transfers are considered to occur annually, generally on December 31. If you use the loan proceeds in your trade or business, you can deduct the forgone interest each year as a business interest expense. The lender must report it as interest income.

**Limit on forgone interest for gift loans of $100,000 or less.** For gift loans between individuals, forgone interest treated as transferred back to the lender is limited to the borrower's net investment income for the year. This limit applies if the outstanding loans between the lender and borrower total $100,000 or less. If the borrower's net investment income is $1,000 or less, it is treated as zero. This limit does not apply to a loan if the avoidance of any federal tax is one of the main purposes of the interest arrangement.

**Treatment of term loans.** If you receive a below-market term loan other than a gift or demand loan, you are treated as receiving an additional cash payment (as a dividend, etc.) on the date the loan is made. This payment is equal to the loan amount minus the present value, at the AFR, of all payments due under the loan. The same amount is treated as OID on the loan. See *Original issue discount (OID)* under *Interest You Can Deduct*, earlier.

**Exceptions for loans of $10,000 or less.** The rules for below-market loans do not apply to any day on which the total outstanding loans between the borrower and lender is $10,000 or less. This exception applies only to the following.

1. Gift loans between individuals if the loan is not directly used to buy or carry income-producing assets.

2. Compensation-related loans or corporation-shareholder loans if the avoidance of any federal tax is not a principal purpose of the interest arrangement.

This exception does not apply to a term loan described in (2) above that was previously subject to the below-market loan rules. Those rules will continue to apply even if the outstanding balance is reduced to $10,000 or less.

**Exceptions for loans without significant tax effect.** The following loans are specifically exempted from the rules for below-market loans because their interest arrangements do not have a significant effect on the federal tax liability of the borrower or the lender.

1. Loans made available by lenders to the general public on the same terms and conditions that are consistent with the lender's customary business practices.

2. Loans subsidized by a federal, state, or municipal government that are made available under a program of general application to the public.

3. Certain employee-relocation loans.

4. Certain loans to or from a foreign person, unless the interest income would be effectively connected with the conduct of a U.S. trade or business and not exempt from U.S. tax under an income tax treaty.

5. Any other loan if the taxpayer can show that the interest arrangement has no significant effect on the federal tax liability of the lender or the borrower. Whether an interest arrangement has a significant effect on the federal tax liability of the lender or the borrower will be determined by all the facts and circumstances. Consider all the following factors.

   a. Whether items of income and deduction generated by the loan offset each other.

b. The amount of the items.

c. The cost of complying with the below-market loan provisions if they were to apply.

d. Any reasons, other than taxes, for structuring the transaction as a below-market loan.

**Exception for loans to qualified continuing care facilities.** The below-market interest rules do not apply to a loan owed by a qualified continuing care facility under a continuing care contract if the lender or lender's spouse is age 62 or older by the end of the calendar year.

A qualified continuing care facility is one or more facilities (excluding nursing homes) meeting the requirements listed below.

1. Designed to provide services under continuing care contracts (defined below).

2. Includes an independent living unit, and either an assisted living or nursing facility, or both.

3. Substantially all of the independent living unit residents are covered by continuing care contracts.

A "continuing care contract" is a written contract between an individual and a qualified continuing care facility that includes all of the following conditions.

1. The individual or individual's spouse must be entitled to use the facility for the rest of their life or lives.

2. The individual or individual's spouse will be provided with housing, as appropriate for the health of the individual or individual's spouse in an:

   a. Independent living unit (which has additional available facilities outside the unit for the provision of meals and other personal care), and

   b. Assisted living or nursing facility available in the continuing care facility.

3. The individual or individual's spouse will be provided with assisted living or nursing care available in the continuing care facility, as required for the health of the individual or the individual's spouse.

For more information, see section 7872(h).

**Sale or exchange of property.** Different rules generally apply to a loan connected with the sale or exchange of property. If the loan does not provide adequate stated interest, part of the principal payment may be considered interest. However, there are exceptions that may require you to apply the below-market interest rate rules to these loans. See *Unstated Interest and Original Issue Discount (OID)* in Pub. 537.

**More information.** For more information on below-market loans, see section 7872 and Regulations section 1.7872-5.

# 5.

# Taxes

## Introduction

You can deduct various federal, state, local, and foreign taxes directly attributable to your trade or business as business expenses.

⚠️ **CAUTION** *You cannot deduct federal income taxes, estate and gift taxes, or state inheritance, legacy, and succession taxes.*

## Topics
This chapter discusses:

- When to deduct taxes
- Real estate taxes
- Income taxes
- Employment taxes
- Other taxes

## Useful Items
You may want to see:

### Publication

❏ **15**   (Circular E), Employer's Tax Guide

❏ **334** Tax Guide for Small Business

❏ **510** Excise Taxes

❏ **538** Accounting Periods and Methods

❏ **551** Basis of Assets

### Form (and Instructions)

❏ **1040 or 1040-SR** U.S. Individual Income Tax Return

❏ **Schedule A (Form 1040)** Itemized Deductions

❏ **Schedule SE (Form 1040)** Self-Employment Tax

❏ **3115** Application for Change in Accounting Method

❏ **8959** Additional Medicare Tax

See chapter 12 for information about getting publications and forms.

## When To Deduct Taxes

Generally, you can only deduct taxes in the year you pay them. This applies whether you use the cash method or an accrual method of accounting.

Under an accrual method, you can deduct a tax before you pay it if you meet the exception for recurring items discussed under *Economic Performance* in Pub. 538. You can also elect to ratably accrue real estate taxes as discussed later under *Real Estate Taxes*. See also *Foreign income taxes*, discussed later.

**Limitation on acceleration of accrual of taxes.** A taxing jurisdiction can require the use of a date for accruing taxes that is earlier than the date it originally required. However, if you use an accrual method, and can deduct the tax before you pay it, use the original accrual date for the year of change and all future years to determine when you can deduct the tax.

*Example.* Your state imposes a tax on personal property used in a trade or business conducted in the state. This tax is assessed and becomes a lien as of July 1 (accrual date). In 2022, the state changed the assessment and lien dates from July 1, 2023, to December 31, 2022, for property tax year 2023. Use the original accrual date (July 1, 2023) to determine when you can deduct the tax. You must also use the July 1 accrual date for all future years to determine when you can deduct the tax.

**Uniform capitalization rules.** Uniform capitalization rules apply to certain taxpayers who produce real property or tangible personal property for use in a trade or business or for sale to customers. They also apply to certain taxpayers who acquire property for resale. Under these rules, you either include certain costs in inventory or capitalize certain expenses related to the property, such as taxes. For more information, see chapter 1.

**Carrying charges.** Carrying charges include taxes you pay to carry or develop real estate or to carry, transport, or install personal property. You can elect to capitalize carrying charges not subject to the uniform capitalization rules if they are otherwise deductible. For more information, see chapter 7.

**Refunds of taxes.** If you receive a refund for any taxes you deducted in an earlier year, include the refund in income to the extent the deduction reduced your federal income tax in the earlier year. For more information, see *Recovery of amount deducted (tax benefit rule)* in chapter 1.

**TIP** *You must include in income any interest you receive on tax refunds.*

## Real Estate Taxes

Deductible real estate taxes are any state or local taxes, including taxes imposed by U.S. possessions, on real estate levied for the general public welfare. The taxing authority must base the taxes on the assessed value of the real estate and charge them uniformly against all property under its jurisdiction. Deductible real estate taxes generally do not include taxes charged for local benefits and improvements that increase the value of the property. See *Taxes for local benefits*, later.

Real estate taxes imposed by a foreign country are not deductible unless paid or accrued in connection with the conduct of a trade or business or for the production of income. For individual tax filers, the amount of deductible state and local real estate taxes may be subject to a $10,000 limitation. See *State and local income taxes*, later.

If you use an accrual method, you generally cannot accrue real estate taxes until you pay them to the government authority. However, you can elect to ratably accrue the taxes during the year. See *Electing to ratably accrue*, later.

**Taxes for local benefits.** Generally, you cannot deduct taxes charged for local benefits and improvements that tend to increase the value of your property. These include assessments for streets, sidewalks, water mains, sewer lines, and public parking facilities. You should increase the basis of your property by the amount of the assessment.

You can deduct taxes for these local benefits only if the taxes are for maintenance, repairs, or interest charges related to those benefits. If part of the tax is for maintenance, repairs, or interest, you must be able to show how much of the tax is for these expenses to claim a deduction for that part of the tax.

*Example.* To improve downtown commercial business, Waterfront City converted a downtown business area street into an enclosed pedestrian mall. The city assessed the full cost of construction, financed with 10-year bonds, against the affected properties. The city is paying the principal and interest with the annual payments made by the property owners.

The assessments for construction costs are not deductible as taxes or as business expenses, but are depreciable capital expenses. The part of the payments used to pay the interest charges on the bonds is deductible as taxes.

**Charges for services.** Water bills, sewerage, and other service charges assessed against your business property are not real estate taxes, but are deductible as business expenses.

**Purchase or sale of real estate.** If real estate is sold, the real estate taxes must be allocated between the buyer and the seller.

The buyer and seller must allocate the real estate taxes according to the number of days in the real property tax year (the period to which the tax imposed relates) that each owned the property. Treat the seller as paying the taxes up to but not including the date of sale. Treat the buyer as paying the taxes beginning with the date of sale. You can usually find this information on the settlement statement you received at closing.

If you (the seller) use an accrual method and have not elected to ratably accrue real estate taxes, you are considered to have accrued your part of the tax on the date you sell the property.

*Example.* Lynn and Curt are calendar year accrual method taxpayers who own real estate in Olmo County. They have not elected to ratably accrue property taxes. November 30 of each year is the assessment and lien date for the current real property tax year, which is the calendar year. They sold the property on June 30, 2022. Under their accounting method, they would not be able to claim a deduction for the taxes because the sale occurred before November 30. They are treated as having accrued their part of the tax, $181/365$ (January 1–June 29), on June 30, and they can deduct it for 2022.

**Electing to ratably accrue.** If you use an accrual method, you can elect to accrue real estate tax related to a definite period ratably over that period.

*Example.* Lea and Joey are calendar year taxpayers who use an accrual method. Their real estate taxes for the real property tax year, July 1, 2022, to June 30, 2023, are $1,200. July 1 is the assessment and lien date.

If the Lea and Joey elect to ratably accrue the taxes, $600 will accrue in 2022 ($1,200 × $6/12$, July 1–December 31) and the balance will accrue in 2023.

**Separate elections.** You can elect to ratably accrue the taxes for each separate trade or business and for nonbusiness activities if you account for them separately. Once you elect to ratably accrue real estate taxes, you must use that method unless you get permission from the IRS to change your accounting method. See *Form 3115*, later.

**Making the election.** If you elect to ratably accrue the taxes for the first year in which you incur real estate taxes, attach a statement to your income tax return for that year. The statement should show all the following items.

- The trades or businesses to which the election applies and the accounting method or methods used.
- The period to which the taxes relate.
- The calculation of the real estate tax deduction for that first year.

Generally, you must file your return by the due date (including extensions). However, if you timely filed your return for the year without electing to ratably accrue, you can still make the election by filing an amended return within 6 months after the due date of the return (excluding extensions). Attach the statement to the amended return and write "Filed pursuant to section 301.9100-2" on the statement. File the amended return at the same address where you filed the original return.

**Form 3115.** If you elect to ratably accrue real estate taxes for a year after the first year in which you incur real estate taxes, or if you want to revoke your election to ratably accrue real estate taxes, file Form 3115. For more information, including applicable time frames for filing, see the Instructions for Form 3115.

## Income Taxes

This section discusses federal, state, local, and foreign income taxes.

**Federal income taxes.** You cannot deduct federal income taxes.

**State and local income taxes.** A corporation or partnership can deduct state and local income taxes imposed on the corporation or partnership as business expenses.

An individual can deduct state and local income taxes only as an itemized deduction on Schedule A (Form 1040), subject to limitations. The deduction is limited to $10,000 as a total of the following taxes.

1. State and local income taxes or general sales taxes. See the Schedule A (Form 1040) instructions.

2. State and local real estate taxes. See the Schedule A (Form 1040) instructions. See also *Real Estate Taxes*, earlier.

3. State and local personal property taxes.

However, an individual can deduct a state tax on gross income (as distinguished from net income) directly attributable to a trade or business as a business expense.

**Accrual of contested income taxes.** If you use an accrual method, and you contest a state or local income tax liability, you must accrue and deduct any contested amount in the tax year in which the liability is finally determined.

If additional state or local income taxes for a prior year are assessed in a later year, you can deduct the taxes in the year in which they were originally imposed (the prior year) if the tax liability is not contested. You cannot deduct them in the year in which the liability is finally determined.

**TIP** *The filing of an income tax return is not considered a contest and, in the absence of an overt act of protest, you can deduct the tax in the prior year. Also, you can deduct any additional taxes in the prior year if you do not show some affirmative evidence of denial of the liability.*

However, if you consistently deduct additional assessments in the year they are paid or finally determined (including those for which there was no contest), you must continue to do so. You cannot take a deduction in the earlier year unless you receive permission to change your method of accounting. For more information on accounting methods, see *When Can I Deduct an Expense* in chapter 1.

If you contest a state or local tax liability, and you transfer money or other property as a provisional payment of the contested tax liability, you can accrue and deduct the amount of the contested tax liability for which you made the provisional payment in the year in which you made the payment, even though the liability is not determined until a later year.

If any portion of the contested amount which was deducted in the year the provisional payment was made is later refunded when the contest is settled, you must include such portion in your gross income in the year the refund is received.

Notwithstanding the exception that allows accrual and deduction of contested state or local income tax liability upon payment, current accrual and deduction is not allowed for income, war profits, and excess profits taxes imposed by a foreign country or possession of the United States.

**Foreign income taxes.** Generally, you can take either a deduction or a credit for income taxes imposed on you by a foreign country or a U.S. possession, subject to limitations. However, an individual cannot take a deduction or credit for foreign income taxes paid on income that is exempt from U.S. tax under the foreign earned income exclusion or the foreign housing exclusion. For information on these exclusions,

see Pub. 54. For information on the foreign tax credit, see Pub. 514.

**Accrual of foreign income taxes.** If you use an accrual method and choose to take a deduction (rather than a credit) for foreign income taxes, you can deduct the taxes in the year in which the fact of the liability becomes fixed and the amount of the liability can be determined with reasonable accuracy. Generally, this is the year with or within which the tax year that applies for foreign tax purposes ends or, in the case of a contested tax, the year in which the contest is resolved. Different rules may apply to determine when a foreign income tax is considered to accrue for purposes of the foreign tax credit. For more information on the foreign tax credit, see Pub. 514.

## Employment Taxes

If you have employees, you must withhold various taxes from your employees' pay. Most employers must withhold their employees' share of social security, Medicare taxes, and Additional Medicare Tax (if applicable), along with state and federal income taxes. You may also need to pay certain employment taxes from your own funds. These include your share of social security and Medicare taxes as an employer, along with unemployment taxes.

Your deduction for wages paid is not reduced by the social security and Medicare taxes, Additional Medicare Tax, and income taxes you withhold from your employees. You can deduct the employment taxes you must pay from your own funds as taxes.

**Example.** You pay your employee $18,000 a year. However, after you withhold various taxes, your employee receives $14,500. You also pay an additional $1,500 in employment taxes. You should deduct the full $18,000 as wages. You can deduct the $1,500 you pay from your own funds as taxes.

**Additional Medicare Tax.** You must withhold a 0.9% Additional Medicare Tax from wages you pay to an employee in excess of $200,000 in a calendar year. The Additional Medicare Tax is only imposed on the employee. There is no employer share of Additional Medicare Tax.

For more information on the Additional Medicare Tax, see Form 8959 and its instructions.

**TIP** *For more information on employment taxes, see Pub. 15 (Circular E).*

**Unemployment fund taxes.** As an employer, you may have to make payments to a state unemployment compensation fund or to a state disability benefit fund. Deduct these payments as taxes.

**Self-employment tax.** You can deduct part of your self-employment tax as a business expense in figuring your adjusted gross income. This deduction only affects your income tax. It does not affect your net earnings from self-employment or your self-employment tax.

To deduct the tax, enter on Schedule 1 (Form 1040), line 15, the amount shown on the

Deduction for one-half of self-employment tax line of Schedule SE (Form 1040).

For more information on self-employment tax, see Pub. 334.

**Additional Medicare Tax.** You may be required to pay Additional Medicare Tax on self-employment income. See Form 8959 and the Instructions for Form 8959 for more information on the Additional Medicare Tax.

## Other Taxes

The following are other taxes you can deduct if you incur them in the ordinary course of your trade or business.

**Excise taxes.** Generally, you can deduct as a business expense all excise taxes that are ordinary and necessary expenses of carrying on your trade or business. However, see *Fuel taxes*, later.

For more information on excise taxes, see Pub. 510.

**Franchise taxes.** You can deduct corporate franchise taxes as a business expense.

**Fuel taxes.** Generally, taxes on gasoline, diesel fuel, and other motor fuels that you use in your business are included as part of the cost of the fuel. Do not deduct these taxes as a separate item.

You may be entitled to a credit or refund for federal excise tax you paid on fuels used for certain purposes. For more information, see Pub. 510.

**Occupational taxes.** You can deduct as a business expense an occupational tax charged at a flat rate by a locality for the privilege of working or conducting a business in the locality.

**Personal property tax.** You can deduct any tax imposed by a state or local government on personal property used in your trade or business.

**Sales tax.** Any sales tax you pay on a service for your business, or on the purchase or use of property in your business is treated as part of the cost of the service or property. If the service or the cost or use of the property is a deductible business expense, you can deduct the tax as part of that service or cost. If the property is merchandise bought for resale, the sales tax is part of the cost of the merchandise. If the property is depreciable, add the sales tax to the basis for depreciation. For more information on basis, see Pub. 551.

**CAUTION** *Do not deduct state and local sales taxes imposed on the buyer that you must collect and pay over to the state or local government. Also, do not include these taxes in gross receipts or sales.*

# 6.

# Insurance

## Reminder

**Premium tax credit.** You may have to use the worksheets in Pub. 974 instead of the worksheet in this chapter. Use the worksheets in Pub. 974 if the insurance plan established, or considered to be established, under your business was obtained through the Health Insurance Marketplace and you are claiming the premium tax credit. See Pub. 974 for details.

## Introduction

You can generally deduct the ordinary and necessary cost of insurance as a business expense if it is for your trade, business, or profession. However, you may have to capitalize certain insurance costs under the uniform capitalization rules. For more information, see *Capitalized Premiums*, later.

### Topics
This chapter discusses:

- Deductible premiums
- Nondeductible premiums
- Capitalized premiums
- When to deduct premiums

### Useful Items
You may want to see:

#### Publication

- ❑ **15-B** Employer's Tax Guide to Fringe Benefits
- ❑ **525** Taxable and Nontaxable Income
- ❑ **538** Accounting Periods and Methods
- ❑ **547** Casualties, Disasters, and Thefts

#### Form (and Instructions)

- ❑ **1040** U.S. Individual Income Tax Return
- ❑ **1040-NR** U.S. Nonresident Alien Income Tax Return
- ❑ **Schedule 1 (Form 1040)** Additional Income and Adjustments to Income
- ❑ **Schedule A (Form 1040)** Itemized Deductions
- ❑ **Schedule C (Form 1040)** Profit or Loss From Business
- ❑ **Schedule F (Form 1040)** Profit or Loss From Farming
- ❑ **Schedule SE (Form 1040)** Self-Employment Tax
- ❑ **Schedule K-1 (Form 1065)** Partner's Share of Income, Deductions, Credits, etc.

- ❑ **2555** Foreign Earned Income
- ❑ **W-2** Wage and Tax Statement

See chapter 12 for information about getting publications and forms.

## Deductible Premiums

You can generally deduct premiums you pay for the following kinds of insurance related to your trade or business.

1. Insurance that covers fire, storm, theft, accident, or similar losses.

2. Credit insurance that covers losses from business bad debts.

3. Group hospitalization and medical insurance for employees, including long-term care insurance.

   a. If a partnership pays accident and health insurance premiums for its partners, it can generally deduct them as guaranteed payments to partners.

   b. If an S corporation pays accident and health insurance premiums for its more-than-2% shareholder-employees, it can generally deduct them, but must also include them in the shareholder's wages subject to federal income tax withholding. See Pub.15-B.

4. Liability insurance.

5. Malpractice insurance that covers your personal liability for professional negligence resulting in injury or damage to patients or clients.

6. Workers' compensation insurance set by state law that covers any claims for bodily injuries or job-related diseases suffered by employees in your business, regardless of fault.

   a. If a partnership pays workers' compensation premiums for its partners, it can generally deduct them as guaranteed payments to partners.

   b. If an S corporation pays workers' compensation premiums for its more-than-2% shareholder-employees, it can generally deduct them, but must also include them in the shareholder's wages.

7. Contributions to a state unemployment insurance fund are deductible as taxes if they are considered taxes under state law.

8. Overhead insurance that pays for business overhead expenses you have during long periods of disability caused by your injury or sickness.

9. Car and other vehicle insurance that covers vehicles used in your business for liability, damages, and other losses. If you operate a vehicle partly for personal use and partly for business use, deduct only the part of the insurance premium that applies to the business use of the vehicle. If you use the standard mileage rate to figure your car expenses, you can't deduct any car insurance premiums.

10. Life insurance covering your officers and employees if you aren't directly or indirectly a beneficiary under the contract.

11. Business interruption insurance that pays for lost profits if your business is shut down due to a fire or other cause.

## Self-Employed Health Insurance Deduction

You may be able to deduct the amount you paid for medical and dental insurance and qualified long-term care insurance for yourself, your spouse, and your dependents. The health insurance can cover your child who was under age 27 at the end of 2022, even if the child wasn't your dependent. A child includes your son, daughter, stepchild, adopted child, or foster child. A foster child is any child placed with you by an authorized placement agency or by judgment, decree, or other order of any court of competent jurisdiction.

One of the following statements must be true.

- You were self-employed and had a net profit for the year reported on Schedule C (Form 1040) or Schedule F (Form 1040).
- You were a partner with net earnings from self-employment for the year reported on Schedule K-1 (Form 1065), box 14, code A.
- You used one of the optional methods to figure your net earnings from self-employment on Schedule SE.
- You received wages in 2022 from an S corporation in which you were a more-than-2% shareholder. Health insurance premiums paid or reimbursed by the S corporation are shown as wages on Form W-2.

The insurance plan must be established, or considered to be established, as discussed in the following bullets, under your business.

- For self-employed individuals filing a Schedule C (Form 1040) or Schedule F (Form 1040), a policy can be either in the name of the business or in the name of the individual.
- For partners, a policy can be either in the name of the partnership or in the name of the partner. You can either pay the premiums yourself or the partnership can pay them and report the premium amounts on Schedule K-1 (Form 1065) as guaranteed payments to be included in your gross income. However, if the policy is in your name and you pay the premiums yourself, the partnership must reimburse you and report the premium amounts on Schedule K-1 (Form 1065) as guaranteed payments to be included in your gross income. Otherwise, the insurance plan won't be considered to be established under your business.
- For more-than-2% shareholders, a policy can be either in the name of the S corporation or in the name of the shareholder. You can either pay the premiums yourself or the S corporation can pay them and report the premium amounts on Form W-2 as wages to be included in your gross income. However, if the policy is in your name and

you pay the premiums yourself, the S corporation must reimburse you and report the premium amounts in box 1 of Form W-2 as wages to be included in your gross income. Otherwise, the insurance plan won't be considered to be established under your business.

Medicare premiums you voluntarily pay to obtain insurance in your name that is similar to qualifying private health insurance can be used to figure the deduction. Amounts paid for health insurance coverage from retirement plan distributions that were nontaxable because you are a retired public safety officer can't be used to figure the deduction.

You can claim the deduction for self-employed health insurance on Schedule 1 (Form 1040), line 17.

**Qualified long-term care insurance.** You can include premiums paid on a qualified long-term care insurance contract when figuring your deduction. But, for each person covered,

you can include only the smaller of the following amounts.

1. The amount of premiums paid for that person.
2. The amount shown below. Use the person's age at the end of the tax year.

    a. Age 40 or younger — $450
    b. Age 41 to 50 — $850
    c. Age 51 to 60 — $1,690
    d. Age 61 to 70 — $4,510
    e. Age 71 or older — $5,640

***Qualified long-term care insurance contract.*** A qualified long-term care insurance contract is an insurance contract that only provides coverage of qualified long-term care services. The contract must meet all the following requirements.
- It must be guaranteed renewable.
- It must provide that refunds, other than refunds on the death of the insured or complete surrender or cancellation of the contract, and dividends under the contract

may be used only to reduce future premiums or increase future benefits.
- It must not provide for a cash surrender value or other money that can be paid, assigned, pledged, or borrowed.
- It must generally not pay or reimburse expenses incurred for services or items that would be reimbursed under Medicare, except where Medicare is a secondary payer or the contract makes per diem or other periodic payments without regard to expenses.

***Qualified long-term care services.*** Qualified long-term care services are:
- Necessary diagnostic, preventive, therapeutic, curing, treating, mitigating, and rehabilitative services; and
- Maintenance or personal care services.

The services must be required by a chronically ill individual and prescribed by a licensed health care practitioner.

Worksheet 6-A. **Self-Employed Health Insurance Deduction Worksheet**     *Keep for Your Records*

**Caution.** You may have to use the worksheets in Pub. 974 instead of this worksheet if the insurance plan established, or considered to be established, under your business was obtained through the Health Insurance Marketplace and you are claiming the premium tax credit. See Pub. 974 for details.

**Note.** Use a separate worksheet for each trade or business under which an insurance plan is established.

1. Enter the total amount paid in 2022 for health insurance coverage established under your business (or the S corporation in which you were a more-than-2% shareholder) for 2022 for you, your spouse, and your dependents. Your insurance can also cover your child who was under age 27 at the end of 2022, even if the child was not your dependent. But **don't** include the following.
   - Amounts for any month you were eligible to participate in a health plan subsidized by your employer or your spouse's employer or the employer of either your dependent or your child who was under the age of 27 at the end of 2022.
   - Any amounts paid from retirement plan distributions that were nontaxable because you are a retired public safety officer.
   - Any payments for qualified long-term care insurance (see line 2) ...................... 1. _____
2. For coverage under a qualified long-term care insurance contract, enter for each person covered the **smaller** of (a) or (b).
   a) Total payments made for that person during the year.
   b) The amount shown below. Use the person's age at the end of the tax year.
      $450— if that person is age 40 or younger
      $850— if age 41 to 50
      $1,690— if age 51 to 60
      $4,510— if age 61 to 70
      $5,640— if age 71 or older
      Note. The amount of long-term care premiums that can be included as a medical expense is limited by the person's age. **Don't** include payments for any month you were eligible to participate in a long-term care insurance plan subsidized by your employer or your spouse's employer or the employer of either your dependent or your child who was under the age of 27 at the end of 2022. If more than one person is covered, figure separately the amount to enter for each person. Then enter the total of those amounts ..................... 2. _____
3. Add lines 1 and 2 ............................................................. 3. _____
4. Enter your net profit* and any other earned income** from the trade or business under which the insurance plan is established. Don't include Conservation Reserve Program payments exempt from self-employment tax. If the business is an S corporation, skip to line 11 ............... 4. _____
5. Enter the total of all net profits* from Schedule C (Form 1040), line 31; Schedule F (Form 1040), line 34; or Schedule K-1 (Form 1065), box 14, code A, plus any other income allocable to the profitable businesses. Don't include Conservation Reserve Program payments exempt from self-employment tax. See the Instructions for Schedule SE (Form 1040). **Don't** include any net losses shown on these schedules ............................................... 5. _____
6. Divide line 4 by line 5 ........................................................ 6. _____
7. Multiply Schedule 1 (Form 1040), line 15, deductible part of self-employment tax, by the percentage on line 6 ............................................................. 7. _____
8. Subtract line 7 from line 4 .................................................... 8. _____
9. Enter the amount, if any, from Schedule 1 (Form 1040), line 16, self-employed SEP, SIMPLE, and qualified plans, attributable to the same trade or business in which the insurance plan is established ................................................................. 9. _____
10. Subtract line 9 from line 8 ................................................... 10. _____
11. Enter your Medicare wages (box 5 of Form W-2) from an S corporation in which you are a more-than-2% shareholder and in which the insurance plan is established ................ 11. _____
12. Enter any amount from Form 2555, line 45, attributable to the amount entered on line 4 or 11 above ....................................................................... 12. _____
13. Subtract line 12 from line 10 or 11, whichever applies ......................... 13. _____
14. **Self-employed health insurance deduction.** Enter the **smaller** of line 3 or line 13 here and on Schedule 1 (Form 1040), line 17. **Don't** include this amount when figuring any medical expense deduction on Schedule A (Form 1040) ....................................... 14. _____

\* If you used either optional method to figure your net earnings from self-employment from any business, don't enter your net profit from the business. Instead, enter the amount attributable to that business from Schedule SE (Form 1040), Part I, line 4b.
\*\* **Earned Income** includes net earnings and gains from the sale, transfer, or licensing of property you created. However, it doesn't include capital gain income.

**Chronically ill individual.** A chronically ill individual is a person who has been certified as one of the following.
- An individual who has been unable, due to loss of functional capacity for at least 90 days, to perform at least two activities of daily living without substantial assistance from another individual. Activities of daily living are eating, toileting, transferring

(general mobility), bathing, dressing, and continence.
- An individual who requires substantial supervision to be protected from threats to health and safety due to severe cognitive impairment.

The certification must have been made by a licensed health care practitioner within the previous 12 months.

**Benefits received.** For information on excluding benefits you receive from a long-term care contract from gross income, see Pub. 525.

**Other coverage.** You can't take the deduction for any month you were eligible to participate in any employer (including your spouse's) subsidized health plan at any time during that month, even if you didn't actually participate. In addition, if you were eligible for any month or part of a month to participate in any subsidized health plan maintained by the employer of either your dependent or your child who was under age 27 at the end of 2022, don't use amounts paid for coverage for that month to figure the deduction.

These rules are applied separately to plans that provide long-term care insurance and plans that don't provide long-term care insurance. However, any medical insurance payments not deductible on Schedule 1 (Form 1040), line 17, can be included as medical expenses on Schedule A (Form 1040) if you itemize deductions.

**Effect on itemized deductions.** Subtract the health insurance deduction from your medical insurance when figuring medical expenses on Schedule A (Form 1040) if you itemize deductions.

**Effect on self-employment tax.** You can't subtract the self-employed health insurance deduction when figuring net earnings for your self-employment tax from the business under which the insurance plan is established, or considered to be established, as discussed earlier. For more information, see Schedule SE (Form 1040).

**How to figure the deduction.** Generally, you can use the worksheet in the Form 1040 instructions to figure your deduction. However, if any of the following apply, you must use Worksheet 6-A in this chapter.
- You had more than one source of income subject to self-employment tax.
- You file Form 2555.
- You are using amounts paid for qualified long-term care insurance to figure the deduction.

*More than one health plan and business.* If you have more than one health plan during the year and each plan is established under a different business, you must use separate worksheets (Worksheet 6-A) to figure each plan's net earnings limit. Include the premium you paid under each plan on line 1 or line 2 of that separate worksheet and your net profit (or wages) from that business on line 4 (or line 11). For a plan that provides long-term care insurance, the total of the amounts entered for each person on line 2 of all worksheets can't be more than the appropriate limit shown on line 2 for that person.

## Nondeductible Premiums

You can't deduct premiums on the following kinds of insurance.

1. Self-insurance reserve funds. You can't deduct amounts credited to a reserve set up for self-insurance. This applies even if you can't get business insurance coverage for certain business risks. However, your actual losses may be deductible. See Pub. 547.

2. Loss of earnings. You can't deduct premiums for a policy that pays for lost earnings due to sickness or disability. However, see

the discussion on overhead insurance, item (8), under *Deductible Premiums*, earlier.

3. Certain life insurance and annuities.

    a. For contracts issued before June 9, 1997, you can't deduct the premiums on a life insurance policy covering you, an employee, or any person with a financial interest in your business if you are directly or indirectly a beneficiary of the policy. You are included among possible beneficiaries of the policy if the policy owner is obligated to repay a loan from you using the proceeds of the policy. A person has a financial interest in your business if the person is an owner or part owner of the business or has lent money to the business.

    b. For contracts issued after June 8, 1997, you generally can't deduct the premiums on any life insurance policy, endowment contract, or annuity contract if you are directly or indirectly a beneficiary. The disallowance applies without regard to whom the policy covers.

    c. Partners. If, as a partner in a partnership, you take out an insurance policy on your own life and name your partners as beneficiaries to induce them to retain their investments in the partnership, you are considered a beneficiary. You can't deduct the insurance premiums.

4. Insurance to secure a loan. If you take out a policy on your life or on the life of another person with a financial interest in your business to get or protect a business loan, you can't deduct the premiums as a business expense. Nor can you deduct the premiums as interest on business loans or as an expense of financing loans. In the event of death, the proceeds of the policy are generally not taxed as income even if they are used to liquidate the debt.

## Capitalized Premiums

Under the uniform capitalization rules, you must capitalize the direct costs and part of the indirect costs for certain production or resale activities. Include these costs in the basis of property you produce or acquire for resale, rather than claiming them as a current deduction. You recover the costs through depreciation, amortization, or cost of goods sold when you use, sell, or otherwise dispose of the property.

Indirect costs include premiums for insurance on your plant or facility, machinery, equipment, materials, property produced, or property acquired for resale.

**Uniform capitalization rules.** You may be subject to the uniform capitalization rules if you do any of the following, unless the property is produced for your use other than in a business or an activity carried on for profit.

1. Produce real property or tangible personal property. For this purpose, tangible personal property includes a film, sound recording, videotape, book, or similar property.

2. Acquire property for resale.

However, these rules don't apply to the following property.

1. Personal property you acquire for resale if your average annual gross receipts are $27 million or less for the 3 prior tax years.

2. Property you produce if you meet either of the following conditions.

    a. Your indirect costs of producing the property are $200,000 or less.

    b. You use the cash method of accounting and don't account for inventories.

**More information.** For more information on these rules, see *Uniform Capitalization Rules* in Pub. 538 and the regulations under section 263A.

## When To Deduct Premiums

You can usually deduct insurance premiums in the tax year to which they apply.

**Cash method.** If you use the cash method of accounting, you generally deduct insurance premiums in the tax year you actually paid them, even if you incurred them in an earlier year. However, see *Prepayment*, later.

**Accrual method.** If you use an accrual method of accounting, you can't deduct insurance premiums before the tax year in which you incur a liability for them. In addition, you can't deduct insurance premiums before the tax year in which you actually pay them (unless the exception for recurring items applies). For more information about the accrual method of accounting, see chapter 1. For information about the exception for recurring items, see Pub. 538.

**Prepayment.** You can't deduct expenses in advance, even if you pay them in advance. This rule applies to any expense paid far enough in advance to, in effect, create an asset with a useful life extending substantially beyond the end of the current tax year.

Expenses such as insurance are generally allocable to a period of time. You can deduct insurance expenses for the year to which they are allocable.

*Example.* In 2022, you signed a 3-year insurance contract. Even though you paid the premiums for 2022, 2023, and 2024 when you signed the contract, you can only deduct the premium for 2022 on your 2022 tax return. You can deduct in 2023 and 2024 the premiums allocable to those years.

**Dividends received.** If you receive dividends from business insurance and you deducted the premiums in prior years, at least part of the dividends are generally income. For more information, see *Recovery of amount deducted (tax benefit rule)* in chapter 1 under *How Much Can I Deduct*.

# 7.

# Costs You Can Deduct or Capitalize

## What's New

**Research and experimental costs.** Beginning January 1, 2022, research and experimental expenditures, generally, have to be amortized over a 5-year period. A business cannot elect to deduct their total research expenses in the current year. See Research and Experimental Costs in chapter 7 and chapter 8.

## Introduction

This chapter discusses costs you can elect to deduct or capitalize.

You generally deduct a cost as a current business expense by subtracting it from your income in either the year you incur it or the year you pay it.

If you capitalize a cost, you may be able to recover it over a period of years through periodic deductions for amortization, depletion, or depreciation. When you capitalize a cost, you add it to the basis of property to which it relates.

A partnership, corporation, estate, or trust makes the election to deduct or capitalize the costs discussed in this chapter except for exploration costs for mineral deposits. Each individual partner, shareholder, or beneficiary elects whether to deduct or capitalize exploration costs.

⚠️ **CAUTION** *Individuals, estates, and trusts may be subject to AMT if they deduct certain research and experimental, intangible drilling, exploration, development, circulation, or business organizational costs.*

For more information on the AMT, see the Instructions for Form 6251 and the Instructions for Schedule I (Form 1041).

## Topics

This chapter discusses:

- Carrying charges
- Research and experimental costs
- Intangible drilling costs
- Exploration costs
- Development costs
- Circulation costs
- Business startup and organizational costs
- Reforestation costs

- Retired asset removal costs
- Barrier removal costs
- Film and television production costs
- Repair and maintenance costs

## Useful Items

You may want to see:

**Publication**

☐ **544** Sales and Other Dispositions of Assets

**Form (and Instructions)**

☐ **Schedule C (Form 1040)** Profit or Loss From Business

☐ **3468** Investment Credit

☐ **6765** Credit for Increasing Research Activities

☐ **8826** Disabled Access Credit

☐ **T (Timber)** Forest Activities Schedule

See chapter 12 for information about getting publications and forms.

## Carrying Charges

Carrying charges include the taxes and interest you pay to carry or develop real property or to carry, transport, or install personal property. Certain carrying charges must be capitalized under the uniform capitalization rules. (For information on capitalization of interest, see chapter 4.) You can elect to capitalize carrying charges not subject to the uniform capitalization rules, but only if they are otherwise deductible.

You can elect to capitalize carrying charges separately for each project you have and for each type of carrying charge. Your election is good for only 1 year for unimproved and unproductive real property. You must decide whether to capitalize carrying charges each year the property remains unimproved and unproductive. For other real property, your election to capitalize carrying charges remains in effect until construction or development is completed. For personal property, your election is effective until the date you install or first use it, whichever is later.

**How to make the election.** To make the election to capitalize a carrying charge, attach a statement to your original tax return for the year the election is to be effective indicating which charges you are electing to capitalize. However, if you timely filed your return for the year without making the election, you can still make the election by filing an amended return within 6 months of the due date of the return (excluding extensions). Attach the statement to the amended return and write "Filed pursuant to section 301.9100-2" on the statement. File the amended return at the same address you filed the original return.

## Research and Experimental Costs

Research or experimental expenditures paid or incurred in tax years beginning after December

31, 2021, must be charged to a separate specified research or experimental capital account and amortized ratably over a 5-year period or a 15-year period for foreign research. The expenses cannot be deducted in full in the current year.

For information on amortizing these costs, see *Research and Experimental Costs* in chapter 8.

**Research and experimental costs defined.** Research or experimental expenditures, as used in section 174, are research and development costs, including costs incident to research in the experimental or laboratory sense, you incur in connection with your trade or business for activities intended to provide information that would eliminate uncertainty about the development or improvement of a product. Uncertainty exists if the information available to you does not establish how to develop or improve a product or the appropriate design of a product. Whether costs qualify as research and experimental expenditures depends on the nature of the activity to which the costs relate rather than on the nature of the product or improvement being developed or the level of technological advancement.

The costs of obtaining a patent, including attorneys' fees paid or incurred in making and perfecting a patent application, are research and experimental expenditures. However, costs paid or incurred to obtain another's patent are not research and experimental expenditures.

The costs related to developing software are treated as research and experimental expenditures.

**Product.** The term "product" includes any of the following items.

- Formula.
- Invention.
- Patent.
- Pilot model.
- Process.
- Technique.
- Property similar to the items listed above.

It also includes products used by you in your trade or business or held for sale, lease, or license.

**Costs not included.** Research and experimental expenditures do not include expenses for any of the following activities.

- Advertising or promotions.
- Consumer surveys.
- Efficiency surveys.
- Land, including acquisition and improvement costs for land.
- Acquisition and improvement costs of depreciable property.
- Exploration costs for the purpose of ascertaining the existence, location, extent, or quality of any deposit of ore or other mineral.
- Management studies.
- Quality control testing.
- Research in connection with literary, historical, or similar projects.
- The acquisition of another's patent, model, production, or process.

**Research credit.** If you pay or incur costs that may be treated as research or experimental costs, you may be able to take the research credit. For more information, see Form 6765 and its instructions.

**Payroll tax credit.** The payroll tax credit is an annual election made by a qualified small business specifying the amount of research credit, not to exceed $250,000, that may be used against the employer portion of social security liability. The credit is the smallest of the current year research credit, an elected amount not to exceed $250,000, or the general business credit carryforward for the tax year (before the application of the payroll tax credit election for the tax year). The election must be made on or before the due date of the originally filed return (including extensions). An election cannot be made for a tax year if an election was made for 5 or more preceding tax years. The election made by a partnership or S corporation is made at the entity level.

A qualified small business that elects to claim the payroll tax credit will claim the payroll tax credit against the employer's portion of social security tax on its employment tax return for the first quarter that begins after it files the return reflecting the payroll tax election. For more information, see the Instructions for Form 6765.

## Intangible Drilling Costs

The costs of developing oil, gas, or geothermal wells are ordinarily capital expenditures. You can usually recover them through depreciation or depletion. However, you can elect to deduct intangible drilling costs (IDCs) as a current business expense. These are certain drilling and development costs for wells in the United States in which you hold an operating or working interest. You can deduct only costs for drilling or preparing a well for the production of oil, gas, or geothermal steam or hot water.

You can elect to deduct only the costs of items with no salvage value. These include wages, fuel, repairs, hauling, and supplies related to drilling wells and preparing them for production. Your cost for any drilling or development work done by contractors under any form of contract is also an IDC. However, see *Amounts paid to contractor that must be capitalized*, later.

You can also elect to deduct the cost of drilling exploratory bore holes to determine the location and delineation of offshore hydrocarbon deposits if the shaft is capable of conducting hydrocarbons to the surface on completion. It does not matter whether there is any intent to produce hydrocarbons.

If you do not elect to deduct your IDCs as a current business expense, you can elect to deduct them over the 60-month period beginning with the month they were paid or incurred.

**Amounts paid to contractor that must be capitalized.** Amounts paid to a contractor must be capitalized if they are either:
- Amounts properly allocable to the cost of depreciable property, or
- Amounts paid only out of production or proceeds from production if these amounts are depletable income to the recipient.

**How to make the election.** You elect to deduct IDCs as a current business expense by taking the deduction on your income tax return for the first tax year you have eligible costs. No formal statement is required. If you file Schedule C (Form 1040), enter these costs under "Other expenses."

For oil and gas wells, your election is binding for the year it is made and for all later years. For geothermal wells, your election can be revoked by the filing of an amended return on which you do not take the deduction. You can file the amended return for the year up to the normal time of expiration for filing a claim for credit or refund, generally, within 3 years after the date you filed the original return or within 2 years after the date you paid the tax, whichever is later.

**Energy credit for costs of geothermal wells.** If you capitalize the drilling and development costs of geothermal wells that you place in service during the tax year, you may be able to claim a business energy credit. See the Instructions for Form 3468 for more information.

**Nonproductive well.** If you capitalize your IDCs, you have another option if the well is nonproductive. You can deduct the IDCs of the nonproductive well as an ordinary loss. You must indicate and clearly state your election on your tax return for the year the well is completed. Once made, the election for oil and gas is binding for all later years. You can revoke your election for a geothermal well by filing an amended return that does not claim the loss.

**Costs incurred outside the United States.** You cannot deduct as a current business expense all the IDCs paid or incurred for an oil, gas, or geothermal well located outside the United States. However, you can elect to include the costs in the adjusted basis of the well to figure depletion or depreciation. If you do not make this election, you can deduct the costs over the 10-year period beginning with the tax year in which you paid or incurred them. These rules do not apply to a nonproductive well.

## Exploration Costs

The costs of determining the existence, location, extent, or quality of any mineral deposit are ordinarily capital expenditures if the costs lead to the development of a mine. You recover these costs through depletion as the mineral is removed from the ground. However, you can elect to deduct domestic exploration costs paid or incurred before the beginning of the development stage of the mine (except those for oil and gas wells).

**How to make the election.** You elect to deduct exploration costs by taking the deduction on your income tax return, or on an amended income tax return, for the first tax year for which you wish to deduct the costs paid or incurred during the tax year. Your return must adequately describe and identify each property or mine, and clearly state how much is being deducted for each one. The election applies to the tax year you make this election and all later years.

*Partnerships and S corporations.* Each partner, not the partnership, elects whether to capitalize or to deduct that partner's share of exploration costs. Each shareholder, not the S corporation, elects whether to capitalize or to deduct that shareholder's share of exploration costs.

**Reduced corporate deductions for exploration costs.** A corporation (other than an S corporation) can deduct only 70% of its domestic exploration costs. It must capitalize the remaining 30% of costs and amortize them over the 60-month period starting with the month the exploration costs are paid or incurred. A corporation may also elect to capitalize and amortize mining exploration costs over a 10-year period. For more information on this method of amortization, see section 59(e).

The 30% that the corporation capitalizes cannot be added to its basis in the property to figure cost depletion. However, the amount amortized is treated as additional depreciation and is subject to recapture as ordinary income on a disposition of the property. See *Section 1250 Property* under *Depreciation Recapture* in chapter 3 of Pub. 544.

These rules also apply to the deduction of development costs by corporations. See *Development Costs*, later.

**Recapture of exploration expenses.** When your mine reaches the producing stage, you must recapture any exploration costs you elected to deduct. Use either of the following methods.

Method 1—Include the deducted costs in gross income for the tax year the mine reaches the producing stage. Your election must be clearly indicated on the return. Increase your adjusted basis in the mine by the amount included in income. Generally, you must elect this recapture method by the due date (including extensions) of your return. However, if you timely filed your return for the year without making the election, you can still make the election by filing an amended return within 6 months of the due date of the return (excluding extensions). Make the election on your amended return and write "Filed pursuant to section 301.9100-2" on the form where you are including the income. File the amended return at the same address you filed the original return.

Method 2—Do not claim any depletion deduction for the tax year the mine reaches the producing stage and any later tax years until the depletion you would have deducted equals the exploration costs you deducted.

You must also recapture deducted exploration costs if you receive a bonus or royalty from mine property before it reaches the producing stage. Do not claim any depletion deduction for the tax year you receive the bonus or royalty and any later tax years until the depletion you would have deducted equals the exploration costs you deducted.

Generally, if you dispose of the mine before you have fully recaptured the exploration costs you deducted, recapture the balance by treating all or part of your gain as ordinary income.

Under these circumstances, you generally treat as ordinary income all of your gain if it is less than your adjusted exploration costs with respect to the mine. If your gain is more than your adjusted exploration costs, treat as ordinary income only a part of your gain, up to the amount of your adjusted exploration costs.

**Foreign exploration costs.** If you pay or incur exploration costs for a mine or other natural deposit located outside the United States, you cannot deduct all the costs in the current year. You can elect to include the costs (other than for an oil, gas, or geothermal well) in the adjusted basis of the mineral property to figure cost depletion. (Cost depletion is discussed in chapter 9.) If you do not make this election, you must deduct the costs over the 10-year period beginning with the tax year in which you pay or incur them. These rules also apply to foreign development costs.

## Development Costs

You can deduct costs paid or incurred during the tax year for developing a mine or any other natural deposit (other than an oil or gas well) located in the United States. These costs must be paid or incurred after the discovery of ores or minerals in commercially marketable quantities. Development costs also include depreciation on improvements used in the development of ores or minerals and costs incurred for you by a contractor. Development costs do not include the costs for the acquisition or improvement of depreciable property.

Instead of deducting development costs in the year paid or incurred, you can elect to treat the costs as deferred expenses and deduct them ratably as the units of produced ores or minerals benefited by the expenses are sold. This election applies each tax year to expenses paid or incurred in that year. Once made, the election is binding for the year and cannot be revoked for any reason.

**How to make the election.** The election to deduct development costs ratably as the ores or minerals are sold must be made for each mine or other natural deposit by a clear indication on your return or by a statement filed with the IRS office where you file your return. Generally, you must make the election by the due date of the return (including extensions). However, if you timely filed your return for the year without making the election, you can still make the election by filing an amended return within 6 months of the due date of the return (excluding extensions). Clearly indicate the election on your amended return and write "Filed pursuant to section 301.9100-2." File the amended return at the same address you filed the original return.

**Foreign development costs.** The rules discussed earlier for *Foreign exploration costs* apply to foreign development costs.

**Reduced corporate deductions for development costs.** The rules discussed earlier for *Reduced corporate deductions for exploration costs* also apply to corporate deductions for development costs.

## Circulation Costs

A publisher can deduct as a current business expense the costs of establishing, maintaining, or increasing the circulation of a newspaper, magazine, or other periodical. For example, a publisher can deduct the cost of hiring extra employees for a limited time to get new subscriptions through telephone calls. Circulation costs may be deducted even if they would normally be capitalized.

This rule does not apply to the following costs that must be capitalized.
- The purchase of land or depreciable property.
- The acquisition of circulation through the purchase of any part of the business of another publisher of a newspaper, magazine, or other periodical, including the purchase of another publisher's list of subscribers.

**Other treatment of circulation costs.** If you do not want to deduct circulation costs as a current business expense, you can elect one of the following ways to recover these costs.
- Capitalize all circulation costs that are properly chargeable to a capital account (see chapter 1).
- Amortize circulation costs over the 3-year period beginning with the tax year they were paid or incurred.

**How to make the election.** You elect to capitalize circulation costs by attaching a statement to your return for the first tax year the election applies. Your election is binding for the year it is made and for all later years, unless you get IRS approval to revoke it.

## Business Startup and Organizational Costs

Business startup and organizational costs are generally capital expenditures. However, you can elect to deduct up to $5,000 of business startup and $5,000 of organizational costs paid or incurred after October 22, 2004. The $5,000 deduction is reduced by the amount your total startup or organizational costs exceed $50,000. Any remaining costs must be amortized. For information about amortizing startup and organizational costs, see chapter 8.

Startup costs include any amounts paid or incurred in connection with creating an active trade or business or investigating the creation or acquisition of an active trade or business. Organizational costs include the costs of creating a corporation or partnership.

**How to make the election.** You elect to deduct the startup or organizational costs by claiming the deduction on your income tax return (filed by the due date including extensions) for the tax year in which the active trade or business begins. For costs paid or incurred after September 8, 2008, you are not required to attach a statement to your return to elect to deduct such costs. However, for startup or organizational costs paid or incurred before September 9, 2008, you may be required to at-

tach a statement to your return to elect to deduct such costs. If you timely filed your return for the year without making the election, you can still make the election by filing an amended return within 6 months of the due date of the return (excluding extensions). Clearly indicate the election on your amended return and write "Filed pursuant to section 301.9100-2."

File the amended return at the same address you filed the original return. The election applies when figuring taxable income for the current tax year and all subsequent years. Once made, the election is irrevocable. For more information on startup and organizational costs, see chapter 8.

## Reforestation Costs

Reforestation costs are generally capital expenditures. However, you can elect to deduct up to $10,000 ($5,000 if married filing separately; $0 for a trust) of qualifying reforestation costs paid or incurred after October 22, 2004, for each qualified timber property. The remaining costs can be amortized over an 84-month period. For information about amortizing reforestation costs, see chapter 8.

Qualifying reforestation costs are the direct costs of planting or seeding for forestation or reforestation. Qualified timber property is property that contains trees in significant commercial quantities. See chapter 8 for more information on qualifying reforestation costs and qualified timber property.

If you elect to deduct qualified reforestation costs, create and maintain separate timber accounts for each qualified timber property and include all reforestation costs and the dates each was applied. Do not include this qualified timber property in any account (for example, depletion block) for which depletion is allowed.

**How to make the election.** You elect to deduct qualifying reforestation costs by claiming the deduction on your timely filed income tax return (including extensions) for the tax year the expenses were paid or incurred. If Form T (Timber) is required, complete Part IV of the form. If Form T (Timber) is not required, attach a statement containing the following information for each qualified timber property for which an election is being made.
- The unique stand identification numbers.
- The total number of acres reforested during the tax year.
- The nature of the reforestation treatments.
- The total amounts of qualified reforestation expenditures eligible to be amortized or deducted.

If you timely filed your return for the year without making the election, you can still make the election by filing an amended return within 6 months of the due date of the return (excluding extensions). Clearly indicate the election on your amended return and write "Filed pursuant to section 301.9100-2." File the amended return at the same address you filed the original return. The election applies when figuring taxable income for the current tax year and all subsequent years.

For additional information on reforestation costs, see chapter 8.

**Recapture.** This deduction may have to be recaptured as ordinary income under section 1245 when you sell or otherwise dispose of the property that would have received an addition to basis if you had not elected to deduct the expenditure. For more information on recapturing the deduction, see *Depreciation Recapture* in Pub. 544.

## Retired Asset Removal Costs

If you retire and remove a depreciable asset in connection with the installation or production of a replacement asset, you can deduct the costs of removing the retired asset. However, if you replace a component (part) of a depreciable asset, capitalize the removal costs if the replacement is an improvement and deduct the costs if the replacement is a repair.

## Barrier Removal Costs

The cost of an improvement to a business asset is normally a capital expense. However, you can elect to deduct the costs of making a facility or public transportation vehicle more accessible to and usable by those who are disabled or elderly. You must own or lease the facility or vehicle for use in connection with your trade or business.

A facility is all or any part of buildings, structures, equipment, roads, walks, parking lots, or similar real or personal property. A public transportation vehicle is a vehicle, such as a bus or railroad car, that provides transportation service to the public (including service for your customers, even if you are not in the business of providing transportation services).

You cannot deduct any costs that you paid or incurred to completely renovate or build a facility or public transportation vehicle or to replace depreciable property in the normal course of business.

**Deduction limit.** The most you can deduct as a cost of removing barriers to the disabled and the elderly for any tax year is $15,000. However, you can add any costs over this limit to the basis of the property and depreciate these excess costs.

**Partners and partnerships.** The $15,000 limit applies to a partnership and also to each partner in the partnership. A partner can allocate the $15,000 limit in any manner among the partner's individually incurred costs and the partner's distributive share of partnership costs. If the partner cannot deduct the entire share of partnership costs, the partnership can add any costs not deducted to the basis of the improved property.

A partnership must be able to show that any amount added to basis was not deducted by the partner and that it was over a partner's $15,000 limit (as determined by the partner). If the partnership cannot show this, it is presumed

that the partner was able to deduct the distributive share of the partnership's costs in full.

***Example.*** Emilio Azul's distributive share of ABC partnership's deductible expenses for the removal of architectural barriers was $14,000. Emilio had $12,000 of similar expenses in his sole proprietorship. He elected to deduct $7,000 of them. Emilio allocated the remaining $8,000 of the $15,000 limit to his share of ABC's expenses. Emilio can add the excess $5,000 of his own expenses to the basis of the property used in his business. Also, if ABC can show that Emilio could not deduct $6,000 ($14,000 – $8,000) of his share of the partnership's expenses because of how Emilio applied the limit, ABC can add $6,000 to the basis of its property.

**Qualification standards.** You can deduct your costs as a current expense only if the barrier removal meets the guidelines and requirements issued by the Architectural and Transportation Barriers Compliance Board under the Americans with Disabilities Act (ADA) of 1990. You can view the ADA at *ADA.gov/pubs/ada.htm*.

The following is a list of some architectural barrier removal costs that can be deducted.
- Ground and floor surfaces.
- Walks.
- Parking lots.
- Ramps.
- Entrances.
- Doors and doorways.
- Stairs.
- Floors.
- Toilet rooms.
- Water fountains.
- Public telephones.
- Elevators.
- Controls.
- Signage.
- Alarms.
- Protruding objects.
- Symbols of accessibility.

You can find the ADA guidelines and requirements for architectural barrier removal at *USDOJ.gov/crt/ada/reg3a.html*.

The costs for removal of transportation barriers from rail facilities, buses, and rapid and light rail vehicles are deductible. You can find the guidelines and requirements for transportation barrier removal at *transit.dot.gov*.

Also, you can access the ADA website at *ADA.gov* for additional information.

***Other barrier removals.*** To be deductible, expenses of removing any barrier not covered by the above standards must meet all three of the following tests.

1. The removed barrier must be a substantial barrier to access or use of a facility or public transportation vehicle by persons who have a disability or are elderly.

2. The removed barrier must have been a barrier for at least one major group of persons who have a disability or are elderly (such as people who are blind, deaf, or wheelchair users).

3. The barrier must be removed without creating any new barrier that significantly impairs access to or use of the facility or vehicle by a major group of persons who have a disability or are elderly.

**How to make the election.** If you elect to deduct your costs for removing barriers to the disabled or the elderly, claim the deduction on your income tax return (partnership return for partnerships) for the tax year the expenses were paid or incurred. Identify the deduction as a separate item. The election applies to all the qualifying costs you have during the year, up to the $15,000 limit. If you make this election, you must maintain adequate records to support your deduction.

For your election to be valid, you must generally file your return by its due date, including extensions. However, if you timely filed your return for the year without making the election, you can still make the election by filing an amended return within 6 months of the due date of the return (excluding extensions). Clearly indicate the election on your amended return and write "Filed pursuant to section 301.9100-2." File the amended return at the same address you filed the original return. Your election is irrevocable after the due date, including extensions, of your return.

**Disabled access credit.** If you make your business accessible to persons with disabilities and your business is an eligible small business, you may be able to claim the disabled access credit. If you choose to claim the credit, you must reduce the amount you deduct or capitalize by the amount of the credit.

For more information, see Form 8826.

## Film, Television, and Live Theatrical Production Costs

Film, television, and theatrical production costs are generally capital expenses. However, you can elect to deduct certain costs of a qualified film, television, or live theatrical production commencing before January 1, 2026 (after December 31, 2015, and before January 1, 2026, for a live theatrical production), if the aggregate cost of the production doesn't exceed $15 million. There is a higher dollar limitation for productions in certain areas. The deduction is subject to recapture under section 1245 if the election is voluntarily revoked or the production fails to meet the requirements for the deduction. For more information, see section 181 and the related regulations.

Certain qualified film, television, or live theatrical productions acquired and placed in service after September 27, 2017, may be eligible for the special depreciation allowance under section 168(k). For more information, see Pub. 946, How To Depreciate Property.

**Note.** No other depreciation or amortization deduction is allowed for costs of qualified film or television production or any qualified live theatrical production if an election is made to deduct such costs.

## Repair and Maintenance Costs

Generally, you can deduct amounts paid for repairs and maintenance to tangible property if the amounts paid are not otherwise required to be capitalized. However, you may elect to capitalize amounts paid for repair and maintenance consistent with the treatment on your books and records. If you make this election, it applies to all amounts paid for repair and maintenance to tangible property that you treat as capital expenditures on your books and records for the tax year.

**How to make the election.** To make the election to treat repairs and maintenance as capital expenditures, attach a statement titled "Section 1.263(a)-3(n) Election" to your timely filed return (including extensions). For more information on what to include in the statement, see Regulations section 1.263(a)-3(n). If you timely filed your return without making the election, you can still make the election by filing an amended return within 6 months of the due date of the return (excluding extensions). Attach the statement to the amended return and write "Filed pursuant to section 301.9100-2" on the statement. File the amended return at the same address you filed the original return.

# 8.

# Amortization

## What's New

**Amortization of research and experimental expenditures.** Specified research or experimental costs paid or incurred in tax years beginning after 2021 must be capitalized and amortized ratably over a 5-year period (15-year period for any expenditures related to foreign research). See *Research and Experimental Costs*, later.

## Introduction

Amortization is a method of recovering (deducting) certain capital costs over a fixed period of time. It is similar to the straight line method of depreciation.

The various amortizable costs covered in this chapter are included in the list below. However, this chapter doesn't discuss amortization of bond premium. For information on that topic, see chapter 3 of Pub. 550, Investment Expenses.

## Topics
This chapter discusses:

- Deducting amortization
- Amortizing costs of starting a business
- Amortizing costs of getting a lease
- Amortizing costs of section 197 intangibles
- Amortizing reforestation costs
- Amortizing costs of geological and geophysical costs
- Amortizing costs of pollution control facilities
- Amortizing costs of research and experimentation
- Amortizing costs of certain tax preferences

## Useful Items
You may want to see:

### Publication

- ☐ **544** Sales and Other Dispositions of Assets
- ☐ **550** Investment Income and Expenses
- ☐ **946** How To Depreciate Property

### Form (and Instructions)

- ☐ **3115** Application for Change in Accounting Method
- ☐ **4562** Depreciation and Amortization
- ☐ **6251** Alternative Minimum Tax—Individuals

See chapter 12 for information about getting publications and forms.

## How To Deduct Amortization

To deduct amortization that begins during the current tax year, complete Part VI of Form 4562 and attach it to your income tax return.

To report amortization from previous years, in addition to amortization that begins in the current year, list on Form 4562 each item separately. For example, in 2021, you began to amortize a lease. In 2022, you began to amortize a second lease. Report amortization from the new lease on line 42 of your 2022 Form 4562. Report amortization from the 2021 lease on line 43 of your 2022 Form 4562.

If you don't have any new amortizable expenses for the current year, you aren't required to complete Form 4562 (unless you are claiming depreciation). Report the current year's deduction for amortization that began in a prior year directly on the "Other deduction" or "Other expense" line of your return.

## Starting a Business

When you start a business, treat all eligible costs you incur before you begin operating the business as capital expenditures that are part of your basis in the business. Generally, you recover costs for particular assets through depreciation deductions. However, you generally can't recover other costs until you sell the business or otherwise go out of business. For a discussion on how to treat these costs, see *If your attempt to go into business is unsuccessful* under *Capital Expenses* in chapter 1.

For costs paid or incurred after September 8, 2008, you can deduct a limited amount of startup and organizational costs. The costs that aren't deducted currently can be amortized ratably over a 180-month period. The amortization period starts with the month you begin operating your active trade or business. You aren't required to attach a statement to make this election. You can choose to forgo this election by affirmatively electing to capitalize your startup costs on your income tax return filed by the due date (including extensions) for the tax year in which the active trade or business begins. Once made, the election to either amortize or capitalize startup costs is irrevocable and applies to all startup costs that are related to your trade or business. See Regulations sections 1.195-1, 1.248-1, and 1.709-1.

For costs paid or incurred after October 22, 2004, and before September 9, 2008, you can elect to deduct a limited amount of business startup and organizational costs in the year your active trade or business begins. Any costs not deducted can be amortized ratably over a 180-month period, beginning with the month you begin business. If the election is made, you must attach any statement required by Regulations sections 1.195-1(b), 1.248-1(c), and 1.709-1(c), as in effect before September 9, 2008.

**Note.** You can apply the provisions of Regulations sections 1.195-1, 1.248-1, and 1.709-1 to all business startup and organizational costs paid or incurred after October 22, 2004, provided the period of limitations on assessment hasn't expired for the year of the election. Otherwise, for business startup and organizational costs paid or incurred after October 22, 2004, and before September 9, 2008, the provisions under Regulations sections 1.195-1(b), 1.248-1(c), and 1.709-1(c), as in effect before September 9, 2008, will apply.

For costs paid or incurred before October 23, 2004, you can elect to amortize business startup and organizational costs over an amortization period of 60 months or more. See *How To Make the Election*, later.

The cost must qualify as one of the following.

- A business startup cost.
- An organizational cost for a corporation.
- An organizational cost for a partnership.

## Business Startup Costs

Startup costs are amounts paid or incurred for **(a)** creating an active trade or business, or **(b)** investigating the creation or acquisition of an active trade or business. Startup costs include amounts paid or incurred in connection with an existing activity engaged in for profit, and for the production of income in anticipation of the activity becoming an active trade or business.

**Qualifying costs.** A startup cost is amortizable if it meets both of the following tests.
- It is a cost you could deduct if you paid or incurred it to operate an existing active trade or business (in the same field as the one you entered into).
- It is a cost you pay or incur before the day your active trade or business begins.

Startup costs include amounts paid for the following.
- An analysis or survey of potential markets, products, labor supply, transportation facilities, etc.
- Advertisements for the opening of the business.
- Salaries and wages for employees who are being trained and their instructors.
- Travel and other necessary costs for securing prospective distributors, suppliers, or customers.
- Salaries and fees for executives and consultants, or for similar professional services.

**Nonqualifying costs.** Startup costs don't include deductible interest, taxes, or research and experimental costs. See *Research and Experimental Costs*, later.

**Purchasing an active trade or business.** Amortizable startup costs for purchasing an active trade or business include only investigative costs incurred in the course of a general search for or preliminary investigation of the business. These are costs that help you decide whether to purchase a business. Costs you incur in an attempt to purchase a specific business are capital expenses that you can't amortize.

*Example.* On June 1, you hired an accounting firm and a law firm to assist you in the potential purchase of XYZ, Inc. They researched XYZ's industry and analyzed the financial projections of XYZ, Inc. In September, the law firm prepared and submitted a letter of intent to XYZ, Inc. The letter stated that a binding commitment would result only after a purchase agreement was signed. The law firm and accounting firm continued to provide services, including a review of XYZ's books and records and the preparation of a purchase agreement. On October 22, you signed a purchase agreement with XYZ, Inc.

All amounts paid or incurred to investigate the business before October 22 are amortizable investigative costs. Amounts paid on or after that date relate to the attempt to purchase the business and therefore must be capitalized.

**Disposition of business.** If you completely dispose of your business before the end of the amortization period, you can deduct any remaining deferred startup costs. However, you can deduct these deferred startup costs only to the extent they qualify as a loss from a business.

## Costs of Organizing a Corporation

Amounts paid to organize a corporation are the direct costs of creating the corporation.

**Qualifying costs.** To qualify as an organizational cost, it must be:
- For the creation of the corporation,
- Chargeable to a capital account (see chapter 1),
- Amortized over the life of the corporation if the corporation had a fixed life, and
- Incurred before the end of the first tax year in which the corporation is in business.

A corporation using the cash method of accounting can amortize organizational costs incurred within the first tax year, even if it doesn't pay them in that year.

Examples of organizational costs include the following.
- The cost of temporary directors.
- The cost of organizational meetings.
- State incorporation fees.
- The cost of legal services.

**Nonqualifying costs.** The following items are capital expenses that can't be amortized.
- Costs for issuing and selling stock or securities, such as commissions, professional fees, and printing costs.
- Costs associated with the transfer of assets to the corporation.

## Costs of Organizing a Partnership

The costs to organize a partnership are the direct costs of creating the partnership.

**Qualifying costs.** A partnership can amortize an organizational cost only if it meets all the following tests.
- It is for the creation of the partnership and not for starting or operating the partnership trade or business.
- It is chargeable to a capital account (see chapter 1).
- It could be amortized over the life of the partnership if the partnership had a fixed life.
- It is incurred by the due date of the partnership return (excluding extensions) for the first tax year in which the partnership is in business. However, if the partnership uses the cash method of accounting and pays the cost after the end of its first tax year, see *Cash method partnership* under *How To Amortize*, later.
- It is for a type of item normally expected to benefit the partnership throughout its entire life.

Organizational costs include the following fees.
- Legal fees for services incident to the organization of the partnership, such as negotiation and preparation of the partnership agreement.
- Accounting fees for services incident to the organization of the partnership.
- Filing fees.

**Nonqualifying costs.** The following costs can't be amortized.
- The cost of acquiring assets for the partnership or transferring assets to the partnership.
- The cost of admitting or removing partners, other than at the time the partnership is first organized.
- The cost of making a contract concerning the operation of the partnership trade or business, including a contract between a partner and the partnership.
- The costs for issuing and marketing interests in the partnership such as brokerage, registration, and legal fees and printing costs. These "syndication fees" are capital expenses that can't be depreciated or amortized.

**Liquidation of partnership.** If a partnership is liquidated before the end of the amortization period, the unamortized amount of qualifying organizational costs can be deducted in the partnership's final tax year. However, these costs can be deducted only to the extent they qualify as a loss from a business.

## How To Amortize

Deduct startup and organizational costs in equal amounts over the applicable amortization period (discussed earlier under *Business Startup Costs*). You can choose an amortization period for startup costs that is different from the period you choose for organizational costs, as long as both aren't less than the applicable amortization period. Once you choose an amortization period, you can't change it.

To figure your deduction, divide your total startup or organizational costs by the months in the amortization period. The result is the amount you can deduct for each month.

**Cash method partnership.** A partnership using the cash method of accounting can deduct an organizational cost only if it has been paid by the end of the tax year. However, any cost the partnership could have deducted as an organizational cost in an earlier tax year (if it had been paid that year) can be deducted in the tax year of payment.

### How To Make the Election

To elect to amortize startup or organizational costs, you must complete and attach Form 4562 to your return for the first tax year you are in business. You may also be required to attach an organizational costs election statement (described later) to your return.

For startup or organizational costs paid or incurred after September 8, 2008, an accompanying statement isn't required. Generally, for startup or organizational costs paid or incurred before September 9, 2008, and after October 22, 2004, unless you choose to apply Regulations sections 1.195-1, 1.248-1, and 1.709-1, you must also attach an accompanying statement to elect to amortize the costs.

If you have both startup and organizational costs, attach a separate statement (if required) to your return for each type of cost. See *Starting a Business*, earlier, for more information.

Generally, you must file the return by the due date (including any extensions). However, if you timely filed your return for the year without making the election, you can still make the election by filing an amended return within 6 months of the due date of the return (excluding extensions). For more information, see the instructions for Part VI of Form 4562.

You can choose to forgo the election to amortize by affirmatively electing to capitalize your startup or organizational costs on your income tax return filed by the due date (including extensions) for the tax year in which the active trade or business begins.

**Note.** The election to either amortize or capitalize startup or organizational costs is irrevocable and applies to all startup and organizational costs that are related to the trade or business.

If your business is organized as a corporation or partnership, only the corporation or partnership can elect to amortize its startup or organizational costs. A shareholder or partner can't make this election. You, as a shareholder or partner, can't amortize any costs you incur in setting up your corporation or partnership. Only the corporation or partnership can amortize these costs.

However, you, as an individual, can elect to amortize costs you incur to investigate an interest in an existing partnership. These costs qualify as business startup costs if you acquire the partnership interest.

**Startup costs election statement.** If you elect to amortize your startup costs, attach a separate statement (if required) that contains the following information.
- A description of the business to which the startup costs relate.
- A description of each startup cost incurred.
- The month your active business began (or was acquired).
- The number of months in your amortization period (which is generally 180 months).

*Filing the statement early.* You can elect to amortize your startup costs by filing the statement with a return for any tax year before the year your active business begins. If you file the statement early, the election becomes effective in the month of the tax year your active business begins.

*Revised statement.* You can file a revised statement to include any startup costs not included in your original statement. However, you can't include on the revised statement any cost you previously treated on your return as a cost other than a startup cost. You can file the revised statement with a return filed after the return on which you elected to amortize your startup costs.

**Organizational costs election statement.** If you elect to amortize your corporation's or partnership's organizational costs, attach a separate statement (if required) that contains the following information.
- A description of each cost.
- The amount of each cost.
- The date each cost was incurred.

- The month your corporation or partnership began active business (or acquired the business).
- The number of months in your amortization period (which is generally 180 months).

*Partnerships.* The statement prepared for a cash basis partnership must also indicate the amount paid before the end of the year for each cost.

You don't need to separately list any partnership organizational cost that is less than $10. Instead, you can list the total amount of these costs with the dates the first and last costs were incurred.

After a partnership makes the election to amortize organizational costs, it can later file an amended return to include additional organizational costs not included in the partnership's original return and statement.

# Getting a Lease

If you get a lease for business property, you may recover the cost of acquiring the lease by amortizing it over the term of the lease. The term of the lease for amortization purposes generally includes all renewal options (and any other period for which you and the lessor reasonably expect the lease to be renewed). However, renewal periods aren't included if 75% or more of the cost of acquiring the lease is for the term of the lease remaining on the acquisition date (not including any period for which you may choose to renew, extend, or continue the lease).

For more information on the costs of getting a lease, see *Cost of Getting a Lease* in chapter 3.

**How to amortize.** Enter your deduction in Part VI of Form 4562 if you are deducting amortization that begins during the current year, or on the appropriate line of your tax return if you aren't otherwise required to file Form 4562.

# Section 197 Intangibles

Generally, you may amortize the capitalized costs of "section 197 intangibles" (see *Section 197 Intangibles Defined*, later) ratably over a 15-year period. You must amortize these costs if you hold the section 197 intangibles in connection with your trade or business or in an activity engaged in for the production of income.

⚠ *You may not be able to amortize section 197 intangibles acquired in a transaction that didn't result in a significant change in ownership or use. See* Anti-Churning Rules, *later.*

Your amortization deduction each year is the applicable part of the intangible's adjusted basis (for purposes of determining gain), figured by amortizing it ratably over 15 years (180 months). The 15-year period begins with the later of:
- The month the intangible is acquired, or
- The month the trade or business or activity engaged in for the production of income begins.

You can't deduct amortization for the month you dispose of the intangible.

If you pay or incur an amount that increases the basis of an amortizable section 197 intangible after the 15-year period begins, amortize it over the remainder of the 15-year period beginning with the month the basis increase occurs.

You aren't allowed any other depreciation or amortization deduction for an amortizable section 197 intangible.

**Tax-exempt use property subject to a lease.** The amortization period for any section 197 intangible leased under a lease agreement entered into after March 12, 2004, to a tax-exempt organization, governmental unit, or foreign person or entity (other than a partnership), shall not be less than 125% of the lease term.

**Cost attributable to other property.** The rules for section 197 intangibles don't apply to any amount that is included in determining the cost of property that isn't a section 197 intangible. For example, if the cost of computer software isn't separately stated from the cost of hardware or other tangible property and you consistently treat it as part of the cost of the hardware or other tangible property, these rules don't apply. Similarly, none of the cost of acquiring real property held for the production of rental income is considered the cost of goodwill, going concern value, or any other section 197 intangible.

# Section 197 Intangibles Defined

The following assets are section 197 intangibles and must be amortized over 180 months.

1. Goodwill.
2. Going concern value.
3. Workforce in place.
4. Business books and records, operating systems, or any other information base, including lists or other information concerning current or prospective customers.
5. A patent, copyright, formula, process, design, pattern, know-how, format, or similar item.
6. A customer-based intangible.
7. A supplier-based intangible.
8. Any item similar to items 3 through 7.
9. A license, permit, or other right granted by a governmental unit or agency (including issuances and renewals).
10. A covenant not to compete entered into in connection with the acquisition of an interest in a trade or business.
11. Any franchise, trademark, or trade name.
12. A contract for the use of, or a term interest in, any item in this list.

You can't amortize any of the intangibles listed in items 1 through 8 that you created rather than acquired unless you created them in acquiring assets that make up a trade or business or a substantial part of a trade or business.

**Goodwill.** This is the value of a trade or business based on expected continued customer patronage due to its name, reputation, or any other factor.

**Going concern value.** This is the additional value of a trade or business that attaches to property because the property is an integral part of an ongoing business activity. It includes value based on the ability of a business to continue to function and generate income even though there is a change in ownership (but doesn't include any other section 197 intangible). It also includes value based on the immediate use or availability of an acquired trade or business, such as the use of earnings during any period in which the business wouldn't otherwise be available or operational.

**Workforce in place, etc.** This includes the composition of a workforce (for example, its experience, education, or training). It also includes the terms and conditions of employment, whether contractual or otherwise, and any other value placed on employees or any of their attributes.

For example, you must amortize the part of the purchase price of a business that is for the existence of a highly skilled workforce. Also, you must amortize the cost of acquiring an existing employment contract or relationship with employees or consultants.

**Business books and records, etc.** This includes the intangible value of technical manuals, training manuals or programs, data files, and accounting or inventory control systems. It also includes the cost of customer lists; subscription lists; insurance expirations; patient or client files; and lists of newspaper, magazine, radio, and television advertisers.

**Patents, copyrights, etc.** This includes package design, computer software, and any interest in a film, sound recording, videotape, book, or other similar property, except as discussed later under *Assets That Aren't Section 197 Intangibles*.

**Customer-based intangible.** This is the composition of market, market share, and any other value resulting from the future provision of goods or services because of relationships with customers in the ordinary course of business. For example, you must amortize the part of the purchase price of a business that is for the existence of the following intangibles.

- A customer base.
- A circulation base.
- An undeveloped market or market growth.
- Insurance in force.
- A mortgage servicing contract.
- An investment management contract.
- Any other relationship with customers involving the future provision of goods or services.

Accounts receivable or other similar rights to income for goods or services provided to customers before the acquisition of a trade or business aren't section 197 intangibles.

**Supplier-based intangible.** A supplier-based intangible is the value resulting from the future acquisitions (through contract or other relationships with suppliers in the ordinary course of business) of goods or services that you will sell or use. The amount you pay or incur for supplier-based intangibles includes, for example, any portion of the purchase price of an acquired trade or business that is attributable to the existence of a favorable relationship with persons providing distribution services (such as a favorable shelf or display space or a retail outlet), or the existence of favorable supply contracts. Don't include any amount required to be paid for the goods or services to honor the terms of the agreement or other relationship. Also, see *Assets That Aren't Section 197 Intangibles*, later.

**Government-granted license, permit, etc.** This is any right granted by a governmental unit or an agency or instrumentality of a governmental unit. For example, you must amortize the capitalized costs of acquiring (including issuing or renewing) a liquor license, a taxicab medallion or license, or a television or radio broadcasting license.

**Covenant not to compete.** Section 197 intangibles include a covenant not to compete (or similar arrangement) entered into in connection with the acquisition of an interest in a trade or business, or a substantial portion of a trade or business. An interest in a trade or business includes an interest in a partnership or a corporation engaged in a trade or business.

An arrangement that requires the former owner to perform services (or to provide property or the use of property) isn't similar to a covenant not to compete to the extent the amount paid under the arrangement represents reasonable compensation for those services or for that property or its use.

**Franchise, trademark, or trade name.** A franchise, trademark, or trade name is a section 197 intangible. You must amortize its purchase or renewal costs, other than certain contingent payments that you can deduct currently. For information on currently deductible contingent payments, see chapter 11.

*Professional sports franchise.* A franchise engaged in professional sports and any intangible assets acquired in connection with acquiring the franchise (including player contracts) is a section 197 intangible amortizable over a 15-year period.

**Contract for the use of, or a term interest in, a section 197 intangible.** Section 197 intangibles include any right under a license, contract, or other arrangement providing for the use of any section 197 intangible. It also includes any term interest in any section 197 intangible, whether the interest is outright or in trust.

## Assets That Aren't Section 197 Intangibles

The following assets aren't section 197 intangibles.

1. Any interest in a corporation, partnership, trust, or estate.
2. Any interest under an existing futures contract, foreign currency contract, notional principal contract, interest rate swap, or similar financial contract.
3. Any interest in land.
4. Most computer software. (See *Computer software*, later.)
5. Any of the following assets not acquired in connection with the acquisition of a trade or business or a substantial part of a trade or business.
   a. An interest in a film, sound recording, videotape, book, or similar property.
   b. A right to receive tangible property or services under a contract or from a governmental agency.
   c. An interest in a patent or copyright.
   d. Certain rights that have a fixed duration or amount. (See *Rights of fixed duration or amount*, later.)
6. An interest under either of the following.
   a. An existing lease or sublease of tangible property.
   b. A debt that was in existence when the interest was acquired.
7. A right to service residential mortgages unless the right is acquired in connection with the acquisition of a trade or business or a substantial part of a trade or business.
8. Certain transaction costs incurred by parties to a corporate organization or reorganization in which any part of a gain or loss isn't recognized.

Intangible property that isn't amortizable under the rules for section 197 intangibles can be depreciated if it meets certain requirements. You must generally use the straight line method over its useful life. For certain intangibles, the depreciation period is specified in the law and regulations. For example, the depreciation period for computer software that isn't a section 197 intangible is generally 36 months.

For more information on depreciating intangible property, see *Intangible Property* under *What Method Can You Use To Depreciate Your Property?* in chapter 1 of Pub. 946.

**Computer software.** Section 197 intangibles don't include the following types of computer software.

1. Software that meets all the following requirements.
   a. It is, or has been, readily available for purchase by the general public.
   b. It is subject to a nonexclusive license.

c. It hasn't been substantially modified. This requirement is considered met if the cost of all modifications isn't more than the greater of 25% of the price of the publicly available unmodified software or $2,000.

2. Software that isn't acquired in connection with the acquisition of a trade or business or a substantial part of a trade or business.

**Computer software defined.** Computer software includes all programs designed to cause a computer to perform a desired function. It also includes any database or similar item that is in the public domain and is incidental to the operation of qualifying software.

**Rights of fixed duration or amount.** Section 197 intangibles don't include any right under a contract or from a governmental agency if the right is acquired in the ordinary course of a trade or business (or in an activity engaged in for the production of income) but not as part of a purchase of a trade or business and either:
- Has a fixed life of less than 15 years; or
- Is of a fixed amount that, except for the rules for section 197 intangibles, would be recovered under a method similar to the unit-of-production method of cost recovery.

However, this doesn't apply to the following intangibles.
- Goodwill.
- Going concern value.
- A covenant not to compete.
- A franchise, trademark, or trade name.
- A customer-related information base, customer-based intangible, or similar item.

## Safe Harbor for Creative Property Costs

If you are engaged in the trade or business of film production, you may be able to amortize the creative property costs for properties not set for production within 3 years of the first capitalized transaction. You may amortize these costs ratably over a 15-year period beginning on the first day of the second half of the tax year in which you properly write off the costs for financial accounting purposes. If, during the 15-year period, you dispose of the creative property rights, you must continue to amortize the costs over the remainder of the 15-year period.

Creative property costs include costs paid or incurred to acquire and develop screenplays, scripts, story outlines, motion picture production rights to books and plays, and other similar properties for purposes of potential future film development, production, and exploitation.

Amortize these costs using the rules of Revenue Procedure 2004-36. For more information, see Revenue Procedure 2004-36, 2004-24 I.R.B. 1063, available at IRS.gov/irb/2004-24_IRB#RP-2004-36.

⚠️ **CAUTION** *A change in the treatment of creative property costs is a change in method of accounting.*

## Anti-Churning Rules

Anti-churning rules prevent you from amortizing most section 197 intangibles if the transaction in which you acquired them didn't result in a significant change in ownership or use. These rules apply to goodwill and going concern value, and to any other section 197 intangible that isn't otherwise depreciable or amortizable.

Under the anti-churning rules, you can't use 15-year amortization for the intangible if any of the following conditions apply.

1. You or a related person (defined later) held or used the intangible at any time from July 25, 1991, through August 10, 1993.
2. You acquired the intangible from a person who held it at any time during the period in (1) and, as part of the transaction, the user didn't change.
3. You granted the right to use the intangible to a person (or a person related to that person) who held or used it at any time during the period in (1). This applies only if the transaction in which you granted the right and the transaction in which you acquired the intangible are part of a series of related transactions. See Related person, later, for more information.

**Exceptions.** The anti-churning rules don't apply in the following situations.
- You acquired the intangible from a decedent and its basis was stepped up to its fair market value.
- The intangible was amortizable as a section 197 intangible by the seller or transferor you acquired it from. This exception doesn't apply if the transaction in which you acquired the intangible and the transaction in which the seller or transferor acquired it are part of a series of related transactions.
- The gain-recognition exception, discussed later, applies.

**Related person.** For purposes of the anti-churning rules, the following are related persons.
- An individual and his or her brothers, sisters, half brothers, half sisters, spouse, ancestors (parents, grandparents, etc.), and lineal descendants (children, grandchildren, etc.).
- A corporation and an individual who owns, directly or indirectly, more than 20% of the value of the corporation's outstanding stock.
- Two corporations that are members of the same controlled group as defined in section 1563(a), except that "more than 20%" is substituted for "at least 80%" in that definition and the determination is made without regard to subsections (a)(4) and (e)(3)(C) of section 1563. For an exception, see section 1.197-2(h)(6)(iv) of the regulations.
- A trust fiduciary and a corporation if more than 20% of the value of the corporation's outstanding stock is owned, directly or indirectly, by or for the trust or grantor of the trust.

- The grantor and fiduciary, and the fiduciary and beneficiary, of any trust.
- The fiduciaries of two different trusts, and the fiduciaries and beneficiaries of two different trusts, if the same person is the grantor of both trusts.
- The executor and beneficiary of an estate.
- A tax-exempt educational or charitable organization and a person who directly or indirectly controls the organization (or whose family members control it).
- A corporation and a partnership if the same persons own more than 20% of the value of the outstanding stock of the corporation and more than 20% of the capital or profits interest in the partnership.
- Two S corporations, and an S corporation and a regular corporation, if the same persons own more than 20% of the value of the outstanding stock of each corporation.
- Two partnerships if the same persons own, directly or indirectly, more than 20% of the capital or profits interests in both partnerships.
- A partnership and a person who owns, directly or indirectly, more than 20% of the capital or profits interests in the partnership.
- Two persons who are engaged in trades or businesses under common control (as described in section 41(f)(1)).

**When to determine relationship.** Persons are treated as related if the relationship existed at the following time.
- In the case of a single transaction, immediately before or immediately after the transaction in which the intangible was acquired.
- In the case of a series of related transactions (or a series of transactions that comprise a qualified stock purchase under section 338(d)(3)), immediately before the earliest transaction or immediately after the last transaction.

**Ownership of stock.** In determining whether an individual directly or indirectly owns any of the outstanding stock of a corporation, the following rules apply.

**Rule 1.** Stock directly or indirectly owned by or for a corporation, partnership, estate, or trust is considered owned proportionately by or for its shareholders, partners, or beneficiaries.

**Rule 2.** An individual is considered to own the stock directly or indirectly owned by or for his or her family. Family includes only brothers and sisters, half brothers and half sisters, spouse, ancestors, and lineal descendants.

**Rule 3.** An individual owning (other than by applying Rule 2) any stock in a corporation is considered to own the stock directly or indirectly owned by or for their partner.

**Rule 4.** For purposes of applying Rule 1, 2, or 3, treat stock constructively owned by a person under Rule 1 as actually owned by that person. Don't treat stock constructively owned by an individual under Rule 2 or 3 as owned by the individual for reapplying Rule 2 or 3 to make another person the constructive owner of the stock.

**Gain-recognition exception.** This exception to the anti-churning rules applies if the person you acquired the intangible from (the transferor) meets both of the following requirements.

- That person wouldn't be related to you (as described under *Related person*, earlier) if the 20% test for ownership of stock and partnership interests were replaced by a 50% test.
- That person chose to recognize gain on the disposition of the intangible and pay income tax on the gain at the highest tax rate. See chapter 2 of Pub. 544 for information on making this choice.

If this exception applies, the anti-churning rules apply only to the amount of your adjusted basis in the intangible that is more than the gain recognized by the transferor.

**Notification.** If the person you acquired the intangible from chooses to recognize gain under the rules for this exception, that person must notify you in writing by the due date of the return on which the choice is made.

**Anti-abuse rule.** You can't amortize any section 197 intangible acquired in a transaction for which the principal purpose was either of the following.

- To avoid the requirement that the intangible be acquired after August 10, 1993.
- To avoid any of the anti-churning rules.

**More information.** For more information about the anti-churning rules, including additional rules for partnerships, see Regulations section 1.197-2(h).

## Incorrect Amount of Amortization Deducted

If you later discover that you deducted an incorrect amount for amortization for a section 197 intangible in any year, you may be able to make a correction for that year by filing an amended return. See *Amended Return* next. If you aren't allowed to make the correction on an amended return, you can change your accounting method to claim the correct amortization. See *Changing Your Accounting Method*, later.

### Amended Return

If you deducted an incorrect amount for amortization, you can file an amended return to correct the following.

- A mathematical error made in any year.
- A posting error made in any year.
- An amortization deduction for a section 197 intangible for which you haven't adopted a method of accounting.

**When to file.** If an amended return is allowed, you must file it by the later of the following dates.

- 3 years from the date you filed your original return for the year in which you didn't deduct the correct amount. (A return filed early is considered filed on the due date.)
- 2 years from the time you paid your tax for that year.

## Changing Your Accounting Method

Generally, you must get IRS approval to change your method of accounting. File Form 3115 to request a change to a permissible method of accounting for amortization.

The following are examples of a change in method of accounting for amortization.
- A change in the amortization method, period of recovery, or convention of an amortizable asset.
- A change in the accounting for amortizable assets from a single asset account to a multiple asset account (pooling), or vice versa.
- A change in the accounting for amortizable assets from one type of multiple asset account to a different type of multiple asset account.

Changes in amortization that aren't a change in method of accounting include the following.
- A change in figuring amortization in the tax year in which your use of the asset changes.
- An adjustment in the useful life of an amortizable asset.
- Generally, the making of a late amortization election or the revocation of a timely valid amortization election.
- Any change in the placed-in-service date of an amortizable asset.

See Regulations section 1.446-1(e)(2)(ii)(a) for more information and examples.

**Automatic approval.** In some instances, you may be able to get automatic approval from the IRS to change your method of accounting for amortization. For a list of automatic accounting method changes, see the Instructions for Form 3115. Also, see the Instructions for Form 3115 for more information on getting approval, automatic approval procedures, and a list of exceptions to the automatic approval process.

## Disposition of Section 197 Intangibles

A section 197 intangible is treated as depreciable property used in your trade or business. If you held the intangible for more than 1 year, any gain on its disposition, up to the amount of allowable amortization, is ordinary income (section 1245 gain). If multiple section 197 intangibles are disposed of in a single transaction or a series of related transactions, treat all of the section 197 intangibles as if they were a single asset for purposes of determining the amount of gain that is ordinary income. Any remaining gain, or any loss, is a section 1231 gain or loss. If you held the intangible 1 year or less, any gain or loss on its disposition is an ordinary gain or loss. For more information on ordinary or capital gain or loss on business property, see chapter 3 of Pub. 544.

**Nondeductible loss.** You can't deduct any loss on the disposition or worthlessness of a section 197 intangible that you acquired in the same transaction (or series of related transac-

tions) as other section 197 intangibles you still have. Instead, increase the adjusted basis of each remaining amortizable section 197 intangible by a proportionate part of the nondeductible loss. Figure the increase by multiplying the nondeductible loss on the disposition of the intangible by the following fraction.
- The numerator is the adjusted basis of each remaining intangible on the date of the disposition.
- The denominator is the total adjusted basis of all remaining amortizable section 197 intangibles on the date of the disposition.

**Covenant not to compete.** A covenant not to compete, or similar arrangement, isn't considered disposed of or worthless before you dispose of your entire interest in the trade or business for which you entered into the covenant.

**Nonrecognition transfers.** If you acquire a section 197 intangible in a nonrecognition transfer, you are treated as the transferor with respect to the part of your adjusted basis in the intangible that isn't more than the transferor's adjusted basis. You amortize this part of the adjusted basis over the intangible's remaining amortization period in the hands of the transferor. Nonrecognition transfers include transfers to a corporation, partnership contributions and distributions, like-kind exchanges, and involuntary conversions.

In a like-kind exchange or involuntary conversion of a section 197 intangible, you must continue to amortize the part of your adjusted basis in the acquired intangible that isn't more than your adjusted basis in the exchanged or converted intangible over the remaining amortization period of the exchanged or converted intangible. Amortize over a new 15-year period the part of your adjusted basis in the acquired intangible that is more than your adjusted basis in the exchanged or converted intangible.

**Example.** You own a section 197 intangible you have amortized for 4 full years. It has a remaining unamortized basis of $30,000. You exchange the asset plus $10,000 for a like-kind section 197 intangible. The nonrecognition provisions of like-kind exchanges apply. You amortize $30,000 of the $40,000 adjusted basis of the acquired intangible over the 11 years remaining in the original 15-year amortization period for the transferred asset. You amortize the other $10,000 of adjusted basis over a new 15-year period. For more information, see Regulations section 1.197-2(g).

## Reforestation Costs

You can elect to deduct a limited amount of reforestation costs paid or incurred during the tax year. See *Reforestation Costs* in chapter 7. You can elect to amortize the qualifying costs that aren't deducted currently over an 84-month period. There is no limit on the amount of your amortization deduction for reforestation costs paid or incurred during the tax year.

The election to amortize reforestation costs incurred by a partnership, S corporation, or estate must be made by the partnership, corporation, or estate. A partner, shareholder, or beneficiary can't make that election.

A partner's or shareholder's share of amortizable costs is figured under the general rules for allocating items of income, loss, deduction, etc., of a partnership or S corporation. The amortizable costs of an estate are divided between the estate and the income beneficiary based on the income of the estate allocable to each.

**Qualifying costs.** Reforestation costs are the direct costs of planting or seeding for forestation or reforestation. Qualifying costs include only those costs you must capitalize and include in the adjusted basis of the property. They include costs for the following items.

- Site preparation.
- Seeds or seedlings.
- Labor.
- Tools.
- Depreciation on equipment used in planting and seeding.

Qualifying costs don't include costs for which the government reimburses you under a cost-sharing program, unless you include the reimbursement in your income.

**Qualified timber property.** Qualified timber property is property that contains trees in significant commercial quantities. It can be a woodlot or other site that you own or lease. The property qualifies only if it meets all of the following requirements.

- It is located in the United States.
- It is held for the growing and cutting of timber you will use in, or sell for use in, the commercial production of timber products.
- It consists of at least one acre planted with tree seedlings in the manner normally used in forestation or reforestation.

Qualified timber property doesn't include property on which you have planted shelter belts or ornamental trees, such as Christmas trees.

**Amortization period.** The 84-month amortization period starts on the first day of the first month of the second half of the tax year you incur the costs (July 1 for a calendar year taxpayer), regardless of the month you actually incur the costs. You can claim amortization deductions for no more than 6 months of the first and last (eighth) tax years of the period.

**Life tenant and remainderman.** If one person holds the property for life with the remainder going to another person, the life tenant is entitled to the full amortization for qualifying reforestation costs incurred by the life tenant. Any remainder interest in the property is ignored for amortization purposes.

**Recapture.** If you dispose of qualified timber property within 10 years after the tax year you incur qualifying reforestation expenses, report any gain as ordinary income up to the amortization you took. See chapter 3 of Pub. 544 for more information.

**How to make the election.** To elect to amortize qualifying reforestation costs, complete Part VI of Form 4562 and attach a statement that contains the following information.

- A description of the costs and the dates you incurred them.
- A description of the type of timber being grown and the purpose for which it is grown.

Attach a separate statement for each property for which you amortize reforestation costs.

Generally, you must make the election on a timely filed return (including extensions) for the tax year in which you incurred the costs. However, if you timely filed your return for the year without making the election, you can still make the election by filing an amended return within 6 months of the due date of the return (excluding extensions). Attach Form 4562 and the statement to the amended return and write "Filed pursuant to section 301.9100-2" on Form 4562. File the amended return at the same address you filed the original return.

**Revoking the election.** You must get IRS approval to revoke your election to amortize qualifying reforestation costs. Your application to revoke the election must include your name, address, the years for which your election was in effect, and your reason for revoking it. Provide your daytime telephone number (optional), in case we need to contact you. You, or your duly authorized representative, must sign the application and file it at least 90 days before the due date (without extensions) for filing your income tax return for the first tax year for which your election is to end.

Send the application to:

Internal Revenue Service
Associate Chief Counsel
Passthroughs and Special Industries
CC:PSI:6
1111 Constitution Ave. NW, IR-5300
Washington, DC 20224

# Geological and Geophysical Costs

You can amortize the cost of geological and geophysical expenses paid or incurred in connection with oil and gas exploration or development within the United States. These costs can be amortized ratably over a 24-month period beginning on the midpoint of the tax year in which the expenses were paid or incurred. For major integrated oil companies (as defined in section 167(h)(5)), these costs must be amortized ratably over a 7-year period for costs paid or incurred after December 19, 2007 (a 5-year period for costs paid or incurred after May 17, 2006, and before December 20, 2007).

If you retire or abandon the property during the amortization period, no amortization deduction is allowed in the year of retirement or abandonment.

# Pollution Control Facilities

You can elect to amortize the cost of a certified pollution control facility over 60 months. However, see *Atmospheric pollution control facilities*, later, for an exception. The cost of a pollution control facility that isn't eligible for amortization can be depreciated under the regular rules for depreciation. Also, you can claim a special depreciation allowance on a certified pollution control facility that is qualified property even if you elect to amortize its cost. You must reduce its cost (amortizable basis) by the amount of any special allowance you claim. See chapter 3 of Pub. 946.

A certified pollution control facility is a new identifiable treatment facility used in connection with a plant or other property in operation before 1976 to reduce or control water or atmospheric pollution or contamination. The facility must do so by removing, changing, disposing, storing, or preventing the creation or emission of pollutants, contaminants, wastes, or heat. The facility must be certified by state and federal certifying authorities.

The facility must not significantly increase the output or capacity, extend the useful life, or reduce the total operating costs of the plant or other property. Also, it must not significantly change the nature of the manufacturing or production process or facility.

The federal certifying authority won't certify your property to the extent it appears you will recover (over the property's useful life) all or part of its cost from the profit based on its operation (such as through sales of recovered wastes). The federal certifying authority will describe the nature of the potential cost recovery. You must then reduce the amortizable basis of the facility by this potential recovery.

***New identifiable treatment facility.*** A new identifiable treatment facility is tangible depreciable property that is identifiable as a treatment facility. It doesn't include a building and its structural components unless the building is exclusively a treatment facility.

**Atmospheric pollution control facilities.** Certain atmospheric pollution control facilities can be amortized over 84 months. To qualify, the following must apply.

- The facility must be acquired and placed in service after April 11, 2005. If acquired, the original use must begin with you after April 11, 2005.
- The facility must be used in connection with an electric generation plant or other property placed in operation after December 31, 1975, that is primarily coal fired.
- If you construct, reconstruct, or erect the facility, only the basis attributable to the construction, reconstruction, or erection completed after April 11, 2005, qualifies.

**Basis reduction for corporations.** A corporation must reduce the amortizable basis of a pollution control facility by 20% before figuring the amortization deduction.

**More information.** For more information on the amortization of pollution control facilities, see sections 169 and 291(c) and the related regulations.

## Research and Experimental Costs

You must amortize specified research or experimental costs paid or incurred in tax years beginning after 2021.

You must amortize specified research or experimental costs ratably over a 5-year period beginning with the midpoint of the tax year in which the expenditures were paid or incurred. Research or experimental expenditures attributable to foreign research conducted outside the United States, Puerto Rico, or any possession of the United States must be amortized ratably over a 15-year period beginning with the midpoint of the tax year in which the expenditures were paid or incurred. This includes any amounts paid or incurred in connection with the development of software which are not otherwise excluded expenditures under Internal Revenue Code section 174 and Treasury Regulations section 1.174-2. For a definition of "research and experimental costs," see chapter 7.

**How to make the election.** To change to the required method of accounting for specified research or experimental expenditures in the first tax year beginning after December 31, 2021, attach the statement in lieu of Form 3115 as described in section 7.02(5) of *Revenue Procedure 2023-11* to your income tax return. You must also complete Part VI of Form 4562 and attach it to your income tax return. Generally, you must file the return by due date (including extensions). However, if you timely filed your return for the year without attaching the statement in lieu of Form 3115 or completed Part VI of Form 4562, you can make the election by filing an amended return within 6 months of the due date of the return (including extensions). Attach the required statement and completed Form 4562 to the amended return and write "Filed pursuant to section 301.9100-2" on Form 4562. File the amended return at the same address you filed the original return.

## Optional Write-off of Certain Tax Preferences

You can elect to amortize certain tax preference items over an optional period beginning in the tax year in which you incurred the costs. If you make this election, there is no alternative minimum tax adjustment. The applicable costs and the optional recovery periods are as follows.
- Circulation costs—3 years.
- Intangible drilling and development costs—60 months.
- Mining exploration and development costs—10 years.
- Research and experimental expenditures paid or incurred in tax years beginning before January 1, 2022 (section 174(a) prior to amendment by section 13206(a) of P.L.

115-97)—10 years. Amortization for these costs should be reported on line 43 of Form 4562.

**How to make the election.** To elect to amortize qualifying costs over the optional recovery period, complete Part VI of Form 4562 and attach a statement containing the following information to your return for the tax year in which the election begins.
- Your name, address, and taxpayer identification number.
- The type of cost and the specific amount of the cost for which you are making the election.

Generally, the election must be made on a timely filed return (including extensions) for the tax year in which you incurred the costs. However, if you timely filed your return for the year without making the election, you can still make the election by filing an amended return within 6 months of the due date of the return (excluding extensions). Attach Form 4562 to the amended return and write "Filed pursuant to section 301.9100-2" on Form 4562. File the amended return at the same address you filed the original return.

**Note.** The amortization deduction and research and experimental expenditures under former section 174(b) or the dollar amount of research and experimental expenditures for which you elected to amortize over the 10-year period under section 59(e) must be reported on line 43 of Form 4562. Attach a statement that shows (a) a description of the costs, (b) the date amortization began, (c) the amortizable amount, (d) the applicable Code section, (e) the amortization period, (f) the accumulated amortization, and (g) the amortization amount for this year.

**Revoking the election.** You must obtain consent from the IRS to revoke your section 59(e) election. Your request to revoke the election must be submitted to the IRS in the form of a letter ruling before the end of the tax year in which the optional recovery period ends. The request must contain all of the information necessary to demonstrate the rare and unusual circumstances that would justify granting revocation. If the request for revocation is approved, any unamortized costs are deductible in the year the revocation is effective.

# 9.

# Depletion

## What's New

**Corporate alternative minimum tax reinstated in 2023.** P.L. 117-169, August 16, 2022,

amended section 55 to impose a corporate alternative minimum tax. The amendment applies to tax years beginning after 2022.

**Excise tax to fund Black Lung Benefits.** P.L. 117-169 also amended section 4121 to eliminate the reduction in tax on coal from mines located in the United States sold by the producer. The amendment applies to sales in calendar quarters beginning after August 17, 2022.

## Reminders

**Domestic production activities deduction repealed.** P.L. 115-97, December 22, 2017, repealed section 199, which provided a deduction for income attributable to domestic production activities. The amendment applies to tax years beginning after 2017.

**Qualified business income deduction enacted.** P.L. 115-97 also added section 199A, which provides a deduction for qualified business income. The amendment applies to tax years beginning after 2017. Section 199A does not apply to tax years beginning after 2025.

## Introduction

Depletion is the using up of natural resources extracted from a mineral property by mining, drilling, quarrying stone, or cutting timber. The depletion deduction allows an owner or operator to account for the reduction of the mineral property's value or basis as a result of the extraction of the natural resource.

There are two ways of figuring depletion: cost depletion and percentage depletion. For oil and gas wells, mines, other natural deposits (including geothermal deposits), and mineral property, you must generally use the method that gives you the larger deduction. For standing timber, you must use cost depletion.

## Topics
This chapter discusses:
- Who can claim depletion
- Mineral property
- Timber

## Useful Items
You may want to see:

**Publication**
- ❏ **544** Sales and Other Dispositions of Assets
- ❏ **551** Basis of Assets

**Form (and Instructions)**
- ❏ **Schedule E (Form 1040)** Supplemental Income and Loss
- ❏ **Schedule K-1 (Form 1065)** Partner's Share of Income, Deductions, Credits, etc.
- ❏ **Schedule K-1 (Form 1120-S)** Shareholder's Share of Income, Deductions, Credits, etc.
- ❏ **6198** At-Risk Limitations

❑ **8582** Passive Activity Loss Limitations

❑ **T (Timber)** Forest Activities Schedule

See chapter 12 for information about getting publications and forms.

# Who Can Claim Depletion?

If you have an economic interest in mineral property or standing timber, you can take a deduction for depletion. More than one person can have an economic interest in the same mineral deposit or timber. In the case of leased property, the depletion deduction is divided between the lessor and the lessee.

You have an economic interest if both the following apply.
- You have acquired by investment any interest in mineral deposits or standing timber.
- You have a legal right to income from the extraction of the mineral or cutting of the timber to which you must look for a return of your capital investment.

A contractual relationship that allows you an economic or monetary advantage from products of the mineral deposit or standing timber is not, in itself, an economic interest.

*Depletion is an item of tax preference under the Alternative Minimum Tax (AMT). See section 57.*

**Basis adjustment for depletion.** You must reduce the basis of your property by the depletion allowed or allowable, whichever is greater, but not below zero.

# Mineral Property

Mineral property includes oil and gas wells, mines, and other natural deposits (including geothermal deposits). For this purpose, the term "property" means each separate interest you own in each mineral deposit in each separate tract or parcel of land. You can treat two or more separate interests as one property or as separate properties. See section 614 and the related regulations for rules on how to treat separate mineral interests.

There are two ways of figuring depletion on mineral property.
- Cost depletion.
- Percentage depletion.

Generally, you must use the method that gives you the larger deduction. However, unless you are an independent producer or royalty owner, you generally cannot use percentage depletion for oil and gas wells. See *Oil and Gas Wells*, later.

## Cost Depletion

To figure cost depletion, you must first determine the following.
- The property's basis for depletion.
- The total recoverable units of mineral in the property's natural deposit.

- The number of units of mineral sold during the tax year.

**Basis for depletion.** To figure the property's basis for depletion, subtract all the following from the property's adjusted basis.

1. Amounts recoverable through:
   a. Depreciation deductions,
   b. Deferred expenses (including deferred exploration and development costs), and
   c. Deductions other than depletion.
2. The residual value of land and improvements at the end of operations.
3. The cost or value of land acquired for purposes other than mineral production.

*Adjusted basis.* The adjusted basis of your property is your original cost or other basis, plus certain additions and improvements, and minus certain deductions such as depletion allowed or allowable and casualty losses. Your adjusted basis can never be less than zero. See Pub. 551 for more information on adjusted basis.

**Total recoverable units.** The total recoverable units is the sum of the following.
- The number of units of mineral remaining at the end of the year (including units recovered but not sold).
- The number of units of mineral sold during the tax year (determined under your method of accounting, as explained next).

You must estimate or determine recoverable units (tons, pounds, ounces, barrels, thousands of cubic feet, or other measure) of mineral products using the current industry method and the most accurate and reliable information you can obtain. You must include ores and minerals that are developed, in sight, blocked out, or assured. You must also include probable or prospective ores or minerals that are believed to exist based on good evidence. But see *Elective safe harbor for owners of oil and gas property*, later.

**Number of units sold during the tax year.** You determine the number of units sold during the tax year based on your method of accounting. Use the following table to make this determination.

| IF you use ... | THEN the units sold during the tax year are ... |
|---|---|
| the cash method of accounting | the units sold for which you receive payment during the tax year (regardless of the year of sale). |
| an accrual method of accounting | the units sold based on your inventories and method of accounting for inventory. |

The number of units sold during the tax year does not include any for which depletion deductions were allowed or allowable in earlier years.

**Figuring the cost depletion deduction.** Once you have figured your property's basis for depletion, the total recoverable units, and the number of units sold during the tax year, you

can figure your cost depletion deduction by taking the following steps.

| Step | Action | Result |
|---|---|---|
| 1 | Divide your property's basis for depletion by total recoverable units. | Depletion unit. |
| 2 | Multiply the depletion unit by units sold during the tax year. | Cost depletion deduction. |

You must keep accounts for the depletion of each property and adjust these accounts each year for units sold and depletion claimed.

**Elective safe harbor for owners of oil and gas property.** Instead of using the method described earlier to determine the total recoverable units, you can use an elective safe harbor to determine the property's recoverable reserves for purposes of figuring cost depletion. If you choose the elective safe harbor, the total recoverable units equal 105% of a property's proved reserves (both developed and undeveloped). For details, see Revenue Procedure 2004-19 on page 563 of I.R.B. 2004-10, available at IRS.gov/irb/2004-10_IRB#RP-2004-19.

To make the election, attach a statement to your timely filed (including extensions) original return for the first tax year for which the safe harbor is elected. The statement must indicate that you are electing the safe harbor provided by Revenue Procedure 2004-19. The election, if made, is effective for the tax year in which it is made and all later years. It cannot be revoked for the tax year in which it is elected, but it may be revoked in a later year. Once revoked, it cannot be re-elected for the next 5 years.

## Percentage Depletion

To figure percentage depletion, you multiply a certain percentage, specified for each mineral, by your gross income from the property during the tax year.

The rates to be used and other rules for oil and gas wells are discussed later under *Independent Producers and Royalty Owners* and under *Natural Gas Wells*. Rates and other rules for percentage depletion of other specific minerals are found later under *Mines and Geothermal Deposits*.

**Gross income.** When figuring percentage depletion, subtract from your gross income from the property the following amounts.
- Any rents or royalties you paid or incurred for the property.
- The part of any bonus you paid for a lease on the property allocable to the product sold (or that otherwise gives rise to gross income) for the tax year.

A bonus payment includes amounts you paid as a lessee to satisfy a production payment retained by the lessor.

Use the following fraction to figure the part of the bonus you must subtract.

$$\frac{\text{No. of units sold in the tax year}}{\text{Recoverable units from the property}} \times \text{Bonus Payments}$$

For oil and gas wells and geothermal deposits, more information about the definition of gross income from the property is under *Oil and Gas Wells*, later. For other property, more information about the definition of gross income from the property is under *Mines and Geothermal Deposits*, later.

**Taxable income limit.** The percentage depletion deduction generally cannot be more than 50% (100% for oil and gas property) of your taxable income from the property figured without the depletion deduction, and any deduction under section 199A.

Taxable income from the property means gross income from the property minus all allowable deductions (except any deduction for depletion or qualified business income) attributable to mining processes, including limited mining transportation. These deductible items include, but are not limited to, the following.

- Operating expenses.
- Certain selling expenses.
- Administrative and financial overhead.
- Depreciation.
- Intangible drilling and development costs.
- Exploration and development expenditures.
- Deductible taxes (see chapter 5), but not taxes that you capitalize or take as a credit.
- Losses sustained.

The following rules apply when figuring your taxable income from the property for purposes of the taxable income limit.

- Do not deduct any net operating loss (NOL) deduction from the gross income from the property.
- Corporations do not deduct charitable contributions from the gross income from the property.
- If, during the year, you dispose of an item of section 1245 property that was used in connection with mineral property, reduce any allowable deduction for mining expenses by the part of any gain you must report as ordinary income that is allocable to the mineral property. See Regulations section 1.613-5(b)(1) for information on how to figure the ordinary gain allocable to the property.

## Oil and Gas Wells

You cannot claim percentage depletion for an oil or gas well unless at least one of the following applies.

- You are either an independent producer or a royalty owner.
- The well produces one of the following: regulated natural gas, natural gas sold under a fixed contract, or natural gas from geopressured brine.

If you are an independent producer or royalty owner, see *Independent Producers and Royalty Owners* next.

For information on the depletion deduction for wells that produce regulated natural gas, natural gas sold under a fixed contract, or natural gas from geopressured brine, see *Natural Gas Wells*, later.

### Independent Producers and Royalty Owners

If you are an independent producer or royalty owner, you figure percentage depletion using a rate of 15% of the gross income from the property based on your average daily production of domestic crude oil or domestic natural gas up to your depletable oil or natural gas quantity. However, an independent producer or royalty owner that also acts as a retailer or refiner may be excluded from claiming percentage depletion. For information on figuring the deduction, see *Figuring percentage depletion*, later.

**Refiners who cannot claim percentage depletion.** You cannot claim percentage depletion if you or a related person refines crude oil and you and the related person refined more than 75,000 barrels on any day during the tax year based on average (rather than actual) daily refinery runs for the tax year. The average daily refinery run is figured by dividing total refinery runs for the tax year by the total number of days in the tax year.

*Related person.* You and another person are related persons if either of you holds a significant ownership interest in the other person or if a third person holds a significant ownership interest in both of you.

For example, a corporation, partnership, estate, or trust and anyone who holds a significant ownership interest in it are related persons. A partnership and a trust are related persons if one person holds a significant ownership interest in each of them.

For purposes of the related person rules, significant ownership interest means direct or indirect ownership of 5% or more in any one of the following.

- The value of the outstanding stock of a corporation.
- The interest in the profits or capital of a partnership.
- The beneficial interests in an estate or trust.

Any interest owned by or for a corporation, partnership, trust, or estate is considered to be owned directly both by itself and proportionately by its shareholders, partners, or beneficiaries.

**Retailers who cannot claim percentage depletion.** You cannot claim percentage depletion if both the following apply.

1. You sell oil or natural gas or their byproducts directly or through a related person in any of the following situations.

    a. Through a retail outlet operated by you or a related person.

    b. To any person who is required under an agreement with you or a related person to use a trademark, trade name, or service mark or name owned by you or a related person in marketing or distributing oil, natural gas, or their byproducts.

    c. To any person given authority under an agreement with you or a related

person to occupy any retail outlet owned, leased, or controlled by you or a related person.

2. The combined gross receipts from sales (not counting resales) of oil, natural gas, or their byproducts by all retail outlets taken into account in (1) are more than $5 million for the tax year.

For the purpose of determining if this rule applies, do not count the following.

- Bulk sales (sales in very large quantities) of oil or natural gas to commercial or industrial users.
- Bulk sales of aviation fuels to the Department of Defense.
- Sales of oil or natural gas or their byproducts outside the United States if none of your domestic production or that of a related person is exported during the tax year or the prior tax year.

*Related person.* To determine if you and another person are related persons, see *Related person* under *Refiners who cannot claim percentage depletion*, earlier.

*Sales through a related person.* You are considered to be selling oil or natural gas (or a product derived therefrom) through a related person if any sale by the related person produces gross income from which you may benefit because of your direct or indirect ownership interest in the related person.

You are **not** considered to be selling oil or natural gas (or a product derived therefrom) through a related person who is a retailer if all of the following apply.

- You do not own a significant ownership interest in the retailer.
- You sell your production to persons who are not related to either you or the retailer.
- The retailer does not buy oil or natural gas from your customers or persons related to your customers.
- There are no arrangements for the retailer to acquire oil or natural gas you produced for resale or made available for purchase by the retailer.
- Neither you nor the retailer knows of, or controls, the final disposition of the oil or natural gas you sold or the original source of the petroleum products the retailer acquired for resale.

**Transferees who cannot claim percentage depletion.** You cannot claim percentage depletion if you received your interest in a proven oil or gas property by transfer after 1974 and before October 12, 1990. For a definition of the term "transfer," see Regulations section 1.613A-7(n). For a definition of the term "interest in proven oil or gas property," see Regulations section 1.613A-7(p).

**Figuring percentage depletion.** Generally, as an independent producer or royalty owner, you figure your percentage depletion by figuring your average daily production of domestic oil or gas and comparing it to your depletable oil or gas quantity. If your average daily production does not exceed your depletable oil or gas quantity, you figure your percentage depletion by multiplying the gross income from the oil or gas property (as defined under *Gross income* *from the property*, later) by 15% (0.15). If your average daily production of domestic oil or gas exceeds your depletable oil or gas quantity, you must make an allocation as explained later under *Average daily production*.

In addition, there is a limit on the percentage depletion deduction. See *Taxable income limit*, later.

**Average daily production.** Figure your average daily production by dividing your total domestic production of oil or gas for the tax year by the number of days in your tax year.

*Partial interest.* If you have a partial interest in the production from a property, figure your share of the production by multiplying total production from the property by your percentage participation in the revenues from the property.

You have a partial interest in the production from a property if you have a net profits interest in the property. To figure the share of production for your net profits interest, you must first determine your percentage participation (as measured by the net profits) in the gross revenue from the property. To figure this percentage, you divide the income you receive for your net profits interest by the gross revenue from the property. Then multiply the total production from the property by your percentage participation to figure your share of the production.

*Example.* Riley owns oil property in which Finley owns a 20% net profits interest. During the year, the property produced 10,000 barrels of oil, which Riley sold for $200,000. Riley had expenses of $90,000 attributable to the property. The property generated a net profit of $110,000 ($200,000 − $90,000). Finley received income of $22,000 ($110,000 × 20% (0.20)) as Finley's net profits interest.

The percentage participation that Finley determined was 11%, figured by dividing $22,000 (income received) by $200,000 (the gross revenue from the property). Finley's share of the oil production was determined to be 1,100 barrels (10,000 barrels × 11% (0.11)).

**Depletable oil or natural gas quantity.** Generally, your depletable oil quantity is 1,000 barrels. Your depletable natural gas quantity is 6,000 cubic feet multiplied by the number of barrels of your depletable oil quantity that you choose to apply. If you claim depletion on both oil and natural gas, you must reduce your depletable oil quantity (1,000 barrels) by the number of barrels you use to figure your depletable natural gas quantity.

*Example.* You have both oil and natural gas production. To figure your depletable natural gas quantity, you choose to apply 360 barrels of your 1,000-barrel depletable oil quantity. Your depletable natural gas quantity is 2.16 million cubic feet of gas (360 × 6,000). You must reduce your depletable oil quantity to 640 barrels (1,000 − 360).

If you have production from marginal wells, see section 613A(c)(6) to figure your depletable oil or natural gas quantity. See also Notice 2022-24, available at *IRS.gov/irb/2022-21_IRB*.

*Business entities and family members.* You must allocate the depletable oil or gas

quantity among the following related persons in proportion to each business entity's or family member's production of domestic oil or gas for the year.

- Corporations, trusts, and estates if 50% or more of the beneficial interest is owned by the same or related persons (considering only persons that own at least 5% of the beneficial interest).
- You and your spouse and minor children.

A related person is anyone mentioned in the related persons discussion under *Nondeductible loss* in chapter 2 of Pub. 544, except that for purposes of this allocation, item (1) in that discussion includes only an individual, spouse, and their minor children.

*Controlled group of corporations.* Members of the same controlled group of corporations are treated as one taxpayer when figuring the depletable oil or natural gas quantity. They share the depletable quantity. A controlled group of corporations is defined in section 1563(a), except that, for this purpose, the stock ownership requirement is "more than 50%" rather than "at least 80%," as described in section 1563(a).

**Gross income from the property.** For purposes of percentage depletion, gross income from the property (in the case of oil and gas wells) is the amount you receive from the sale of the oil or gas in the immediate vicinity of the well. If you do not sell the oil or gas on the property but manufacture or convert it into a refined product before sale, or transport it before sale, the gross income from the property is the representative market or field price (RMFP) of the oil or gas before conversion or transportation.

However, if you sold gas after you transported it from the premises for a price that is lower than the RMFP, determine gross income from the property for percentage depletion purposes without regard to the RMFP.

Gross income from the property does not include lease bonuses, advance royalties, or other amounts payable without regard to production from the property.

**Average daily production exceeds depletable quantities.** If your average daily production for the year is more than your depletable oil or natural gas quantity, figure your allowance for depletion for each domestic oil or natural gas property as follows.

1. Figure your average daily production of oil or natural gas for the year.

2. Figure your depletable oil or natural gas quantity for the year.

3. Figure depletion for all oil or natural gas produced from the property using a percentage depletion rate of 15% (0.15).

4. Multiply the result figured in (3) by a fraction, the numerator of which is the result figured in (2) and the denominator of which is the result figured in (1). This is your depletion allowance for that property for the year.

**Taxable income limit.** If you are an independent producer or royalty owner of oil and gas,

your deduction for percentage depletion is limited to the smaller of the following.

- 100% of your taxable income from the property figured without the deduction for depletion and the deduction for qualified business income under section 199A. For a definition of taxable income from the property, see *Taxable income limit*, earlier, under *Mineral Property*.
- 65% of your taxable income for the year figured without the deduction for depletion, the deduction for qualified business income under section 199A, any net operating loss carryback to the tax year under section 172, any capital loss carryback to the tax year under section 1212, and in the case of a trust, any distribution to its beneficiary (with certain exceptions).

You can carry over to the following year any amount you cannot deduct because of the 65%-of-taxable-income limit. Add it to your depletion allowance (before applying any limits) for the following year.

## Partnerships and S Corporations

Generally, each partner or S corporation shareholder, and not the partnership or S corporation, figures the depletion allowance separately. Each partner or shareholder must decide whether to use cost or percentage depletion. A partner or shareholder using percentage depletion must apply the 65%-of-taxable-income limit using its taxable income from all sources.

**Partner's or shareholder's adjusted basis.** The partnership or S corporation must allocate to each partner or shareholder its share of the adjusted basis of each oil or gas property held by the partnership or S corporation. The partnership or S corporation makes the allocation as of the date it acquires the oil or gas property.

Each partner's share of the adjusted basis of the oil or gas property is generally figured according to that partner's interest in partnership capital. However, in some cases, it is figured according to the partner's interest in partnership income.

The partnership or S corporation adjusts the partner's or shareholder's share of the adjusted basis of the oil and gas property for any capital expenditures made for the property and for any change in partnership or S corporation interests.

*Recordkeeping.* Each partner or shareholder must separately keep records of its share of the adjusted basis in each oil and gas property of the partnership or S corporation. The partner or shareholder must reduce its applicable adjusted basis by the depletion allowed or allowable on the property each year. The partner or shareholder must use that reduced adjusted basis to figure cost depletion, or its gain or loss, if the partnership or S corporation disposes of the property.

**Reporting the deduction.** Information that you, as a partner or shareholder, use to figure your depletion deduction on oil and gas properties is reported by the partnership or S corporation on Schedule K-1 (Form 1065) or on Schedule K-1 (Form 1120-S). Deduct oil and gas depletion for your partnership or S corporation interest on Schedule E (Form 1040). The depletion deducted on Schedule E is included in figuring income or loss from rental real estate or royalty properties. The Instructions for Schedule E (Form 1040) explain where to report this income or loss and whether you need to file either of the following forms.

- Form 6198.
- Form 8582.

## Natural Gas Wells

You can use percentage depletion for a well that produces natural gas that is either:

- Regulated natural gas,
- Sold under a fixed contract, or
- Produced from geopressured brine.

**Regulated natural gas.** Regulated natural gas qualifies for a percentage depletion rate of 22%. Regulated natural gas is domestic natural gas produced and sold by the producer before July 1, 1976, and is regulated by the Federal Power Commission. The price for regulated gas cannot be adjusted to reflect any increase in the seller's tax liability because of the repeal of percentage depletion for gas. Price increases after February 1, 1975, are presumed to take the increase in tax liability into account unless demonstrated otherwise by clear and convincing evidence.

**Natural gas sold under a fixed contract.** Natural gas sold under a fixed contract qualifies for a percentage depletion rate of 22%. Natural gas sold under a fixed contract is domestic natural gas sold by the producer under a contract that does not provide for a price increase to reflect any increase in the seller's tax liability because of the repeal of percentage depletion for gas. The contract must have been in effect from February 1, 1975, until the date of sale of the gas. Price increases after February 1, 1975, are presumed to take the increase in tax liability into account unless demonstrated otherwise by clear and convincing evidence.

**Natural gas from geopressured brine.** Qualified natural gas from geopressured brine is eligible for a percentage depletion rate of 10%. This is natural gas that meets both of the following conditions.

- Produced from a well you began to drill after September 1978 and before 1984.
- Determined in accordance with section 503 of the Natural Gas Policy Act of 1978 to be produced from geopressured brine.

## Mines and Geothermal Deposits

Certain mines, oil and gas wells, and other natural deposits, including geothermal deposits, qualify for percentage depletion.

**Mines, oil and gas wells, and other natural deposits.** The percentage of your gross income from the property that you can deduct as depletion depends on the type of deposit.

See section 613(b) for the percentage depletion rates.

**Corporate deduction for iron ore and coal.** The percentage depletion deduction of a corporation for iron ore and coal (including lignite) is reduced by 20% (0.20) of:

- The percentage depletion deduction for the tax year (figured without this reduction), minus
- The adjusted basis of the property at the close of the tax year (figured without the depletion deduction for the tax year).

**Gross income from the property.** For property other than a geothermal deposit or an oil or gas well, gross income from the property means the gross income from mining. Mining includes all of the following.

- Extracting ores or minerals from the ground.
- Applying certain treatment processes described below.
- Transporting ores or minerals (generally, not more than 50 miles) from the point of extraction to the plants or mills in which the treatment processes are applied.

**Excise tax.** Gross income from mining includes the separately stated excise tax received by a mine operator from the sale of coal to compensate the operator for the excise tax the mine operator must pay to finance the benefits provided under the Black Lung Benefits Revenue Act of 1977.

**Extraction.** Extracting ores or minerals from the ground includes extraction by mine owners or operators of ores or minerals from the waste or residue of prior mining. This does not apply to extraction from waste or residue of prior mining by the purchaser of the waste or residue or the purchaser of the rights to extract ores or minerals from the waste or residue.

**Treatment processes.** The processes included as mining depend on the ore or mineral mined. To qualify as mining, the treatment processes must be applied by the mine owner or operator. For a listing of treatment processes considered as mining, see section 613(c)(4) and the related regulations.

**Transportation of more than 50 miles.** If ore or mineral must be transported more than 50 miles to plants or mills to be treated because of physical and other requirements, the additional authorized transportation may be considered mining and included in the calculation of gross income from mining if authorized by the IRS.

If you wish to include transportation of more than 50 miles in the calculation of gross income from mining, request an advance ruling from the IRS. Include in the request the facts about the physical and other requirements that prevented the construction and operation of the plant (in which mining processes are applied) within 50 miles of the point of extraction. For more information about requesting an advance ruling, see Rev. Proc. 2022-1, available at *IRS.gov/irb/2022-01_IRB*, modified by Rev. Proc. 2022-10, available at *IRS.gov/irb/2022-06_IRB*, AND superseded by Rev. Proc. 2023-1, available at *IRS.gov/irb/2023-01_IRB*.

**Disposal of coal or iron ore.** You cannot take a percentage depletion deduction for coal (including lignite) or iron ore mined in the United States if both of the following apply.

- You disposed of it after holding it for more than 1 year.
- You disposed of it under a contract under which you retain an economic interest in the coal or iron ore.

Treat any gain on the disposition as a capital gain.

**Disposal to related person.** This rule does not apply if you dispose of the coal or iron ore to one of the following persons.

- A related person (as listed in chapter 2 of Pub. 544).
- A person owned or controlled by the same interests that own or control you.

**Geothermal deposits.** Geothermal deposits located in the United States or its possessions qualify for a percentage depletion rate of 15%. A geothermal deposit is a geothermal reservoir of natural heat stored in rocks or in a watery liquid or vapor (whether or not under pressure). For percentage depletion purposes, a geothermal deposit is not considered a gas well.

Figure gross income from the property for a geothermal steam well in the same way as for oil and gas wells. See *Gross income from the property*, earlier, under *Oil and Gas Wells*. Percentage depletion on a geothermal deposit cannot be more than 50% of your taxable income from the property.

## Lessor's Gross Income

In the case of leased property, the depletion deduction is divided between the lessor and the lessee.

A lessor's gross income from the property that qualifies for percentage depletion is usually the total of the royalties received from the lease.

**Bonuses and advanced royalties.** Bonuses and advanced royalties are payments a lessee makes before production to a lessor for the grant of rights in a lease or for minerals, gas, or oil to be extracted from leased property. If you are the lessor, your income from bonuses and advanced royalties received is subject to an allowance for depletion, as explained in the next two paragraphs.

**Figuring cost depletion.** To figure cost depletion on a bonus, multiply your adjusted basis in the property by a fraction, the numerator of which is the bonus and the denominator of which is the total bonus and royalties expected to be received. To figure cost depletion on advanced royalties, use the calculation explained earlier under *Cost Depletion*, treating the number of units for which the advanced royalty is received as the number of units sold.

**Figuring percentage depletion.** In the case of mines, wells, and other natural deposits other than gas, oil, or geothermal property, you may use the percentage rates discussed earlier under *Mines and Geothermal Deposits*. Any bonus or advanced royalty payments are generally part of the gross income from the property to which the rates are applied in making the calculation. However, for oil, gas, or geothermal property, gross income does not include lease bonuses, advanced royalties, or other amounts payable without regard to production from the property.

***Ending the lease.*** If you receive a bonus on a lease that ends or is abandoned before you derive any income from mineral extraction or the cutting of timber, include in income the depletion deduction you took on the bonus. Do this for the year the lease ends or is abandoned. Also, increase your adjusted basis in the property to restore the depletion deduction you previously subtracted.

For advanced royalties, include in income the depletion claimed on minerals or timber for which the advanced royalties were paid, if the minerals were not produced or timber not cut before the lease ended. Include this amount in income for the year the lease ends. Increase your adjusted basis in the property by the amount you include in income.

**Delay rentals.** These are payments for deferring development of the property. Since delay rentals are ordinary rent, they are ordinary income to the payee that is not subject to depletion. These rentals can be avoided by either abandoning the lease, beginning development operations, or obtaining production.

## Timber

You can figure timber depletion only by the cost method. Percentage depletion does not apply to timber. Base your depletion on your cost or other basis in the timber. Your cost does not include the cost of land or any amounts recoverable through depreciation.

Depletion takes place when you cut standing timber. You can figure your depletion deduction when the quantity of cut timber is first accurately measured in the process of exploitation.

**Figuring cost depletion.** To figure your cost depletion allowance, you multiply the number of timber units cut by your depletion unit.

***Timber units.*** When you acquire timber property, you must make an estimate of the quantity of marketable timber reasonably known, or on good evidence believed to exist on the property. You measure the timber using feet board measure (FBM), log scale, cords, or other units. If you later determine that you have more or less units of timber, you must adjust the original estimate.

The term "timber property" means your economic interest in standing timber in each tract or block representing a separate timber account.

***Depletion unit.*** You figure your depletion unit each year by taking the following steps.

1. Determine your cost or adjusted basis of the timber on hand at the beginning of the year. Adjusted basis is defined under *Cost Depletion* in the discussion on *Mineral Property*, earlier.

2. Add to the amount determined in (1) the cost of any timber units acquired during the year and any additions to capital.

3. Figure the number of timber units to take into account by adding the number of timber units acquired during the year to the number of timber units on hand in the account at the beginning of the year and then adding (or subtracting) any correction to the estimate of the number of timber units remaining in the account.

4. Divide the result of (2) by the result of (3). This is your depletion unit.

***Example.*** You bought a timber tract for $160,000 and the land was worth as much as the timber. Your basis for the timber is $80,000. Based on an estimated 1 million feet board measure (FBM) or 1,000 "thousand board feet" (MFBM) of standing timber, you figure your depletion unit to be $80 per MFBM ($80,000 ÷ 1,000). If you cut 500 MFBM of timber, your depletion allowance would be $40,000 (500 MFBM × $80).

**When to claim depletion.** Claim your depletion allowance as a deduction in the year of sale or other disposition of the products cut from the timber, unless you choose to treat the cutting of timber as a sale or exchange (explained below). Include allowable depletion for timber products not sold during the tax year the timber is cut as a cost item in the closing inventory of timber products for the year. The inventory is your basis for determining gain or loss in the tax year you sell the timber products.

***Example.*** The facts are the same as in the previous example, except that you sold only half of the timber products in the cutting year. You would deduct $20,000 of the $40,000 depletion that year. You would add the remaining $20,000 depletion to your closing inventory of timber products.

**Electing to treat the cutting of timber as a sale or exchange.** You can elect, under certain circumstances, to treat the cutting of timber held for more than 1 year as a sale or exchange. You must make the election on your income tax return for the tax year to which it applies. The election can't be made on an amended return. If you make this election, subtract the adjusted basis for depletion from the fair market value (FMV) of the timber on the first day of the tax year in which you cut it to figure the gain or loss on the cutting. You generally report the gain as long-term capital gain. The FMV then becomes your basis for figuring your ordinary gain or loss on the sale or other disposition of the products cut from the timber. For more information, see *Timber* in chapter 2 of Pub. 544.

You may revoke an election to treat the cutting of timber as a sale or exchange, without the IRS's consent, by the due date (including extensions) for the return. The prior election (and revocation) is disregarded for purposes of making a subsequent election. See Form T (Timber, Forest Activities Schedule) for more information.

**Form T (Timber, Forest Activities Schedule).** Complete and attach Form T (Timber, Forest Activities Schedule) to your income tax return if you claim a deduction for timber depletion, choose to treat the cutting of timber as a sale or exchange, or make an outright sale of timber.

# 10.

# Business Bad Debts

## Introduction

You have a bad debt if you cannot collect money owed to you. A bad debt is either a business bad debt or a nonbusiness bad debt. This chapter discusses only business bad debts.

Generally, a business bad debt is one that comes from operating your trade or business. You can deduct business bad debts on Schedule C (Form 1040) or your applicable business income tax return.

All other bad debts are nonbusiness bad debts and are deductible only as short-term capital losses. For more information on nonbusiness bad debts, see Pub. 550.

## Topics
This chapter discusses:

- Definition of business bad debt
- When a debt becomes worthless
- How to claim a business bad debt
- Recovery of a bad debt

## Useful Items
You may want to see:

### Publication
- ❏ **525** Taxable and Nontaxable Income
- ❏ **536** Net Operating Losses (NOLs) for Individuals, Estates, and Trusts
- ❏ **544** Sales and Other Dispositions of Assets
- ❏ **550** Investment Income and Expenses
- ❏ **556** Examination of Returns, Appeal Rights, and Claims for Refund

### Form (and Instructions)
- ❏ **Schedule C (Form 1040)** Profit or Loss From Business
- ❏ **1040-X** Amended U.S. Individual Income Tax Return
- ❏ **1045** Application for Tentative Refund
- ❏ **1065** U.S. Return of Partnership Income
- ❏ **1065-X** Amended Return or Administrative Adjustment Request (AAR)
- ❏ **1120-S** U.S. Income Tax Return for an S Corporation

❏ **1120-X** Amended U.S. Corporation Income Tax Return

❏ **1139** Corporation Application for Tentative Refund

❏ **3115** Application for Change in Accounting Method

See chapter 12 for information about getting publications and forms.

## Definition of Business Bad Debt

A business bad debt is a loss from the worthlessness of a debt that was either:
- Created or acquired in your trade or business, or
- Closely related to your trade or business when it became partly or totally worthless.

A debt is closely related to your trade or business if your primary motive for incurring the debt is business related. Bad debts of a corporation (other than an S corporation) are always business bad debts.

**Credit sales.** Business bad debts are mainly the result of credit sales to customers. Goods that have been sold, but not yet paid for, and services that have been performed, but not yet paid for, are recorded in your books as either accounts receivable or notes receivable. After a reasonable period of time, if you have tried to collect the amount due, but are unable to do so, the uncollectible part of the receivables becomes a business bad debt.

Accounts or notes receivable valued at fair market value (FMV) when received are deductible only at that value, even though the FMV may be less than the face value. If you purchased an account receivable for less than its face value, and the receivable subsequently becomes worthless, the most you're allowed to deduct is the amount you paid to acquire it.

⚠️ You can claim a business bad debt deduction only if the amount owed to you *was previously included in gross income. This applies to amounts owed to you from all sources of taxable income, including sales, services, rents, and interest.*

***Accrual method.*** If you use an accrual method of accounting, you generally report income as you earn it. You can only claim a bad debt deduction for an uncollectible receivable if you have previously included the uncollectible amount in income.

If you qualify, you can use the nonaccrual-experience method of accounting, discussed later. Under this method, you don't have to accrue income that, based on your experience, you don't expect to collect.

***Cash method.*** If you use the cash method of accounting, you generally report income when you receive payment. You can't claim a bad debt deduction for amounts owed to you because you never included those amounts in income. For example, a cash basis architect can't claim a bad debt deduction if a client fails to pay the bill because the architect's fee was never included in income.

**Debts from a former business.** If you sell your business but retain its receivables, these debts are business debts because they arose out of your trade or business. If any of these receivables subsequently become worthless, the loss is still a business bad debt.

***Debt acquired from a decedent.*** The character of a loss from debts of a business acquired from a decedent is determined in the same way as debts acquired on the purchase of a business. The executor of the decedent's estate treats any loss from the debts as a business bad debt if the debts were closely related to the decedent's trade or business when they became worthless. Otherwise, a loss from these debts becomes a nonbusiness bad debt for the decedent's estate.

***Liquidation.*** If you liquidate your business and some of the accounts receivable that you retain become worthless, they're treated as business bad debts.

## Types of Business Bad Debts

Business bad debts may result from the following.

**Loans to clients and suppliers.** If you loan money to a client, supplier, employee, or distributor for a business reason and you're unable to collect the loan after attempting to do so, you have a business bad debt.

**Debts owed by political parties.** If a political party (or other organization that accepts contributions or spends money to influence elections) owes you money and the debt becomes worthless, you can claim a bad debt deduction only if all of the following requirements are met.

1. You use an accrual method of accounting.
2. The debt arose from the sale of goods or services in the ordinary course of your trade or business.
3. More than 30% of your receivables accrued in the year of the sale were from sales to political parties.
4. You made substantial and continuing efforts to collect on the debt.

**Loan or capital contribution.** You cannot claim a bad debt deduction for a loan you made to a corporation if, based on the facts and circumstances, the loan is actually a contribution to capital.

**Debts of an insolvent partner.** If your business partnership breaks up and one of your former partners becomes insolvent, you may have to pay more than your pro rata share of the partnership's debts. If you pay any part of the insolvent partner's share of the debts, you can claim a bad debt deduction for the amount you paid that is attributable to the insolvent partner's share.

**Business loan guarantee.** If you guarantee a debt that subsequently becomes worthless, the

debt can qualify as a business bad debt if all of the following requirements are met.
- You made the guarantee in the course of your trade or business.
- You have a legal duty to pay the debt.
- You made the guarantee before the debt became worthless. You meet this requirement if you reasonably expected you wouldn't have to pay the debt without full reimbursement from the borrower.
- You received reasonable consideration for making the guarantee. You meet this requirement if you made the guarantee according to normal business practice or for a good faith business purpose.

***Example.*** Jane Zayne owns the Zayne Dress Company. She guaranteed payment of a $20,000 note for Elegant Fashions, a dress outlet. Elegant Fashions is one of Zayne's largest clients. Elegant Fashions later defaulted on the loan. As a result, Ms. Zayne paid the remaining balance of the loan in full to the bank.

She can claim a business bad debt deduction only for the amount she paid because her guarantee was made in the course of her trade or business for a good faith business purpose. She was motivated by the desire to retain one of her better clients and keep a sales outlet.

***Deductible in the year paid.*** If you make a payment on a loan you guaranteed, you can deduct it in the year paid, unless you have rights against the borrower.

***Rights against a borrower.*** When you make payment on a loan you guaranteed, you may have the right to take the place of the lender. The debt is then owed to you. If you have this right, or some other right to demand payment from the borrower, you can't claim a bad debt deduction until these rights become partly or totally worthless.

**Joint debtor.** If two or more debtors jointly owe you money, your inability to collect from one doesn't enable you to deduct a proportionate amount as a bad debt.

**Sale of mortgaged property.** If mortgaged or pledged property is sold for less than the debt, the unpaid, uncollectible balance of the debt is a bad debt.

## When a Debt Becomes Worthless

A debt becomes worthless when there is no longer any chance the amount owed will be paid. This may occur on the date the debt is due or prior to that date.

To demonstrate worthlessness, you must only show that you have taken reasonable steps to collect the debt but were unable to do so. It isn't necessary to go to court if you can show that a judgment from the court would be uncollectible. Bankruptcy of your debtor is generally good evidence of the worthlessness of at least a part of an unsecured and unpreferred debt.

**Property received for debt.** If you receive property in partial settlement of a debt, reduce the debt by the property's FMV, which becomes the property's basis. You can deduct the remaining debt as a bad debt if and when it becomes worthless.

If you later sell the property for more than its basis, any gain on the sale is due to the appreciation of the property. It isn't a recovery of a bad debt. For information on the sale of an asset, see Pub. 544.

## How To Claim a Business Bad Debt

There are two methods to claim a business bad debt.
- The specific charge-off method.
- The nonaccrual-experience method.

Generally, you must use the specific charge-off method. However, you may use the nonaccrual-experience method if you meet the requirements discussed later under *Nonaccrual-Experience Method*.

### Specific Charge-off Method

If you use the specific charge-off method, you can deduct specific business bad debts that become either partly or totally worthless during the tax year. However, with respect to partly worthless bad debts, your deduction is limited to the amount you charged off on your books during the year.

**Partly worthless debts.** You can deduct specific bad debts that become partly uncollectible during the tax year. Your tax deduction is limited to the amount you charge off on your books during the year. You don't have to charge off and deduct your partly worthless debts annually. You can delay the charge-off until a later year. However, you can't deduct any part of a debt after the year it becomes totally worthless.

*Significantly modified debt.* An exception to the charge-off rule exists for debt that has been significantly modified and on which the holder recognized gain. For more information, see Regulations section 1.166-3(a)(3).

*Deduction disallowed.* Generally, you can claim a partial bad debt deduction only in the year you make the charge-off on your books. If, under audit, the IRS doesn't allow your deduction and the debt becomes partly worthless in a later tax year, you can deduct the amount you charged off in that year plus the disallowed amount charged off in the earlier year. The charge-off in the earlier year, unless reversed on your books, fulfills the charge-off requirement for the later year.

**Totally worthless debts.** If a debt becomes totally worthless in the current tax year, you can deduct the entire amount minus any amount deducted in an earlier tax year when the debt was only partly worthless.

You don't have to make an actual charge-off on your books to claim a bad debt deduction for a totally worthless debt. However, you may want to do so. If you don't and the IRS later

rules the debt is only partly worthless, you will not be allowed a deduction for the debt in that tax year because a deduction of a partly worthless bad debt is limited to the amount actually charged off. See *Partly worthless debts*, earlier.

**Filing a claim for refund.** If you didn't deduct a bad debt on your original return for the year it became worthless, you can file a claim for a credit or refund. If the bad debt was totally worthless, you must file the claim by the later of the following dates.
- 7 years from the date your original return was due (not including extensions).
- 2 years from the date you paid the tax.

If the claim is for a partly worthless bad debt, you must file the claim by the later of the following dates.
- 3 years from the date you filed your original return.
- 2 years from the date you paid the tax.

You may have longer to file the claim if you were unable to manage your financial affairs due to a physical or mental impairment. Such an impairment requires proof of existence.

For details and more information about filing a claim, see Pub. 556. Use one of the following forms to file a claim. For more information, see the instructions for the applicable form.

Table 10-1. **Forms Used To File a Claim**

| IF you filed as a... | THEN file... |
|---|---|
| sole proprietor or farmer | Form 1040-X. |
| corporation | Form 1120-X. |
| S corporation | Form 1120-S and check box H(4). |
| partnership | Form 1065-X if filing on paper or Form 1065 and check box G(5) if filing electronically. |

## Nonaccrual-Experience Method

Generally, a person using accrual accounting isn't required to accrue a service-provided receivable that experience shows won't be collected if:
- The service provided is health, law, engineering, architecture, accounting, actuarial science, performing arts, or consulting; or
- The person's average annual gross receipts for all previous 3-tax-year periods don't exceed $27 million.

See section 448 for details and exceptions.

## Recovery of a Bad Debt

If you claim a deduction for a bad debt on your income tax return and later recover (collect) all or part of it, you may have to include all or part of the recovery in gross income. The amount you include is limited to the amount you actually deducted. However, you can exclude the

amount deducted that did not reduce your tax. Report the recovery as "Other income" on the appropriate business form or schedule.

See *Recoveries* in Pub. 525 for more information.

*NOL carryover.* If a bad debt deduction increases an NOL carryover that has not expired before the beginning of the tax year in which the recovery takes place, you treat the deduction as having reduced your tax. A bad debt deduction that contributes to an NOL helps lower taxes in the year to which you carry the NOL. For more information about NOLs for individuals, see Pub. 536. Also, see the Instructions for Form 1045, and the Instructions for Form 1139.

# 11.

# Other Expenses

## What's New

**Standard mileage rate.** For tax year 2022, the standard mileage rate for the cost of operating your car, van, pickup, or panel truck for business use is:
- 58.5 cents per mile from January 1, 2022, through June 30, 2022; and
- 62.5 cents per mile from July 1, 2022, through December 31, 2022.

For more information, see *Car and truck expenses* under *Miscellaneous Expenses*, later.

## Reminders

**No miscellaneous itemized deductions allowed.** You can no longer claim any miscellaneous itemized deductions, including the deduction for repayments (claim of right). Miscellaneous itemized deductions are those deductions that would have been subject to the 2%-of-adjusted-gross-income limitation.

**Qualified business income deduction.** For tax years beginning after 2017, individual taxpayers and some trusts and estates may be entitled to a deduction of up to 20% of their qualified business income (QBI) from a trade or business, including income from a pass-through entity, but not from a C corporation, plus 20% of qualified real estate investment trust (REIT) dividends and qualified publicly traded partnership (PTP) income. The deduction is subject to multiple limitations, such as the type of trade or business, the taxpayer's taxable income, the amount of W-2 wages paid in the trade or business, and the unadjusted basis immediately after acquisition (UBIA) of qualified property held by the trade or business. The deduction can be taken in addition to the standard or itemized deductions. See the Instructions for Form 8995 and the Instructions for Form 8995-A for more information.

**Travel, meals, and entertainment.** In general, entertainment expenses are no longer deductible. For more information on travel and non-entertainment-related meals, including deductibility, see Pub. 463.

**Certain payments made in sexual harassment or sexual abuse cases.** For amounts paid or incurred after December 22, 2017, new section 162(q) provides that no deduction is allowed under section 162 for any settlement or payment related to sexual harassment or sexual abuse if it is subject to a nondisclosure agreement. In addition, attorney's fees related to such a settlement or payment aren't allowed as a deduction.

## Introduction

This chapter covers business expenses that may not have been explained to you, as a business owner, in previous chapters of this publication.

### Topics
This chapter discusses:

- Travel and non-entertainment-related meals
- Bribes and kickbacks
- Charitable contributions
- Education expenses
- Lobbying expenses
- Penalties and fines
- Repayments (claim of right)
- Other miscellaneous expenses

### Useful Items
You may want to see:

#### Publication

- ❏ **15-B** Employer's Tax Guide to Fringe Benefits
- ❏ **463** Travel, Gift, and Car Expenses
- ❏ **526** Charitable Contributions
- ❏ **529** Miscellaneous Deductions
- ❏ **544** Sales and Other Dispositions of Assets
- ❏ **946** How To Depreciate Property
- ❏ **970** Tax Benefits for Education

#### Form (and Instructions)

- ❏ **Schedule A (Form 1040)** Itemized Deductions
- ❏ **Schedule C (Form 1040)** Profit or Loss From Business
- ❏ **Schedule F (Form 1040)** Profit or Loss From Farming
- ❏ **1099-MISC** Miscellaneous Information
- ❏ **1120** U.S. Corporation Income Tax Return
- ❏ **4562** Depreciation and Amortization
- ❏ **8949** Sales and Other Dispositions of Capital Assets

- ❏ **8995** Qualified Business Income Deduction Simplified Computation
- ❏ **8995-A** Qualified Business Income Deduction
- ❏ **W-2** Wage and Tax Statement

See chapter 12 for information about getting publications and forms.

## Reimbursement of Travel and Non-Entertainment-Related Meals

The following discussion explains how to handle any reimbursements or allowances you may provide to your employees under a reimbursement or allowance arrangement for travel and non-entertainment-related meals expenses. If you are self-employed and report your income and expenses on Schedule C (Form 1040), see Pub. 463.

To be deductible for tax purposes, expenses incurred for travel and non-entertainment-related meals must be ordinary and necessary expenses incurred while carrying on your trade or business. For more information on travel and non-entertainment-related meals, including deductibility, see Pub. 463.

### Reimbursements

A "reimbursement or allowance arrangement" provides for payment of advances, reimbursements, and allowances for travel and non-entertainment-related meals expenses incurred by your employees during the ordinary course of business. If the expenses are substantiated, you can deduct the allowable amount on your tax return. Because of differences between accounting methods and tax law, the amount you can deduct for tax purposes may not be the same as the amount you deduct on your business books and records. For example, you can deduct 100% of the cost of meals on your business books and records. However, only 50% of these costs are allowed by law as a tax deduction.

How you deduct a business expense under a reimbursement or allowance arrangement depends on whether you have:
- An accountable plan, or
- A nonaccountable plan.

If you reimburse these expenses under an accountable plan, deduct them as travel and non-entertainment-related meals expenses.

If you reimburse these expenses under a nonaccountable plan, report the reimbursements as wages on Form W-2, and deduct them as wages on the appropriate line of your tax return. If you make a single payment to your employees and it includes both wages and an expense reimbursement, you must specify the amount of the reimbursement and report it accordingly. See Table 11-1.

## Accountable Plans

An accountable plan requires your employees to meet all of the following requirements. Each employee must:

1. Have paid or incurred deductible expenses while performing services as your employee,
2. Adequately account to you for these expenses within a reasonable period of time, and
3. Return any excess reimbursement or allowance within a reasonable period of time.

An arrangement under which you advance money to employees is treated as meeting (3) above only if the following requirements are also met.
- The advance is reasonably calculated not to exceed the amount of anticipated expenses.
- You make the advance within a reasonable period of time of your employee paying or incurring the expense.

If any expenses reimbursed under this arrangement aren't substantiated, or an excess reimbursement isn't returned within a reasonable period of time by an employee, you can't treat these expenses as reimbursed under an accountable plan. Instead, treat the reimbursed expenses as paid under a nonaccountable plan, discussed later.

**Adequate accounting.** Your employees must adequately account to you for their travel and non-entertainment-related meals expenses. They must give you documentary evidence of their travel, mileage, and other employee business expenses. This evidence should include items such as receipts, along with either a statement of expenses, an account book, a day planner, or similar record in which the employee entered each expense at or near the time the expense was incurred.

**Excess reimbursement or allowance.** An excess reimbursement or allowance is any amount you pay to an employee that is more than the business-related expenses for which the employee adequately accounted. The employee must return any excess reimbursement or other expense allowance to you within a reasonable period of time.

**Reasonable period of time.** A reasonable period of time depends on the facts and circumstances. Generally, actions that take place within the times specified in the following list will be treated as taking place within a reasonable period of time.

1. You give an advance within 30 days of the time the employee pays or incurs the expense.
2. Your employees adequately account for their expenses within 60 days after the expenses were paid or incurred.
3. Your employees return any excess reimbursement within 120 days after the expenses were paid or incurred.

4. You give a periodic statement (at least quarterly) to your employees that asks them to either return or adequately account for outstanding advances *and* they comply within 120 days of the date of the statement.

**How to deduct.** You can claim a deduction for travel and non-entertainment-related meals expenses if you reimburse your employees for these expenses under an accountable plan. Generally, the amount you can deduct for non-entertainment-related meals is subject to a 50% limit, discussed later. If you are a sole proprietor, or are filing as a single member limited liability company, deduct the travel reimbursement on line 24a and the deductible part of the non-entertainment-related meals reimbursement on line 24b of Schedule C (Form 1040).

If you are filing an income tax return for a corporation, include the reimbursement on the *Other deductions* line of Form 1120. If you are filing any other business income tax return, such as a partnership or S corporation return, deduct the reimbursement on the appropriate line of the return as provided in the instructions for that return.

## Per Diem and Car Allowances

You can reimburse your employees under an accountable plan based on travel days, miles, or some other fixed allowance. In these cases, your employee is considered to have accounted to you for the amount of the expense that doesn't exceed the rates established by the federal government. Your employee must actually substantiate to you the other elements of the expense, such as time, place, and business purpose.

**Federal rate.** The federal rate can be figured using any one of the following methods.

1. For car expenses:
   a. The standard mileage rate.
   b. A fixed and variable rate (FAVR).
2. For per diem amounts:
   a. The regular federal per diem rate.
   b. The standard meal allowance.
   c. The high-low rate.

**Car allowance.** Your employee is considered to have accounted to you for car expenses that don't exceed the standard mileage rate. For tax year 2022, the standard business mileage rate is:

- 58.5 cents per mile for January 1, 2022, through June 30, 2022; and
- 62.5 cents per mile for July 1, 2022, through December 31, 2022.

To find the standard mileage rate for 2023, go to *IRS.gov/Tax-Professionals/Standard-Mileage-Rates*.

You can choose to reimburse your employees using an FAVR allowance. This is an allowance that includes a combination of payments covering fixed and variable costs, such as a cents-per-mile rate to cover your employees' variable operating costs (such as gas, oil, etc.) plus a flat amount to cover your employees'

Table 11-1. **Reporting Reimbursements**

| IF the type of reimbursement (or other expense allowance) arrangement is under | THEN the employer reports on Form W-2 |
| --- | --- |
| **An accountable plan with:** | |
| *Actual expense reimbursement:* Adequate accounting made and excess returned | No amount. |
| *Actual expense reimbursement:* Adequate accounting and return of excess both required but excess not returned | The excess amount as wages in box 1. |
| *Per diem or mileage allowance up to the federal rate:* Adequate accounting made and excess returned | No amount. |
| *Per diem or mileage allowance up to the federal rate:* Adequate accounting and return of excess both required but excess not returned | The excess amount as wages in box 1. The amount up to the federal rate is reported only in box 12—it isn't reported in box 1. |
| *Per diem or mileage allowance exceeds the federal rate:* Adequate accounting made up to the federal rate only and excess not returned | The excess amount as wages in box 1. The amount up to the federal rate is reported only in box 12—it isn't reported in box 1. |
| **A nonaccountable plan with:** | |
| Either adequate accounting or return of excess, or both, not required by plan | The entire amount as wages in box 1. |
| No reimbursement plan | The entire amount as wages in box 1. |

fixed costs (such as depreciation, insurance, etc.). For information on using an FAVR allowance, see Revenue Procedure 2019-46, available at *IRS.gov/irb/2019-49_IRB#RP-2019-46*, and Notice 2022-03, available at *IRS.gov/irb/2022-02_IRB*.

**Per diem allowance.** If your employee actually substantiates to you the other elements (discussed earlier) of the expenses reimbursed using the per diem allowance, how you report and deduct the allowance depends on whether the allowance is for lodging and meal expenses or for meal expenses only and whether the allowance is more than the federal rate.

*Regular federal per diem rate.* The regular federal per diem rate is the highest amount the federal government will pay to its employees while away from home on travel. It has the following two components.

1. Lodging expense.
2. Meal and incidental expenses (M&IE).

The rates are different for different locations. See *GSA.gov/perdiem* for the per diem rates in the continental United States.

*Standard meal allowance.* The federal rate for M&IE is the standard meal allowance. You can pay only an M&IE allowance to employees who travel away from home if:

- You pay the employee for actual expenses for lodging based on receipts submitted to you,
- You provide for the lodging,
- You pay for the actual expense of the lodging directly to the provider,
- You don't have a reasonable belief that lodging expenses were incurred by the employee, or
- The allowance is figured on a basis similar to that used in figuring the employee's wages (that is, number of hours worked or miles traveled).

*Per diem rates online.* You can access per diem rates at *GSA.gov/perdiem*.

*High-low method.* This is a simplified method of figuring the federal per diem rate for travel within the continental United States. It eliminates the need to keep a current list of the per diem rate for each city.

Under the high-low method, the per diem amount for travel during January through September of 2022 is $296 ($74 for M&IE) for certain high-cost locations. All other areas have a per diem amount of $202 ($64 for M&IE). The high-cost localities eligible for the higher per diem amount under the high-low method are listed in Notice 2021-52, available at *IRS.gov/irb/2021-38_IRB#NOT-2021-52*.

Effective October 1, 2023, the per diem rate for high-cost locations will increase to $297 ($74 for M&IE). The rate for all other locations will increase to $204 ($64 for M&IE). For October, November, and December 2023, you can either continue to use the rates described in the preceding paragraph or change to the new rates. However, you must use the same rate for all employees reimbursed under the high-low method.

For more information about the high-low method, see Notice 2022-44, available at *IRS.gov/irb/2022-41_IRB#NOT-2022-44*. See *GSA.gov/perdiem* for the current per diem rates for all locations.

**Reporting per diem and car allowances.** The following discussion explains how to report per diem and car allowances. The manner in which you report them depends on how the allowance compares to the federal rate. See *Table 11-1*.

*Allowance less than or equal to the federal rate.* If your allowance for the employee is less than or equal to the appropriate federal rate, that allowance isn't included as part of the employee's pay in box 1 of the employee's Form W-2. Deduct the allowance as travel expenses (including meals that may be subject to the 50% limit, discussed later). See *How to deduct* under *Accountable Plans*, earlier.

**Allowance more than the federal rate.** If your employee's allowance is more than the appropriate federal rate, you must report the allowance as two separate items.

Include the allowance amount up to the federal rate in box 12 (code L) of the employee's Form W-2. Deduct it as travel expenses (explained above). This part of the allowance is treated as reimbursed under an accountable plan.

Include the amount that is more than the federal rate in box 1 (and in boxes 3 and 5 if they apply) of the employee's Form W-2. Deduct it as wages subject to income tax withholding, social security, Medicare, and federal unemployment taxes. This part of the allowance is treated as reimbursed under a *Nonaccountable Plans* (explained later) under *Nonaccountable Plans*.

## Meals

Under an accountable plan, you can generally deduct only 50% of any otherwise deductible business-related meal expenses you reimburse your employees. The deduction limit applies even if you reimburse them for 100% of the expenses.

**Application of the 50% limit.** The 50% deduction limit applies to reimbursements you make to your employees for expenses they incur for meals while traveling away from home on business and meals for business customers at your place of business, a restaurant, or another location. It applies to expenses incurred at a business convention or reception, business meeting, or business luncheon at a club. The deduction limit may also apply to meals you furnish on your premises to your employees.

**TIP** *Section 210 of the Taxpayer Certainty and Disaster Tax Relief Act of 2020 provides for the temporary allowance of a 100% business meal deduction for food or beverages provided by a restaurant and paid or incurred after December 31, 2020, and before January 1, 2023.*

**Related expenses.** Taxes and tips relating to a meal you reimburse to your employee under an accountable plan are included in the amount subject to the 50% limit. However, the cost of transportation to and from an otherwise allowable business meal isn't subject to the 50% limit.

**Amount subject to 50% limit.** If you provide your employees with a per diem allowance only for meal and incidental expenses, the amount treated as an expense for food and beverages is the lesser of the following.
• The per diem allowance.
• The federal rate for M&IE.

If you provide your employees with a per diem allowance that covers lodging, meals, and incidental expenses, you must treat an amount equal to the federal M&IE rate for the area of travel as an expense for food and beverages. If the per diem allowance you provide is less than the federal per diem rate for the area of travel, you can treat 40% of the per diem allowance as the amount for food and beverages.

**Meal expenses when subject to "hours of service" limits.** You can deduct 80% of the cost of reimbursed meals your employees consume while away from their tax home on business during, or incident to, any period subject to the Department of Transportation's "hours of service" limits.

See Pub. 463 for a detailed discussion of individuals subject to the Department of Transportation's "hours of service" limits.

**De minimis (minimal) fringe benefit.** P.L. 115-97, Tax Cuts and Jobs Act, changed the rules for the deduction of food or beverage expenses that are excludable from employee income as a de minimis fringe benefit. For amounts incurred or paid after 2017, the 50% limit on deductions for food or beverage expenses also applies to food or beverage expenses excludable from employee income as a de minimis fringe benefit. While your business deduction may be limited, the rules that allow you to exclude certain de minimis meals and meals on your business premises from your employee's wages still apply. See *Meals* in section 2 of Pub. 15-B.

**Company cafeteria or executive dining room.** The cost of food and beverages you provide primarily to your employees on your business premises is deductible. This includes the cost of maintaining the facilities for providing the food and beverages. These expenses are subject to the 50% limit unless they are compensation to your employees (explained later).

**Employee activities.** The expense of providing recreational, social, or similar activities (including the use of a facility) for your employees is deductible and isn't subject to the 50% limit. The benefit must be primarily for your employees who aren't highly compensated.

For this purpose, a highly compensated employee is an employee who meets either of the following requirements.

1. Owned a 5%-or-more interest in the business during the year or the preceding year. An employee is treated as owning any interest owned by their sibling, spouse, ancestors, and lineal descendants.

2. Received more than $130,000 in pay for the preceding year. You can choose to include only employees who were also in the top 20% of employees when ranked by pay for the preceding year.

For example, the expenses for food, beverages, and entertainment for a company-wide picnic aren't subject to the 50% or 100% limit.

**Meals or entertainment treated as compensation.** The 50% limit doesn't apply to either of the following.

1. Expenses for meals or entertainment that you treat as:
   a. Compensation to an employee who was the recipient of the meals or entertainment, and
   b. Wages subject to withholding of federal income tax.

2. Expenses for meals or entertainment if:
   a. A recipient of the meals or entertainment who isn't your employee has to include the expenses in gross income as compensation for services or as a prize or award; and
   b. You include that amount on a Form 1099-MISC issued to the recipient, if a Form 1099-MISC is required.

**Sales of meals or entertainment.** You can deduct the cost of meals or entertainment (including the use of facilities) you sell to the public. For example, if you run a nightclub, your expense for the entertainment you furnish to your customers, such as a floor show, is a business expense that is fully deductible. The 100% limit doesn't apply to this expense.

**Providing meals or entertainment to general public to promote goodwill.** You can deduct the cost of providing meals, entertainment, or recreational facilities to the general public as a means of advertising or promoting goodwill in the community. The 50% or 100% limit doesn't apply to this expense.

**Director, stockholder, or employee meetings.** You can deduct entertainment expenses directly related to business meetings of your employees, partners, stockholders, agents, or directors. You can provide some minor social activities, but the main purpose of the meeting must be your company's business. These expenses are subject to the 100% limit.

**Trade association meetings.** You can deduct expenses directly related to, and necessary for, attending business meetings or conventions of certain tax-exempt organizations. These organizations include business leagues, chambers of commerce, real estate boards, and trade and professional associations.

## Nonaccountable Plans

A nonaccountable plan is an arrangement that doesn't meet the requirements for an accountable plan. All amounts paid, or treated as paid, under a nonaccountable plan are reported as wages on Form W-2. The payments are subject to income tax withholding, social security, Medicare, and federal unemployment taxes. You can deduct the reimbursement as compensation or wages only to the extent it meets the deductibility tests for employees' pay in chapter 2. Deduct the allowable amount as compensation or wages on the appropriate line of your income tax return, as provided in its instructions.

# Miscellaneous Expenses

In addition to travel, meal, and certain entertainment expenses, there are other expenses you can deduct.

**Advertising expenses.** You can generally deduct reasonable advertising expenses that are directly related to your business activities. Generally, you can't deduct amounts paid to influence legislation (for example, lobbying). For more information, see *Lobbying expenses*, later.

You can usually deduct as a business expense the cost of institutional or goodwill advertising to keep your name before the public if it relates to business you reasonably expect to gain in the future. For example, the cost of advertising that encourages people to contribute to the Red Cross, to buy U.S. savings bonds, or to participate in similar causes is usually deductible.

**Anticipated liabilities.** Anticipated liabilities or reserves for anticipated liabilities aren't deductible. For example, assume you sold 1-year TV service contracts this year totaling $50,000. From experience, you know you will have expenses of about $15,000 in the coming year for these contracts. You can't deduct any of the $15,000 this year by charging expenses to a reserve or liability account. You can deduct your expenses only when you actually pay or accrue them, depending on your accounting method.

**Bribes and kickbacks.** Engaging in the payment of bribes or kickbacks is a serious criminal matter. Such activity could result in criminal prosecution. Any payments that appear to have been made, either directly or indirectly, to an official or employee of any government or an agency or instrumentality of any government aren't deductible for tax purposes and are in violation of the law.

Payments paid directly or indirectly to a person in violation of any federal or state law (but only if that state law is generally enforced, defined below) that provides for a criminal penalty or for the loss of a license or privilege to engage in a trade or business aren't allowed as a deduction for tax purposes.

*Meaning of "generally enforced."* A state law is considered generally enforced unless it is never enforced or enforced only for infamous persons or persons whose violations are extraordinarily flagrant. For example, a state law is generally enforced unless proper reporting of a violation of the law results in enforcement only under unusual circumstances.

*Kickbacks.* A kickback is a payment for referring a client, patient, or customer. The common kickback situation occurs when money or property is given to someone as payment for influencing a third party to purchase from, use the services of, or otherwise deal with the person who pays the kickback. In many cases, the person whose business is being sought or enjoyed by the person who pays the kickback isn't aware of the payment.

For example, the Yard Corporation is in the business of repairing ships. It returns 10% of the repair bills as kickbacks to the captains and chief officers of the vessels it repairs. Although this practice is considered an ordinary and necessary expense of getting business, it is clearly a violation of a state law that is generally enforced. These expenditures aren't deductible for tax purposes, whether or not the owners of the shipyard are subsequently prosecuted.

*Form 1099-MISC.* It doesn't matter whether any kickbacks paid during the tax year are deductible on your income tax return in regards to information reporting. See Form 1099-MISC for more information.

**Car and truck expenses.** The costs of operating a car, truck, or other vehicle in your business may be deductible. For more information on how to figure your deduction, see Pub. 463.

**Charitable contributions.** Cash payments to an organization, charitable or otherwise, may be deductible as business expenses if the payments aren't charitable contributions or gifts and are directly related to your business. If the payments are charitable contributions or gifts, you can't deduct them as business expenses. However, corporations (other than S corporations) can deduct charitable contributions on their income tax returns, subject to limitations. See the Instructions for Form 1120 for more information. Sole proprietors, partners in a partnership, or shareholders in an S corporation may be able to deduct charitable contributions made by their businesses on Schedule A (Form 1040).

*Example.* You paid $15 to a local church for a half-page ad in a program for a concert it is sponsoring. The purpose of the ad was to encourage readers to buy your products. Your payment isn't a charitable contribution. You can deduct it as an advertising expense.

*Example.* You made a $100,000 donation to a committee organized by the local Chamber of Commerce to bring a convention to your city, intended to increase business activity, including yours. Your payment isn't a charitable contribution. You can deduct it as a business expense.

See Pub. 526 for a discussion of donated inventory, including capital gain property.

**Club dues and membership fees.** Generally, you can't deduct amounts paid or incurred for membership in any club organized for business, pleasure, recreation, or any other social purpose. This includes country clubs, golf and athletic clubs, hotel clubs, sporting clubs, airline clubs, and clubs operated to provide meals under circumstances generally considered to be conducive to business discussions.

*Exception.* The following organizations aren't treated as clubs organized for business, pleasure, recreation, or other social purpose unless one of the main purposes is to conduct entertainment activities for members or their guests or to provide members or their guests with access to entertainment facilities.

- Boards of trade.
- Business leagues.
- Chambers of commerce.
- Civic or public service organizations.
- Professional organizations such as bar associations and medical associations.
- Real estate boards.
- Trade associations.

**Credit card convenience fees.** Credit card companies charge a fee to businesses who accept their cards. This fee when paid or incurred by the business can be deducted as a business expense.

**Damages recovered.** Special rules apply to compensation you receive for damages sustained as a result of patent infringement, breach of contract or fiduciary duty, or antitrust violations. You must include this compensation in your income. However, you may be able to take a special deduction. The deduction applies only to amounts recovered for actual economic injury, not any additional amount. The deduction is the smaller of the following.

- The amount you received or accrued for damages in the tax year reduced by the amount you paid or incurred in the year to recover that amount.
- Your losses from the injury you haven't deducted.

**Demolition expenses or losses.** Amounts paid or incurred to demolish a structure aren't deductible. These amounts are added to the basis of the land where the demolished structure was located. Any loss for the remaining undepreciated basis of a demolished structure wouldn't be recognized until the property is disposed of.

**Education expenses.** Ordinary and necessary expenses paid for the cost of the education and training of your employees are deductible. See *Education Expenses* in chapter 2.

You can also deduct the cost of your own education (including certain related travel) related to your trade or business. You must be able to show the education maintains or improves skills required in your trade or business, or that it is required by law or regulations, for keeping your license to practice, status, or job. For example, an attorney can deduct the cost of attending Continuing Legal Education (CLE) classes that are required by the state bar association to maintain their license to practice law.

Education expenses you incur to meet the minimum requirements of your present trade or business, or those that qualify you for a new trade or business, aren't deductible. This is true even if the education maintains or improves skills presently required in your business. For more information on education expenses, see Pub. 970.

**Franchise, trademark, trade name.** If you buy a franchise, trademark, or trade name, you can deduct the amount you pay or incur as a business expense only if your payments are part of a series of payments that are:

1. Contingent on productivity, use, or disposition of the item;
2. Payable at least annually for the entire term of the transfer agreement; and
3. Substantially equal in amount (or payable under a fixed formula).

When determining the term of the transfer agreement, include all renewal options and any other period for which you and the transferor reasonably expect the agreement to be renewed.

A franchise includes an agreement that gives one of the parties to the agreement the right to distribute, sell, or provide goods, services, or facilities within a specified area.

**Impairment-related expenses.** If you are disabled, you can deduct expenses necessary for you to be able to work (impairment-related expenses) as a business expense, rather than as a medical expense.

You are disabled if you have either of the following.

- A physical or mental disability (for example, blindness or deafness) that functionally limits your being employed.
- A physical or mental impairment that substantially limits one or more of your major life activities.

The expense qualifies as a business expense if all the following apply.

- Your work clearly requires the expense for you to satisfactorily perform that work.
- The goods or services purchased are clearly not needed or used, other than incidentally, in your personal activities.
- Their treatment isn't specifically provided for under other tax law provisions.

**Example.** You are blind. You must use a reader to do your work, both at and away from your place of work. The reader's services are only for your work. You can deduct your expenses for the reader as a business expense.

**Internet-related expenses.** Generally, you can deduct Internet-related expenses including domain registration fees and webmaster consulting costs. If you are starting a business, you may have to amortize these expenses as startup costs. For more information about amortizing startup and organizational costs, see chapter 8.

**Interview expense allowances.** Reimbursements you make to job candidates for transportation or other expenses related to interviews for possible employment aren't wages. You can deduct the reimbursements as a business expense. However, expenses for food and beverages are subject to the 50% limit discussed earlier under *Meals*.

**Legal and professional fees.** Fees charged by accountants and attorneys that are ordinary and necessary expenses directly related to operating your business are deductible as business expenses. However, legal fees you pay to acquire business assets usually aren't deductible. These costs are added to the basis of the property.

Fees that include payments for work of a personal nature (such as drafting a will or damages arising from a personal injury) aren't allowed as a business deduction on Schedule C (Form 1040). If the invoice includes both business and personal charges, figure the business portion as follows: multiply the total amount of the bill by a fraction, the numerator of which is the amount attributable to business matters, and the denominator of which is the total amount paid. The result is the portion of the invoice attributable to business expenses. The portion attributable to personal matters is the difference between the total amount and the business portion (figured above).

Legal fees related to doing or keeping your job, such as those you paid to defend yourself against criminal charges arising out of your

trade or business, may be deductible on Schedule A (Form 1040) if you itemize deductions. For more information, see Pub. 529.

***Certain payments made in sexual harassment or sexual abuse cases.*** For amounts paid or incurred after December 22, 2017, new section 162(q) provides that no deduction is allowed under section 162 for any settlement or payment related to sexual harassment or sexual abuse if it is subject to a nondisclosure agreement. In addition, attorney's fees related to such a settlement or payment aren't allowed as a deduction.

***Tax preparation fees.*** The cost of hiring a tax professional, such as a certified public accountant (CPA), to prepare that part of your tax return relating to your business as a sole proprietor is deductible on Schedule C (Form 1040). You can deduct the expenses of preparing tax schedules relating to rental properties on Schedule E or farm income and expenses on Schedule F. Expenses for completing the remainder of the return are miscellaneous deductions and are no longer deductible.

You can also claim a business deduction for amounts paid or incurred in resolving asserted tax deficiencies for your business operated as a sole proprietor.

**Licenses and regulatory fees.** Licenses and regulatory fees for your trade or business paid annually to state or local governments are generally deductible. Some licenses and fees may have to be amortized. See chapter 8 for more information.

**Lobbying expenses.** Generally, lobbying expenses aren't deductible. Lobbying expenses include amounts paid or incurred for any of the following activities.

- Influencing legislation.
- Participating in or intervening in any political campaign for, or against, any candidate for public office.
- Attempting to influence the general public, or segments of the public, about elections, legislative matters, or referendums.
- Communicating directly with covered executive branch officials (defined later) in any attempt to influence the official actions or positions of those officials.
- Researching, preparing, planning, or coordinating any of the preceding activities.

Your expenses for influencing legislation and communicating directly with a covered executive branch official include a portion of your labor costs and general and administrative costs of your business. For information on making this allocation, see section 1.162-28 of the regulations.

You can't claim a charitable or business expense deduction for amounts paid to an organization if both of the following apply.

- The organization conducts lobbying activities on matters of direct financial interest to your business.
- A principal purpose of your contribution is to avoid the rules discussed earlier that prohibit a business deduction for lobbying expenses.

If a tax-exempt organization, other than a section 501(c)(3) organization, provides you

with a notice on the part of dues that is allocable to nondeductible lobbying and political expenses, you can't deduct that part of the dues.

***Covered executive branch official.*** For purposes of this discussion, a "covered executive branch official" is any of the following.

1. The President.
2. The Vice President.
3. Any officer or employee of the White House Office of the Executive Office of the President and the two most senior level officers of each of the other agencies in the Executive Office.
4. Any individual who:
   a. Is serving in a position in Level I of the Executive Schedule under section 5312 of title 5, United States Code;
   b. Has been designated by the President as having Cabinet-level status; or
   c. Is an immediate deputy of an individual listed in item (a) or (b).

***Exceptions to denial of deduction.*** The general denial of the deduction doesn't apply to the following.

- Any in-house expenses for influencing legislation and communicating directly with a covered executive branch official if those expenses for the tax year don't exceed $2,000 (excluding overhead expenses).
- Expenses incurred by taxpayers engaged in the trade or business of lobbying (professional lobbyists) on behalf of another person (but does apply to payments by the other person to the lobbyist for lobbying activities).

**Moving machinery.** Generally, the cost of moving machinery from one city to another is a deductible expense. So is the cost of moving machinery from one plant to another, or from one part of your plant to another. You can deduct the cost of installing the machinery in the new location. However, you must capitalize the costs of installing or moving newly purchased machinery.

**Outplacement services.** The costs of outplacement services you provide to your employees to help them find new employment, such as career counseling, resume assistance, skills assessment, etc., are deductible.

The costs of outplacement services may cover more than one deduction category. For example, deduct as a utilities expense the cost of telephone calls made under this service and deduct as a rental expense the cost of renting machinery and equipment for this service.

For information on whether the value of outplacement services is includible in your employees' income, see Pub. 15-B.

**Penalties and fines.** Penalties paid for late performance or nonperformance of a contract are generally deductible. For instance, you own and operate a construction company. Under a contract, you are to finish construction of a building by a certain date. Due to construction delays, the building isn't completed and ready for occupancy on the date stipulated in the contract. You are now required to pay an additional amount for each day that completion is delayed beyond the completion date stipulated in the contract. These additional costs are deductible business expenses.

On the other hand, generally, no deduction is allowed for penalties and fines paid to a government or specified nongovernmental entity for the violation of any law except the following.

- Amounts that constitute restitution.
- Amounts paid to come into compliance with the law.
- Amounts paid or incurred as the result of certain court orders in which no government or specified nongovernmental agency is a party.
- Amounts paid or incurred for taxes due.

On or after December 22, 2017, no deduction is allowed for the restitution amount or amount paid to come into compliance with the law unless the amounts are specifically identified in the settlement agreement or court order. Also, any amount paid or incurred as reimbursement to a government for the costs of any investigation or litigation aren't eligible for the exceptions and are nondeductible.

See section 162(f), as amended by P.L. 115-97, section 13306.

Examples of nondeductible penalties and fines include the following.

- Amounts paid because of a conviction for a crime or after a plea of guilty or no contest in a criminal proceeding.
- Amounts paid as a penalty imposed by federal, state, or local law in a civil action, including certain additions to tax and additional amounts and assessable penalties imposed by the Internal Revenue Code.
- Amounts paid in settlement of actual or possible liability for a fine or penalty, whether civil or criminal.
- Amounts forfeited as collateral posted for a proceeding that could result in a fine or penalty.
- Fines paid for violating city housing codes.
- Fines paid by truckers for violating state maximum highway weight laws.
- Fines paid for violating air quality laws.
- Civil penalties paid for violating federal laws regarding mining safety standards and discharges into navigable waters.

A fine or penalty doesn't include any of the following.

- Legal fees and related expenses to defend yourself in a prosecution or civil action for a violation of the law imposing the fine or civil penalty.
- Court costs or stenographic and printing charges.
- Compensatory damages paid to a government.

**Political contributions.** Contributions or gifts paid to political parties or candidates aren't deductible. In addition, expenses paid or incurred to take part in any political campaign of a candidate for public office aren't deductible.

**Indirect political contributions.** You can't deduct indirect political contributions and costs of taking part in political activities as business expenses. Examples of nondeductible expenses include the following.

- Advertising in a convention program of a political party, or in any other publication if any of the proceeds from the publication are for, or intended for, the use of a political party or candidate.
- Admission to a dinner or program (including, but not limited to, galas, dances, film presentations, parties, and sporting events) if any of the proceeds from the function are for, or intended for, the use of a political party or candidate.
- Admission to an inaugural ball, gala, parade, concert, or similar event if identified with a political party or candidate.

**Repairs.** The cost of repairing or improving property used in your trade or business is either a deductible or capital expense. Routine maintenance that keeps your property in a normal efficient operating condition, but that doesn't materially increase the value or substantially prolong the useful life of the property, is deductible in the year that it is incurred. Otherwise, the cost must be capitalized and depreciated. See Form 4562 and its instructions for how to figure and claim the depreciation deduction.

The cost of repairs includes the costs of labor, supplies, and certain other items. The value of your own labor isn't deductible. Examples of repairs include:

- Reconditioning floors (but not replacement),
- Repainting the interior and exterior walls of a building,
- Cleaning and repairing roofs and gutters, and
- Fixing plumbing leaks (but not replacement of fixtures).

**Repayments.** If you had to repay an amount you included in your income in an earlier year, you may be able to deduct the amount repaid for the year in which you repaid it. Or, if the amount you repaid is more than $3,000, you may be able to take a credit against your tax for the year in which you repaid it. In most cases, you can claim a deduction or credit only if the repayment qualifies as an expense or loss incurred in your trade or business or in a for-profit transaction.

**Type of deduction.** The type of deduction you are allowed in the year of repayment depends on the type of income you included in the earlier year. For instance, if you repay an amount you previously reported as a capital gain, deduct the repayment as a capital loss as explained in the Instructions for Schedule D (Form 1040). If you reported it as self-employment income, deduct it as a business expense on Schedule C (Form 1040), or a farm expense on Schedule F (Form 1040).

If you reported the amount as wages, unemployment compensation, or other nonbusiness ordinary income, you may be able to deduct it as an other itemized deduction if the amount repaid is over $3,000.

*Beginning in 2018, due to the suspension of miscellaneous itemized deductions subject to the 2% floor under section 67(a), you aren't able to deduct the repayment as an itemized deduction if it is $3,000 or less.*

**Repayment—$3,000 or less.** If the amount you repaid was $3,000 or less, deduct it from your income in the year you repaid it.

**Repayment—Over $3,000.** If the amount you repaid was more than $3,000, you can deduct the repayment as an other itemized deduction on Schedule A (Form 1040), line 16, if you included the income under a "claim of right." This means that at the time you included the income, it appeared that you had an unrestricted right to it. However, you can choose to take a credit for the year of repayment. Figure your tax under both methods and use the method that results in less tax.

**Method 1.** Figure your tax for 2022 claiming a deduction for the repaid amount.

**Method 2.** Figure your tax for 2022 claiming a credit for the repaid amount. Follow these steps.

1. Figure your tax for 2022 without deducting the repaid amount.
2. Refigure your tax from the earlier year without including in income the amount you repaid in 2022.
3. Subtract the tax in (2) from the tax shown on your return for the earlier year. This is the amount of your credit.
4. Subtract the answer in (3) from the tax for 2022 figured without the deduction (step 1).

If Method 1 results in less tax, deduct the amount repaid as discussed earlier under *Type of deduction.*

If Method 2 results in less tax, claim the credit on Schedule 3 (Form 1040), line 13z, and write "I.R.C. 1341" next to line 13z.

**Example.** For 2021, you filed a return and reported your income on the cash method. In 2022, you repaid $5,000 included in your 2021 gross income under a claim of right. Your filing status in 2022 and 2021 is single. Your income and tax for both years are as follows:

| | 2021 With Income | 2021 Without Income |
|---|---|---|
| Taxable Income | $15,000 | $10,000 |
| Tax | $1,604 | $1,004 |

| | 2022 Without Deduction | 2022 With Deduction |
|---|---|---|
| Taxable Income | $49,950 | $44,950 |
| Tax | $6,606 | $5,506 |

Your tax under Method 1 is $5,506. Your tax under Method 2 is $6,006, figured as follows:

Tax previously determined for
2021 . . . . . . . . . . . . . . . . . . . . . . . . $ 1,604
Less: Tax as refigured . . . . . . . . . . . – 1,004
Decrease in 2021 tax . . . . . . . . . . . . $600
Regular tax liability for 2022 . . . . . . $6,606
Less: Decrease in 2021 tax . . . . . . . – 600
**Refigured tax for 2022** . . . . . . . . **$6,006**

Because you pay less tax under Method 1, you should take a deduction for the repayment in 2022.

**Repayment does not apply.** This discussion doesn't apply to the following.
- Deductions for bad debts.
- Deductions from sales to customers, such as returns and allowances, and similar items.
- Deductions for legal and other expenses of contesting the repayment.

**Year of deduction (or credit).** If you use the cash method of accounting, you can take the deduction (or credit, if applicable) for the tax year in which you actually make the repayment. If you use any other accounting method, you can deduct the repayment or claim a credit for it only for the tax year in which it is a proper deduction under your accounting method. For example, if you use the accrual method, you are entitled to the deduction or credit in the tax year in which the obligation for the repayment accrues.

**Supplies and materials.** Unless you have deducted the cost in any earlier year, you can generally deduct the cost of materials and supplies actually consumed and used during the tax year.

If you keep incidental materials and supplies on hand, you can deduct the cost of the incidental materials and supplies you bought during the tax year if all the following requirements are met.
- You don't keep a record of when they are used.
- You don't take an inventory of the amount on hand at the beginning and end of the tax year.
- This method doesn't distort your income.

You can also deduct the cost of books, professional instruments, equipment, etc., if you normally use them within a year. However, if the usefulness of these items extends substantially beyond the year they are placed in service, you must generally recover their costs through depreciation. For more information regarding depreciation, see Pub. 946.

**Utilities.** Business expenses for heat, lights, power, telephone service, and water and sewerage are deductible. However, any part due to personal use isn't deductible.

**Telephone.** You can't deduct the cost of basic local telephone service (including any taxes) for the first telephone line you have in your home, even if you have an office in your home. However, charges for business long-distance phone calls on that line, as well as the cost of a second line into your home used exclusively for business, are deductible business expenses.

# 12.

# How To Get Tax Help

If you have questions about a tax issue; need help preparing your tax return; or want to download free publications, forms, or instructions, go to *IRS.gov* to find resources that can help you right away.

**TTY/TDD and Federal Relay Service.** People who are deaf, hard of hearing, or have a speech disability and who have access to TTY/TDD equipment can call toll free 800-829-4059 to ask tax questions or to order forms and publications. Deaf or hard of hearing customers may call any of our toll-free numbers using their choice of relay service.

**Coronavirus.** Go to *IRS.gov/Coronavirus* for links to information on the impact of the coronavirus, as well as tax relief available for individuals and families, small and large businesses, and tax-exempt organizations.

**Preparing and filing your tax return.** After receiving all your wage and earning statements (Forms W-2, W-2G, 1099-R, 1099-MISC, 1099-NEC, etc.); unemployment compensation statements (by mail or in a digital format) or other government payment statements (Form 1099-G); and interest, dividend, and retirement statements from banks and investment firms (Forms 1099), you have several options to choose from to prepare and file your tax return. You can prepare the tax return yourself, see if you qualify for free tax preparation, or hire a tax professional to prepare your return.

**Free options for tax preparation.** Go to *IRS.gov* to see your options for preparing and filing your return online or in your local community, if you qualify, which include the following.
- **Free File.** This program lets you prepare and file your federal individual income tax return for free using brand-name tax-preparation-and-filing software or Free File fillable forms. However, state tax preparation may not be available through Free File. Go to *IRS.gov/FreeFile* to see if you qualify for free online federal tax preparation, e-filing, and direct deposit or payment options.
- **VITA.** The Volunteer Income Tax Assistance (VITA) program offers free tax help to people with low-to-moderate incomes, persons with disabilities, and limited-English-speaking taxpayers who need help preparing their own tax returns. Go to *IRS.gov/VITA*, download the free IRS2Go app, or call 800-906-9887 for information on free tax return preparation.
- **TCE.** The Tax Counseling for the Elderly (TCE) program offers free tax help for all taxpayers, particularly those who are 60 years of age and older. TCE volunteers specialize in answering questions about pensions and retirement-related issues

unique to seniors. Go to *IRS.gov/TCE*, download the free IRS2Go app, or call 888-227-7669 for information on free tax return preparation.
- **MilTax.** Members of the U.S. Armed Forces and qualified veterans may use MilTax, a free tax service offered by the Department of Defense through Military One-Source. For more information, go to *MilitaryOneSource* (*MilitaryOneSource.mil/MilTax*).

Also, the IRS offers Free Fillable Forms, which can be completed online and then filed electronically regardless of income.

**Employers can register to use Business Services Online.** The Social Security Administration (SSA) offers online service at *SSA.gov/Employer* for fast, free, and secure online W-2 filing options to certified public accountants (CPAs), accountants, enrolled agents, and individuals who process Forms W-2, Wage and Tax Statement, and Forms W-2c, Corrected Wage and Tax Statement.

**Tax reform.** Tax reform legislation affects individuals, businesses, and tax-exempt and government entities. Go to *IRS.gov/TaxReform* for information and updates on how this legislation affects your taxes.

**A–Z index for business.** *Find it fast!* Know what you're looking for and want to find it fast? Select business topics using our A–Z listing, or by business type such as sole proprietor, corporation, etc. We also provide links to major business subjects, such as Business Expenses, which provide a gateway to all related information on those subjects.
- *Small Business Forms and Publications*. You can download forms and publications for small businesses and self-employed individuals.
- *Employer ID Numbers (EINs)*. Find out about EINs or apply for one online.
- *e-File Form 940, 941, 944, or 945 for Small Businesses*. Learn your options for *e-filing* Form 940, 941, 944, or 945 for small businesses.
- *Employment Taxes*. Federal income tax, social security and Medicare taxes, FUTA tax, self-employment tax, and more.
- *Independent Contractor (Self-Employed) or Employee*. It is critical that you, the employer, correctly determine whether the individuals providing services are employees or independent contractors.
- *Self-Employed Individuals Tax Center*. The basics on self-employment, filing requirements, and reporting responsibilities for independent contractors.
- *Information Return Filing Requirements*. If you made or received a payment as a small business or self-employed individual, you are most likely required to file an information return with the IRS.
- *IRS Video Portal*. Videos, webinars, and audio presentations for small businesses, individuals, and tax pros.
- *Small Business Events*. Workshops and webinars on a variety of topics for small businesses.
- *Online Tools & Educational Products*. Choose from a variety of products,

including the Tax Calendar desktop tool, to help you learn about business taxes on your own time, and at your own pace.

- *Subscribe to e-News.* A free electronic mail service keeping you up to date on tax topics.

**Requirements for filing.** If you made or received a payment during the calendar year as a small business or self-employed individual, you are most likely required to file an information return with the IRS. For more information, see *Am I Required To File a Form 1099 or Other Information Return?* on IRS.gov.

**Getting answers to your tax questions.** On *IRS.gov,* you can get up-to-date information on current events and changes in tax law.

- *IRS.gov/Help*: A variety of tools to help you get answers to some of the most common tax questions.
- *IRS.gov/ITA*: The Interactive Tax Assistant, a tool that will ask you questions and, based on you input, provide answers on a number of tax law topics.
- *IRS.gov/Forms*: Find forms, instructions, and publications. You will find details on the most recent tax changes and interactive links to help you find answers to your questions.
- You may also be able to access tax law information in your electronic filing software.

**IRS social media.** Go to *IRS.gov/SocialMedia* to see the various social media tools the IRS uses to share the latest information on tax changes, scam alerts, initiatives, products, and services. At the IRS, privacy and security are our highest priority. We use these tools to share public information with you. **Don't** post your social security number (SSN) or other confidential information on social media sites. Always protect your identity when using any social networking site.

The following IRS YouTube channels provide short, informative videos on various tax-related topics in English, Spanish, and ASL.

- *Youtube.com/irsvideos*.
- *Youtube.com/irsvideosmultilingua*.
- *Youtube.com/irsvideosASL*.

**Watching IRS videos.** The IRS Video portal (*IRSVideos.gov*) contains video and audio presentations for individuals, small businesses, and tax professionals.

**Online tax information in other languages.** You can find information on *IRS.gov/MyLanguage* if English isn't your native language.

**Free Over-the-Phone Interpreter (OPI) Service.** The IRS is committed to serving our multilingual customers by offering OPI services. The OPI Service is a federally funded program and is available at Taxpayer Assistance Centers (TACs), other IRS offices, and every VITA/TCE return site. The OPI Service is accessible in more than 350 languages.

**Accessibility Helpline available for taxpayers with disabilities.** Taxpayers who need in-

formation about accessibility services can call 833-690-0598. The Accessibility Helpline can answer questions related to current and future accessibility products and services available in alternative media formats (for example, braille, large print, audio, etc.). The Accessibility Helpline does not have access to your IRS account. For help with tax law, refunds, or account-related issues, go to *IRS.gov/LetUsHelp.*

**Note.** Form 9000, Alternative Media Preference, or Form 9000(SP) allows you to elect to receive certain types of written correspondence in the following formats.

- Standard Print.
- Large Print.
- Braille.
- Audio (MP3).
- Plain Text File (TXT).
- Braille Ready File (BRF).

**Disasters.** Go to *Disaster Assistance and Emergency Relief for Individuals and Businesses* to review the available disaster tax relief.

**Getting tax forms and publications.** Go to *IRS.gov/Forms* to view, download, or print all of the forms, instructions, and publications you may need. Or, you can go to *IRS.gov/OrderForms* to place an order and have them mailed to you within 10 business days.

**Getting tax publications and instructions in eBook format.** You can also download and view popular tax publications and instructions (including the Instructions for Form 1040) on mobile devices as eBooks at *IRS.gov/eBooks.*

**Note.** IRS eBooks have been tested using Apple's iBooks for iPad. Our eBooks haven't been tested on other dedicated eBook readers, and eBook functionality may not operate as intended.

**Access your online account (individual taxpayers only).** Go to *IRS.gov/Account* to securely access information about your federal tax account.

- View the amount you owe and a breakdown by tax year.
- See payment plan details or apply for a new payment plan.
- Make a payment or view 5 years of payment history and any pending or scheduled payments.
- Access your tax records, including key data from your most recent tax return and transcripts.
- View digital copies of select notices from the IRS.
- Approve or reject authorization requests from tax professionals.
- View your address on file or manage your communication preferences.

**Tax Pro Account.** This tool lets your tax professional submit an authorization request to access your individual taxpayer *IRS online account*. For more information, go to *IRS.gov/TaxProAccount.*

**Using direct deposit.** The fastest way to receive a tax refund is to file electronically and

choose direct deposit, which securely and electronically transfers your refund directly into your financial account. Direct deposit also avoids the possibility that your check could be lost, stolen, or returned undeliverable to the IRS. Eight in 10 taxpayers use direct deposit to receive their refunds. If you don't have a bank account, go to *IRS.gov/DirectDeposit* for more information on where to find a bank or credit union that can open an account online.

**Need someone to prepare your tax return?** There are various types of tax return preparers, including enrolled agents, CPAs, attorneys, and many others who don't have professional credentials. If you choose to have someone prepare your tax return, choose that preparer wisely. A paid tax preparer is:

- Primarily responsible for the overall substantive accuracy of your return,
- Required to sign the return, and
- Required to include their preparer tax identification number (PTIN).

Although the tax preparer always signs the return, you're ultimately responsible for providing all the information required for the preparer to accurately prepare your return. Anyone paid to prepare tax returns for others should have a thorough understanding of tax matters. For more information on how to choose a tax preparer, go to *Tips for Choosing a Tax Preparer* on IRS.gov.

For your convenience, the IRS provides an online database for all Authorized IRS *e-file* Providers that choose to be included in the database. You can locate the closest Authorized IRS *e-file* Providers in your area where you can electronically file your tax return. For more information on finding a tax return preparer who provides IRS *e-file,* see *Authorized IRS e-file Providers for Individuals* on IRS.gov, or go to *IRS.gov/uac/Authorized-IRS-e-file-Providers-for-Individuals.* The inclusion in this database does not constitute any endorsement by the IRS of the *e-file* Providers listed in this database or any of the products or services that they provide. You should always be sure to conduct your own due diligence when selecting an *e-file* Provider. In addition to the Authorized IRS *e-file* Provider locator tool above, you can also find professional help through the *IRS Tax Professional Partner* page at *IRS.gov/Tax-Professionals/IRSTaxProAssociationPartners.*

Choose a tax return preparer you will be able to contact in case the IRS examines your return and has questions regarding how your return was prepared. You can designate your paid tax return preparer or another third party to speak to the IRS concerning the preparation of your return, payment/refund issues, and mathematical errors. The third party authorization checkbox on Form 1040 or 1040-SR gives the designated party the authority to receive and inspect returns and return information for 1 year from the original due date of your return (without regard to extensions). You can extend the authority to receive and inspect returns and return information to a third party using *Form 8821, Tax Information Authorization.*

The following points will assist you when selecting a tax return preparer.

- **Check the preparer's qualifications.** All paid tax return preparers are required to have a PTIN.
- **Check the preparer's history.** You can check with the Better Business Bureau to find out if a preparer has a questionable history. Check for disciplinary actions and the license status for credentialed preparers. For CPAs, check with the State Board of Accountancy. For attorneys, check with the State Bar Association. For Enrolled Agents (EAs), go to *IRS.gov/Tax-Professionals/Verify-the-Status-of-an-Enrolled-Agent* and follow the instructions for requesting EA status verification.
- **Ask about service fees.** Avoid preparers who base their fee on a percentage of your refund or those who say they can get larger refunds than others can. Always make sure any refund due is sent directly to you or deposited into your bank account. You should **not** have your refund deposited into a preparer's bank account.
- **Ask to e-file your return.** Make sure your preparer offers IRS *e-file*. Any paid preparer who prepares and files more than 10 returns must generally *e-file* their clients' returns. The IRS has safely processed more than 1.3 billion *e-filed* tax returns.
- **Make sure the preparer is available.** You need to ensure that you can contact the tax preparer after you file your return. That's true even after the April 17, 2023, due date for individual returns. The due date for partnerships and S corporations using a calendar year is March 15, 2023. You may need to contact the preparer if questions come up about your tax return at a later time.
- **Provide tax records.** A good preparer will ask to see your records and receipts. They ask you questions to report your total income and the tax benefits you're entitled to claim. These may include tax deductions, tax credits, and other items. Do not use a preparer who is willing to *e-file* your return using your last pay stub instead of your *Form W-2*. This is against IRS *e-file* rules.
- **Never sign a blank tax return.** Do not use a tax preparer who asks you to sign a blank tax form.
- **Review your return before signing.** Before you sign your tax return, review it thoroughly. Ask questions if something is not clear to you. Make sure you're comfortable with the information on the return before you sign it.
- **Preparer must sign returns and include their PTIN.** A paid preparer **must** sign returns and include his or her PTIN as required by law. The preparer must also give you a copy of the return.
- **Report abusive tax preparers to the IRS.** You can report abusive tax preparers and suspected tax fraud to the IRS. Use *Form 14157, Complaint: Tax Return Preparer*. If you suspect a return preparer filed or changed the return without your consent, you should also file *Form 14157-A, Return Preparer Fraud or Misconduct Affidavit*. You can download and print these forms from IRS.gov. If you need a paper form mailed to you, go to *IRS.gov/OrderForms* to order online. For more information, go to *How Do You Report Suspected Tax Fraud Activity?* on IRS.gov.

**Using online tools to help prepare your return.** Go to *IRS.gov/Tools* for the following.

- The *Earned Income Tax Credit Assistant* (*IRS.gov/EITCAssistant*) determines if you're eligible for the earned income credit (EIC).
- The *Online EIN Application* (*IRS.gov/EIN*) helps you get an employer identification number (EIN) at no cost.
- The *Tax Withholding Estimator* (*IRS.gov/W4app*) makes it easier for you to estimate the federal income tax you want your employer to withhold from your paycheck. This is tax withholding. See how your withholding affects your refund, take-home pay, or tax due.
- The *First-Time Homebuyer Credit Account Look-up* (*IRS.gov/HomeBuyer*) tool provides information on your repayments and account balance.
- The *Sales Tax Deduction Calculator* (*IRS.gov/SalesTax*) figures the amount you can claim if you itemize deductions on Schedule A (Form 1040).
- Go to *IRS.gov/Pub17* to get Pub. 17, Your Federal Income Tax for Individuals, which features details on tax-saving opportunities, 2022 tax changes, and thousands of interactive links to help you find answers to your questions. View it online in HTML or as a PDF or, better yet, download it to your mobile device to enjoy eBook features.
- You may also be able to access tax law information in your electronic filing software.
- Go to IRS.gov and click on the Help & Resources tab for more information.

**Getting a transcript or copy of a return.** Tax transcripts are summaries of tax returns. IRS transcripts are best and most often used to validate past income and tax filing status for mortgage, student, and small business loan applications, and to help with tax preparation. Taxpayers can also use transcripts to obtain their prior-year adjusted gross income (AGI), which they need in order to *e-file* their returns. You can get a transcript by mail to view your tax account transactions or line-by-line tax return information for a specific tax year. The method you used to file your return and whether you have a refund or balance due affects your current tax year transcript availability. Generally, these transcript types are available for the current tax year and 3 prior years. The quickest way to get a copy of your tax transcript is to go to *IRS.gov/Transcripts*. Click on either "Get Transcript Online" or "Get Transcript by Mail" to order a free copy of your transcript. If you need an account transcript for an older tax year, a wage and income transcript, or a verification of nonfiling letter, you'll need to complete Form 4506-T, Request for Transcript of Tax Return, available at *IRS.gov/Forms-Pubs/About-Form-4506-T*, and send it to us as instructed on the form. If you made estimated tax payments and/or applied your overpayment from a prior-year tax return to your current-year tax return, you can request a tax account transcript to confirm these payments or credits a few weeks after the beginning of the calendar year prior to filing your current-year return. For the list of the various types of transcripts available for you to order, see *Transcript Types and Ways to Order Them* at *IRS.gov/Individuals/Tax-Return-Transcript-Types-and-Ways-to-Order-Them*. To order your transcript, you can choose from one of the following convenient options.

- Request a return or account transcript using *Get Transcript* at *IRS.gov/Individuals/Get-Transcript*.
- Download the free IRS2Go app to your mobile device and use it to order transcripts of your tax returns or tax account.
- Call the automated transcript toll-free line at 800-908-9946 to receive your transcript by mail.
- Go to *Get Transcript* at *IRS.gov/Individuals/Get-Transcript*, and click on "Get Transcript by Mail." You will need your SSN or your individual taxpayer identification number (ITIN), date of birth, and address from your latest tax return. Transcripts arrive in 5 to 10 calendar days at the address we have on file for you.
- Mail *Form 4506-T, Request for Transcript of Tax Return*, or *Form 4506T-EZ, Short Form Request for Individual Tax Return Transcript* (both available on IRS.gov).

The IRS never sends email requesting that you obtain or access your transcripts. Report all unsolicited email claiming to be from the IRS or an IRS-related function to *phishing@irs.gov*.

A transcript isn't a photocopy of your return. If you need a photocopy of your original return, complete and mail *Form 4506, Request for Copy of Tax Return*, available at *IRS.gov/Pub/irs-pdf/F4506.pdf*, along with the applicable fee.

**Reporting and resolving your tax-related identity theft issues.**

- Tax-related identity theft happens when someone steals your personal information to commit tax fraud. Your taxes can be affected if your SSN is used to file a fraudulent return or to claim a refund or credit.
- The IRS doesn't initiate contact with taxpayers by email, text messages (including shortened links), telephone calls, or social media channels to request or verify personal or financial information. This includes requests for personal identification numbers (PINs), passwords, or similar information for credit cards, banks, or other financial accounts.
- Go to *IRS.gov/IdentityTheft*, the IRS Identity Theft Central webpage, for information on identity theft and data security protection for taxpayers, tax professionals, and businesses. If your SSN has been lost or stolen or you suspect you're a victim of tax-related identity theft, you can learn what steps you should take.
- Get an Identity Protection PIN (IP PIN). IP PINs are six-digit numbers assigned to taxpayers to help prevent the misuse of their SSNs on fraudulent federal income tax returns. When you have an IP PIN, it prevents someone else from filing a tax return with your SSN. To learn more, go to *IRS.gov/IPPIN*.
- The IRS stops and flags suspicious or duplicate federal tax returns that falsely

represent your identity, such as your name or SSN. If the IRS suspects tax ID theft, the agency will send a *5071C* letter to your home address. If you receive this letter, verify your identity at *IDVerify.IRS.gov* or call the toll-free number listed in the letter. If you did not receive an IRS notice but believe you've been the victim of ID theft, contact the IRS Identity Protection Specialized Unit at 800-908-4490 right away so we can take steps to secure your tax account and match your SSN or ITIN.

- Also, fill out and submit the IRS *Form 14039, Identity Theft Affidavit*. Please write legibly and follow the directions on the back of the form that relate to your specific circumstances.
- If you are a victim of state tax ID theft, contact your state's taxation department or comptroller's office about the next steps you need to take.
- You should protect the information that you keep, and properly dispose of what you no longer need. And, of course, you should create a plan to respond to security incidents. As part of its long-standing efforts to promote good data security practices, the Federal Trade Commission (FTC) has undertaken extensive efforts to educate businesses and has brought more than 50 law enforcement actions related to data security issues. For more information, see Protecting Personal Information: A Guide for Business, available at *FTC.gov/Tips-advice/business-center/guidance/protecting-personal-information-guide-business*, for practical tips on creating and implementing a plan for safeguarding personal information used in your business. Most recently, the FTC released Start with Security: A Guide for Business, available at *FTC.gov/Tips-advice/business-center/guidance/start-security-guide-business?utm_source=govdelivery*, which draws on the lessons learned from the FTC's enforcement actions.

The IRS, the states, and the tax industry joined together to enact new safeguards and take additional actions to combat tax-related identity theft. Many of these safeguards will be invisible to you, but invaluable to our fight against these criminal syndicates. If you prepare your own return with tax software, you will see new log-on standards. Some states also have taken additional steps. See your *state revenue agency's web site* for additional details.

The FTC works for consumers to prevent fraudulent, deceptive, and unfair business practices and to provide information to help spot, stop, and avoid them. To file a complaint, for example, to report someone falsely claiming to be from the government, a business, or a family member, visit the FTC's online *Report Fraud Assistant* or call 877-FTC-HELP (877-382-4357). The FTC enters complaints into Consumer Sentinel, a secure, online database available to more than 2,000 civil and criminal law enforcement agencies in the United States and abroad. Complaints from consumers help the FTC detect patterns of fraud and

abuse. The FTC's website provides free information on a variety of consumer topics, in English and in Spanish.

Consumer complaints regarding international scams can be reported online through *Econsumer.gov*. These are also entered into Consumer Sentinel, the complaint database maintained by the FTC, and are made available to enforcers and regulators in countries with participating agencies. Those agencies may use the complaints to investigate cross-border issues, uncover new scams, pursue regulatory or enforcement actions, and spot consumer trends.

### Ways to check on the status of your refund.
- Go to *IRS.gov/Refunds*.
- Download the official IRS2Go app to your mobile device to check your refund status.
- Call the automated refund hotline at 800-829-1954.

**Note.** The IRS can't issue refunds before mid-February for returns that claimed the EIC or the additional child tax credit (ACTC). This applies to the entire refund, not just the portion associated with these credits.

**Making a tax payment.** Go to *IRS.gov/Payments* for information on how to make a payment using any of the following options.

- *IRS Direct Pay*: Pay your individual tax bill or estimated tax payment directly from your checking or savings account at no cost to you.
- *Debit or Credit Card*: Choose an approved payment processor to pay online or by phone.
- *Electronic Funds Withdrawal*: Schedule a payment when filing your federal taxes using tax return preparation software or through a tax professional.
- *Electronic Federal Tax Payment System*: Best option for businesses. Enrollment is required.
- *Check or Money Order*: Mail your payment to the address listed on the notice or instructions.
- *Cash*: You may be able to pay your taxes with cash at a participating retail store.
- *Same-Day Wire*: You may be able to do same-day wire from your financial institution. Contact your financial institution for availability, cost, and time frames.

**Note.** The IRS uses the latest encryption technology to ensure that the electronic payments you make online, by phone, or from a mobile device using the IRS2Go app are safe and secure. Paying electronically is quick, easy, and faster than mailing in a check or money order.

**What if I can't pay now?** Go to *IRS.gov/Payments* for more information about your options.

- Apply for an *online payment agreement* (*IRS.gov/OPA*) to meet your tax obligation in monthly installments if you can't pay your taxes in full today. Once you complete the online process, you will receive immediate notification of whether your agreement has been approved.

- Use the *Offer in Compromise Pre-Qualifier* to see if you can settle your tax debt for less than the full amount you owe. For more information on the Offer in Compromise program, go to *IRS.gov/OIC*. If you are a sole proprietor or independent contractor, apply for a payment agreement as an individual.

**Filing an amended return.** Go to *IRS.gov/Form1040X* for information and updates.

**Checking the status of an amended return.** Go to *IRS.gov/WMAR* to track the status of Form 1040-X amended returns.

**Note.** It can take up to 3 weeks from the date you filed your amended return for it to show up in our system, and processing it can take up to 16 weeks.

**Filing past due tax returns.** File all tax returns that are due, regardless of whether or not you can pay in full. File your past due return the same way and to the same location where you would file an on-time return. If you have received a notice, make sure to send your past due return to the location indicated on the notice you received. If you have a past due return, filing your past due return now can help you do the following.

- **Avoid interest and penalties.** File your past due return and pay now to limit interest charges and late payment penalties.
- **Claim a refund.** You risk losing your refund if you don't file your return. If you are due a refund for withholding or estimated taxes, you must file your return to claim it within 3 years of the return due date. The same rule applies to a right to claim tax credits such as the EIC. We hold income tax refunds in cases where our records show that one or more income tax returns are past due. We hold them until we get the past due return or receive an acceptable reason for not filing a past due return.
- **Protect social security benefits.** If you are self-employed and do not file your federal income tax return, any self-employment income you earned will not be reported to the SSA and you will not receive credits toward social security retirement or disability benefits.
- **Avoid issues obtaining loans.** Loan approvals may be delayed if you don't file your return. Copies of filed tax returns must be submitted to financial institutions, mortgage lenders/brokers, etc., whenever you want to buy or refinance a home, get a loan for a business, or apply for federal aid for higher education.

For more information, go to *Filing Past Due Tax Returns* on IRS.gov.

**Substitute return.** If you fail to file voluntarily, we may file a substitute return for you, based on income reported to the IRS. This return might not give you credit for deductions and exemptions you may be entitled to receive. We will send you a *Notice of Deficiency CP3219N* (90-day letter) proposing a tax assessment. You will have 90 days to file your past due tax return or file a petition in Tax Court. If you do neither, we will proceed with our proposed assessment. If you have received a Notice of Deficiency CP3219N, you can't request an extension to file. Call us if you think you don't have to file.

If any of the income listed is incorrect, you may do the following.

- Contact us toll free at 866-681-4271 to let us know.
- Contact the payer (source) of the income to request a corrected Form W-2 or 1099.
- Attach the corrected forms when you send us your completed tax returns.

If the IRS files a substitute return, it is still in your best interest to file your own tax return to take advantage of any exemptions, credits, and deductions you are entitled to receive. The IRS will generally adjust your account to reflect the correct figures. If you filed a past due return and have received a notice, you should send us a copy of the past due return to the address contained in the notice. It takes approximately 6 weeks for us to process an accurately completed past due tax return.

**Understanding an IRS notice or letter.** Go to *IRS.gov/Notices* to find additional information about responding to an IRS notice or letter. We will send you a notice or letter if any of the following apply.

- You have a balance due.
- You are due a larger or smaller refund.
- We have a question about your tax return.
- We need to verify your identity.
- We need additional information.
- We changed your return.
- We are notifying you of delays in processing your return.

When you receive correspondence from us, read the entire notice or letter carefully. Typically, we only need a response if you don't agree with the information, we need additional information, or you have a balance due. If we changed your tax return, compare the information we provided in the notice or letter with the information in your original return. If we receive a return that we suspect is ID theft, we will ask you to verify your identity using the web address provided in the letter.

If we ask for a response within a specific time frame, you must respond on time to minimize additional interest and penalty charges or to preserve your appeal rights if you don't agree. Pay as much as you can, even if you can't pay the full amount you owe. You can pay online or apply for an OPA or OIC. See *What if I can't pay now*, earlier, or visit our *Payments* page, *IRS.gov/Payments*, for more information.

We provide our contact phone number on the top right-hand corner of our correspondence. Be sure you have your tax return and any related documentation available when you call. You can also write to us at the address in the correspondence to explain why you disagree. If you write, allow at least 30 days for our response. Keep a copy of all correspondence with your tax records.

**Note.** You can use Schedule LEP (Form 1040), Request for Change in Language Preference, to state a preference to receive notices, letters, or other written communications from the IRS in an alternative language. The IRS's commitment to LEP taxpayers is part of a multi-year timeline that is scheduled to begin providing translations in 2023. You will continue to receive communications, including notices and letters, in English until they are translated to your preferred language.

**Collection and enforcement actions.** The return we prepare for you (our proposed assessment) will lead to a tax bill, which, if unpaid, will trigger the collection process. This can include such actions as a levy on your wages or bank account or the filing of a notice of federal tax lien. If you repeatedly do not file, you could be subject to additional enforcement measures, such as additional penalties and/or criminal prosecution.

**Contacting your local IRS office.** Keep in mind, many questions can be answered on IRS.gov without visiting an IRS TAC. Go to *IRS.gov/LetUsHelp* for the topics people ask about most. If you still need help, IRS TACs provide tax help when a tax issue can't be handled online or by phone. All TACs now provide service by appointment, so you'll know in advance that you can get the service you need without long wait times. Before you visit, go to *IRS.gov/TACLocator* to find the nearest TAC and to check hours, available services, and appointment options. Or, on the IRS2Go app, under the Stay Connected tab, choose the Contact Us option and click on "Local Offices."

**Recognizing and reporting tax scams.** The *Dirty Dozen* is compiled annually by the IRS and lists a variety of common scams taxpayers may encounter any time during the year. Many of these con games peak during filing season as people prepare their tax returns or hire someone to do so. Aggressive and threatening phone calls by criminals impersonating IRS agents remain near the top of the annual Dirty Dozen list of tax scams for the filing season.

Scammers are able to alter caller identification (caller ID) numbers to make it look like the IRS is calling. They use fake names and bogus IRS identification or badge numbers. They often leave "urgent" callback requests. They prey on the most vulnerable people, such as the elderly, newly arrived immigrants, and those whose first language is not English. Scammers have been known to impersonate agents of *IRS Criminal Investigation* as well.

Be cautious when receiving suspicious calls at home or at work from sources claiming to be from the IRS, other agencies, or outside sources asking for money or credit card information, or threatening to have you arrested for not paying. These callers may demand money or may say you have a refund due and try to trick you into sharing private information. These con artists can sound convincing when they call. They may know a lot about you.

Here are five things the scammers often do but the IRS will **not** do. Any one of these five things is a tell-tale sign of a scam.

**The IRS will never do any of the following.**

- Call to demand immediate payment, nor will the agency call about taxes owed without first having mailed you a bill.
- Demand that you pay taxes without giving you the opportunity to question or appeal the amount they say you owe.
- Require you to use a specific payment method for your taxes, such as a prepaid debit card.
- Ask for credit or debit card numbers over the phone.
- Threaten to bring in local police or other law-enforcement groups to have you arrested for not paying.

If you get a phone call from someone claiming to be from the IRS and asking for money, do not disclose your personal information. You should make notes of all information regarding the call and/or the caller, for example, any caller ID information, then hang up immediately and do the following.

- If you know you owe taxes or think you might owe, call the IRS toll free at 800-829-1040. The IRS assistors can help you with a payment issue.
- If you know you don't owe taxes or have no reason to believe that you do, report the incident to the Treasury Inspector General for Tax Administration (TIGTA) toll free at 800-366-4484 or at *TIGTA.gov*.
- If you've been targeted by this scam, also contact the FTC and use their *Report Fraud Assistant* at *FTC.gov*. Please add "IRS Telephone Scam" to the comments of your complaint.

Remember, too, the IRS does **not** use email, text messages, or any social media to discuss your personal tax issue involving bills or refunds. If you get a phone call from someone claiming to be from the IRS regarding a refund owed to you and asking you for your SSN and bank account information, do **not** give them this information. You should make notes of all information regarding the call and/or the caller, for example, any caller ID information, and report this scam. For more information on reporting tax scams, go to IRS.gov and type "scam" in the search box. You can verify any potential refunds owed to you by contacting the IRS directly.

# The Taxpayer Advocate Service (TAS) Is Here To Help You

## What Is TAS?

TAS is an *independent* organization within the IRS that helps taxpayers and protects taxpayer rights. Their job is to ensure that every taxpayer is treated fairly and that you know and understand your rights under the *Taxpayer Bill of Rights*.

## How Can You Learn About Your Taxpayer Rights?

The Taxpayer Bill of Rights describes 10 basic rights that all taxpayers have when dealing with the IRS. Go to *TaxpayerAdvocate.IRS.gov* to help you understand what these mean to you and how they apply. These are **your** rights. Know them. Use them.

You can find a list of your rights and the IRS's obligations to protect them in *Pub. 1, Your Rights as a Taxpayer*. It includes the following.

1. **The Right To Be Informed.** Taxpayers have the right to know what they need to do to comply with the tax laws. They are entitled to clear explanations of the laws and IRS procedures in all tax forms, instructions, publications, notices, and correspondence. They have the right to be informed of IRS decisions about their tax accounts and to receive clear explanations of the outcomes.

2. **The Right to Quality Service.** Taxpayers have the right to receive prompt, courteous, and professional assistance in their dealings with the IRS, to be spoken to in a way they can easily understand, to receive clear and easily understandable communications from the IRS, and to speak to a supervisor about inadequate service.

3. **The Right To Pay No More Than the Correct Amount of Tax.** Taxpayers have the right to pay only the amount of tax legally due, including interest and penalties, and to have the IRS apply all tax payments properly.

4. **The Right To Challenge the IRS's Position and Be Heard.** Taxpayers have the right to raise objections and provide additional documentation in response to formal IRS actions or proposed actions, to expect that the IRS will consider their timely objections and documentation promptly and fairly, and to receive a response if the IRS does not agree with their position.

5. **The Right To Appeal an IRS Decision in an Independent Forum.** Taxpayers are entitled to a fair and impartial administrative appeal of most IRS decisions, including many penalties, and have the right to receive a written response regarding the Office of Appeals' decision. Taxpayers generally have the right to take their cases to court.

6. **The Right to Finality.** Taxpayers have the right to know the maximum amount of time they have to challenge the IRS's position as well as the maximum amount of time the IRS has to audit a particular tax year or collect a tax debt. Taxpayers have the right to know when the IRS has finished an audit.

7. **The Right to Privacy.** Taxpayers have the right to expect that any IRS inquiry, examination, or enforcement action will comply with the law and be no more intrusive

than necessary, and will respect all due process rights, including search and seizure protections, and will provide, where applicable, a collection due process hearing.

8. **The Right to Confidentiality.** Taxpayers have the right to expect that any information they provide to the IRS will not be disclosed unless authorized by the taxpayer or by law. Taxpayers have the right to expect appropriate action will be taken against employees, return preparers, and others who wrongfully use or disclose taxpayer return information.

9. **The Right To Retain Representation.** Taxpayers have the right to retain an authorized representative of their choice to represent them in their dealings with the IRS. Taxpayers have the right to seek assistance from a Low Income Taxpayer Clinic if they cannot afford representation.

10. **The Right to a Fair and Just Tax System.** Taxpayers have the right to expect the tax system to consider facts and circumstances that might affect their underlying liabilities, ability to pay, or ability to provide information timely. Taxpayers have the right to receive assistance from TAS if they are experiencing financial difficulty or if the IRS has not resolved their tax issues properly and timely through its normal channels.

The IRS is working to increase the number of Americans who know and understand their rights under the tax law. To expand awareness, the IRS makes *Pub. 1* available in multiple languages on IRS.gov. This important publication is available in the following languages:

- English, *Your Rights as a Taxpayer*, at *IRS.gov/Pub/irs-pdf/P1.pdf*.
- Chinese, *Chinese- Your Rights as a Taxpayer (Pub 1)*, at *IRS.gov/Chinese*.
- Korean, *Korean- Your Rights as a Taxpayer (Pub 1)*, at *IRS.gov/Korean*.
- Russian, *Ваши права в качестве налогоплательщика (Публикацию № 1)*, at *IRS.gov/Russian*.
- Spanish, *Publicación 1SP, Derechos del Contribuyente*, at *IRS.gov/Spanish*.
- Vietnamese, *Quyền Hạn của Người Đóng Thuế, Your Rights as a Taxpayer (Pub 1)*, at *IRS.gov/Vietnamese*.

The IRS will include Pub. 1 when sending notices to taxpayers on a range of issues, such as an audit or collection matter. All IRS facilities will publicly display the rights for taxpayers and employees to see.

## What Can TAS Do for You?

TAS can help you resolve problems that you can't resolve with the IRS. And their service is free. If you qualify for their assistance, you will be assigned to one advocate who will work with you throughout the process and will do everything possible to resolve your issue. TAS can help you if:

- Your problem is causing financial difficulty for you, your family, or your business;
- You face (or your business is facing) an immediate threat of adverse action; or
- You've tried repeatedly to contact the IRS but no one has responded, or the IRS hasn't responded by the date promised.

## How Can You Reach TAS?

TAS has offices *in every state, the District of Columbia, and Puerto Rico*. Your local advocate's number is in your local directory and at *TaxpayerAdvocate.IRS.gov/Contact-Us*. You can also call them at 877-777-4778.

## How Else Does TAS Help Taxpayers?

TAS works to resolve large-scale problems that affect many taxpayers. If you know of one of these broad issues, report it to them at *IRS.gov/SAMS*.

## TAS for Tax Professionals

TAS can provide a variety of information for tax professionals, including tax law updates and guidance, TAS programs, and ways to let TAS know about systemic problems you've seen in your practice.

## Low Income Taxpayer Clinics (LITCs)

LITCs are independent from the IRS. LITCs represent individuals whose income is below a certain level and need to resolve tax problems with the IRS, such as audits, appeals, and tax collection disputes. In addition, LITCs can provide information about taxpayer rights and responsibilities in different languages for individuals who speak English as a second language. Services are offered for free or a small fee for eligible taxpayers. To find an LITC near you, go to *TaxpayerAdvocate.IRS.gov/about-us/Low-Income-Taxpayer-Clinics-LITC* or see IRS Pub. 4134, *Low Income Taxpayer Clinic List*.

## Index

To help us develop a more useful index, please let us know if you have ideas for index entries. See "Comments and Suggestions" in the "Introduction" for the ways you can reach us.

Publication 535 (2022)

129

130

651121

☐ Final K-1     ☐ Amended K-1     OMB No. 1545-0123

**Schedule K-1**
**(Form 1065)**
Department of the Treasury
Internal Revenue Service

20**22**

For calendar year 2022, or tax year

beginning ___ / ___ / 2022   ending ___ / ___ / ___

**Partner's Share of Income, Deductions,**
**Credits, etc.**          See separate instructions.

| Part I | Information About the Partnership |
|---|---|
| A | Partnership's employer identification number |
| B | Partnership's name, address, city, state, and ZIP code |

C   IRS center where partnership filed return:
D   ☐ Check if this is a publicly traded partnership (PTP)

| Part II | Information About the Partner |
|---|---|
| E | Partner's SSN or TIN (Do not use TIN of a disregarded entity. See instructions.) |
| F | Name, address, city, state, and ZIP code for partner entered in E. See instructions. |

G   ☐ General partner or LLC member-manager     ☐ Limited partner or other LLC member
H1  ☐ Domestic partner     ☐ Foreign partner
H2  ☐ If the partner is a disregarded entity (DE), enter the partner's:
    TIN _____   Name _____
I1  What type of entity is this partner? _____
I2  If this partner is a retirement plan (IRA/SEP/Keogh/etc.), check here  . ☐
J   Partner's share of profit, loss, and capital (see instructions):

|  | Beginning | Ending |
|---|---|---|
| Profit | % | % |
| Loss | % | % |
| Capital | % | % |

Check if decrease is due to sale or exchange of partnership interest  .  . ☐
K   Partner's share of liabilities:

|  | Beginning | Ending |
|---|---|---|
| Nonrecourse | $ | $ |
| Qualified nonrecourse financing | $ | $ |
| Recourse | $ | $ |

Check this box if item K includes liability amounts from lower-tier partnerships ☐

L            **Partner's Capital Account Analysis**
Beginning capital account  .  .  . $ _____
Capital contributed during the year .  . $ _____
Current year net income (loss)  .  .  . $ _____
Other increase (decrease) (attach explanation) $ _____
Withdrawals and distributions  .  .  . $ (_____)
Ending capital account  .  .  .  . $ _____

M   Did the partner contribute property with a built-in gain (loss)?
    ☐ Yes   ☐ No   If "Yes," attach statement. See instructions.
N   **Partner's Share of Net Unrecognized Section 704(c) Gain or (Loss)**
    Beginning  .  .  .  .  .  .  .  . $ _____
    Ending  .  .  .  .  .  .  .  . $ _____

| Part III | Partner's Share of Current Year Income, Deductions, Credits, and Other Items |
|---|---|

| 1 | Ordinary business income (loss) | 14 | Self-employment earnings (loss) |
|---|---|---|---|
| 2 | Net rental real estate income (loss) | | |
| 3 | Other net rental income (loss) | 15 | Credits |
| 4a | Guaranteed payments for services | | |
| 4b | Guaranteed payments for capital | 16 | Schedule K-3 is attached if checked  .  .  .  .  .  . ☐ |
| 4c | Total guaranteed payments | 17 | Alternative minimum tax (AMT) items |
| 5 | Interest income | | |
| 6a | Ordinary dividends | | |
| 6b | Qualified dividends | 18 | Tax-exempt income and nondeductible expenses |
| 6c | Dividend equivalents | | |
| 7 | Royalties | | |
| 8 | Net short-term capital gain (loss) | | |
| 9a | Net long-term capital gain (loss) | 19 | Distributions |
| 9b | Collectibles (28%) gain (loss) | | |
| 9c | Unrecaptured section 1250 gain | 20 | Other information |
| 10 | Net section 1231 gain (loss) | | |
| 11 | Other income (loss) | | |
| 12 | Section 179 deduction | 21 | Foreign taxes paid or accrued |
| 13 | Other deductions | | |

22 ☐ More than one activity for at-risk purposes*
23 ☐ More than one activity for passive activity purposes*
*See attached statement for additional information.

For IRS Use Only

For Paperwork Reduction Act Notice, see the Instructions for Form 1065.     www.irs.gov/Form1065     Cat. No. 11394R     **Schedule K-1 (Form 1065) 2022**

**SCHEDULE C**
**(Form 1040)**

Department of the Treasury
Internal Revenue Service

# Profit or Loss From Business
## (Sole Proprietorship)

Go to *www.irs.gov/ScheduleC* for instructions and the latest information.
**Attach to Form 1040, 1040-SR, 1040-NR, or 1041; partnerships must generally file Form 1065.**

OMB No. 1545-0074

**2022**

Attachment
Sequence No. **09**

Name of proprietor | Social security number (SSN)

| A | Principal business or profession, including product or service (see instructions) | **B** Enter code from instructions |
|---|---|---|

| C | Business name. If no separate business name, leave blank. | **D** Employer ID number (EIN) (see instr.) |
|---|---|---|

E  Business address (including suite or room no.) _____
   City, town or post office, state, and ZIP code _____

F  Accounting method:  **(1)** ☐ Cash  **(2)** ☐ Accrual  **(3)** ☐ Other (specify) _____

G  Did you "materially participate" in the operation of this business during 2022? If "No," see instructions for limit on losses  .  ☐ **Yes**  ☐ **No**

H  If you started or acquired this business during 2022, check here  .  .  .  .  .  .  .  .  .  ☐

I  Did you make any payments in 2022 that would require you to file Form(s) 1099? See instructions  .  .  .  .  .  ☐ **Yes**  ☐ **No**

J  If "Yes," did you or will you file required Form(s) 1099?  .  .  .  .  .  .  .  .  .  .  .  .  .  .  ☐ **Yes**  ☐ **No**

## Part I  Income

| 1 | Gross receipts or sales. See instructions for line 1 and check the box if this income was reported to you on Form W-2 and the "Statutory employee" box on that form was checked  .  .  .  .  .  .  .  .  ☐ | 1 | |
|---|---|---|---|
| 2 | Returns and allowances  .  .  .  .  .  .  .  .  .  . | 2 | |
| 3 | Subtract line 2 from line 1  .  .  .  .  .  .  .  . | 3 | |
| 4 | Cost of goods sold (from line 42)  .  .  .  .  .  .  . | 4 | |
| 5 | **Gross profit.** Subtract line 4 from line 3  .  .  .  . | 5 | |
| 6 | Other income, including federal and state gasoline or fuel tax credit or refund (see instructions)  .  . | 6 | |
| 7 | **Gross income.** Add lines 5 and 6  .  .  .  .  .  .  .  .  .  .  .  .  .  .  .  . | 7 | |

## Part II  Expenses. Enter expenses for business use of your home only on line 30.

| 8 | Advertising  .  .  .  .  . | 8 | | 18 | Office expense (see instructions)  . | 18 | |
|---|---|---|---|---|---|---|---|
| 9 | Car and truck expenses (see instructions)  .  .  . | 9 | | 19 | Pension and profit-sharing plans  . | 19 | |
| 10 | Commissions and fees  . | 10 | | 20 | Rent or lease (see instructions): | | |
| 11 | Contract labor (see instructions) | 11 | | a | Vehicles, machinery, and equipment | 20a | |
| 12 | Depletion  .  .  .  . | 12 | | b | Other business property  .  .  . | 20b | |
| 13 | Depreciation and section 179 expense deduction (not included in Part III) (see instructions)  .  . | 13 | | 21 | Repairs and maintenance  .  .  . | 21 | |
| | | | | 22 | Supplies (not included in Part III)  . | 22 | |
| | | | | 23 | Taxes and licenses  .  .  .  . | 23 | |
| | | | | 24 | Travel and meals: | | |
| 14 | Employee benefit programs (other than on line 19)  . | 14 | | a | Travel  .  .  .  .  .  .  . | 24a | |
| | | | | b | Deductible meals (see instructions)  .  .  .  .  . | 24b | |
| 15 | Insurance (other than health) | 15 | | 25 | Utilities  .  .  .  .  .  . | 25 | |
| 16 | Interest (see instructions): | | | 26 | Wages (less employment credits) | 26 | |
| a | Mortgage (paid to banks, etc.) | 16a | | 27a | Other expenses (from line 48)  .  . | 27a | |
| b | Other  .  .  .  .  .  . | 16b | | b | **Reserved for future use**  .  .  . | 27b | |
| 17 | Legal and professional services | 17 | | | | | |

| 28 | **Total expenses** before expenses for business use of home. Add lines 8 through 27a  .  .  .  .  .  . | 28 | |
|---|---|---|---|
| 29 | Tentative profit or (loss). Subtract line 28 from line 7  .  .  .  .  .  .  .  .  .  . | 29 | |

30  Expenses for business use of your home. Do not report these expenses elsewhere. Attach Form 8829 unless using the simplified method. See instructions.
**Simplified method filers only:** Enter the total square footage of (a) your home: _____
and (b) the part of your home used for business: _____. Use the Simplified
Method Worksheet in the instructions to figure the amount to enter on line 30  .  .  .  .  .  .  . | **30** | |

31  **Net profit or (loss).** Subtract line 30 from line 29.

• If a profit, enter on both **Schedule 1 (Form 1040), line 3,** and on **Schedule SE, line 2.** (If you checked the box on line 1, see instructions.) Estates and trusts, enter on **Form 1041, line 3.**
• If a loss, you **must** go to line 32. | **31** | |

32  If you have a loss, check the box that describes your investment in this activity. See instructions.

• If you checked 32a, enter the loss on both **Schedule 1 (Form 1040), line 3,** and on **Schedule SE, line 2.** (If you checked the box on line 1, see the line 31 instructions.) Estates and trusts, enter on **Form 1041, line 3.**
• If you checked 32b, you **must** attach **Form 6198.** Your loss may be limited.

32a ☐ All investment is at risk.
32b ☐ Some investment is not at risk.

**For Paperwork Reduction Act Notice, see the separate instructions.**  Cat. No. 11334P  **Schedule C (Form 1040) 2022**

Schedule C (Form 1040) 2022 — Page **2**

**Part III   Cost of Goods Sold** (see instructions)

33 Method(s) used to value closing inventory: **a** ☐ Cost   **b** ☐ Lower of cost or market   **c** ☐ Other (attach explanation)

34 Was there any change in determining quantities, costs, or valuations between opening and closing inventory?
If "Yes," attach explanation . . . . . . . . . . . . . . . . . . . . ☐ Yes   ☐ No

| | | |
|---|---|---|
| 35 Inventory at beginning of year. If different from last year's closing inventory, attach explanation | 35 | |
| 36 Purchases less cost of items withdrawn for personal use | 36 | |
| 37 Cost of labor. Do not include any amounts paid to yourself | 37 | |
| 38 Materials and supplies | 38 | |
| 39 Other costs | 39 | |
| 40 Add lines 35 through 39 | 40 | |
| 41 Inventory at end of year | 41 | |
| 42 **Cost of goods sold.** Subtract line 41 from line 40. Enter the result here and on line 4 | 42 | |

**Part IV   Information on Your Vehicle.** Complete this part **only** if you are claiming car or truck expenses on line 9 and are not required to file Form 4562 for this business. See the instructions for line 13 to find out if you must file Form 4562.

43 When did you place your vehicle in service for business purposes? (month/day/year) ___/___/___

44 Of the total number of miles you drove your vehicle during 2022, enter the number of miles you used your vehicle for:

a Business _____  b Commuting (see instructions) _____  c Other _____

45 Was your vehicle available for personal use during off-duty hours? . . . . . . ☐ Yes  ☐ No

46 Do you (or your spouse) have another vehicle available for personal use? . . . ☐ Yes  ☐ No

47a Do you have evidence to support your deduction? . . . . . . . . . . ☐ Yes  ☐ No

b If "Yes," is the evidence written? . . . . . . . . . . . . . . . . ☐ Yes  ☐ No

**Part V   Other Expenses.** List below business expenses not included on lines 8–26 or line 30.

| | |
|---|---|
| | |
| | |
| | |
| | |
| | |
| | |
| | |
| | |
| 48 **Total other expenses.** Enter here and on line 27a | 48 |

Schedule C (Form 1040) 2022

C.A. KNUCKLES

**Form 1065**

**U.S. Return of Partnership Income**

OMB No. 1545-0123

Department of the Treasury
Internal Revenue Service

For calendar year 2022, or tax year beginning _____, 2022, ending _____, 20____.

Go to *www.irs.gov/Form1065* for instructions and the latest information.

**2022**

| | |
|---|---|
| **A** Principal business activity | Name of partnership |
| **B** Principal product or service | Number, street, and room or suite no. If a P.O. box, see instructions. |
| **C** Business code number | City or town, state or province, country, and ZIP or foreign postal code |

Type or Print

**D** Employer identification number

**E** Date business started

**F** Total assets (see instructions) $

**G** Check applicable boxes: **(1)** ☐ Initial return **(2)** ☐ Final return **(3)** ☐ Name change **(4)** ☐ Address change **(5)** ☐ Amended return
**H** Check accounting method: **(1)** ☐ Cash **(2)** ☐ Accrual **(3)** ☐ Other (specify): _____
**I** Number of Schedules K-1. Attach one for each person who was a partner at any time during the tax year: _____
**J** Check if Schedules C and M-3 are attached . . . . . . . . . . . . . . . . . . . ☐
**K** Check if partnership: **(1)** ☐ Aggregated activities for section 465 at-risk purposes **(2)** ☐ Grouped activities for section 469 passive activity purposes

**Caution:** Include **only** trade or business income and expenses on lines 1a through 22 below. See instructions for more information.

**Income**

| | | | |
|---|---|---|---|
| 1a | Gross receipts or sales | 1a | |
| b | Returns and allowances | 1b | |
| c | Balance. Subtract line 1b from line 1a | 1c | |
| 2 | Cost of goods sold (attach Form 1125-A) | 2 | |
| 3 | Gross profit. Subtract line 2 from line 1c | 3 | |
| 4 | Ordinary income (loss) from other partnerships, estates, and trusts (attach statement) | 4 | |
| 5 | Net farm profit (loss) (attach Schedule F (Form 1040)) | 5 | |
| 6 | Net gain (loss) from Form 4797, Part II, line 17 (attach Form 4797) | 6 | |
| 7 | Other income (loss) (attach statement) | 7 | |
| 8 | **Total income (loss).** Combine lines 3 through 7 | 8 | |

**Deductions** (see instructions for limitations)

| | | | |
|---|---|---|---|
| 9 | Salaries and wages (other than to partners) (less employment credits) | 9 | |
| 10 | Guaranteed payments to partners | 10 | |
| 11 | Repairs and maintenance | 11 | |
| 12 | Bad debts | 12 | |
| 13 | Rent | 13 | |
| 14 | Taxes and licenses | 14 | |
| 15 | Interest (see instructions) | 15 | |
| 16a | Depreciation (if required, attach Form 4562) | 16a | |
| b | Less depreciation reported on Form 1125-A and elsewhere on return | 16b | |
| | | 16c | |
| 17 | Depletion **(Do not deduct oil and gas depletion.)** | 17 | |
| 18 | Retirement plans, etc. | 18 | |
| 19 | Employee benefit programs | 19 | |
| 20 | Other deductions (attach statement) | 20 | |
| 21 | **Total deductions.** Add the amounts shown in the far right column for lines 9 through 20 | 21 | |
| 22 | **Ordinary business income (loss).** Subtract line 21 from line 8 | 22 | |

**Tax and Payment**

| | | | |
|---|---|---|---|
| 23 | Interest due under the look-back method—completed long-term contracts (attach Form 8697) | 23 | |
| 24 | Interest due under the look-back method—income forecast method (attach Form 8866) | 24 | |
| 25 | BBA AAR imputed underpayment (see instructions) | 25 | |
| 26 | Other taxes (see instructions) | 26 | |
| 27 | **Total balance due.** Add lines 23 through 26 | 27 | |
| 28 | Payment (see instructions) | 28 | |
| 29 | Amount owed. If line 28 is smaller than line 27, enter amount owed | 29 | |
| 30 | Overpayment. If line 28 is larger than line 27, enter overpayment | 30 | |

**Sign Here**

Under penalties of perjury, I declare that I have examined this return, including accompanying schedules and statements, and to the best of my knowledge and belief, it is true, correct, and complete. Declaration of preparer (other than partner or limited liability company member) is based on all information of which preparer has any knowledge.

Signature of partner or limited liability company member _____ Date _____

May the IRS discuss this return with the preparer shown below? See instructions. ☐ Yes ☐ No

**Paid Preparer Use Only**

| Print/Type preparer's name | Preparer's signature | Date | Check ☐ if self-employed | PTIN |
|---|---|---|---|---|
| Firm's name | | | Firm's EIN | |
| Firm's address | | | Phone no. | |

**For Paperwork Reduction Act Notice, see separate instructions.**

Cat. No. 11390Z

Form **1065** (2022)

134

Form 1065 (2022)     Page **2**

| Schedule B | Other Information | | |
|---|---|---|---|

| | | Yes | No |
|---|---|---|---|
| **1** | What type of entity is filing this return? Check the applicable box: | | |
| **a** ☐ Domestic general partnership    **b** ☐ Domestic limited partnership | | | |
| **c** ☐ Domestic limited liability company    **d** ☐ Domestic limited liability partnership | | | |
| **e** ☐ Foreign partnership    **f** ☐ Other: _____ | | | |
| **2** | At the end of the tax year: | | |
| **a** | Did any foreign or domestic corporation, partnership (including any entity treated as a partnership), trust, or tax-exempt organization, or any foreign government own, directly or indirectly, an interest of 50% or more in the profit, loss, or capital of the partnership? For rules of constructive ownership, see instructions. If "Yes," attach Schedule B-1, Information on Partners Owning 50% or More of the Partnership . . . . . . . . . . . . | | |
| **b** | Did any individual or estate own, directly or indirectly, an interest of 50% or more in the profit, loss, or capital of the partnership? For rules of constructive ownership, see instructions. If "Yes," attach Schedule B-1, Information on Partners Owning 50% or More of the Partnership . . . . . . . . . . . . . | | |
| **3** | At the end of the tax year, did the partnership: | | |
| **a** | Own directly 20% or more, or own, directly or indirectly, 50% or more of the total voting power of all classes of stock entitled to vote of any foreign or domestic corporation? For rules of constructive ownership, see instructions. If "Yes," complete (i) through (iv) below . . . . . . . . . . . . . . . . | | |

| (i) Name of Corporation | (ii) Employer Identification Number (if any) | (iii) Country of Incorporation | (iv) Percentage Owned in Voting Stock |
|---|---|---|---|
| | | | |
| | | | |
| | | | |
| | | | |

| | | Yes | No |
|---|---|---|---|
| **b** | Own directly an interest of 20% or more, or own, directly or indirectly, an interest of 50% or more in the profit, loss, or capital in any foreign or domestic partnership (including an entity treated as a partnership) or in the beneficial interest of a trust? For rules of constructive ownership, see instructions. If "Yes," complete (i) through (v) below . . | | |

| (i) Name of Entity | (ii) Employer Identification Number (if any) | (iii) Type of Entity | (iv) Country of Organization | (v) Maximum Percentage Owned in Profit, Loss, or Capital |
|---|---|---|---|---|
| | | | | |
| | | | | |
| | | | | |
| | | | | |

| | | Yes | No |
|---|---|---|---|
| **4** | Does the partnership satisfy all **four** of the following conditions? | | |
| **a** | The partnership's total receipts for the tax year were less than $250,000. | | |
| **b** | The partnership's total assets at the end of the tax year were less than $1 million. | | |
| **c** | Schedules K-1 are filed with the return and furnished to the partners on or before the due date (including extensions) for the partnership return. | | |
| **d** | The partnership is not filing and is not required to file Schedule M-3 . . . . . . . . . . | | |
| | If "Yes," the partnership is not required to complete Schedules L, M-1, and M-2; item F on page 1 of Form 1065; or item L on Schedule K-1. | | |
| **5** | Is this partnership a publicly traded partnership, as defined in section 469(k)(2)? . . . . . . . . . . | | |
| **6** | During the tax year, did the partnership have any debt that was canceled, was forgiven, or had the terms modified so as to reduce the principal amount of the debt? . . . . . . . . . . . . . . . . | | |
| **7** | Has this partnership filed, or is it required to file, Form 8918, Material Advisor Disclosure Statement, to provide information on any reportable transaction? . . . . . . . . . . . . . . . . . . . | | |
| **8** | At any time during calendar year 2022, did the partnership have an interest in or a signature or other authority over a financial account in a foreign country (such as a bank account, securities account, or other financial account)? See instructions for exceptions and filing requirements for FinCEN Form 114, Report of Foreign Bank and Financial Accounts (FBAR). If "Yes," enter the name of the foreign country _____ | | |
| **9** | At any time during the tax year, did the partnership receive a distribution from, or was it the grantor of, or transferor to, a foreign trust? If "Yes," the partnership may have to file Form 3520, Annual Return To Report Transactions With Foreign Trusts and Receipt of Certain Foreign Gifts. See instructions . . . . . . . . . . . . | | |
| **10a** | Is the partnership making, or had it previously made (and not revoked), a section 754 election? . . . . . . See instructions for details regarding a section 754 election. | | |
| **b** | Did the partnership make for this tax year an optional basis adjustment under section 743(b) or 734(b)? If "Yes," attach a statement showing the computation and allocation of the basis adjustment. See instructions . . . . | | |
| **c** | Is the partnership required to adjust the basis of partnership assets under section 743(b) or 734(b) because of a substantial built-in loss (as defined under section 743(d)) or substantial basis reduction (as defined under section 734(d))? If "Yes," attach a statement showing the computation and allocation of the basis adjustment. See instructions | | |

Form **1065** (2022)

135

| | Schedule B | Other Information *(continued)* | Yes | No |
|---|---|---|---|---|

**11** Check this box if, during the current or prior tax year, the partnership distributed any property received in a like-kind exchange or contributed such property to another entity (other than disregarded entities wholly owned by the partnership throughout the tax year) . . . . . . . . . . . . . . . . . . . . . . . . . . ☐

**12** At any time during the tax year, did the partnership distribute to any partner a tenancy-in-common or other undivided interest in partnership property? . . . . . . . . . . . . . . . . . . . . .

**13** If the partnership is required to file Form 8858, Information Return of U.S. Persons With Respect to Foreign Disregarded Entities (FDEs) and Foreign Branches (FBs), enter the number of Forms 8858 attached. See instructions . . . . . . . . . . . . . . . . . . . . . . . . . . . . . . . . .

**14** Does the partnership have any foreign partners? If "Yes," enter the number of Forms 8805, Foreign Partner's Information Statement of Section 1446 Withholding Tax, filed for this partnership . . . . . .

**15** Enter the number of Forms 8865, Return of U.S. Persons With Respect to Certain Foreign Partnerships, attached to this return . . . . . . . . . . . . . . . . . . . . . . . . . . . . . . . .

**16a** Did you make any payments in 2022 that would require you to file Form(s) 1099? See instructions . . . . .
**b** If "Yes," did you or will you file required Form(s) 1099? . . . . . . . . . . . . . . . . . .

**17** Enter the number of Forms 5471, Information Return of U.S. Persons With Respect to Certain Foreign Corporations, attached to this return . . . . . . . . . . . . . . . . . . . . . . . . . . . . . . .

**18** Enter the number of partners that are foreign governments under section 892 . . . . . . . . .

**19** During the partnership's tax year, did the partnership make any payments that would require it to file Forms 1042 and 1042-S under chapter 3 (sections 1441 through 1464) or chapter 4 (sections 1471 through 1474)? . . . . .

**20** Was the partnership a specified domestic entity required to file Form 8938 for the tax year? See the Instructions for Form 8938 . . . . . . . . . . . . . . . . . . . . . . . . . . . . . .

**21** Is the partnership a section 721(c) partnership, as defined in Regulations section 1.721(c)-1(b)(14)? . . . . . .

**22** During the tax year, did the partnership pay or accrue any interest or royalty for which one or more partners are not allowed a deduction under section 267A? See instructions . . . . . . . . . . . . .
If "Yes," enter the total amount of the disallowed deductions . . . . . . . . . $

**23** Did the partnership have an election under section 163(j) for any real property trade or business or any farming business in effect during the tax year? See instructions . . . . . . . . . . . . . .

**24** Does the partnership satisfy one or more of the following? See instructions . . . . . . . . .
**a** The partnership owns a pass-through entity with current, or prior year carryover, excess business interest expense.
**b** The partnership's aggregate average annual gross receipts (determined under section 448(c)) for the 3 tax years preceding the current tax year are more than $27 million and the partnership has business interest expense.
**c** The partnership is a tax shelter (see instructions) and the partnership has business interest expense.
If "Yes" to any, complete and attach Form 8990.

**25** Is the partnership attaching Form 8996 to certify as a Qualified Opportunity Fund? . . . . . . . .
If "Yes," enter the amount from Form 8996, line 15 . . . . . . . . . . . . . $

**26** Enter the number of foreign partners subject to section 864(c)(8) as a result of transferring all or a portion of an interest in the partnership or of receiving a distribution from the partnership . . . . . . . .
Complete Schedule K-3 (Form 1065), Part XIII, for each foreign partner subject to section 864(c)(8) on a transfer or distribution.

**27** At any time during the tax year, were there any transfers between the partnership and its partners subject to the disclosure requirements of Regulations section 1.707-8? . . . . . . . . . . . . . . .

**28** Since December 22, 2017, did a foreign corporation directly or indirectly acquire substantially all of the properties constituting a trade or business of your partnership, and was the ownership percentage (by vote or value) for purposes of section 7874 greater than 50% (for example, the partners held more than 50% of the stock of the foreign corporation)? If "Yes," list the ownership percentage by vote and by value. See instructions.
Percentage: By vote: _____ By value: _____

**29** Reserved for future use . . . . . . . . . . . . . . . . . . . . . . . . .

**30** Is the partnership electing out of the centralized partnership audit regime under section 6221(b)? See instructions.
If "Yes," the partnership must complete Schedule B-2 (Form 1065). Enter the total from Schedule B-2, Part III, line 3 . . . . . . . . . . . . . . . . . . . . . . . . . . . . .
If "No," complete Designation of Partnership Representative below.

**Designation of Partnership Representative** (see instructions)
Enter below the information for the partnership representative (PR) for the tax year covered by this return.

Name of PR

| U.S. address of PR | _____ | U.S. phone number of PR |
|---|---|---|

If the PR is an entity, name of the designated individual for the PR

| U.S. address of designated individual | _____ | U.S. phone number of designated individual |
|---|---|---|

Form **1065** (2022)

Form 1065 (2022)     Page **4**

## Schedule K — Partners' Distributive Share Items

| | | | | Total amount |
|---|---|---|---|---|
| **Income (Loss)** | **1** | Ordinary business income (loss) (page 1, line 22) | **1** | |
| | **2** | Net rental real estate income (loss) (attach Form 8825) | **2** | |
| | **3a** | Other gross rental income (loss)   **3a** | | |
| | **b** | Expenses from other rental activities (attach statement)   **3b** | | |
| | **c** | Other net rental income (loss). Subtract line 3b from line 3a | **3c** | |
| | **4** | Guaranteed payments: **a** Services **4a**    **b** Capital **4b** | | |
| | **c** | Total. Add lines 4a and 4b | **4c** | |
| | **5** | Interest income | **5** | |
| | **6** | Dividends and dividend equivalents: **a** Ordinary dividends | **6a** | |
| | **b** | Qualified dividends **6b**    **c** Dividend equivalents **6c** | | |
| | **7** | Royalties | **7** | |
| | **8** | Net short-term capital gain (loss) (attach Schedule D (Form 1065)) | **8** | |
| | **9a** | Net long-term capital gain (loss) (attach Schedule D (Form 1065)) | **9a** | |
| | **b** | Collectibles (28%) gain (loss) **9b** | | |
| | **c** | Unrecaptured section 1250 gain (attach statement) **9c** | | |
| | **10** | Net section 1231 gain (loss) (attach Form 4797) | **10** | |
| | **11** | Other income (loss) (see instructions)   Type: _____ | **11** | |
| **Deductions** | **12** | Section 179 deduction (attach Form 4562) | **12** | |
| | **13a** | Contributions | **13a** | |
| | **b** | Investment interest expense | **13b** | |
| | **c** | Section 59(e)(2) expenditures: **(1)** Type: _____ **(2)** Amount: | **13c(2)** | |
| | **d** | Other deductions (see instructions)   Type: _____ | **13d** | |
| **Self-Employ-ment** | **14a** | Net earnings (loss) from self-employment | **14a** | |
| | **b** | Gross farming or fishing income | **14b** | |
| | **c** | Gross nonfarm income | **14c** | |
| **Credits** | **15a** | Low-income housing credit (section 42(j)(5)) | **15a** | |
| | **b** | Low-income housing credit (other) | **15b** | |
| | **c** | Qualified rehabilitation expenditures (rental real estate) (attach Form 3468, if applicable) | **15c** | |
| | **d** | Other rental real estate credits (see instructions)   Type: _____ | **15d** | |
| | **e** | Other rental credits (see instructions)   Type: _____ | **15e** | |
| | **f** | Other credits (see instructions)   Type: _____ | **15f** | |
| **Inter-national** | **16** | Attach Schedule K-2 (Form 1065), Partners' Distributive Share Items—International, and check this box to indicate that you are reporting items of international tax relevance ☐ | | |
| **Alternative Minimum Tax (AMT) Items** | **17a** | Post-1986 depreciation adjustment | **17a** | |
| | **b** | Adjusted gain or loss | **17b** | |
| | **c** | Depletion (other than oil and gas) | **17c** | |
| | **d** | Oil, gas, and geothermal properties—gross income | **17d** | |
| | **e** | Oil, gas, and geothermal properties—deductions | **17e** | |
| | **f** | Other AMT items (attach statement) | **17f** | |
| **Other Information** | **18a** | Tax-exempt interest income | **18a** | |
| | **b** | Other tax-exempt income | **18b** | |
| | **c** | Nondeductible expenses | **18c** | |
| | **19a** | Distributions of cash and marketable securities | **19a** | |
| | **b** | Distributions of other property | **19b** | |
| | **20a** | Investment income | **20a** | |
| | **b** | Investment expenses | **20b** | |
| | **c** | Other items and amounts (attach statement) | | |
| | **21** | Total foreign taxes paid or accrued | **21** | |

Form **1065** (2022)

## Analysis of Net Income (Loss) per Return

| | | | | | | | |
|---|---|---|---|---|---|---|---|
| **1** | Net income (loss). Combine Schedule K, lines 1 through 11. From the result, subtract the sum of Schedule K, lines 12 through 13d, and 21 . . . . . . . . . . . . . . . . . **1** | | | | | | |

| **2** | Analysis by partner type: | **(i)** Corporate | **(ii)** Individual (active) | **(iii)** Individual (passive) | **(iv)** Partnership | **(v)** Exempt Organization | **(vi)** Nominee/Other |
|---|---|---|---|---|---|---|---|
| **a** | General partners | | | | | | |
| **b** | Limited partners | | | | | | |

### Schedule L — Balance Sheets per Books

| | Assets | Beginning of tax year (a) | (b) | End of tax year (c) | (d) |
|---|---|---|---|---|---|
| **1** | Cash . . . . . . . . . . . | | | | |
| **2a** | Trade notes and accounts receivable . . . . . . | | | | |
| **b** | Less allowance for bad debts . . . . . . | | | | |
| **3** | Inventories . . . . . . . . | | | | |
| **4** | U.S. Government obligations . . . . . . . . | | | | |
| **5** | Tax-exempt securities . . . . . . . . . | | | | |
| **6** | Other current assets (attach statement) . . . . | | | | |
| **7a** | Loans to partners (or persons related to partners) . | | | | |
| **b** | Mortgage and real estate loans . . . . . . . | | | | |
| **8** | Other investments (attach statement) . . . . . . | | | | |
| **9a** | Buildings and other depreciable assets . . . . | | | | |
| **b** | Less accumulated depreciation . . . . . . | | | | |
| **10a** | Depletable assets . . . . . . . . . . . | | | | |
| **b** | Less accumulated depletion . . . . . . . | | | | |
| **11** | Land (net of any amortization) . . . . . . . . | | | | |
| **12a** | Intangible assets (amortizable only) . . . . . | | | | |
| **b** | Less accumulated amortization . . . . . . . | | | | |
| **13** | Other assets (attach statement) . . . . . . | | | | |
| **14** | Total assets . . . . . . . . . . . . | | | | |
| | **Liabilities and Capital** | | | | |
| **15** | Accounts payable . . . . . . . . . . | | | | |
| **16** | Mortgages, notes, bonds payable in less than 1 year | | | | |
| **17** | Other current liabilities (attach statement) . . . | | | | |
| **18** | All nonrecourse loans . . . . . . . . . | | | | |
| **19a** | Loans from partners (or persons related to partners) . | | | | |
| **b** | Mortgages, notes, bonds payable in 1 year or more . | | | | |
| **20** | Other liabilities (attach statement) . . . . . . | | | | |
| **21** | Partners' capital accounts . . . . . . . . | | | | |
| **22** | Total liabilities and capital . . . . . . . . | | | | |

### Schedule M-1 — Reconciliation of Income (Loss) per Books With Analysis of Net Income (Loss) per Return

**Note:** The partnership may be required to file Schedule M-3. See instructions.

| | | | | | |
|---|---|---|---|---|---|
| **1** | Net income (loss) per books . . . . | | **6** | Income recorded on books this year not included on Schedule K, lines 1 through 11 (itemize): | |
| **2** | Income included on Schedule K, lines 1, 2, 3c, 5, 6a, 7, 8, 9a, 10, and 11, not recorded on books this year (itemize): _____ | | **a** | Tax-exempt interest $_____ _____ | |
| **3** | Guaranteed payments (other than health insurance) . . . . . . . . . | | **7** | Deductions included on Schedule K, lines 1 through 13d, and 21, not charged against book income this year (itemize): | |
| **4** | Expenses recorded on books this year not included on Schedule K, lines 1 through 13d, and 21 (itemize): | | **a** | Depreciation $_____ _____ | |
| **a** | Depreciation $_____ | | **8** | Add lines 6 and 7 . . . . . . . . | |
| **b** | Travel and entertainment $_____ | | **9** | Income (loss) (Analysis of Net Income (Loss), line 1). Subtract line 8 from line 5 | |
| **5** | Add lines 1 through 4 . . . . . | | | | |

### Schedule M-2 — Analysis of Partners' Capital Accounts

| | | | | | |
|---|---|---|---|---|---|
| **1** | Balance at beginning of year . . . | | **6** | Distributions: **a** Cash . . . . . | |
| **2** | Capital contributed: **a** Cash . . . | | | **b** Property . . . . . | |
| | **b** Property . . | | **7** | Other decreases (itemize): _____ | |
| **3** | Net income (loss) (see instructions) . | | | | |
| **4** | Other increases (itemize): _____ | | **8** | Add lines 6 and 7 . . . . . . . | |
| **5** | Add lines 1 through 4 . . . . . . | | **9** | Balance at end of year. Subtract line 8 from line 5 | |

Form **1065** (2022)

# BANKING TO BUILD WEALTH

# BANKING EXPLAINED

"If people only understood the rank of the injustice of our money and banking system, there would be a revolution by morning." –Andrew Jackson

Starting off with a quote from Andrew Jackson seems a bit crazy. Still, the fact that it was written before all these banking institutions, regulations, the Federal Reserve Bank, etc., seems to show the predicted future of what was about to sweep over America. In the simplest terms, banking is the business of protecting money for others. Banks lend money that generates interest, which creates profits for the bank. Those profits are mainly generated through what's called "Fractional Banking." A banking system that requires that banks only hold onto a portion of the money deposited with them as reserves. Andrew Jackson's quote starts within this secret system of banking. It developed during the Great Depression when depositors made many withdrawals, and lending to banks fell. It was created so banks couldn't invest all their money into risky investments.

Example: $100 $\Rightarrow$Bank $\Rightarrow$$90 created $\Rightarrow$$ Loan % $\Rightarrow$$80

Example: ⌂10% Interest $\Rightarrow$Loan $10 $\Rightarrow$$11

Because banks use this system, 95% of all money is numbers and digits, not physical. Banks are allowed to loan 90% of all money deposited into their vaults and earn interest on it, usually at higher rates, which translates to higher profits, as the examples show. Banks you or your family use can create money out of "thin air" using this fractional Banking system.

$1000 goes in the bank $\Rightarrow$⌂$ $\Rightarrow$Loans your money out $ $\Rightarrow$$Collects interest $\Rightarrow$CREDIT INTEREST is 20%; way higher than the bank gives you [0.2%] $\Rightarrow$for every $1000 you put in the bank, the bank creates $900 and lends it to someone else $\Rightarrow$TOTAL amount created from your $1000=$1,900 for the bank. Understand the process of banking to build wealth. While the bank continues to this day to scam you by telling you to hold your money in the bank, the wealthy, who know this, flip it around to do the opposite to build wealth.

Before we get into that, let's briefly drive back to Italy. The word Bank means Bench in Italian because back in the day, people gathered to show coins from different countries in large quantities on benches or tables for the purpose of exchanging. So, remember, the bank is derived from the old Italian word "Banca," which means "bench or money exchange table." History is important to understand. Know the financial system; know how to build wealth within that system.

Fractional banking, as discussed above, made banks interconnected. This started leveraging against each other, creating a money multiplier effect. Created Leveraged Money! Banks are sold to the public and media as Financial Middlemen, but over time, they have evolved into Banks: Creators of Money. This was the best described by a man who you probably never heard of but authored one of the greatest books about money, finances, and banking. It's not a prisoner-favored book, Rich Dad, Poor Dad! [In my next book, I will show how the cash flow chart from that book doesn't create income]. His name is Richard Cantillon, a banker; the book is Essay on Nature of Trading in General [1775]. This book is from 1775, but it still lives on today, even developed on a financial model: The Cantillon Effect. To this day, this is one of the most important financial instruments in the banking and financial markets. What is this Cantillon Effect? It describes the inequalities of inflation while stressing the importance of entrepreneurs as the drivers of economic activity, traders, and innovators who take on risks. Money, in other words, is not neutral; money printing has distributional consequences that operate through the price system, which is known as the Cantillon Effect. This Cantillon Effect helps show how banks are the creators of money and how it is distributed, for instance. When new money enters the economy, it's not equally distributed across the economy sectors or asset classes. But more importantly, it's not equally distributed among people and businesses. The first to receive new money created by these banks goes to bankers, bureaucrats, and politicians, who benefit first from new money.

This unequal distribution of money impacts individual wealth. It is the key cause and driver of injustices in our modern society because when banks give their friends money, they spend it on whatever they want, usually commodities and other valuable assets. They are also allowed to take advantage of Arbitrage since they get the new money first, enabling them to buy real estate, which pumps new money into the real estate sector and causes prices to increase. By the time the money trickles back down to regular people like you and your family, you are unfortunately priced out. For example, new money was introduced when the Federal Reserve bank turned on the money printer during the Covid-19 pandemic to prop up the economy; at the same time, stocks went up, and all the bankers, politicians, etc. got their money they were the first to buy stocks and by the time you and I got our money, stocks, of course, were already climbing, thus missing out on growth. Because of this, the middle class and poor miss out on wealth creation that would otherwise lift them out of their financial demise. Don't feel sorry for yourself, and the key is this knowledge! We have a problem complaining about finances or our own economic conditions as if this knowledge is a secret. Reading and learning about financial literacy will push you forward. All these so-called financial gurus teach you about everything but the PROCESS OF THE SYSTEM! The Cantillon Effect is the process of how the current banking system and lending works. While also showing the inequalities in the flow of money. We are in a recession, with inflation at a high of 8.2% in September 2022, down 0.1% from the previous month, but still at almost 35-40-year highs. Don't get caught up on the news about all the bull-crap about inflation; the real cause of inflation that happens is the above Cantillon Effect; that's really a government-imposed, non-legislative, and regressive tax on your purchasing power as middle-class and poor citizens. This is how the government does business with the wealthy to enrich them while continuing to impoverish the financially illiterate, which is the main cause of how the middle class keeps on falling apart - no matter how much you try to tax the wealthy to make up for the unequal distribution of wealth.

To take advantage of these same opportunities, you have to know the system process first, not sell products or offer services. There are many solutions for you to get new money first and get the benefits of the wealthy, bankers, politicians, and private equity funds. Remember, new money travels through these institutions owned and run by the wealthy. The first thing you need to:

Increase Income Streams by ultimately becoming entrepreneurs who take on risks to create value for the world and get rewarded for it through earning profit. Remember, when you have a fixed income, it comes from working for someone else. Living this way, you become a victim of inflating the cost of living, which means your fixed income is becoming less and less valuable over time. If you've only got one job working for someone, you only have one source of income, which can be risky. In addition to your income already being fixed as an entrepreneur, you can transition to a non-fixed income situation. Entrepreneurs find gaps in the market, find opportunities to solve problems in the world, and affect real positive change in the world, all while providing cash flow for themselves.

Another positive aspect of this system is monetary expansion. That's necessary for economic growth, so when the banks create money for a person or company to grow a business on your own, your business creates and performs valuable goods and services that create economic growth without inflation. These types of loans create jobs that foster innovation. So, become an entrepreneur and use banks to create new money through loans for you, which in turn puts you at the top of the line for new money to flow to you as the wealthy do. You have the process: go out and build your business and remove yourself from the normal 9-to-5 that prevents you from having access to this form of wealth! Remember the quote above by Andrew Jackson: this is the system that he predicted we would be in.

---

## Pro se Tip: (!)

Leverage: Is what happens when you earn interest on not just your money, but also on someone else's money.

---

# PROS AND CONS OF BANKS

As mentioned previously, banks are financial institutions licensed to receive deposits and make loans. These pros extend to financial services such as wealth management, currency exchange, and safe deposit boxes. Several kinds of banks exist, including retail, commercial, and corporate. Other pros include checking and savings accounts and certificate deposits [CDs], which are paired with traditional banking transactions like deposits, withdrawals, check writing, and bill payments.

You can save money and earn interest on your account [although not much]. Also, credit is provided for people and corporations [i.e., car loans, credit cards, mortgages]; their goal is to earn a profit for their owners. [i.e., banks pay 1% interest on savings accounts and charge 6% interest for loans, which earns a gross profit of 5% for its owners.]

Some cons are the 1% interest paid on your money in these checking and savings accounts. These accounts, like savings, should only be for emergencies, 3 to 12 months of savings, purchases [i.e., houses, cars, etc.], and investments [i.e., rental property, businesses, etc.]. Other than these accounts above, you are becoming poor by saving. Banks' savings rate doesn't keep up with inflation:

Inflation Rate $\Rightarrow$Goes faster than $\Rightarrow$Savings Rate.


Bank Loss/Don't Save

$1,000 $\Rightarrow$1% a year

8% inflation = $70 loss

$100,000 $\Rightarrow$1% a year

8% inflation = $7,000 loss

$1,000,000 $\Rightarrow$1% a year

8% inflation = $70,000 loss

All the losses above are ones you will take on the money you deposit in the bank and let it sit there for a year.

Of course, inflation will deteriorate the value of your savings if you decide to stash your cash in a bank account. This is a con of letting your money sit for years in your neighborhood bank. Over the long run, you'll be better off investing now, even if the expected returns are lower. Banks keep money safe and are FDIC-insured, but they also have predatory practices that hurt middle- and low-income citizens. Somethings include:

- **Credit Card Fees**: Too high-fixed rate = 13.02%. An example of this might be if the bank can borrow money from the Federal Reserve at 0.75%. The bank will profit from the difference because the fixed rate is 13.02%! Credit card debt usually is 15% of the median annual household income.
- **Foreclosures**: Bankers lose in the majority of these cases brought to court, but most people don't have money to hire lawyers to fight these banks, and these banks know this. They also lose up to $78,000 per foreclosure [30% of the loan] to you, the borrower! The reason why it's a con is that foreclosures make you lose hard-earned equity in the home. Plus, once processed by the banks, foreclosures are the most damaging item that can appear in a credit report. What has been happening behind the scenes to people who use banks like this is that the IRS sees this foreclosure as unpaid debt, making it a tax liability for the borrower, on top of you losing your home.
- **Pay Day Lenders**: These are among the worst predatory lenders ever. Their practices prey on the poor; I'm talking about this in the banking section because banks help these lenders exist, and, furthermore, they help them with payroll deductions on direct deposits. They have a high-interest rate, with annual rates of 322%! This also builds. Typically, these services are only offered to people who earn $30,000 a year, and 18% get some of their income from public assistance.

## Pro se Tip: (!)

Idle time is mentally killing prisoners and their dreams/goals. Use your time to solve problems in your life, with a little work, and a focused mind." –Unknown

#1 on the list of cons of the banks and their system is what I talked about earlier: The **Fractional Reserve system**. Ex. Deposit $100 into a bank; the bank loans out 90% and holds onto 10% [turns out $90 of $100]. Banks are creators of money; just know you are producing more inflation by saving money; for every dollar you deposit, it creates $20. Fractional banking allows banks to lend out money they don't have. This is just what our financial system has grown into. In this system, only a fraction of bank deposits need to be held in cash. Our modern economy allows banks to create money when they extend credit [i.e., create loans, etc.]. Proving my point of why you lose keeping money in the bank, creating money out of thin air is the genius of banks. Also, the banks make two entries on their balance sheets, #1 on the assets side and #2 on the liabilities side.

Example:

Loan $ Assets ⟹ Is offset by the new deposit ⟹ Which is a liability of the bank depositor holder ⟹The loan then creates deposits.

Above is the process of how banks create money from nothing. They lend first, then look for reserves later, which is "you" in this process, the new customer. [i.e., the reserve] Currently, the Fed Fund Rate that controls this system is 3.75%-4%, the interest rate banks charge each other to borrow or lend excess reserves overnight. Financially speaking, entering the banking system has pros and cons; you have to know the difference and build wealth like the wealthy and not like the poor people who just save money and never want to understand the system to move up the economic ladder.

# FEDERAL RESERVE BANK:
# WHY IT MATTERS

The most complicated financial institution in the world. While also being connected to ½ of all transactions in the U.S., It's the Central Bank of the U.S.A. and the most powerful in the world. Let's start here: the Federal Reserve Bank isn't "Federal" and "Not a bank" in the traditional sense. You can't deposit money there, and you can't obtain money from there. What it is, is a private bank created in 1913 because of the panic of 1907, when Wall Street and the U.S. Government turned to J.P. Morgan to steer the country and bail it out. What followed was a complete monopoly over the ability to create money. Based on one meeting between the wealthy and the government, J.P. Morgan represented their interest. This meeting took place on Jekyll Island with people of influence in the government, such as Nelson Aldrich [R-RI], and on Wall Street with people, such as Paul Warburg, director of Wells Fargo. Remember, money travels through wealthy families, along with power, and the Warburg family name was a powerful force in the world. Not to jump off course with this family, but like Paul, Max Warburg before he funded Vladimir Lenin, while James Warburg, Paul's son, became an advisor to FDR [President] who also changed the banking system around whom they could lend to [i.e., not blacks in red districts]. This meeting wasn't known to the U.S. Citizens because they knew people wouldn't have wanted the rules of money to be written by Wall Street backers and approved by a select few of the U.S. government. Thus, what was created was a Federal Reserve Bank, with what's known as "The Dual Mandate"? Which has two elements in it, which are:

- Maximum Employment
- Stabilize Prices [moderate long-term interest rates]

Maximum employment looks good on paper, but in reality, it doesn't work and doesn't mean anything in reality, just a plan of words. There is no way to do this, so what sounded cool on paper really breaks down to "Just Print Money." All this does is create inflation, not employment. Question what you don't understand and what doesn't make logical sense; more than likely, it's not doing what they say it was supposed to do. Next, Stabilize Prices, which is how the Federal Reserve controls the interest rates for the U.S.A. The process they use does not help the average citizen, but the crazy thing is that if they wanted to, they could create great conditions for the poor and middle class to win. This quote sums up this system:

"The establishment of a Central Bank is 90% of communizing a nation" –Vladimir Lenin

Republicans say they are capitalists, and Democrats love to promote socialism – not all, but a lot. The reality is to look at what they built and what they let be created: The Federal Reserve Bank. It's funny when you think about it that they fight about these two forms of economic thought; both allow a bank [Private bank] to exist by government powers that really control ½ of every trade/transaction in the U.S. [i.e., the FED]], that half of the economy. So, check out the quote above; being as though the FED is the Central bank of the U.S., the financial system is already 90% communized! [The irony]

The U.S. Government doesn't make money; their main source of income is taxes! Treasury bonds allow the U.S.A. government to obtain money from other people and countries as a loan. Once the U.S. wants money, the FED prints the money. See the illustration below.

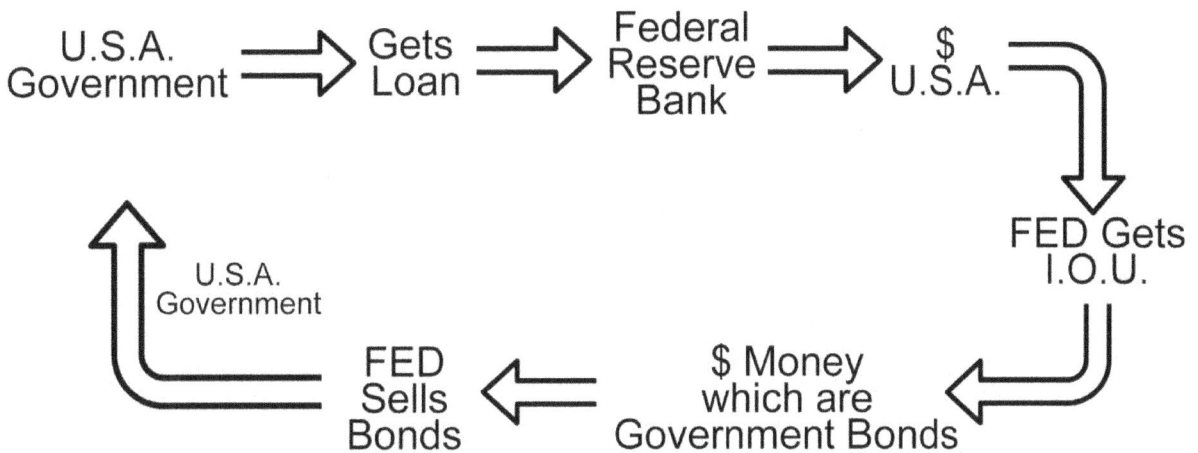

This shows you that we borrow all of our currency into existence. Ex: If you borrow the first dollar into existence, the only dollar that exists on the planet, but you promise to pay it back with interest, where do you get the second $1?

Ultimately, you must borrow that; it's really the definition of a Ponzi Scheme because you can never pay it off. Thus, we keep going deeper into debt. This is the reason why the F.E.D. is the most important financial institution in the World. Every country values its currency against the U.S. Dollar. If countries stop loaning money to the U.S., the whole Ponzi Scheme will fall. When the FED prints money, it devalues our currency [Hence Inflation], affecting citizens' living costs.

Central banks like the Federal Reserve Bank tell you that 2%-3% inflation is better than 0%. This narrative is crazy because they associate these % percentages with wages, telling Americans that their wage will increase by 2%-3% and inflation is better than 0%. This narrative is crazy because they associate these % percentages with wages, telling Americans that their wage will increase by 2%-3% because of inflation. Core Inflation, which the FED promotes like sweet candy, is a target number that doesn't matter. It disguises the real headline inflation, including much more, like energy prices and sudden tax rises. If we used the CPI [Consumer

147

Price Index] that President Carter used when he was President, the inflation rate today would be 2x higher, which is the real numbers under the surface the FED tries to hide.

When You Print $

⇓

With nothing backing it

⇓

Debasing it

⇓

Causes Inflation

Understanding this financial institution and learning why they matter if you ever want to build wealth in this country. Debasing money, as the FED does, is on purpose and is coordinated at the highest levels of the U.S. Government. The people who get hurt in this Ponzi Scheme are regular citizens who work for a paycheck. Look at it this way: Wage based on the 2022 Dollar [CPI] has been unchanged in 50 years, only making $0.12 more than in 1972. The bottom 90% wages ↑ 28.2%, while the people who benefit because they have the knowledge are ↑179.3% [Top 1%], and the top 0.1% is ↑289.1%. Now, you have the knowledge to take control of your finances. If you don't understand money/and its systems with proper financial education, you will be screwed by that same system.

There are 12 Federal Reserve Banks spread across the country; each bank was strategically placed, based on the meeting during its inception on Jekyll Island in Georgia. Today, the Federal Reserve Banks [FOMC] Federal Open Market Committee meets [8x] times a year to set the Federal Funds Rate, which determines where banks/lenders will set their interest rates. The higher the FED Rate, the more expensive borrowing is. This is the reason why the Federal Reserve Bank matters. That same Fed Rate acts as a lever for yields on savings accounts and Certificate Deposits [CDs] while also affecting portfolio and retirement accounts. Your money is impacted and controlled by this one secret financial institution that many Americans don't know about or understand how it operates. Far too many people lack the basic knowledge of what the FED does and how it controls 100% of the financial transactions of money that the lower and middle classes do. Directly or indirectly, they affect your money. So how would you begin to build wealth not knowing this? A two-fold attack occurs when the FED increases the monetary supply: growth or inflation. While what you feel at the bottom is consumer prices of goods and services rise, like what's happening now. It's November 2022; the Fed Rate has just increased again by 0.75% to slow growth and stop inflation, so now car loans, credit card payments, and consumer prices are going to rise. So, pay attention!

As spoken about earlier, the FED buys U.S. Treasury Bonds – not directly because that is illegal – through others to influence the interest rates you pay on your credit card or mortgage. Bond prices ↑ while yield prices ↓ in this process. Before 1813 and the creation of the Federal Reserve Bank, the banking industry was decentralized. Since then, impacts have directly caused massive wealth transfers that have not allowed the lower class and middle class to benefit. To beat this system and get ahead, check out the "Pros" part before this one so you can develop a plan to execute.

# INSURANCE AS A BANK

Did you know the average person can become their own bank? Look at this from the perspective of creating generational wealth. Using insurance as your own bank would ensure that you will never have to borrow money from a bank or private lender again. Always remember that banks don't lose money. They loan money out and then charge interest back to themselves. So, what if you could use those same principles but use insurance as the vehicle by which you become your own bank?

> ## Pro se Tip: (!)
> "You can't expect to grow and also stay the same."

What I'm speaking of is using a financial tool that allows you to save inside your life insurance policy instead of doing what most people do and putting it in a bank account. Use your policy to lend money to yourself and earn certain tax advantages. All this is conducted by using your policy's cash value! Plans such as whole life insurance have a cash value, the actual policy's death benefit that becomes liquid by the insurance company. It's the portion of the whole life insurance that earns interest. Therefore, if we look at it from the "insurance as a bank" perspective, the cash value of your whole life policy can be used for policy loans as long as you pay the premiums. The more money deposited into your policy each month, instead of a bank account, the faster your cash value increases. Plus, all growth on your cash value is "Tax-Free"! It also covers you during your entire life and could be used to withdraw or borrow cash [borrowing cash won't be tax-free]. As a bank, insurance is a stable financial plan, nothing more, nothing less! **Step One: Cash Value Life Insurance**. During this period, it's called the "Capitalization Phase". Once you fund the policy, you will accumulate cash value from the start. Dividend-paying life insurance is the best vehicle because of the tax advantages of IRC Section 7702. Remember, under this code, policy interest accrued or the dividends paid are taxable. So, this vehicle grows tax-deferred via a policy loan. We only want to maximize the cash value and minimize the initial death benefit. This will allow more of the premium to go into your policy. Make sure you try to stay in this "Capitalization Phase" for about 6-12 months and push funding into the policy. **Step Two Life Insurance Riders**. Simply put, Paid additions Riders allow you to purchase more death benefits, which will ultimately increase the policy's cash value growth.

Another Rider is the "Life Insurance Supplement," which blends low-cost term life with permanent life insurance. Term life goes down once you start making payments, with permanent life insurance as the only thing left. Three other Riders are:

- **Additional Life Insurance Rider**. Allows the policy owner to make increased premium payments to purchase additional participating paid-up life insurance, which actually increases the policy's death benefit and cash value growth.
- **Term Life Rider**: Term Life Rider or Renewable term Rider offers term life insurance that can be converted to permanent life insurance sometime in the future.
- **Guaranteed Insurability Rider**: GIR guarantees that you can purchase additional insurance without answering health questions. This is a great option for children, as it provides options to increase their coverage down the line.

**Step Three: Funding Your Bank**. Once the policy is set up, you would need to put money in it. From the start, to make the greatest impact, you have to over-fund your policy up to the point. Never go over the point because it would turn into a "MEC" [Modified Endowment Contract]. Also, what you are learning can be applied now with your outside network; if you trust someone out there, you have to sign a "Power of Attorney," giving them Financial Power of Attorney to act on your behalf. You can open a bank account and apply for Life Insurance this way. Utilize your network and build a solid, reliable group, each that can do something different than the other. NEVER PUT TOO MUCH ON ONE PERSON! Let's get back to it! The IRS has set strict rules that prohibit you from putting too much money into a life insurance policy to avoid it being a tax haven. But our plan is to fill it up with cash up to that IRS tipping point to maximize early cash value accumulation and growth. Use Step Three combined with Step Two Riders, which helps to give your policy speed to charge up your cash value growth right from the start. Check and see if you can qualify to "Backdate your policy to save age," which lets you fund your policy with more money in the first year than normally would be allowed. I hope you see what we are doing with this Insurance Bank. We are building from the ground up to the roof. The secret is to stack the policy, riders, and funding maximums on top of each other, along with a backdating policy to save age and increase 1st year funding above normal limits. You must stack on top of these policies to get the full value of using cash-value life insurance as your own bank. It's a process that must be done correctly, and shortcuts are not allowed.

**Step Four: Borrowing for Purchases!** Sticking with the process, we have been following, you must borrow from the policy rather than withdraw money. Borrowing allows you to still build cash value; withdrawing money forces you to deplete your cash value. Now, you get the loan, using your cash value as collateral, to purchase assets that produce income. Real estate is the perfect purchase, offering its own tax incentives and breaks for you. First, buy a rental property and use the monthly income from the tenants to pay back your policy loan with interest. So basically, you are loaning yourself money as a bank and paying yourself back with interest! Set your interest rate the same as lenders' current interest rates. Thus increasing your death benefit and cash flow growth tax-free. Another aspect of loaning money can be to your business, then have said business pay you back with interest for the loan you made to your business. What this does is like magic; it allows you to recapture your own interest and replenish your policy, but hold on. If it gets better, your business can write off the interest payments [if eligible], making more money appear for you!

All this is called Insurance as a Bank, just a simple concept of being your own bank, which allows you to use a vehicle like insurance to loan money to you/your business, then recapture the interest that you would have given to the bank and put it back into your policy and run up the death benefits.

**Step Five: Recapture that Interest.** Briefly touched on above, it's important that you pay back the loan because it yields the best long-term returns if you follow this process step by step. Plus, your policy grows faster and faster. Simply rinse and repeat these steps over and over again. Pay the loan back to your "Insurance Bank," get another loan, and do it again. Free Game!

## 4 Major Mutual Companies

DIV. 6.00% MassMutual.com

DIV. 5.65% GuardianLife.com

Div. 5.80% NewYorkLife.com

Div. 5.00% NorthwesternMutual.com

# ABOUT THE AUTHOR

C.A. Knuckles is currently incarcerated in Maryland. He has built Pro Se Prisoner into the go-to financial literacy publishing brand. This new book series, Pro se Prisoner: Guide to Build Wealth, is the follow-up to his successful Pro se Prisoner: How to Buy Stocks and Bitcoin. Mr. Knuckles' goal is to help prisoners build wealth and learn about finances by giving them the knowledge to succeed while in prison. If you have questions or ideas or need advice about business-related matters, including investments, please contact him through his investment company.

The Attic Group, LLC

1 East Chase Street, Suite #1101

Baltimore, Maryland 21202

Mr. Knuckles would love to get your feedback about the book, make suggestions for the next one, or just let him know you liked it. Write to the above address. First, Becoming wealthy requires changing your mindset, obtaining knowledge, and taking action! Thanks for becoming a Pro se Prisoner!

# FREEBIRD PUBLISHERS

## Thanks for your interest in Freebird Publishers!

We value our customers and would love to hear from you! Reviews are an important part in bringing you quality publications. We love hearing from our readers-rather it's good or bad (though we strive for the best)!

If you could take the time to review/rate any publication you've purchased with Freebird Publishers we would appreciate it!

If your loved one uses Amazon, have them post your review on the books you've read. This will help us tremendously, in providing future publications that are even more useful to our readers and growing our business.

Amazon works off of a 5 star rating system. When having your loved one rate us be sure to give them your chosen star number as well as a written review. Though written reviews aren't required, we truly appreciate hearing from you.

Sample Review Received on Inmate Shopper

poeticsunshine

☆☆☆☆☆ **Truly a guide**

Reviewed in the United States on June 29, 2023

Verified Purchase

This book is a powerhouse of information. My son had to calm/ground himself to prioritize where to start.

# CURRENT FULL COLOR CATALOG
## 92-Pages filled with books, gifts and services for prisoners

We have created four different versions of our new catalog A: Complete B:No Pen Pal Content C:No Sexy Photo Content D:No Pen Pal and Sexy Content. Available in full Color or B&W (please specify) please make sure you order the correct catalog based on your prison mail room regulations. We are not responsible for rejected or lost in the mail catalogs. Send SASE for info on stamp options.

### Freebird Publishers Book Selection Includes:

- Ask. Believe. Receive.: Our Power to Create Our Own Destiny
- Celebrity Female Star Power
- Cell Chef 1 & 2
- Cellpreneur: The Millionaire Prisoner's Guidebook
- Chapter 7 Bankruptcy: Seven Steps to Financial Freedom
- Convicted Creations Cookbook
- Cooking With Hot Water
- DIY for Prisoners
- Federal Rules of Criminal Procedures Pocket Guide
- Federal Rules of Evidence Pocket Guide
- Fine Dining Cookbook 1, 2, 3
- Freebird Publisher's Gift Look Book
- Get Money: Self Educate, Get Rich, & Enjoy Life (3 book series)
- Habeas Corpus Manual
- Hobo Pete and the Ghost Train
- Hot Girl Safari: Non-Nude Photo Book
- How to Write a Good Letter From Prison
- Ineffective Assistance of Counsel
- Inmate Shopper
- Inmate Shopper Censored
- Introduction to Financial Success
- Kitty Kat: Adult Entertainment Resource Book

- Life With a Record
- Locked Down Cookin'
- Locked Up Love Letters: Becoming the Perfect Pen Pal
- Parent to Parent: Raising Children from Prison
- Penacon Presents: The Prisoners Guide to Being a Perfect Pen Pal
- Pen Pal Success: The Ultimate Guide to Getting & Keeping Pen Pals
- Pen Pals: A Personal Guide for Prisoners
- Pillow Talk: Adult Non-Nude Photo Book
- Post-Conviction Relief Series (Books 1-7)
- Prison Health Handbook
- Prison Legal Guide
- Prison Picasso
- Prisoner's Communication Guidelines for Navigating in Prison
- Prisonyland Adult Coloring Book
- Pro Se Guide to Legal Research & Writing
- Pro Se Prisoner: How to Buy Stocks and Bitcoin
- Pro Se Section 1983 Manual
- Section 2254 Pro Se Guide to Winning Federal Relief
- Soft Shots: Adult Non-Nude Photo Book
- The Best 500 Non-Profit Organizations for Prisoners & Their Families
- Weight Loss Unlocked
- Write & Get Paid

**CATALOG ONLY $5 - SHIPS BY FIRST CLASS MAIL**
**ADDITIONAL OPTION: add $5 for Shipping and Handling with Tracking**

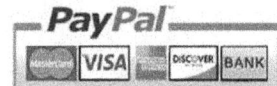

**PayPal** MasterCard VISA DISCOVER BANK

**NO ORDER FORM NEEDED CLEARLY WRITE ON PAPER & SEND PAYMENT TO:**
**FREEBIRD PUBLISHERS** 221 Pearl St., Ste. 541, North Dighton, MA 02764
www.FreebirdPublishers.com Diane@FreebirdPublishers.com Text/Phone: 774-406-8682
**We accept all forms of payment. Plus Venmo & CashApp!** Venmo: @FreebirdPublishers CashApp: $FreebirdPublishers

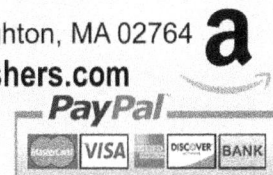

www.ingramcontent.com/pod-product-compliance
Lightning Source LLC
Chambersburg PA
CBHW080555220326
41599CB00032B/6484

* 9 7 8 1 9 5 2 1 5 9 4 6 6 *